WHISPERIN'
AN AUTOBIOGRAPHY
BILL

To Georgia
All My best,

[signature]

4-17-92

Published by
LONGSTREET PRESS, INC.
2150 Newmarket Parkway
Suite 102
Marietta, Georgia 30067

Printed in the United States of America

Published 1989. Paperback Edition 1990

Library of Congress Catalog Number 90-060437

ISBN 0-929264-37-1

This book was printed by R. R. Donnelley and Sons in Harrisonburg, Virginia. The text type was set in Goudy Old Style by Typo-Repro Service, Inc., Atlanta, Georgia. Design by Paulette Lambert. Cover photo by Dennis Carney.

Permissions for lyrics

MOST RICHLY BLESSED (Luther T. Brandon & Archie Campbell)
   © 1964 Peer International Corporation
YOU & YOUR SWEET LOVE (Bill Anderson)
   © 1969 Stallion Music, Inc.
ROLLER COASTER RIDE (Bill Anderson)
   © 1974 Stallion Music, Inc.
CITY LIGHTS (Bill Anderson)
   © 1958 TNT Music, Inc.
A GIRL I USED TO KNOW (Jack Clement)
   © 1962 Jack Music, Inc.
STILL (Bill Anderson)
   © 1962 Johnny Bienstock Music
WE'VE GOT IT ALL (Bill Anderson)
   © 1975 Stallion Music, Inc.
PEEL ME A 'NANNER (Bill Anderson)
   © 1963 Johnny Bienstock Music
COLD HARD FACTS OF LIFE (Bill Anderson)
   © 1967 Stallion Music, Inc.
PO' FOLKS (Bill Anderson)
   © 1961 Tree International
MAMA SANG A SONG (Bill Anderson)
   © 1961 Tree International
STILL #2 (Bill Anderson & Sheb Wooley)
   © 1963 Johnny Bienstock Music
FOR LOVING YOU (Steve Karliski)
   © 1966 Painted Desert Music Corp.
SOMETIMES (Bill Anderson)
   © 1975 Stallion Music, Inc.
I'D RATHER BE SORRY (Kris Kristofferson)
   © 1967 Buckhorn Music Publishers, Inc.
I CAN'T WAIT ANY LONGER (Bill Anderson/Buddy Killen)
   © 1978 Stallion Music, Inc.
FIVE LITTLE FINGERS (Bill Anderson)
   © 1963 Tree International
GARDEN PARTY (Ricky Nelson)
   © Matragum Music, Inc.
YOU'RE CALLING ME SWEETHEART AGAIN
   © Central Songs

WHISPERIN'
AN AUTOBIOGRAPHY
BILL

BILL ANDERSON
A Life of Music, Love, Tragedy & Triumph

LONGSTREET PRESS
Atlanta, Georgia

To Becky,
the most determined person I've ever known,

and to Jamey,
who looked to me for strength and for answers,
never realizing so much of my strength
and so many of my answers came from him . . . .

And to the Fans

" . . . And almost despite myself . . .
I, among men, am
most richly blessed."

From the Decca LP
I Can Do Nothing Alone
Bill Anderson (1967)

Prologue

Every twenty-four hours the world turns over on somebody who's sitting on top of it.

I know. It happened to me.

Well, maybe I wasn't perched *exactly* on top of the world, but I was close. I was approaching my twenty-fifth anniversary as a performer in the country music business, and while my records and my songs weren't burning up the popularity charts at that very moment, I could look back across a career that had spanned nearly a quarter-century and count seventy-two single records of my own that had made those charts* and countless hundreds of songs I had written that had done likewise for other artists who had recorded them. I had released nearly fifty albums, won more songwriting awards than any other writer in the history of country music, been named Male Vocalist of the Year, half of the Duet of the Year with two different singing partners, Songwriter of the Year several times, hosted and starred in the country music Television Series of the Year, written the Song of the Year, twice recorded the Record of the Year, employed the Band of the Year, and had once been voted along with Hank Williams and Harlan Howard, as one of the three Top Songwriters of All-Time!

I had been elected to the Nashville Songwriters Association Hall of Fame and to the Georgia Music Hall of Fame. My biography had appeared in *Who's Who in America*, I had hung gold records on my wall, hosted my own major-network television game show, been an actor in a TV soap opera, appeared in several movies, and was part-owner and national spokesman for one of the fastest growing restaurant chains in America. I had served eleven terms spanning sixteen years as an officer and member of the Board of Directors of the

* The CashBox Country Singles Charts (1958-1982)

international Country Music Association.

I had travelled nearly everywhere in the world that I had ever dreamed of going and met people I'd never dared dream I'd meet. I had been there when my mom and dad celebrated their fiftieth wedding anniversary, and I was the father of three bright, healthy children who had never given me a moment's trouble in their lives. In 1982 I was even honored at a luncheon in Atlanta and given a trophy proclaiming me as Southeast Father of the Year. I had never been super-rich by big-time show business standards, but I had a few dollars in the bank and thought I had a few good investments for the future. I wasn't complaining.

But at almost the stroke of midnight Saturday, October 13, 1984, while I was rambling around inside my sprawling country home near Lebanon, Tennessee, packing my clothes to go on a road trip to play and sing country music, everything changed. At the very moment I was whistling through the house making sure I had clean underwear and enough toothpaste to last me a couple of days, my wife, Becky, was returning to a small condominium we owned near Nashville after having seen a movie with a friend. She was barely more than a mile from her doorstep when an eighteen-year-old boy, so drunk he later admitted he didn't even remember crawling in behind the wheel of his company's faded white pickup truck, appeared from out of nowhere and smashed head-on into her barely moving white Cadillac coupe. The collision was so violent it completely crumpled Becky's car and came within micro-inches of killing her. She was left with crippling brain damage, head injuries so severe that they changed her life, my life, and the lives of everyone close to us forever.

Her very survival hung in the balance for several days. In the space of a heartbeat, I found myself facing the exceedingly real possibility that my wife might die and the stark realization that even if she did survive she might never again be normal.

And we had a six-year-old son.

I loved my little boy more than anything in this world, but he was still not much more than a baby. He was in the first grade, sure, but kids that age can't do very many things for themselves. They need mothers and they need fathers to love them and care for them. Never in my wildest dreams had I ever imagined I might someday have to become both mother and father to my son . . . and for how long, God only knew.

Me, a gypsy, a travelling minstrel man, having to learn how to crawl out of bed at six A.M., fry bacon, scramble eggs, wash a little face, comb hair, tie shoelaces, proofread homework, wash and dry clothes, drive to school, remember lunch money, pick up from school, attend Cub Scout meetings, and join the PTO. Plus, in order for me to do all of the above, I'd have to leave the tranquil estate in the country that seemed more like home to me than anyplace I had ever lived and move into a tiny, cramped apartment with my son, so as not to disrupt his life any more than it might have already been disrupted.

I did it . . . I did it *all* . . . but it wasn't easy. And it took its toll. Four months after the accident, probably buckling from the physical and mental strain of caring for both my son and my brain-injured wife, I suffered a ruptured disc on the lower left side of my back. For almost two years I couldn't walk, stand, sit, or even lie down to sleep without wincing from the excruciating, piercing pain that seemed to be constantly radiating from my back all the way down my long left leg, into my foot, and out the very tips of my toes. It was constant agony, but I wasn't able to take the time and attention away from my duties at home or my work as an entertainer, smiling TV game show host, and national restaurant spokesman long enough to undergo the corrective surgery and lengthy rehabilitation necessary to alleviate the problem. As a result, I strapped myself into a stiff elastic and metal back brace, stuffed painkilling medication into my body like it was popcorn, and whenever I'd find a break in the action I'd make the rounds of doctors' offices, hospitals, and pain clinics anywhere I might find them, searching for a miracle cure that would not come.

At almost this very same time, with so much of my energy and most of my time being sapped by the events unfolding around me, I discovered that some very large business investments, which I had practically ignored, were swiftly going sour on me. I woke up one morning and realized that I owed creditors all over the country sums of money reaching well into the millions of dollars . . . and that I was facing the definite possibility of owing several million dollars more. The totals were staggering. After twenty-five successful years in business and after having been repeatedly called "one of the best businessmen in country music," I found myself suddenly hanging by a very thin financial thread indeed.

But, believe it or not, fate wasn't through. In a matter of only a few more months I was standing at the bedside of my critically ill twenty-five-year-old daughter in a hospital almost a thousand miles away from home, listening to some of the best medical minds in the country tell me that the tumor they'd just removed from her young body was malignant.

It reads like a bad script from a soap opera, but I can assure you it was all very, very real.

Most of what I am about to share in these pages revolves around my life as an entertainer—all the years spent singing, smiling, and laughing—but I've deliberately set it against the backdrop of this seemingly impossible period in my life when the only smiling, laughing, and singing I managed to do for a long time was on the outside . . . and in my memories of a better day and time.

I've chosen this way to tell my story because of the profound effect these recent years have had upon me as a human being. An autobiography is the story of a person, but in my case it may well be the story of two people—the person I was before all the anxiety and turmoil of these past few years and the person I feel I have become as a result of it. I've grown, I've changed, I've discovered, and more importantly I've *re*-discovered. I was taught at an early age most of the things that matter in life. My problem was that somewhere along the way I had managed to lose sight of the fact that what matters isn't always the same as what *counts*.

For better or for worse, I have written every word of this book myself. There have been no ghost writers and no long hours spent talking into a tape recorder only to have another writer come along and attempt to organize and interpret my thoughts. I'll take the blame for it all, and I'll accept the fact that even some of those closest to me will probably be surprised by some of what I have to say.

There is no doubt that my life has been, for the most part, a fairy-tale existence, chock-full of happiness and the savoring of sweet success. One morning fate just decided to serve me a heaping platter of bitter reality for breakfast. From that day to this, my mission has been to try to learn how better to accept life on its own terms . . . all the while seeking to remind myself and those around me that there is a big difference between a dead-end and a fork in the road.

PART I

PART 1

1

It didn't start out to be a very unusual day at all, certainly not one I ever thought I'd be remembering in such detail all these years later.

The sun came up as always in the east, peeking tentatively at first from behind the sloping rooftop of my neighbor Danny Norton's house, then easing its way ever so slowly up into the clear, intensely blue sky. By midmorning its bright beams were streaming down like glistening raindrops upon the shiny new coats of the gold, orange, and coral leaves still clinging to the lower branches of the oak, maple, and walnut trees that dotted my yard. There was just enough of a bite in the air to announce that this was indeed October, my favorite month of the year in Tennessee, the most beautiful and serene of all places. It was truly a morning made for a sleepy country music singer to crack open his eyelids for only a moment, admiringly soak up a quick dose of the beauty all around him, and then roll back over, pull the covers up tightly around his shoulders, and dream until noon of million-selling records, perfectly tuned guitars, and richly tanned ladies all sitting cross-legged on the front row.

But my alarm clock, by design, had other ideas. It woke me promptly at nine A.M., the lone sound penetrating the otherwise total serenity of my country estate. I awoke lying crossways in my custom-made king-sized bed. Alone. The alone part wasn't anything different. Waking up as early as nine o'clock on a Saturday morning at home definitely was different.

Home was, and had been for almost five years, a rambling, six-thousand-square-foot Spanish-styled mansion standing picturesquely atop a grassy knoll overlooking thirty-five acres of rolling farm land some thirty-odd miles east of downtown Nashville. The house, a modern horse barn, an authentic log cabin built in 1816 by slave labor, and a creek that flowed through open land before winding its way to within a few feet of the screened porch that had been added to the back of the cabin, was listed officially as Route 9, Lebanon, Tennessee. Actually, it was nearly five miles from the courthouse in downtown Lebanon, situated just smack-dab in the middle of the country. Wilson County, Tennessee. East of Mount Juliet, west of Crab Orchard, north of Bell Buckle. And I loved it better than any place I had ever lived.

I lifted my body begrudgingly off the cool cotton sheets, rubbed the backs of my fingers gingerly across the tops of my crusty eyelids, and stumbled toward the kitchen. I opened the drapes, raised the blind over the big picture window above the sink, and marvelled for the millionth time at the brilliant colors dancing in the easy breeze that seemed always to be sweeping across the top of my little hill. As I stood listening to the sound of boiling water bouncing off the top of the percolator, I wondered how anybody could possibly not be happy living in a setting as majestic as this.

But my wife, Becky, wasn't, and she hadn't been for quite some time. For the past two-and-a-half years, she had preferred to spend most of her time at a small condominium we had purchased near Nashville. She seemed to have a lot of reasons for wanting to be at our city place. I felt I had just as many reasons for wanting to stay where I was. And now, smugly sipping my coffee and breathing in the fresh, crisp country air all around me, I was more convinced than ever that I had been right.

My six-year-old son, Jamey, would be playing in a YMCA youth league soccer game in Donelson, a Nashville suburb, at eleven, and I had promised him I would be there without fail. There hadn't been many Saturdays in town for Dad this season, and I wanted to be there to cheer him on. Besides, he and I had made big plans to hit one of the nearby fast-food restaurants for some burgers and fries when the game was over and then to drive back out to the country for a friendly game of father-and-son softball. Afterwards, I planned to coax him into taking a short nap so he'd feel like going backstage with me later that night at the Grand Ole Opry.

I finished off half a sweet roll with my second cup of coffee, unplugged the percolator, and tossed the cup carelessly into the dishwasher where it came to rest alongside the remnants of six similar bachelor-style breakfasts and dinners earlier in the week. "Someday I'll have to get an estimate on what it'll cost to wash those dishes," I thought to myself as I swished the trashcan with my paper napkin— "Anderson, a jumper for two!"—and walked sprightly back to my dressing room. I grinned. I whistled the melody to an old country song. I was feeling great and loving the feeling.

I took a quick shower in my spacious coral marble shower stall, shaved my stubble of a beard with a gold-plated razor my daughters had given me the preceding Christmas, then grabbed my cleanest pair of dirty blue jeans from inside my custom-made walnut closet and pulled them on. I dressed them down with a pair of custom-made tan cowboy boots, a luxury item indeed, but one that had seen so many miles the toes were virtually worn away. I didn't have time to blow-dry and style my hair, so I slipped on my faded blue denim baseball cap with "PoFolks" emblazoned in canary-yellow letters across the front. To that I added a colorful albeit non-descript blue-and-white sweatshirt, immediately covering it with a fire-engine red University of Georgia windbreaker with hand-sewn, raised white letters directly over the heart identifying me as "Coach Anderson." In a not-so-concerted effort to look like just another dad at the soccer game, I left the house looking like a cross between Porter Wagoner on a Saturday night and Freddie the Freeloader. But I was running late and really didn't have the time to care.

I made the half-hour trip from Lebanon into Donelson in silence. Most days I'd have had the radio on in the car punching the buttons, trying to pick up on the latest country music sounds. But not this time. As the wheels of the big white Lincoln Town Car hummed westward over the concrete ribbons of Interstate 40, I grew pensive, reflective . . . driving . . . thinking . . . and wondering why. Why, after all these years of happily living together, had Becky and I suddenly come to this particular time and place in our lives where we couldn't seem to resolve this situation over where we wanted to live? And were we ever going to be able to work things out? And if so, how? And when? Oh, sure, we'd had lots of piddling little arguments through the years, like all married folks do, mostly over things that didn't amount to a hill of beans, but this was starting to feel different. Very different. And scary. So scary, in fact, that I was, for the first time since I'd met my wife nearly eighteen years earlier, beginning seriously to ponder the future of our relationship.

"What is it that keeps you from being happy living out here in the country?" I must have asked her a hundred times over the past few years. I loved it *so* much. I just couldn't understand why she didn't.

"It's a combination of things," she said. "For one, Lebanon is just too far away from Nashville. Plus, you've been gone so much since we moved here. I feel awfully isolated."

"You have friends you can spend time with when I'm gone, don't you? You've always seemed to have plenty of friends before."

"I know, and I've really tried to make friends here. But it hasn't been easy. Besides, I miss all my friends back in Nashville. I like the people in Lebanon, but . . . I don't know . . . I just don't seem to fit in." I'd nod and try to understand, recalling ruefully how excited we'd both been just a few years earlier when we'd left our home on Old Hickory Lake to take on small-town life and wide open spaces. Becky and I had both grown up in little towns near big cities, and at the time I had thought she wanted to live in the country and raise our son there just as much as I did.

"I *did* want to live here," she continued, "but things have changed. I'm lonesome and I'm frightened. I mean, this is a big house and it sits out here all by itself in the middle of all this land. When you're gone, it's just me and the baby. I get scared. Can't you see why I might not like it?"

In one way I could see what she meant and yet in another way I couldn't. There had been some incidents—beer cans scattered across our porch one morning, just outside our bedroom window; obscene phone calls; people driving onto our property uninvited, cameras poised—but I wrote it off as part of the price you pay when you choose to live a high-profile lifestyle. I figured it could have happened anywhere. "When you seek a place in the sun, you have to be prepared to get blistered," I said. I thought it was clever but Becky didn't smile.

I guess I was too busy seeing the end of the rainbow—a city boy who had always dreamed of one day living in a big house in the country and finally making it—to see how traumatic this lonely, fearful existence was for my wife. I loved her and I wanted her to like where we lived, but she didn't. To me, being in the country was heaven. To her, it was far less. I'm sure she thought I was selfish—blind to her feelings, deaf to her concerns.

It had all seemed so perfect in the beginning. We didn't have to walk but a few yards from our house down through the woods to our very own little creek where I could teach my son to skip rocks and catch tadpoles; stroll just a few feet from our front door and step inside a cozy log cabin where Becky and I could build fires and I could write songs and we could dream; drive just a few miles to a small downtown square where we could have lunch at a mom-and-pop cafe and shake 'n howdy with all our neighbors. It was all I had ever wanted—the brass ring, the platinum album, the top of the charts. What had gone wrong? And what could be done to straighten things out?

"I don't think I can live here anymore, Bill," Becky finally said to me one spring morning after more than two years of trying to adjust. "Please try to understand. I'll admit it . . . I made a mistake. I want to live in Nashville."

"But I want to live *here*," I pleaded, "and I love you. I love Jamey and I want our family to live together."

"Then come go with me. We've got the condo, the three of us can live there while we look for a new place where we can all be happy. I love you, too, but I can't be happy here."

But I couldn't leave. I knew she was frightened and unhappy and felt isolated, but I was stubborn. Maybe self-centered is a better word, because a lot of the evidence seemed to be pointing to our having made an error in moving so far out into the country.

Our house sat back off the road several hundred yards, the property was fenced, and we'd installed an iron security gate at the end of the driveway, but in spite of all that nothing seemed to deter the flow of traffic. We woke up several mornings to find phonograph records and tapes of songs from would-be singers and songwriters hanging from our outside doorknobs. All kinds of strange correspondence found its way into our mailbox, including one threat on my life and a series of handwritten letters from a lady who said she was destitute and knew we could help her out financially if only we would. After the third or fourth note, I began to feel sorry for the lady and contacted the county welfare office in hopes of finding her some help.

"Why, I know this lady," the social worker told me, "and, my goodness, she's got a good job. Why in the world would she write letters like this?" I didn't have the slightest idea, but as soon as the authorities confronted her, the letters stopped.

A cleaning lady we hired was late coming to work one morning and Becky asked her why. "I had to go to court with my son," she answered casually. "He done kilt some dude."

Jamey's allergies were another problem. His doctor had told us that all the sniffling and sneezing he'd been doing since we'd moved to the country was because he was allergic to something growing out there. "You need to get him back to concrete," the doctor said. Whereupon I lost my cool and snapped, "Well, *I'm* allergic to concrete!" I didn't want to go back to anywhere.

It wasn't like our house was always under seige. Most of the time the area was peaceful and quiet, most people respected our privacy, and to me there was just no more beautiful setting in the whole wide world. I could come home from a long tour or a hectic day at the studio or the office, watch the big iron gate swing shut behind me, gaze at the sun going down over the tops of the tall trees, and feel like the pressures and problems of the world were a million miles away. I'm not a hermit by any means; I like people and I enjoy being around them, but as an entertainer I've made my living being around people, sometimes twenty-four hours a day, for the past almost thirty years. And I'm the kind of person who needs to have a little time every once in a while to be alone, a place to get away from the pressure-packed existence of my daily life in show business, a shelter where I can curl up and hide and recharge my batteries. Some people relax by retreating to a creek bank with a fishing pole in their hands, some seek out a golf course, others head for the back of a noisy pool hall with their fingers wrapped around a cold can of beer. But my house and my property were my refuge. The last thing I wanted to do was leave them behind.

But Becky didn't share my enthusiasm. In fact, she was so nervous and unhappy living where we did that when I was out of town she started sleeping with the lights on. "I've never been afraid to be alone before," she said. "You know that. But this place petrifies me!"

She finally decided she had to move away. She begged me to go with her, but I couldn't do it. So she left without me. And she took our son.

At first, it was no big thing. Not very many people even knew we weren't living together full-time. There was no big fuss made over the fact that Bill Anderson wanted to live in the country and Becky Anderson wanted to live in town. It was hardly front-page news. Oh, one of the supermarket tabloids got wind of it once and ran a three or four-line blurb about us on page 198 underneath an ad for acne cream, but that was about it. I surely didn't go around talking about it and neither did Becky. It was just no big thing. Even after she left, we didn't consider ourselves to be separated. We never talked about divorce. We simply decided, for a while at least, that it might be best if we lived in two separate residences.

For two-and-a-half years we continued to go nearly everywhere together, still considering ourselves very much man and wife. Just the preceding Monday, in fact, we'd spent a wonderful evening together at the annual Country Music Association Awards Show and Party. Becky had shown radiantly in her full-length black sequined gown, her long blonde hair falling gently around her soft white shoulders, her bright brown eyes laughing and dancing in the night as we visited with friends and fans until long after midnight. "Anderson, you married way above yourself," people would say to me, and I'd smile, nod my head and agree. Becky was a very beautiful and a very special lady.

Not only that, she was also my very best friend. We had always enjoyed doing many things together: watching the same TV shows, going to the same kinds of movies, eating in the same kinds of restaurants. Like every couple we'd had our share of day-to-day disputes and squabbles, but this difference of opinion about where we wanted to live was the only major conflict we'd ever had. We had always been so much alike. Maybe we were too much alike. Maybe that was part of what was making this situation so hard to reconcile.

The best answer we were able to come up with was for her to live in the condo near Nashville and for me to continue to live in the big house in the country. But we never considered that to be a permanent solution.

I took a closet for myself at the condominium and kept it stocked with blue jeans, a few shirts, a pair of boots, a razor, and I'd eat dinner there and spend the night with my family every chance I got. Becky, in turn, never cleaned out her closets in Lebanon, never moved out any of the furniture, any of the dishes, or any of the silverware. She took only her essentials. She furnished the condo in early Wal-Mart, trying to get by as inexpensively as she could. We had every intention of this unusual living arrangement being only temporary, and we didn't want to invest any more money than we had to in dressing up a residence we never planned to keep.

Still, it was a strange situation, drawn out and in some ways made even worse by our equally strange interim solution. Not everyone who knew about the way we were living understood our arrangement at all. Most of the time I wasn't sure I even understood it.

Jamey's team, the Cavaliers, played as hard as they could, blocked what appeared to be a last-second game-tying goal by the opposing team, and won the hard-fought soccer game 2-1, which meant they were in first place in their division. He and I gave each other a couple of high-five's as the teams came off the field, then we took off laughing for McDonald's. We got our orders to go and headed out toward the country munching on French fries, balancing soft drink cups on our laps, and discussing such important issues as why catsup is red, why I never played soccer as a boy, and how airplanes are able to fly. As soon as we reached the house and I'd parked the car alongside the fence by the swimming pool, Jamey jumped out, announced to me which pine tree would serve as which base, and the old man and the boy got into a fierce two-man softball game. Becky left the soccer match when we did, headed for her late-morning session at the health club, then drove out to join us in midafternoon.

Somewhere around four o'clock, Jamey became tired enough to put down the bats and balls, lie down across the top of his built-in bunk bed, and close his eyes for a nap. The prospect of his going backstage at the Opry with me and my Po' Folks Band later that night was enticement enough. "Can I play the drums on stage during intermission?" he asked hopefully. "I don't know, son, we'll see," I replied, glowing inside at the thought of this marvelous, fragile little boy perhaps someday wanting to follow his father's footsteps into the music business.

Becky and I decided to rest too, and we stretched out across the top of the king-sized bed she'd had custom-built as a gift for me and my long legs back on our first wedding anniversary. The bed we'd once called ours, but which for the past two-and-a-half years had been mostly mine. We lay there, but we couldn't sleep and we didn't talk. What else was there to say that we hadn't already said hundreds of times before? I wanted her and Jamey to move back home, for us to live there as a family again, and she knew it. She wanted me to close up the house and come live with them in the condo, and I knew it. We had been trying to compromise recently and speed up the process of our living together again when we found nine acres of beautiful wooded hillside property about half-way between the house in Lebanon and the condo in Nashville. Houses were close by, shops, schools and churches only a few miles away, yet this land was at the end of a dead-end street and covered with trees. It offered everything Becky wanted and I liked it, too. I could just see a rustic little house sitting halfway up the hill, a big fire roaring in the fireplace, and me stretched out on a warm bearskin rug writing a hit song. It was perfect—rural enough for me and urban enough for Becky—and we didn't waste any time in buying it, telling ourselves that one day soon we'd sit down together and start designing our dream house.

I drove a For Sale sign deep into the ground down by the road in front of the Lebanon house, knowing we first needed to sell that site before we could even begin to think about building on the new one. It was such a large and unique offering, however, that we

sometimes went months without having even one potential customer come to take a look at it. There could be no new house until
the old one sold, and Becky and I both came to realize that was
going to take some time. But it appeared that the longer it took,
the longer we lived apart, the wider the gulf was beginning to grow
between us.

And now, lying across the bed together in the still and quiet of
the late afternoon, there was simply no new ground left for us to
cover. Nothing left for either one of us to say. The lines of communication between us were taut and strained. So we just lay there.
Man and wife. Without talking. Without touching. Finally, shortly
before five o'clock, she got up without a word and drove back to
Nashville.

I didn't see Becky again until just before my first appearance on
the Opry that night at seven-thirty when she walked into my
dressing room. Jamey was munching on some nachos I had bought
him at the concession stand and sipping from a glass of pink
lemonade he'd found in the artists' lounge backstage. We had
already rehearsed our songs for the upcoming show, and as the
band members filed out and onto the stage, my ear was glued to a
small transistor radio I had brought along.

"Vandy's getting killed," I moaned to Becky as she came in.
"LSU has them twenty-something to three. And it's only the second quarter!" College football was one of the wide variety of
things we had always enjoyed together. Even though I'd graduated
from the University of Georgia and would always be a Bulldog at
heart and even though she was a North Carolinian, Becky and I
had become great fans of Vanderbilt University athletics after we'd
married. There was no real reason for us to support Vanderbilt
except for the fact that they were our local Nashville school, we
had met and grown to like many of the people in the athletic
department there, and over the years I had helped them with the
recruiting of several young student-athletes into their program,
mostly those with parents or relatives who were country music
fans. We had purchased season tickets to both the football and the
basketball games every year, and just one week earlier the University and the *Nashville Banner* newspaper had honored me on the

field at halftime of the Vandy-Tulane game, naming me the winner of their prestigious Commodore Award.

The game, however, couldn't have been farther from Becky's mind. She was concerned that I had not fed Jamey anything very nourishing for dinner and promised she'd take him home for "something better" as soon as my half-hour show was over. I shrugged, walked to the stage, sang my two songs, helped with a couple of radio commercials for Goo-Goo Candy Clusters ("Go Get a Goo-Goo, It's Good!") and Jamey reached up to hug my neck when I came off. "Great show, Dad!" he beamed proudly, and I smiled. "See you when you get back," he added, and squeezing my legs tightly, he turned to take his mother's hand. I watched the two of them walk down the backstage corridor and out the stage door into the night shortly after eight P.M.

The Po' Folks Band and I had one more Opry spot to do at nine-thirty. Then we'd be packing up and climbing aboard our big chartered Silver Eagle tour bus for a midnight-to-dawn ride to Lancaster, South Carolina, where we were scheduled to perform a Sunday afternoon concert for the employees of Springs Industries, Inc. My plan was to crawl into the bunk in the rear stateroom of the lavishly converted coach sometime in the wee hours, do a little serious snoozing, and wake up the next day around noon well-rested and ready to shave, shower, pick and grin. It wasn't anything unusual. I'd done it hundreds of times over the years en route to hundreds of other Lancasters coast to coast.

I had to do a brief radio interview with a Polish announcer from the Voice of America in my dressing room following our second Opry performance, after which I excused myself and headed back out to the farm to pack. I assumed that Becky had taken Jamey home to eat and that they were safely back at the condo, but driving east from Nashville on Interstate 40 just before reaching the exit they would have taken to go home, my heart nearly jumped out of my chest. I topped the crest of a high hill and found myself staring into the teeth of a grinding automobile accident which apparently had occurred only minutes before. "Oh, my God!" I thought as I saw the flashing blue police car lights and heard the sound of an onrushing ambulance. I was almost afraid to look over into the median where a big car was lying on its side, smoldering in the dust. Something told me if I looked I was going to see Becky's white Cadillac.

I slowed down and finally forced a glance. I breathed a huge sigh of relief when I realized it was an older model car than Becky's and a dark-colored one at that. I was tempted to pull off the interstate at the next exit and drop by the condo just to make sure everything was all right, but instead I glanced at the dashboard clock. It was almost eleven. I figured I needed to head on home.

I had only an hour to pack my small overnight suitcase with fresh socks, a clean shirt, a toothbrush and all the related essentials, make sure I had the proper stage apparel in my leather hang-up bag, lock the house, and drive my black Ford pickup truck to the parking lot of the all-night market out by the second Lebanon exit off the interstate. I often left my car or truck there while I was out on tour, and that's where the bus picked me up a little before twelve-thirty A.M.

As the driver eased the big Eagle away from the market and back into the eastbound lane of I-40, I reached for the TV. "Gotta see the Vandy replay," I announced to the band. "I just heard on the radio that they came back and almost beat LSU! I've gotta see how they did it!" And for as far as we could pick up the Nashville channel, I sat glued watching the tape of the football game.

It must have been somewhere between two and three o'clock in the morning when I stood up, stretched, bid the rest of the group a yawning good night and retired to the back of the bus in search of a few zzz's. But as tired as I was, for some reason I had trouble going to sleep. I blamed it on the strange bus.

After having owned my own buses (four of them to be exact) for nearly twenty years, I had decided to cut back on my travel schedule a couple of years earlier and sold my most recent one to singing star Sylvia. I had begun leasing buses on a per-date basis for my more infrequent road trips, and I had learned that while leasing had some definite advantages (no sky-rocketing insurance premiums, for example, and no maintenance expenses), each leased bus with its hired driver was different. Mostly I learned that none of the vehicles I'd come across was quite the home on wheels my own bus had been. And this particular driver, whom we had never had carry us before, sure did keep his bus cold!

I crawled under what seemed like a half-dozen blankets on the bunk in the bus's rear stateroom. I called the driver three or four times over the intercom to ask him why the bus was so cold. Each time he assured me the heat was on high. I assured him that if it was, none of it was making its way to the rear of the coach. Normally I like cool weather for sleeping, but I was afraid to close my eyes too tight at this point for fear they might freeze shut and I'd never be able to get them open again. Exhaustion finally overtook me, though, just as the sun began to show its face across the peaks of the Carolina hills. The last time I checked it was five A.M. I never did get warm.

I had been asleep for what seemed like only a few minutes when the incessant buzzing of the intercom at the foot of my bed woke me again. "If that danged driver woke me up to see if I'm warm enough, I may run this bus over him!" I thought as I struggled with the mountain of wool covering my body and reached for the receiver.

"Whadda you want?" I half-heartedly mumbled into the phone, trying to sound as disgusted as I felt.

"We just got pulled over," the driver answered.

"Well, if you were speeding, pay the dad-blamed ticket and let me sleep," I replied.

"No, that's not it," he said. "The highway patrol's been looking for us all night. You've got an emergency message to call home immediately!"

I looked at my watch. It was 7:13 A.M.

2

I have loved country music as long as I can remember. My parents tell me I could find the "hillbillies" (as they were called then) on the radio long before I could tie my shoelaces, so maybe it's a love I was born with. If so, it dates back to my birth, November 1, 1937, in Columbia, South Carolina.

My mom says I was "just another Bill that came on the first of the month!" Actually, that's not true. My full name is James William Anderson III, and until I was eight years old I wasn't even a Bill at all. I was known as Billy. One day I decided that Billy was a sissy name, and I refused to answer unless I was addressed as Bill. I'm sure I missed supper a few times when Mom or Dad would call out of habit, "Come to the table, Billy," but I wouldn't go until they said it right. Besides, I never thought Billy went with my last name. It always came out Billy Yanderson. Today a lot of people think Bill is my middle name. My first name, they think, is Whisperin'!

My mother and father, Elizabeth (Lib) and James William Anderson, Jr., (Jim) had been married a little over four years when I came along. I was their first child. My sister, Mary Elizabeth, wasn't born until four-and-a-half years later. Although I've written and sung many songs about coming from a large family, in reality there were only the four of us.

Daddy was not a farmer, as I sang in my song "Po' Folks," but rather an employee of the credit service company Dun & Bradstreet when I was born. He later became, like his father before him, an insurance agent. Mama's full-time job was taking care of Dad and us.

I don't know why I've always fantasized about coming from a large family and living on a farm. I wrote that not only into "Po' Folks" ("There was ten of us living in a two-room shack") but into "Mama Sang a Song" as well ("All daddy ever got was a bad-land farm and seven hungry mouths to feed"). I think that's why when I finally bought my home in the country in 1979, I looked upon it as the fulfillment of a lifelong dream.

My parents were both originally from Georgia, having met as teenagers in the small mill town of Griffin where my mother's father, the Reverend Horace Stratton Smith, had been sent to serve as pastor of the First Methodist Church. Mom was the third of four children born to her father and his wife, Mary Jessie Lewis Smith, and I've heard her say many times over the years that she often felt like she was the third verse of a four-stanza hymn. "You know how a lot of times the preacher says, 'We'll sing the first, second, and last verses'?", she'd ask. "The third one is the one that always gets left out!" But she always said it with a smile on her face.

My mother's mother died when Mom was only sixteen, so I never knew her. Her father was an interesting man, though. He worked in the newspaper business for a while, was later employed as a school teacher, and might never have gone into the ministry except for a violent thunderstorm that swept across the Gulf of Mexico and onto the coast of Texas late one night. He was young and single at the time, going to school and living alone in a small room on the second floor of an old wood-framed rooming house in Galveston. For most of this particular evening he'd been lying across the bed in his room studying, listening to the wind howl around the corners of the ancient structure while the flashing bolts of lightning lit up the jagged coastline and the raindrops pounded viciously against the tiny windowpanes. For some reason, around ten o'clock he laid down the book he'd been reading, got up from his bed, and walked downstairs to the kitchen for a glass of milk. When he returned to his room moments later, one entire wall of the house had collapsed under the onslaught of the storm and debris was piled more than three feet high across his bed . . . right in the spot where he'd been lying. There was no doubt that if he'd stayed in his room he would have been killed.

He immediately began to ponder why he'd been spared. What made him rise from his bed and go for that drink of milk at precisely the moment he did? Was God trying to tell him something important? Did He have something special in mind for this young teacher to do with his life?

"I spent the rest of that night wrestling with the devil," he used to say, "and the devil lost." Grandaddy decided almost immediately to change directions in his life. He returned to Georgia and applied for a license to preach, joined the North Georgia Conference of the Methodist church, and began his service as an ordained minister. From a fiery young circuit-riding preacher in his early days to a retired district superintendent many years later, he brought the word of God into thousands of lives. Yet on his deathbed in 1965 at the age of eighty-eight, without his even knowing it, he touched thousands more.

"Billy," he said to me as I leaned over his bed and strained to hear his weakening voice, "I don't know much about this business you're in, but I do know one thing: You're in a position to touch more lives with one song, with one appearance somewhere, than I've been able to touch with every sermon I've ever preached in my life." His words stunned me.

I knew what he'd said was true, yet somehow it seemed so unfair. Here he was, a much more eloquent speaker, a much better person spiritually than I'd ever be, I knew, yet my opportunities would be so much greater than his. Several years later when I was given the chance to record an album of all religious music (*I Can Do Nothing Alone*) I used his last words to me as my inspiration and dedicated the album to his memory.

On the other hand, my dad's father, James William Anderson, Sr., was born and raised on the red clay farm land of middle Georgia, and he worked as a farmer for most of his young life. Things weren't very easy, though, for people in that part of the country who tried to extract a living from soil that was so unyielding. In 1920, my grandpapa, as I've always called him, sold the farm and the little wooden farmhouse in Pike County where my dad was born and moved his wife and their only child seven miles east into Griffin to take up the insurance business. Despite having no experience in the field and only a fifth-grade education, he helped to found the successful Middle Georgia Mutual Insurance Company, where his portrait hangs on the wall to this day.

Grandpapa (his wife and friends all called him "Mr. Jim") was also an old-time fiddle player. He was part of a group that was widely known throughout the central part of the state as simply the Anderson Family Band. I'm told they played for every pie supper, cake walk, square dance, worm wrestlin', and goat ropin' that was held in those parts. Grandpapa had quit playing very much by the time I was born, but I felt the impact of his music many years later at my great uncle's funeral when my Dad introduced me to one of the neighbors, an old-timer who lived way back in the woods of that still extremely rural area.

"This is my son, Bill Anderson," my dad said proudly. "You might have heard of him. He plays up in Nashville, Tennessee, on the Grand Ole Opry!"

The old fellow, who had to be over ninety, looked me up and down, never showing any emotion in his craggy face at all. He spit a mouthful of tobacco juice on the ground in my direction and said, "Shoot, I don't care who he is. He can't make no music like Mr. Jim!"

My grandmother, Elizabeth Williams Anderson (everybody called her "Miss Lizzy") was also a musician, a guitar player, although nobody seems to recall her ever performing in public. Like Grandpapa, she didn't play much in her later years, but I grew up feeling an extreme closeness to both of my Anderson grandparents. I've got to believe it was a bond created and strengthened somehow by the love we all felt for music and for singing, for the joy that only music can bring.

I was always particularly close to my grandpapa. He was a big, strapping man who stood well over six feet tall and weighed close to two hundred pounds. He thought his little curly-headed grandson hung the moon. He'd play ball with me in the front yard of his house in Griffin, he'd go to the movies with me and sit through a double-feature of Red Ryder and Little Beaver, and he'd let me help him mow the lawn, pick turnip greens from the garden, even sleep in the same bedroom with him when I'd go to his house for my summer vacation.

In those days there was a train called the *Nancy Hanks* that ran from Atlanta to Savannah on the old Central of Georgia railroad line, and I'd save my money every year just so I could ride on the *Nancy* some fifty-five minutes south to Griffin. I thought I was really hot stuff when Grandpapa would be there to meet me at the station in his 1941 green Ford coupe and carry me home to Grandmama's dinner table where I would invariably stuff my face so full of her good country cooking that I'd get sick. He'd pamper me all night, then take me to his office with him the next morning. He'd set me up in a back room with my own typewriter and a stack of paper, and I'd amuse myself for hours, typing all sorts of things and playing office. At night after we'd gone to bed, he'd lie on the other side of the room and tell me stories and give me advice.

"Billy, don't you be thinking about getting married now, you hear?" he said to me once when I was about ten or eleven years old and had told him about a pretty girl I kind of liked in my sixth-grade class. And later on he said, "I know how much you like to play ball, Billy, but you be careful now and don't get athlete's foot!" I had to laugh even then, but I knew no boy ever had a better friend than my grandpapa was to me.

People ask me all the time where I got my musical abilities and my desire to write songs and entertain. It certainly didn't come from either one of my parents, so I guess, in truth, it probably goes back to my grandparents on both sides of the family. When you combine an old-time fiddle player with a circuit-ridin' preacher who used to write for a newspaper, then throw in a guitar-pickin' grandma for good measure, you come up with whatever it is that I am!

My mother and dad got married in the parsonage of the First Methodist Church in Decatur, Georgia, where Grandaddy Smith had been transferred, the afternoon of September 27, 1933, then headed south to Savannah Beach for their honeymoon. They had barely gotten inside their hotel room, however, when a bellman knocked on the door and handed Dad a telegram telling him that the company he worked for was transferring him from Atlanta to Meridian, Mississippi, and that they needed him to report immediately.

Jobs weren't easy to come by in 1933, so, honeymoon or not, my parents-to-be decided they'd best leave Savannah right away. Driving Dad's little brown-and-tan Chevrolet coupe farther west than either of them had ever been in their lives, they wound their way to Meridian, a sleepy little east Mississippi town that had only recently achieved a certain amount of fame and notoriety as the hometown of country music's first superstar, Jimmie Rodgers. In later years, honky-tonk wailer Moe Bandy would be born in Meridian, and had my Dad's company not changed its mind again and been so anxious to move him back east to South Carolina in 1936, ole Whisperin' Bill might have been born there as well.

My earliest childhood memories are set in Columbia, however, and I remember it as a happy place to have lived and begun growing up. It was hot as blazes in the summertime, and the streets were constantly filled during the wartime years with marching soldiers from nearby Fort Jackson. But I learned to play baseball at Shandon Park in Columbia, I saw my first college football game when the University of South Carolina defeated Presbyterian College 42-0 during the war, and I was valedictorian of my class in kindergarten. That meant I got to stand up in front of the rest of the kids and all the parents at our little graduation exercises and sing "Deep in the Heart of Texas" and recite a poem about how much fun it was to get mud between my toes. I was a certified ham before I even started to school!

I also got to go inside my very first radio station in Columbia. How could a hometown have given a kid anything more?

Our next-door neighbor's daughter was a receptionist at the biggest station in Columbia at the time, WIS, and she knew that from the time I was three or four years old I had sat faithfully by the radio every morning, noon, and night listening to a group called Byron Parker and the Hillbillies as they played and sang live country music on her station. They had three shows a day, sponsored by people like Seiberling Tires, Good Enough Flour, and Black Draught Laxative, and I never missed a one. I thought Byron Parker was the greatest man alive. In fact, he and General Douglas MacArthur were probably my first honest-to-goodness heroes.

I couldn't have been more than five or six the morning she asked me if I'd like to go to the radio station with her and see a live broadcast of my favorite show, but I remember it like it was yesterday. I was overwhelmed by all the microphones and the wires and cables and turntables in the control room, but what really got me excited was finding myself in the presence of the big man that loomed larger than life. It was him—the real, live Byron Parker—the man who talked to me and sang for me every day in my living room on Dad's little table-model Philco radio.

"Funny," I thought when I saw him for the first time, "he doesn't sound as big and fat on the radio as he looks in person!" But as I came to realize later, that was the beauty of radio: You only listened, and in your mind's eye your heroes could look any way you wanted them to.

Before he went on the air that morning at eight-thirty, Byron Parker came over to where I was seated in the corner of the studio and talked to me, asked me my name, then introduced me to some of the other musicians in the band. They were names I knew as well as I knew his, people like Snuffy Jenkins, Pappy Sherrill, and Greasy Medlin. Then when their show started, Byron Parker, the Old Hired Hand himself, even said my name on the radio so my mother and dad at home could hear that I was there. I honestly don't remember another day in the early years of my life when I was as excited or as happy.

Byron Parker recorded a few songs for RCA Victor during his career, but he never became a star anywhere outside South Carolina, where his name was legend. I'd have given anything, though, if he could have lived long enough to know all the good things that have happened to me in my career and what a big influence he was on me. He died while performing on stage in the late 1940s, and I never had the chance to see him in person but that one time. Yet there's another story involving him that gives me goose bumps every time I think about it.

In the early 1960s I was riding to a show date in Maryland with bluegrass greats Don Reno and Red Smiley on their bus. We had worked a show together the night before in North Carolina, and it was the first time Don and Red had ever seen me perform. Somewhere in the wee hours of the morning, Don got up from where he'd been sitting quietly in the front of the rolling bus and walked to the back where Red and I sat talking. He stood there without saying a word for the longest time and finally he looked down and said, "I've got it! It's been about to drive me crazy, but I've finally figured it out." He was looking directly at me.

"What's that?" I asked, wondering what I'd done.

"Oh, it's nothing really. I've just been sitting up there all night trying to figure out who you remind me of. I saw you working onstage tonight and you reminded me of somebody and I couldn't think who it was. But now I know."

"Well, who is it?" I asked.

"Oh, you probably never heard of him," he answered. "He's not even alive now. He was just a local singer down in South Carolina that I used to listen to when I lived up around Spartanburg. But, boy, you sound like him and you move like him on the stage, and from what I saw tonight you handle an audience just like he did . . . and he was the best. It won't mean anything to you, but his name was Byron Parker."

I don't think I slept a wink that night.

I started school in Columbia and finished the first, second, and half the third grade at Schneider Elementary. A few years ago my mother was rummaging through her basement at home and ran across my last report card from there. In the section on the back where the teacher had space to write her personal comments to the parents, my teacher had prophetically written, "Billy whispers too much." Never let it be said that I didn't start at an early age!

I was halfway through my third-grade year when Mom and Dad decided they needed to move back home to Georgia. Dad was becoming a bit restless in his job and wasn't sure he wanted to spend the rest of his life working for someone else. Too, his being an only child put extra pressure on him to return and live closer to his parents. His folks and Mom's dad and stepmother were all beginning to get along in years, so even though I didn't fully understand and begged and pleaded to stay in Columbia, I finally gave in and tried to smile when in December, 1945, we pulled up stakes and moved to Griffin, some forty miles south of Atlanta.

Actually, Griffin was only a pit stop. We lived there in the house with Grandmama and Grandpapa until the following February when the apartment Dad had rented for us in Decatur was ready. By the time my third-grade year was finally over, I had lived in three different towns, attended three different schools, each of which was teaching on a totally different level from the others, and had changed my name from Billy to Bill. I wasn't really sure at that point just who I was, how smart I was, or where I belonged.

Dad had said Decatur would be a great place for us to live. It was only a ninety-minute drive from his parents, even closer to Mom's family, and "just a few miles outside of Atlanta," he told us. "It takes only a half-hour to get right downtown, and you can ride the streetcar!" he'd say excitedly. "Plus, Decatur is a small town, not a big city like Atlanta. I want you kids to grow up in a small town." Of course, Decatur stayed a small town for about thirty minutes after we got there, and by the time I left home in 1955, Atlanta had dug up the streetcar tracks, replaced them with electric power lines for trackless trolleys, and swallowed up Decatur and a host of other little towns far beyond. Even Griffin was in danger of becoming one of Atlanta's numerous bedroom communities.

My childhood was, on the whole, what I'd call average. I wasn't really very different from most of the kids I grew up around. We didn't live in a house of our own until I was in the sixth grade, living instead in apartments or duplexes. We didn't have a lot of material possessions—Dad drove an old two-door black 1941 Chevrolet until I was well into high school, we never owned an air conditioner, we wore a lot of homemade clothes (Mama was a super seamstress!) and I got a lot of fifty-cent haircuts—but I never remember going to bed hungry. I made pretty good grades in school when I tried, but unfortunately I didn't always try. I had a dog and a cat, and once I even decided I wanted to raise rabbits. I must have been pretty good at raising them, too, because I raised them faster than Dad could give them away.

I was in the 4-H Club, the Cub Scouts, and I played cow pasture baseball and football (this was long before the Little Leagues and Pee Wee Leagues the kids have today) in an honest-to-goodness cow pasture behind Ralph and Jerry Adams's house. I got interested in girls early on and spent many a Saturday afternoon on the back row of the old Decatur Theater watching cowboy movies, munching popcorn, and holding hands. I carried out groceries in a supermarket, delivered newspapers on my bicycle after school, mowed lawns, took pictures of the neighborhood kids at Christmas (for a small fee, of course), and once even started a neighborhood newspaper. I was always industrious and trying to come up with ways to make some spending money.

Money was something we didn't have very much of. Dad came home from work one evening not long after our move to Decatur and announced to the family over dinner that he'd quit his job. "What do you plan to do?" Mama asked nervously. "Oh, I don't know," Dad replied. "I've always kinda wanted to be in business for myself. I think I'll start my own company."

And with that—lots of determination and not much more—my father went into the insurance agency business in 1946. He called his firm "Jim Anderson and Company . . . All Forms Of Insurance." "We can't say 'all *kinds* of insurance,'" he once told me, "because people will think we sell the good kind and the bad kind!" The "and Company" was, in the beginning, the corner of our dining room table and a telephone I was warned never to answer. "It might be business," I was carefully told.

From those humble beginnings, Dad built a very successful agency, which he personally managed for over thirty years. He sold the company to a group of his employees the year he turned sixty-seven. To this day the company still bears his name, and to this day his is a good name.

Being his only son, I guess it was natural for my dad to want me to follow his footsteps into the insurance business. I even worked for him one summer during high-school vacation, but I was a square peg in a round hole. I learned how to type labels for file folders and how to make bank deposits, but I never was too sure just what insurance was or how somebody went about selling it. It was apparent to me early on that I was simply not cut out to be, as many of the Georgia locals called it, "the policy man."

Over the years I've seen a lot of fathers try to force their sons into occupations the sons weren't really suited for. I've seen guys become doctors who wanted to fly airplanes, others become lawyers when they wanted to run off and join the circus. The greatest gift my dad ever gave me, the one he probably had to dig down the deepest to give but the one I'll always appreciate the most, was the freedom he gave me to be myself.

I did enjoy going to his office every day, however, for one reason. Upstairs over Dad's company was a radio station. The call letters were WGLS (they said it stood for World's Greatest Little Station!) and on my lunch hour every day I'd grab a sandwich and go running up the stairs to watch the disc jockeys and announcers at work. I pressed my nose so hard into that soundproof glass out in the hall that my prints are probably still on it today. It was obvious that the show-business bug was beginning to nibble at me even then.

At night I'd sometimes hang around after the station signed off the air and watch people with colorful names like Cowboy Jack, George "Sleepy" Head, and Swain Sheriff & His Deputies tape-record their early morning country music radio shows. They weren't very professional and probably weren't even very good, but I didn't care. I loved the music they played and sang. They each had four or five local musicians who sold cars, laid pipe, or plowed all day, then picked 'n' grinned for a few extra bucks at night, and I'd sometimes sit there watching them for hours, tapping my toes, listening to the melodies they played and the lyrics they sang. I felt like I'd died and gone to heaven.

And, oh, how I wanted to learn to play the guitar like they did! I worked hard and finally saved enough money from my paper route to buy a cheap, flat-top model with the strings about an inch above the fret-board. Now, anyone who has ever tried to learn how to play the guitar will tell you that your fingers get mighty sore when you first start learning, even on a good instrument, but on this ole thing my fingers ached and bled so bad it nearly crippled me. I was determined I was going to learn a few chords, though, so I could accompany myself when I sang. By that time I could imitate any country singer you could name.

That was one of my problems. Being left-handed was also a problem. My natural inclination was to turn the guitar around and strum it upside down, but something told me I'd never really learn to play that way. So I forced myself to flip my instrument back around the way it should be and learn to play right-handed. To this day, playing a guitar is the only thing I don't do left-handed.

I soon learned to play well enough that I began picking and singing songs for my mama while she did her housework. I'd strum and sing up-tempo songs while perched on top of her old wringer washing machine, and she'd tap her toes, sing along, and get her work done in a hurry. If I started singing ballads, though, she'd slow down to the tempo of the music and the house would still be dirty when Daddy got home.

Dad would come in and hear me singing. If I was singing a Hank Williams song, I'd be trying my darnedest to sing it just like ole Hank. Or on an Ernest Tubb song, I'd try to sound like Ernest. Or Webb Pierce, or Carl Smith, or Faron Young, or any of the top stars of the day. I guess Dad enjoyed as much as he could stand, because one day he said, "Son, why don't you try sounding like Bill Anderson?"

I didn't understand what he meant at first and it hurt my feelings. "Listen," he said, "there's already a Hank Williams and an Ernest Tubb. Why do you want to sound like them? Try sounding like yourself."

Today I'd say that was one of the two or three best pieces of advice I've ever received. Lots of people have said over the years that I sound "like the devil" when I sing, but nobody has ever accused me of being an imitator or a copier. You might not like Bill Anderson when you hear him sing, but you darn sure know who it is!

Actually, it wasn't until I began making up some songs of my own to sing that I was *able* to start sounding like myself. For the first time I was singing songs I'd never heard anybody else sing, because nobody else had ever sung them. I *had* to sound like me. I had nothing to imitate.

I was about ten or eleven years old when I wrote my first song. It was called "Carry Me to My Texas Home." I had never been west of Carrollton, Georgia, at the time, but Texas just sounded like something a true country artist ought to be writing and singing about.

I was fifteen years old and in the tenth grade at Avondale High School when three buddies and I decided to form a band and enter the upcoming school talent show. I was selected to emcee our part of the show, play rhythm guitar, and sing. A genuinely talented boy a year or two younger named Charles Wynn would play mandolin and/or lead guitar and sing harmony. A short, chubby little guy my age whom we nicknamed "Meatball" Bell would be our fiddle player, while a big, lumbering, uninhibited goofball of a guy named Tom Schooley, who had no talent whatsoever but enough nerve and brass for all the rest of us combined, would play washtub bass and do comedy. (For the city slickers among you, a washtub bass is a homemade instrument constructed by turning a galvanized tub upside down and drilling a small hole in the bottom, just big enough for a rope or a heavy string to slide through. One end of the rope is knotted underneath the upper side or bottom of the tub, while the other end is connected to a broom handle or stick which then becomes the neck of the instrument. Musical tones can actually be formed by pulling or pushing the neck, which tightens or loosens the rope.)

Schooley, unfortunately, never learned to match the tones of his bass with the tones the rest of the band was attempting to make, but a tenth-grader standing six-foot-two, weighing close to two hundred pounds, wearing bibbed overalls with freckles painted on his cheeks and his front teeth blacked out doesn't have to make beautiful music to get attention. We cleverly named him "Rufus Rainwater, the Red-headed Rodeo Romper." We put a lot of thought into naming the band, too, and came up with the imaginative name the Avondale Playboys.

Meatball, whose real name was Jim, had been studying classical violin and never got around to telling his parents he had joined a hillbilly band. Somehow he feared that after all the money they'd spent on his music lessons they just might not understand. He'd never played any country music at all, so we bought him a copy of "The Orange Blossom Special" and "Boil Them Cabbage Down" and he listened to the records and actually became a pretty good country fiddler . . . as long as we didn't expand the repertoire too much!

I had written a song called "What Good Would It Do to Pretend?" and we decided to perform that and "The Orange Blossom Special" for the talent show. The day before our big debut, we all went down to Decatur Street, in the heart of the black section of downtown Atlanta, and found some matching brown cowboy shirts in the back of a dirty old pawn shop. The guy sold them to us for something like five bucks for the whole lot, and we thought we'd be the cat's meow wearing them in the show.

The act we put on for our teachers and classmates went over pretty well, especially my solo. After our part of the program was over, we went offstage and into the adjoining gymnasium locker room to change from our cowboy shirts and matching brown slacks back into our school clothes. We still had a full day of classes to attend. Suddenly I heard this tremendous roar going up out in the audience, screaming, clapping, cheering coming from everywhere. In a minute somebody stuck his head in the dressing-room door and said, "Hey, you guys just won the show! They want you back out there!"

I got so excited that I forgot I wasn't fully dressed. I just grabbed my guitar and yelled "Let's go!" to the rest of the band, and we went parading out in front of all our classmates, our teachers, and the principal of the school.

It wasn't until I reached the microphone at center stage that I began to feel a draft. I suddenly realized that while I did have my pants on, they were not zipped. To this day if you mention my name around any of the people who were there, they'll say, "Oh yeah . . . Bill Anderson . . . that's the guy who holds his guitar in a real funny position!"

(Come to think of it, zippers and I have never gotten along very well. Once, several years later during my college days, I was invited to Sunday dinner at the home of a young lady that I was rather fond of. I had never met her parents and was naturally very anxious to impress them.

My girlfriend's mother had cooked up a delicious southern-style country dinner, and I was feeding my face furiously when about halfway through the meal I dropped a bit of food into my lap. When I reached down to remove it, I realized to my utter dismay that my shiny new brown pants were completely unzipped. Not partially unzipped, mind you, but staring up at me open as a shark's mouth. How or when they got that way I'll never know, but at the tender age of eighteen I had neither the experience nor the ingenuity to know how to remain the cool cat I was trying so hard to be and at the same time remedy my tenuous situation.

You see, the guest of honor, sitting at the head of the dining room table, can't just reach down and zip up a wide-open fly without attracting attention. In fact, it's virtually impossible to perform such an act while remaining seated. I knew I had to come up with a solution quick, though, because the meal was almost over and we'd all be getting up from the table at almost any moment. And I knew that under no circumstances whatsoever could I possibly get up from that table with my pants unzipped and run the risk of those I was trying so hard to impress seeing my blue boxer shorts. I'd rather have died!

The only thing I could think of was that somehow I had to distract all the other people in that room. Suddenly it hit me. The layout of the house dictated that after the meal we would all adjourn from the dining room, walk a few short steps to our right, and reconvene in the adjacent living room where the big over-stuffed sofa and padded armchairs beckoned invitingly. And on the right-hand wall of that living room was a large picture window facing the front yard and the little country lane that wound its way through the trees beyond. It was a gamble, but it was my only hope.

As I anticipated, we finished the last bites of the meal and rose almost as one from the table. First my girlfriend's parents, a brother, then two sisters, and finally my beloved made their way to the living room. By design I lingered and brought up the rear.

My timing, I thought, was perfect. Just as I pushed back my chair and began to follow the procession away from the table, I looked out the big picture window and saw a young boy roaring down the lane on a shiny red bicycle. Perfect, I thought! God does answer prayers after all! Without pausing, I quickly pointed toward the lad and his bicycle and shouted, "Look, everybody! What's that?"

The entire family immediately ran toward the window in anticipation of sharing my great discovery, whatever it might be, and I quickly pulled my zipper back into place.

"I am so smart and so clever!" I smiled to myself as I made my way toward the window, hastily trying to invent a reason why the kid on the bicycle had been so important in the first place. But by the time I reached the window, the bicycle and its rider were nowhere in sight. Instead, the entire family that I wanted so much to impress was standing transfixed at the glass staring at the per-spiring bodies of two huge black dogs in the act of making wild and passionate doggie-love!

Every mouth in the room hung at half-mast. Nobody spoke a word. Thank goodness. What could I have possibly replied? The only word that came to mind was "Oops!" and somehow that didn't seem like quite enough.

I stood there awkwardly for what seemed like a lifetime, then I asked softly where the restroom was. I excused myself and quietly sneaked out the back door. When my hosts last saw me, I was racing down their driveway, jumping into my car, cranking the engine, and burning rubber like Richard Petty at Talledega. It was several months before I got up enough nerve to drive back past my sweetheart's house. There was a sign in the front yard—"Black puppies for sale!" I kept on driving.)

Anyhow . . . with all the excitement of winning the high school talent show still ringing in our hearts, minds, and ears, we decided to keep our little band together for a while, playing anywhere we could get anybody to listen. Tom Schooley's dad was one of the big shots at the local Chevrolet manufacturing plant and had just given his son a shiny, new red convertible. We figured out a way to take full advantage of that. On weekend nights we'd gather the band together, roll back the top on Tom's car, and drive up into the parking lot of the Avondale Tavern, a beer joint/sandwich shop located along the main drag in the community of Avondale Estates. We'd turn a big cowboy hat upside down and set it out on top of the trunk, stand up in the back seat with our unamplified instruments, and pick and sing for hours for tips. We didn't get rich, but the experience led to a regular Saturday night gig at a fancy restaurant east of town near Stone Mountain. Again we used only acoustical instruments so that we'd be free to wander from table to table and play requests. We weren't guaranteed a salary, but the manager said we could take home as much money in tips as we could siphon off the customers. A big tip in those days was about a dollar.

One slow night around ten P.M. a large party of people from Wisconsin stopped in to eat, and we made a beeline for their table. "Would you folks like to hear a song while you wait for your food?" I asked. One of the men in the party, who had obviously had a bit too much to drink tore into his pocket and ripped out a crisp, new twenty-dollar bill. "You betcha," he shouted. "I'll give you twenty dollars to play 'On Wisconsin!'" All his friends started chiming in, "Yeah, play it . . . we wanta hear 'On Wisconsin!'" Trouble was, there wasn't a one of us Georgia boys who had any idea how to play "On Wisconsin!" But, oh, that twenty-dollar bill sure did look good!

"Sir, I'm afraid we don't . . . ," I started to explain, heartsick to think that we were on the verge of missing out on the biggest payday we'd ever had. But before I could finish telling him we didn't know the song, I felt the sharp jab of a fiddle bow gouging me in the ribs.

"Oh yes, we *do* know it," Meatball, the round little fiddle player interrupted. "I know it real well. You guys join in." And with that, he tore into playing the old country fiddle tune "Boil Them Cabbage Down" and began singing at the top of his voice, "On Wisconsin . . . on Wisconsin!"

It may not have been the worst attempt at making music I had ever heard, but it sure came close. There was no correlation between the lyrics and the melody whatsoever. It was just noise. The good news, though, was that the man with the twenty-dollar bill never knew the difference. In fact, he got so excited to be hearing a song about his home state sung 'way down south in Georgia that he started singing along. I can see him now, jumping up from his seat, dancing around the table, waving his money in the air, singing a college fight song to the tune of a hillbilly hoedown. And when we finished he applauded like he'd just heard Hank Williams yodel the "Lovesick Blues." Better than that, he gave us the twenty dollars.

Later that night, as the four of us sat around dividing up our loot, it dawned on me that I had just learned a valuable lesson: Never admit there's a song you don't know. You might not know it exactly the way it was written, but under the right set of circumstances, a good singer can somehow manage to sing just about anything!

The Avondale Playboys and I ended up with our own Saturday afternoon radio show not long afterward. It was on radio station WBGE, a small station located in the basement of the Georgian Terrace Hotel in downtown Atlanta. But had the program director of the station not had a good sense of humor, we might have lost our show before it ever got on the air.

We rehearsed for days and went down to the studios to audition early one evening. Everything came off perfect, so perfect, in fact, that we were hired on the spot and were told we'd be on the air for thirty minutes every week beginning at four-thirty the following Saturday afternoon. I was so excited I could hardly put my guitar back in the case. Meatball, however, was a bit skeptical.

"How powerful is this station?" he asked the program director moments after we'd been told we had the job.

"Two hundred and fifty watts," the P.D. answered.

To which Meatball replied, "Good Lord, is that all? I've got a light bulb at home that powerful!"

Even with all the success we were having and all the fun I was finding in getting up on stage and performing, music was not my major concern at this point in my life. What I wanted more than anything else in the world was to be a professional baseball player.

I had played football for two years in high school but came to realize that I just wasn't aggressive enough to really be good at the game. Shortly after making first-string right offensive tackle in spring practice prior to my junior year, I quit the team.

But baseball, now that was something else. My freshman year in high school, I played first base, but not very much. Avondale won the State Class A Championship that year, and there were a lot of players on the team better than me. Three or four even signed professional contracts. But at practice one day during my sophomore season, I got to fooling around on the sidelines with pitching. I found I could really throw a slow, tantalizing round-house curve ball and throw it just about anywhere I wanted it to go. I could break it out and away from a left-handed batter, in tight on a right-handed batter, or make it drop down like it was rolling off the edge of a table. I could make it do everything I wanted except go fast.

I worked hard at perfecting my newly discovered talent, and I became a pitcher. I guess I just pitched kinda like I sing . . . soft. My teammates used to tease that my fast ball was so slow the school made extra money on the nights I pitched by selling advertising on the sides of the ball. But whatever I was doing it must have been right, because I started winning ball games doing it.

I moved into the starting rotation my junior year and ended up with a won-lost record of something like 10-2. I pitched both American Legion and Babe Ruth League ball the following summer, and by my senior year some of the pro scouts who combed our area seeking talent for the major league teams were beginning to take notice of me.

I was big for sixteen. I stood over six feet tall, weighed about 175 pounds, and it was obvious I wasn't through growing. The "bird dogs," as the part-time scouts were called, urged me to learn to throw more with my body and not put so much strain on my arm, but I was known for, as one newspaper writer put it, "the cautious left arm of Bill 'Hillbilly' Anderson."

The writers and most of the kids on the other high school teams knew of my interest and involvement in music through the various radio and TV programs I had begun doing around the Atlanta area (by my senior year in high school I'd had my own radio programs not only on WBGE but also on fifty-thousand-watt WEAS, as well as my own television show, on WQXI-TV), and when I'd pitch some of the opposing players would really try to give me a hard time. They'd grab their bats over on the sidelines and act like they were strumming guitars. Then they'd start wailing some awful country song at the top of their lungs, trying to distract me. "Hey, Hillbilly," they'd yell, "sing us a song. Yodel-o-lady-who!" I'd just try to ignore them and keep on throwing round-house curves.

One of the scouts told me during my senior season that he could arrange for me to go to Mesa, Arizona, to the Chicago Cubs training camp the spring following graduation if I'd like to go and work with some of the pitching coaches there. Then, if things worked out—meaning if I ever learned to put my body weight behind my pitches and began throwing a pro-type fastball—he said the Cubs would sign me to a professional contract. Lord, I wanted to go, but the only thing my mom and dad had ever seriously asked me to do in my entire life was to go to college. They had let me play sports, they had let me run all over town at all hours of the night playing music while I was still in school (as long as I kept my grades respectable), but I knew I'd break their hearts if I tried skipping college to play baseball.

I wrestled with it long and hard and finally told the scout that I appreciated his offer but I intended to enroll that fall at the University of Georgia. "Fine," he answered, "you play ball at Georgia and maybe when you get out we can pick up some of your college expenses and you can still sign with the Cubs." It sounded like a good idea to me.

On graduation night the kids in my class all exchanged gag gifts with one another. They called me up front and presented me with a little red-and-yellow plastic guitar with a card attached which read:

To Bill Anderson We Give This Guitar
Because in the World of Music We Know You'll Go Far.

I thought at the time, Now that's silly. I'm not going to be in the music business. I'm going to play professional baseball.

But a funny thing happened on my way to Wrigley Field.

3

I grabbed my blue jeans, sweatshirt, ball cap, socks, and cowboy boots and pulled them all on in less than thirty seconds. On top of my pajamas.

I hardly ever sleep in pajamas on the bus and I don't know to this day how a pair happened to be in my travelling bag this trip, but as cold as I was all night, I'm glad they were. When I reached the stairwell in the front of the bus, I was warmer than I'd been for hours.

"How far are we from a phone?" I asked the driver.

"We're seven miles from Chester," he replied.

"You sure the call is for me? I mean, could it be for somebody in the band?"

"They said 'Bill Anderson,'" he answered. "It was actually some fans who stopped us. They heard on their CB that the sheriff was looking for us."

We plowed through the sleepy Carolina morning as fast as the big burgundy bus could negotiate the winding, bumpy roads. It seemed like an eternity before a combination market-filling station came into view and I spotted a phone booth just off the edge of the road.

"Pull over there," I instructed the driver, pointing to an open space between the phone booth and the store. He nodded and began to gear the bus down.

For the first time since he had buzzed to wake me, I became aware of my heart pounding rapidly inside my chest. My breaths were coming short and fast. There was no one there I wanted to admit it to at the time, but I was scared.

My first thought was that something had happened to my mother or my dad. After all, they were both in their seventies, and although their health had been good, I knew things could happen. Mom had fallen a few years earlier and broken her jaw pretty bad. I was afraid something like that had happened again. Only maybe worse.

And then I thought of the house in Lebanon. It was standing empty. What if it had caught on fire or somebody had broken in? I had a sophisticated alarm system, but . . .

The bus came to a halt between the phone booth and the market. "Cut the engines," I told the driver. "I need to be able to hear." He quickly switched off the main diesel engine and the smaller, gasoline-driven power generator.

My hand was shaking uncontrollably as I ran down the steps of the bus and into the tiny glass cubicle, anxiously sliding the quarter into the slot and dialing our number at the condo. Our babysitter-housekeeper, Pam Hunt, answered the phone.

"Pam, what's the matter?" I asked hurriedly, all the time still assuming it was something to do with my folks and that Pam had just answered the phone while Becky was upstairs, perhaps packing for a necessary trip home.

"Jamey, run upstairs and get me a pencil please," I heard her calmly say to my son. Then I heard his little shriek, and Pam came back on the line.

"Bill," she said quietly, but sounding out of breath, "it's Becky. She's had a horrible automobile accident. She's at General Hospital."

"Becky?" I cried. How could that be? She'd been at the Opry with me until after eight o'clock, and then she left to go get Jamey something to eat. And I already knew Jamey was safe at home.

"When? How?"

"It happened around midnight," Pam said, "on her way home from the movies. She and Kathy Woodard decided at the last minute to go to the late show over by Rivergate. You'd better call Lynne at the hospital. She can give you all the details."

"How bad is it? Is she . . ."

"I don't know. I think it's pretty bad. You'd better call."

"Is Jamey OK?" I asked. "I mean, does he know?"

"No, I haven't told him yet. I figured it's best for you to do that. Or at least somebody who's family. I told him when he woke up this morning that his mother had to go to a meeting. So far that seems to have satisfied him."

I wrote down the number that Lynne, Becky's older sister, had given Pam, hung up the telephone, then had to run back onto the bus for another quarter. I had charged the call to my credit card and my coin should have been returned, but for some reason it wasn't. And I couldn't get a dial tone without another coin.

By the time I hit the aisle of the bus, everybody was up: Mike Johnson, my steel guitar player and band leader of several years; his younger brother, Mark, my bass player and road manager; our guitar player, Les Singer; the keyboard player, Dirk Johnson (no kin to Mike and Mark); drummer, Mike Streeter; background vocalists, LeAnn Folsom and Liana Manis; our audio engineer, Jimmy Corn; and a friend of mine from Lebanon, Don Keaton, a professional photographer, who had come along on the trip to take some pictures and maybe, just maybe, run into an old girlfriend he'd last seen in the vicinity of Spartanburg. They were all bleary-eyed and tousle-haired and nobody said a word, but I could tell by the expressions on their faces that they knew something was wrong. I found out later that Mike Johnson was trying to ask me if something had happened to Jamey but the words had hung in his throat and he couldn't get them out.

I didn't say anything either but ran quickly to the rear of the bus. I grabbed a quarter from the ashtray in my stateroom and raced back down the aisle and out the door to the phone. I had to strain to hold my hand steady enough to slide the coin into the slot and dial the number Pam had just given me. My call went through to a special family waiting room inside the trauma center of General Hospital in Nashville.

"Lynne . . . what's happened? How is she?" I asked breathlessly when Becky's sister came on the line. I held on to the side of the phone booth, not sure I really wanted to know.

"Oh, God, Bill, it's awful. A drunk driver hit her head-on about midnight out on Andrew Jackson Parkway. She's really hurt bad."

For the first time I forced myself to say it: "Is she alive?" I asked in a voice I could barely control.

"She's alive," Lynne answered, "but the doctors say the next forty-eight hours are critical. Most of the damage seems to be from the neck up. She's got a million stitches in her face. She's all cut and bruised. They say her brain is swelled real bad . . . wait, here comes a doctor. Talk to him."

The voice on the other end identified himself as a Dr. Alexander. "Your wife has been in an accident," he began.

"I know," I interrupted. "How is she? Is she going to live?"

"I'd say the chances are about fifty-fifty right now, Mr. Anderson," he replied. "Her brain is bruised and swollen very badly. We have her on some strong medication. If it works it should prevent any more swelling and she should make it. But . . . if it doesn't . . . then we're in trouble. I think you'd best get here as fast as you can."

"Lynne, I'll call you back," I said as soon as the doctor was off the line. "I'm in the middle of nowhere but I'll get a plane somehow. Can somebody pick me up at the airport?"

"I'll have Marion come get you," Lynne answered, referring to her husband. "But please hurry. You really need to be here."

I placed the receiver back in its cradle and stood staring mindlessly for I don't know how long into a thicket of pine trees that dotted the other side of the narrow country highway. The whole world seemed to be on hold . . . a kaleidoscope suspended in midair. Wife . . . death . . . six-year old . . .

The next thing I recall was standing inside the little market tightly clutching a styrofoam cup of hot, black coffee that had somehow gotten into my hand. Mike Streeter, my drummer and close friend of more than seven years, was standing beside me. He didn't say a word. And for the longest time neither did I. Then, almost as if on cue, I reached my arms out around his shoulders and pulled him close.

"Oh, God, Mikey," I cried. "I'm afraid He's given me a mountain this time!"

4

I arrived at the University of Georgia in the fall of 1955 determined to get a degree in journalism as fast as I could and then run all the way, if I had to, to Mesa, Arizona. A baseball player with a college degree. It had a nice ring to it.

I had decided on journalism as my major for two reasons. First, I'd always loved to write. I had been sports editor of the weekly *DeKalb New Era* newspaper in Decatur my last two years in high school and had even latched onto a stringer's job with the daily *Atlanta Constitution* on the side. "Stringer" meant I was given specific assignments to cover, in my case high school football and basketball games (notice I didn't say baseball . . . come baseball season I wanted not to write but to be written about), and I was paid by the job. Not much, mind you, something like five dollars per game and out of that I paid my own expenses, but I enjoyed it. I even thought once or twice that in spite of the obvious lack of significant financial reward, sportswriting might be an enjoyable way to try and make a living after my ball-playing career was over.

The second reason I chose journalism was because it was the only course I could find in searching through the University curriculum that didn't require any courses in math to graduate. Let me go on record here and now as saying that I am not a mathematician. In fact, in my sixteen years of schooling I flunked only two subjects: math and music! (Actually the music course I failed was called Music Appreciation. One day the professor was telling the class something about Beethoven and I asked how that compared to something Hank Williams had once done, and he roared that I was never even so much as to mention the name Hank Williams in the same breath with Beethoven again. I decided not to return to Music Appreciation class after that. It was obvious I didn't appreciate their music and they darn sure didn't appreciate mine!) Of course, math and music are the only two things from school that I've used since I got out!

I enjoyed my first year at Georgia. I lived in the freshman dormitory, sharing a small third-floor room and bunk beds with an older student and freshman counselor from Fitzgerald, Georgia, named Cliff Pickens. My sophomore year I became a counselor myself and shared the same room with a foreign exchange student from Tokyo name Hiroyuki Sugahara. You should have heard me trying to explain country music to *him*!

I studied hard most of the time, made fairly good grades, fell in love every couple of weeks or so, and tried to adjust to life away from home for the first time. I pledged the Kappa Sigma fraternity and, in an effort to prove what a good and loyal brother I'd be, I got myself thrown into jail on the Saturday night before my formal initiation into the brotherhood on Sunday afternoon.

Each of the pledges, most of whom were freshmen like me, was given what were supposed to be ridiculous but harmless little tasks to perform as part of our overall initiation rites. Each of us had a "big brother" in the fraternity, an older member to whom we were responsible, and it was the big brother's job to decide what each little brother's initiation chore was to be. My big brother was an upper-classman from Albany, Georgia, named George Thompson, and George had an old score he wanted settled.

Before he had transferred to Georgia, George had been a student at a military college in the little north Georgia town of Dahlonega, and he had gotten into trouble on more than one occasion while he was there. The Commandant of the school, an Army lieutenant colonel who lived in a nice house next to the campus, had meted out some pretty tough punishment on him a few times, and George had been carrying a grudge for years.

"The whole time I was in school up there," he said to me at the frat house on Friday night, "I tried to figure out a way to get back at that guy. Now you're gonna help me do it!" There was a glow of sweet revenge in his eye.

"Right out in front of the house where he lives, on his lawn, is a little sign. It's nothing fancy, just a small white sign with his name and rank on it . . . and the word 'Commandant.' I used to pass his house and look at that sign every day, and I wanted to yank it up out of the ground and smash it to bits every time I looked at it. Now I'm finally going to get to do it, because *you're* going to go up there tomorrow and get that sign and bring it back to me. Aren't you?"

"Do I have a choice?" I timidly asked.

"No," Big Brother answered.

"Then, yeah, I guess I'm gonna go get it. But won't that be stealing?"

"Not if you don't get caught, it won't. But here's how you'll have to do it: Wait until after dark when everything in town is closed. That won't be very late 'cause they roll up the sidewalks in Dahlonega at ten o'clock. Then, when nobody's looking, you sneak up on the lawn, grab the sign, and run like the devil. It shouldn't take more than just a few seconds and you'll be gone. Bring the sign back here to me and I'll guarantee that you'll become a full-fledged Kappa Sig Sunday afternoon."

I wasn't sure what to say. I'd never stolen anything in my life, and I wasn't real anxious to start. On the other hand, I'd heard through the grapevine that some of my fellow pledges were going to have to eat raw eggs and swallow live goldfish as part of their initiation Saturday night, and stealing a little sign sounded kinda tame compared to that. I smiled at George, stuffed a couple of candy bars into the pockets of my coat, and headed for the dorm to get some sleep. At ten o'clock the next morning I was standing on the north side of Athens trying to thumb a ride to Dahlonega.

I had better luck than I had anticipated in flagging down a couple of cars, and I arrived in the former mining town (they discovered gold there back in the 1800s) in midafternoon. I decided it was too early for me even to begin thinking about carrying out my assignment, so I went to work on trying to pass the time. I wandered in and out of the drugstore a couple of times, checked out the dime store, then bought a newspaper and sat outside on a park bench and read for a while. I started once to go down to the barbershop and watch haircuts, but I never got quite that bored.

The local movie theater opened about seven, so I decided to take in the western that was playing. I bought a box of popcorn and a large cola drink and settled in for a couple of hours of watching the good guys run the bad guys out of town. I should have taken that as an omen.

True to George's prediction, thirty minutes after the movie let out around nine-thirty, downtown Dahlonega was deserted. I sauntered up the hill from the theater and tried to get the lay of the land. Sure enough, right at the top of the hill on the left side of the road was the Commandant's house, and about thirty feet from his front door, square in the middle of his grassy, tree-laden yard, was my target, the little white sign. "Piece of cake," I smiled to myself. I looked to my left and then to my right. There wasn't a soul in sight. Then suddenly I realized I was about to act prematurely. My wait wasn't quite over. There were a couple of lights shining from inside the windows of the Commandant's house. "Probably sitting up reading *War and Peace*," I surmised, and I walked aimlessly on up the hill.

It was a few minutes after midnight when I meandered back down by the house for the umpteenth time and saw that all was finally dark and still. "Perfect," I thought, and I tiptoed quietly up the little bank and into the yard. I slowly eased my way along, careful not so much as to step on a twig. I didn't want to arrouse anyone's attention. I'd come too far and been too careful to blow it all now. I was starting to want the little sign as much as George did.

From one tree to the next, I inched my way, stopping to make sure no one was watching, creeping ever so carefully through the darkness. Ten feet away, then five, three, two, until suddenly I was standing poised directly above my prey. I looked all around one last time. No one was there. I reached for the sign and gave it a tug. It moved a couple of inches but that was all. "Hmmm, this might be a little harder than I thought," I conjectured, but I never got a chance to find out just how difficult removing the sign from the red Georgia clay might have been. I was suddenly distracted by the fierce glare of lights and the piercing scream of sirens!

The front yard of the Commandant's house must have been wired like a mine field. All I know is that in far less time than it takes to tell it, I was standing dead solid center in the penetrating yellow beam of the Army's or the sheriff's or somebody's hot, luminous spotlight and telling some big dude in a uniform that it was all a mistake. I wasn't trying to sabotage the United States Army, I was just a college kid from Athens trying to join a fraternity. You can imagine about how that went over.

In a minute here came the Commandant roaring out his front door to see what was going on. He was dressed in bright red-and-white striped pajamas underneath a dark blue bathrobe. If I hadn't been so nervous, I'm sure I could have come up with a brilliant remark regarding his patriotic choice of nightwear.

"What's going on?" he thundered, and I launched into my story about George Thompson and Kappa Sigma and about how all I wanted was the sign for good ole George, but now that I'd had some time to think about it I really didn't want it all that bad, and why didn't he just keep his sign and go on back to bed and we'd forget the whole thing. About fifteen minutes later I was doing my whole routine again in front of an equally unappreciative audience down at the county jail.

But I've got to hand it to the chief or the sheriff or whoever was in charge, he was OK. He listened to all I had to say, kept me there for a few hours, probably to frighten me more than anything else, then just before daylight he let me go. Even sent me over to a legendary family-style Dahlonega eatery called the Smith House and instructed me to eat a good breakfast and be out of town by ten o'clock. I was out on the side of the road with my thumb in the air long before that.

Rides were hard to come by that morning, though, and I didn't make it back to Athens until just a few minutes before the formal oath-taking ceremonies at the fraternity house at two o'clock. And I walked into the house minus the sign I'd been sent to retrieve.

"It's a long story, big brother," I said to George as he rushed out to meet me, but he didn't even question me as to why I wasn't carrying his prize. He just reached up and hugged my neck. I found out later that he and all the other brothers had been so nervous as to my whereabouts that they didn't care whether I'd carried out my duties or not. They were just thankful I was alive. They had been looking at their watches since early morning and had about decided that I had been kidnapped, killed, or had run off to join the foreign legion. Not that they would have missed me all that much, but they would have been held responsible. If I'd never come back, the dean of men would have probably pulled the permit for their next beer party!

I grabbed a quick shower, put on a borrowed tuxedo, and became a full-fledged brother in Kappa Sigma that afternoon. I guess it was fun and I carry around some good memories from that period of my life, but it wasn't long afterward that I decided I wasn't really cut out to be Joe College. I was starting to get too many other things on my mind.

For one thing, there was a big freshman talent show coming up, and I wanted more than anything to enter. I did, wearing a bright red western shirt with matching fire-engine red pants, a white western belt and a pair of white buck shoes with red soles. Can't you just imagine how that went over on a college campus? I played my guitar and sang the same song I had written and sung for the talent show in high school three years before, "What Good Would It Do to Pretend?" and actually my act went over pretty well. In fact, I won second place. A blind girl who played the piano and sang came in first. I learned another valuable show business lesson that night: Never compete against a kid, a dog, or a blind girl who plays the piano and sings. You'll come in second every time!

But the word quickly spread around campus that there was this oddball kid in the freshman class who went around wearing red cowboy clothes, picking a guitar, and singing through his nose. That prompted a phone call one day from a couple of upperclassmen who had been in the military and had come back to school to study under the GI bill.

"We're thinking about getting together a country band," they told me, "and wondered if you'd like to join us." I asked them, "Is a flat-top guitar flat?" Of course I'd like to join them. What they didn't tell me, though, was that each of them played nothing but guitar (neither of them exceptionally well), and with the addition of my talents, the band would consist of three guitars. That's all, just three guitars. And nobody really played lead. The strength of the group was obviously going to be in its rhythm section!

But we didn't let that stop us. We formed the Classic City Playboys, named after the town of Athens which refers to itself as a "classic city." Norman Vaughn, later to be known as "Sleepy Norman" of all-night disc jockey fame on powerhouse WWVA, Wheeling, West Virginia; Chuck Goddard, who came to Georgia on a football scholarship and who would later introduce me to my first wife; and the young kid with the red clothes. Three rhythm guitars, a couple of weekend bookings at a local service club, and a half-hour show on radio station WRFC every Saturday afternoon. Yet, somehow, it lasted for almost a year.

Norman was also the early morning DJ on WRFC. Our band would go to the station once a week late at night to rehearse our show for the upcoming Saturday. One night in early January after we'd finished practicing, I asked Norman if he could show me how to run the station's control board. He sat me down, gave me a few pointers, and I went crazy. I can picture myself now sitting there between those turntables with a stack of records on one side and pages of news, weather, and commercials on the other and a set of those awesome-looking headphones ("We radio announcers call them 'cans'") stretched across the top of my head. I thought I was Superman. I knew that night that I *had* to get a job as a disc jockey!

I suddenly forgot all about baseball. The pitchers and catchers were beginning to throw and work out indoors, but I couldn't have cared less. I was too busy writing letters and making telephone calls to every radio station within a hundred-mile radius of Athens, trying to find somebody willing to hire an ambitious eighteen-year-old would-be disc jockey.

I got the same answer everywhere. "Have you had any experience?" they'd always ask.

"No," I'd always reply.

"Well, we're only hiring people with experience."

"How can I get any experience if I can't get a job?" I'd ask. And they'd mumble incoherently and I'd start looking up the next number.

When school was out for the summer, I got in my shiny metallic-blue 1947 Ford, the one with just under two million miles on it, and drove to towns like Winder, Monroe, Madison, Griffin, Newnan, Carrollton, LaGrange, looking for a job as a disc jockey. Finally I found one right under my nose, at WGAU-AM and FM in Athens.

A genial, warm-hearted man named Burl Womack was station manager at the time, and he'd had a policy down through the years of hiring college students as part-time radio announcers. The first time I'd called on him he'd had no openings, but near the end of June another student-announcer left town for the summer and I had a job. I still didn't have any experience, but I guess Burl figured I wouldn't be any better or too much worse than any of the others he'd hired. Or maybe he could just see in my eyes how badly I wanted to try.

My first duties at the station consisted of coming in at five-thirty every morning, gathering the news and weather for Burl to read on his *Breakfast with Burl* show, and reading a few commercials myself. Soon I was given a DJ show of my own on the weekends and finally the three to six P.M. slot every weekday afternoon. I was happier than a pig in a mud puddle!

Six weeks into my hard-to-come-by employment, however, my bubble burst. The station was sold to new owners and my friend Mr. Womack was fired. I was heartsick. I just knew I'd be back out pounding the pavement again any day. But, surprisingly, that didn't happen at all. A kind but firm man named H. Randolph Holder bought controlling interest in the station and for some reason didn't run the new kid on the staff out the back door when he came in the front. But he wouldn't let me play any country music.

"This is not going to be a country station," he said to me more than once in the deep, authoritative voice that had distinguished him for years as the town's leading newscaster at crosstown rival WRFC. "If you insist on playing country music, you can look for a job someplace else."

I had already seen that movie, so I followed orders and on my three-hour record show in the afternoons played only the songs listed in *Billboard's* Top 100 pop records chart. Remember, though, this was 1956, and a new thing called rock 'n' roll was just beginning to burst upon the scene. I played a lot of rock 'n' roll! On several occasions Mr. Holder would hear me playing records by Elvis or Carl Perkins and once even Fats Domino, and he'd come charging into the control room to accuse me of playing country music again. I'd calmly get out *Billboard* magazine, show him where the song I was playing was ranked among the Top 100 pop records in the country, and he'd leave me alone. But he didn't like it.

At the time, WGAU was affiliated with the CBS Radio Network, and we had a standard policy at the station that if anything ever went wrong during one of our local broadcasts, we were to "hit the net," that is, punch the button that would replace our local programming with the program currently being aired on the network.

I was manning the control board late one Saturday night when an Atlanta Crackers minor league baseball game we were carrying was halted by rain. My specific instructions were right there in front of me written on an alternate programming log: "In the event of a rainout or a rain delay, continue with programming from CBS." What the person who typed the log didn't know, however, was that on Saturday nights CBS broadcast live from Shreveport, Louisiana, the *Louisiana Hayride*. And the *Hayride* was second only to the *Grand Ole Opry* in those days as the top country music show in America.

Well, the rains didn't let up in Atlanta and I did just as I was told. I punched up the network and sat back in my chair grinning from ear to ear listening to Johnny Horton, Slim Whitman, and all the *Hayride* regulars singing their songs and doing their thing. And then the phone rang. Not the request line nor the news line, but the *hot* line. The one that rang loud and flashed bright red in the control room. The line the boss used when he was mad. Or upset. Or both.

"What in the blankety-blank is that blankety-blank country music doing on my radio station?" Mr. Holder bellowed into my ear. "If I've told you once I've told you a thous . . ."

"But, Mr. Holder," I interrupted, "I only did as I was told. The log said to go to CBS and this is what CBS . . ."

On Monday morning Mr. Holder wanted to see me in his office. He had calmed down but only slightly. "Look, I've been thinking about this, son," he said, "and I know how much you love country music. But we're just not going to play it here. That's all there is to it. We are not a country music station. But I'll tell you what. A good friend of mine has just gotten his permit to put a new station on the air up in Commerce. I called him today and told him about you. He said he'd like for you to drive up next week and meet with him. I think you've got a good chance of being hired there. Of course, Commerce is just a little town compared to Athens, but you can play country music up there to your heart's content."

That was the nicest anybody has ever been fired. And although neither of us had any way of knowing it at the time, Mr. H. Randolph Holder had just proceeded to do Mr. James William Anderson III one of the biggest favors of his young life.

5

For all that had happened over the past few years—in spite of the fact that we'd had a major disagreement and in spite of the fact that we were spending much of our time living in two separate places—never once, not even for one split second, had I ever quit loving Becky Anderson. Not since the Saturday night in January, 1967, when we'd been introduced by a mutual friend backstage at one of my concerts in Charlotte, North Carolina.

She was Becky Davis then, twenty years old, a country girl born and raised in a modest white frame house that didn't even have indoor plumbing until she was five or six years old. The closest town was Marshville, Union County, North Carolina, some thirty-odd miles southeast of Charlotte down U.S. Highway 74, the shortest route to the beach.

As Becky Stegall, she had attended Forest Hills High School where she admits her two favorite subjects were basketball and boys. She graduated in the spring of 1964, but not before marrying a boy she hadn't even been dating for very long. By the time I met her, the marriage was on the rocks, and she had filed for divorce. She had moved back home to live with her mother and stepfather and was working as a secretary in the office of a hydraulics equipment company in Charlotte. She was a charming, attractive lady, but I had by no means been introduced to a movie star.

Still, Becky had a quality about her, a very natural easiness laced with self-assurance, that I instantly liked. Maybe it was warmth. Maybe it was her marvelous sense of humor. Maybe I just sensed that in a world full of "plastic" people she was real. I'm not sure. All I know is that from the beginning I wanted to spend more time with her. I wanted to get to know her better.

Following my concert the night we met, I invited her to join me for breakfast at a pancake house just down the road from the coliseum where we'd played. My band had already left on the bus heading for Pittsburgh where we had two shows scheduled the next day, but I had elected to stay behind and fly out Sunday morning. Over a hot cup of coffee, I asked Becky if she'd come to my motel and pick me up at six A.M. and drive me to the airport. Before she had a chance to answer, I'd already planned my next line: "Easier than that, why don't you just stay?" She saw it coming and cut me off at the pass.

"I can't pick you up at that hour," she replied emphatically, "but I will give you a wake-up call in plenty of time for you to catch a cab." I liked that, and I liked her warm voice when she did call . . . right on time!

I flew on to Pittsburgh and then back home to Nashville, but I couldn't get the lady from North Carolina off my mind. We stayed in touch, she came to see me when I worked shows later that year in Fayetteville and Winston-Salem, and we began to learn more and more about one another. The more I learned, the more attracted to her I became. In the fall she moved to Atlanta, where she got a job working in state politics, first as secretary to Zell Miller, who was then personnel director of the Board of Corrections, then as secretary to the Georgia State Senate Administrative Affairs Committee in the Capitol. She moved to Nashville to work in a political campaign during the summer of 1970, and I asked her to marry me that October.

Our road together hadn't always been smooth, not even since our marriage, but we'd never faced a problem we hadn't been able to work out together. We had climbed mountains together, walked through valleys together, basked in the sunshine together, and huddled together against the rain. And through it all, Becky had become my closest and most trusted friend.

Our relationship had spawned many of my songs, everything from the tender "You and Your Sweet Love" ("Never try to tell me it wasn't God above/Who sent me you and your sweet love") to the caustic "Roller Coaster Ride" ("And the preacher should have said do you want to take a roller coaster ride/Cause that's all it's been since the day that you became my blushing bride"). But "together" was our byword from the very beginning, and even though we were having trouble right then sorting out our differences over where and how we wanted to live, somehow I think both of us always knew there was an answer and that one of these days we were going to find it.

All this and a million other things were churning inside my head as I sat nervously behind a desk inside the little police station near Chester, South Carolina, staring at a telephone, begging it to ring. I couldn't locate an airplane to fly me to Nashville.

It was still early on Sunday morning and code-a-phones and janitors were answering most of the calls I tried to place. I had looked under "Aircraft" in the yellow pages of the local telephone directory and begun dialing every air charter service listed anywhere in the Carolinas, but I was having no luck at all. I'd leave a message everywhere I phoned, but no one was calling me back. Suddenly I remembered a card I'd carried in my wallet for years from Corporate Air Fleet, a company based in Nashville. I had chartered planes from them several times before when I'd had close connections to make en route to a personal appearance. Surely they can find me something, I thought. I took out the card and dialed their number.

I got a live, on-duty person to talk with for a change, but he didn't offer me much encouragement. "I'll put it into the computer, Mr. Anderson, and see what I can come up with," he said.

"I don't want a computer, I want an airplane," I grumbled under my breath, but I tried to control my impatience and told him that would be just fine and to please call me back. I hung up the phone and on a whim reached into my suitcase and pulled out a copy of the Official Airline Guide that I carry everywhere I go. But it was just as I'd suspected. A commercial flight was out of the question. I'd have to drive to Charlotte or Greenville-Spartanburg to catch one, and I just didn't have the time. The doctor had said "fifty-fifty chance" and "come as soon as you can." I had to get home!

And then I remembered that the National Life & Accident Insurance Company, which for years owned the Grand Ole Opry, once had their own jet. In desperation I called Bud Wendell, a former manager of the Opry, who had become president of the entire Opryland-WSM-Nashville Network complex. I think I woke him up. In a sleepy voice but sounding concerned, Bud said the new owners, Gaylord Broadcasting, didn't have a plane but he'd check with his friends at Martha White Flour, one of the longtime Opry sponsors, to see about my using theirs. He called back in a few minutes to tell me we could use the plane, but the pilots had all left for church and couldn't be located.

I tried phoning Clyde Culp, president of PoFolks restaurants, the chain for which I was the national spokesman, to see if he could reach somebody . . . anybody . . . at the Krystal Corporation, PoFolks' parent company in Chattanooga. Krystal had an entire aviation complex there. I knew, I'd seen it. Surely they could get a plane to me, maybe even a jet, but Clyde was nowhere to be found.

The crew on duty at the little police station couldn't have been more accommodating. They provided coffee, two phone lines, and plenty of privacy or company, whichever I needed. I alternated between the two.

Mike Streeter had ridden with me and a police sergeant in a squad car from the market where the bus had stopped to the combination police headquarters and small county jail a few miles away. Mikey, as I've called him for years, was the closest to my age of the band members and was the kind of guy I'd want next to me if we were at war and I were stuck in a foxhole in enemy territory. He's what the folks down home used to call "solid" . . . a strong, quick-thinking, morally straight Iowa farm boy . . . a family man and a Christian but one who lives his faith quietly and never tries to force his beliefs on anyone else. He stayed right beside me during every painful minute of the ordeal I was going through. When I wanted to talk, he listened. When I felt like just sitting and staring at the wall, he sat and stared right along with me. I honestly don't know how I'd have made it through those first few hours without Mikey.

I tried to telephone my mom and dad to tell them what had happened, but they, too, had gone to church. My sister, Mary, who has always thought of Becky as more of a sister than a sister-in-law, broke down sobbing when I called her and told her the news of the accident. She promised she'd pull herself together, though, and drive over to Mom and Dad's house and break it to them as gently as she could when they got home. She and her family lived less than a mile away from our parents.

I phoned my daughters, Terri, twenty-three, and Jenni, eighteen, back in Nashville. Terri wasn't home, but Jenni became extremely upset and concerned when I told her of our impending crisis. She said Terri was in the car on the way over to her house and as soon as she got there they'd both be glad to do anything they could. I asked both of them to be at the airport to meet me when I finally did get home.

I spoke by phone with a representative of Springs Industries, the people who were sponsoring that afternoon's concert for their employees. I told him the Po' Folks Band was on its way to the concert site (all but the drummer who was with me, and someone from the police station would bring him over later) and the show would go on as scheduled even though there was no possible way I could be there. The gentleman I spoke with seemed very understanding, and I was told later that before the performance began at three P.M. the entire audience bowed as one and prayed for Becky's recovery. Springs Industries also insisted on paying me in full for the show. I'll never forget their warm expressions of concern and compassion. In fact, two years later, almost to the day, I went back to South Carolina and gave them a concert for free.

A few minutes before ten o'clock, almost two agonizing hours after my initial phone call to them, Corporate Air Fleet in Nashville finally called back and said they had located a plane and that it was on its way to pick me up. It would be coming from Greer, South Carolina, only a few minutes away. Again, one of the pilots had been in church, but they had succeeded in getting a message to him. At exactly 10:28 A.M. by my watch (I'd never changed it from Nashville time), the blue-and-white twin-engine King Air swept down from the bright morning sky, taxied to the edge of the little landing strip that serves as the Chester airport, and I climbed aboard. The pilots helped hoist my luggage on board and told me it would be about a ninety-minute trip back to Music City.

Except for the two men in the cockpit, I was alone in the plane. I strapped myself into a seat by the right rear window and stared pensively out at the bright sunshine, the scattered fluffy white clouds that floated leisurely by, and the brilliant reds, greens, and oranges of the Carolina autumn below. I tried to relax, but I couldn't turn my mind off. I tried to imagine what Becky must be going through at that particular moment, and I thought, "I've got to be with her." I squirmed in the seat trying to get comfortable and constantly looked at my watch, hoping the pilots had overestimated the flight time and maybe with a little luck we could pick up a tail wind and get home sooner.

Somewhere over the Smoky Mountains, flying along smoothly at seventeen thousand feet, I decided I needed to talk to God . . . real bad. I wasn't sure just what it was that I wanted to say and I was just as unsure of how to say it, but I leaned forward in my seat, bowed my head, and closed my eyes. For a long time I just sat there trying to figure out how to put into words the crazy, mixed-up thoughts that were racing back and forth across my mind. I wanted to ask Him to stay close to Becky, to please not let her die, and then to please give the rest of our family the strength I knew we were all going to need to face the biggest crisis any of us had probably ever faced. But it had been a long time.

> *Uh, hello God . . . this is Bill Anderson. I just uh . . . you know, God, Whisperin' Bill . . . Grand Ole Opry . . . Nashville, Tennessee. Look, I know I haven't been real good about stayin' in touch . . . especially these past couple of years or so . . . but I really need . . .*

I've never been the kind of person who wears his religion on his sleeve, but I've always considered myself a Christian. Or at least a Christian Under Construction. I grew up going to Sunday school and church, and I've never not believed in God. I just hadn't connected with Him for a while, particularly during the past couple of years while I'd been struggling with Becky's and my living arrangements. I wasn't real sure how to go about reopening the lines of communication, but I knew I had to try. Slowly but surely I got a few things out. And when I finished I felt a lot better, confident that He had heard and somehow understood the things I was trying to say.

Terri and Jenni were at the hangar when we landed and taxied in. Even though their mother and I had separated when they were seven and two, respectively, and had divorced not long after, I had tried hard over the years to maintain an honest, open relationship with each of my daughters. I wasn't a live-in daddy during much of their growing-up years, and there were times when that nearly killed me. But I did try to talk with them every day or two, spend as many weekends with them as my crazy schedule allowed, and have them with me as much of the time as I possibly could in the summer and at Christmas. I went to their school programs, birthday parties, piano recitals, dance recitals, horse shows, and anywhere else I could go where they were involved. It hadn't always been easy for either them or me, and there had no doubt been times over the years when they'd needed me and for one reason or another I hadn't been there. But I'll never forget looking out the tiny window of that airplane and seeing them both standing there for me, waiting and willing to prop me up in any way they could. I thought my heart, heavy as it was at the time, was going to melt and run right out on the ground.

Terri: Tall, blonde, statuesque, with the same sensitive but gentle blue eyes she'd been born with, beautifully matured into the youthful, graceful image of her mother. A graduate of Middle Tennessee State University with a degree in criminal justice and employed by the district attorney's office in Nashville. And Jenni: Shorter, with flowing chestnut hair and laughing brown eyes; her round face, her olive complexion, her joyous smile all undeniably Anderson. A freshman at Western Kentucky University in Bowling Green, working her way toward a degree in goodness-knows-what. But working hard at it just the same. I had never been so glad to see any two people in my life.

I stumbled down the rear steps of the plane and literally fell into their arms, squeezing Terri in my left arm and Jenni in my right with all the strength I could muster. Their eyes met mine and lingered in an expression of both love and pain for only a fleeting moment. Nobody spoke a word. Words weren't necessary. With my arms draped around their shoulders and theirs encircling my waist, the three of us quickly made our way out to the parking lot and into the back seat of my brother-in-law's car. With the help of a police escort, we pulled up in front of General Hospital at exactly 12:15.

. . .

The events of the next hour or so all run together in my mind. I talked to Becky's sister and to her mother, and they brought me up-to-date on the sequence of events that had taken place. I talked to several of our closest friends, some of whom had heard the news before daylight and had been there offering their support ever since. And I talked with the doctors, only to learn that little had changed since I had last spoken with them on the phone from South Carolina. After doing his best to prepare me for the sight I was about to see, one of the doctors led me into the trauma center emergency room where Becky was still being attended more than thirteen hours after the accident.

It was a gruesome sight. There were cuts and bruises, stitches and bandages, tubes and life-support systems everywhere. Most of the damage, as Lynne had told me, had been from the neck up. Most of her long, beautiful hair had been shaved so the lacerations in her head could be stitched. The hair that remained was matted with blood. She looked very pale and seemed to be having an extremely hard time breathing. I couldn't help but recall how that same blonde hair had been spread across the pillow on the bed in Lebanon just a few hours earlier. Hours ago when we had nothing to say to each other. And now, suddenly, there was *so much* I wanted to say.

I reached down and took hold of her left hand and felt no response whatsoever. I leaned over the bed and whispered into ears that could not hear me, "Oh, honey, I'm so sorry this has happened. I love you so much. Please fight . . . you've always been a fighter . . . please fight. Jamey and I love you and we need you so much!" The sound of what I was saying shocked even me. I hadn't told Becky I "needed" her in a long time, but then I was standing there feeling a *lot* of things I hadn't felt in a long time. Suddenly *where* we lived and *how* we lived didn't seem important at all. The only thing that mattered was *that* she live.

The doctor quickly reached out and took me by the arm and told me I had to leave. I kissed Becky's hand, then turned and walked swiftly back out to the family waiting room. I grabbed the phone and placed a call to the person I suddenly wanted to talk to more than any other person I could think of at that moment, the preacher who had married us, the Reverend Felix Snell. Actually, he'd married us twice, once on October 2, 1970, then again on

October 2, 1980, when after ten years we'd decided to renew our vows and our commitment to each other. Brother Snell, as I've always called him, was at his home in suburban Madison eating Sunday dinner when my call went through.

I told him as quickly and as calmly as I could everything that had happened. "You don't have to come," I said. "I know it's your afternoon with the family. I just wanted you to know what's happened. And I want you to say a little prayer for all of us."

"I'll be there in fifteen minutes," he said, insisting that nothing would do but for him to jump up from the table and drive to the hospital as quickly as he could. I never will forget the compassionate yet quietly confident way he looked at me when he walked in.

"Just remember, Bill," he said as he took my hand in the hallway outside the trauma center, "the Truth is the same today as it was yesterday. And it will be the same tomorrow. The Hands that made Becky aren't about to let go of her now."

Somehow I knew he was right. Becky's fate was certainly out of *my* hands. The next forty-eight hours were critical. All I could do, as Brother Snell told me, was to trust and believe.

But I was having a hard time letting go. I kept thinking I needed to *do* something . . . make something happen. What I needed to do most of all was relax and realize God was in control, but I couldn't. Not just yet. All my thoughts kept coming back to an innocent little six-year-old boy having to grow up without his mother . . . a frightened country music singing star having to stumble through the rest of his life more lost and alone than anybody he'd ever written or sung about in even his saddest songs.

And the closest thing to a prayer I could come up with at the time was, "Oh, Lord, what in the world am I gonna do now?"

6

Commerce, Georgia, was, in the late 1950s, a dingy, sometimes depressing little country town straddling U.S. Highway 441 eighteen miles north of Athens and just south of the foothills of the Blue Ridge Mountains. The most exciting thing a teenaged kid could find to do after work, if he wasn't into stealing hubcaps, was to go for a double-dip ice cream cone at the local Dairy Bar. There were three or four large textile mills in Commerce (at least one of them manufactured blue jeans), and much of the local citizenry was employed there. There was also a railroad track that ran parallel to the main street, dividing the heart of the business district, but in all the years I lived there I don't think I ever saw a train. Just the tracks. I used to try and figure out which was the right side and which was the wrong side of the tracks, but I never came to any conclusion. I lived on one side and worked on the other, so I really didn't care, but studying on it helped to pass the time.

Commerce was inhabited by approximately forty-two hundred of the kindest, friendliest, just plain nicest down-home folks I think I've ever known, and the radio station there, WJJC, "The Friendly Voice of Jackson County," turned out to be everything the station in Athens had not been.

I was there from the very beginning. I had gone to work at the station in early June, a couple of weeks before we were scheduled to begin broadcasting. My primary job was to organize the record library. I was standing in the control room filing records the morning the telegram arrived from the Federal Communications Commission in Washington saying that as of that moment we were licensed to sign on the air. It was an exciting and tense time. There had never been a radio station in the little town before, and everybody was anxiously awaiting our first broadcast.

The owners of the station, Mr. and Mrs. Albert Hardy, had run the local newspaper in Commerce for years and didn't profess to know much about radio, so they hired a young station manager named Grady Cooper from Cedartown, Georgia, and entrusted him with the job of getting us in business. Mr. Cooper, who turned out to be a very capable and dedicated manager (and in my case a very patient employer) decided we should sign on that first morning by playing a recording of "The Star-Spangled Banner," and then he thought maybe he'd like to open the microphone and say the first few words. That sounded great to me, and I stood nervously poised behind his chair as he flipped the switch to send our national anthem echoing out across the hills and valleys of northeast Georgia. It was a proud moment.

The record ended and Mr. Cooper opened his microphone. "Good morning, ladies and gentlemen," he said authoritatively, "this is Grady Cooper signing on WJJ . . ."

Click. Dead silence.

In all the excitement of trying to get our new radio station on the air, nobody had remembered to check the volume level of the microphone, and when Mr. Cooper threw the switch and started talking, the transmitter overmodulated something fierce. Our new little baby went right back off the air just as quickly as she had come on.

I could picture radios all over town having been jarred off their shelves by the roar and plummeting to the floor. All the planning, all the preparation, and our first broadcast had lasted less than three minutes. Fortunately, our engineer, Bill Evans, was standing by and quickly spotted the source of the problem. He turned down a couple of knobs, and we did it all over again. This time it worked to perfection.

In less than an hour, at eleven-thirty A.M. to be exact, I came on the air for the first time, hosting the station's first country music record show called, in the beginning, the *Dinnerbell Jamboree*. I loved my time on the air and the fact that finally, after more than a year of trying, I could at long last play country music on the radio, but every time I said the name *Dinnerbell Jamboree* I cringed. I thought that was the most awful name for a radio show I had ever heard. I didn't say anything about it at first, but after we'd been on the air for a couple of months and I had begun to build up both a bit of confidence and a bit of a following around the area, I began asking Mr. Cooper if we could change the name of my program. He wasn't too keen about the idea at first, but the more I badgered him the more I began to wear him down. Finally he gave in, more to shut me up than anything else, I think, and from that moment on the entire afternoon's programming became known as the *Bill Anderson Show.* I was off and running!

Mr. Cooper was a super boss, giving me a free hand not only to play the country music I loved but to develop myself into a full-blown radio personality as well. I took advantage (sometimes too much advantage) of my newfound freedom.

My new show came on the air every afternoon at one o'clock, and for the first two-and-a-half hours of my shift I played country music. Nothing but country music and all the country music I wanted. Then about three-thirty, when the area high schools began to let out and just as soon as I figured the kids had had time to get to their cars and head out of the parking lot, I rocked. I mean, up until the sun went down and our little thousand-watt daytime station signed off the air, I played Elvis and Jerry Lee and Chuck Berry and the Coasters and all the rest. And I liked it. Not as much as I liked country music, of course, but in those days rock 'n' roll was new and was a synonym for success. More than anything else in the world I wanted to be successful.

My radio program slowly but surely began to build an audience. The grown folks liked the country music I played and they seemed to respect my knowledge of the subject. The kids loved the loud rock and the fact that they never knew what I was liable to say or do next. I screamed and I yelled, I deliberately screwed up commercials, messed up artists' names and their song titles. I told jokes, I laughed when I should have been serious, and I played it straight when everyone else was cracking up. All over northeast Georgia it became the afternoon thing to do to turn the radio dial to 1270 and partake of the craziness.

There were even a few times when our signal wasn't confined to northeast Georgia. I snooped around and found out where the knob was on the transmitter that controlled the power output of the station, and I learned how to ease it up past our assigned thousand watts. It was illegal as robbing a bank, but when nobody was looking, I'd often do it. Some days when the ground was wet along the creekbank by our tower and nature was helping amplify our signal as well, listeners would phone me from parts of North Carolina, nearly one hundred miles away. I never got called on the carpet for tinkering, but it's a wonder. I could have cost the station a large fine and put our very license to broadcast in jeopardy.

I guess I was just too hyper and too young to realize that what I was involved in was something more than a big toy. To me it was all one big lark . . . making a little money doing something I loved. I even went so far as to create an on-the-air sidekick, a talking duck named Josh.

Actually, Chuck Goddard, my old pickin' buddy from the Classic City Playboys, found the little rubber duck for sale in a store somewhere, bought him, named him, and taught him how to talk on the radio. Chuck and Josh manned the airwaves at WMGE radio in Madison, Georgia, about the same time I was at WGAU in Athens, and, quite truthfully, Chuck taught Josh most of his bad habits. In a couple of years Chuck got an opportunity to move up to WDOL in Athens, and they were so uptown they didn't allow ducks on their station. So I adopted the poor homeless creature and took him to Commerce.

Josh didn't actually speak. He just squeaked. I'd talk, squeeze Josh, he'd squeak his reply into the microphone, and I'd interpret for the listeners what Josh had said. Usually it was something outrageously stupid or else it was the duck trying to get the best of the disc jockey. It was really not much more than my sitting alone in a dark room and talking back and forth to myself, but I had a ball with it and so did the listeners. I've thought since that Josh was just basic training for Edgar, the Talking Jukebox, who was to come later in my life.

The younger kids especially loved Josh. Not long after the adoption papers had been filed and it was legally confirmed that Josh would be with me permanently, I had a contest on the air to give him a middle name, ("Hey, gang, a duck this important *needs* a middle name. There's Harry S Truman, Dwight *David* Eisenhower . . . we've got to have Josh 'Something' McDuck!") and I received thousands of entries, most of them from the kids. We ended up tagging him the distinguished Josh "Waddlesforth" McDuck, and pretty soon he was getting more fan mail than I was. When that started happening, I began to lie and tell the listeners that Josh was sick or out of town on business, and I'd do the shows by myself, leaving the duck on the shelf for days at a time!

I also became known in Commerce as "Peanut Butter Bill," a name that has, pardon the pun, stuck with me all these years in that area. I came upon it quite innocently. I had moved to Commerce by that time and drove to Athens every morning to attend classes at the University until noon. Then I'd drive back along the winding roads from Athens north to Commerce as fast as I safely could every afternoon and run into the radio station only a few minutes before air time, out of breath and always hungry. I'd keep a loaf of bread and a jar of peanut butter in a back room, and while my first record was playing I'd sneak out and make me a sandwich.

One day I mentioned on the air that I was eating a peanut butter sandwich. From that day on, whenever I'd make a mistake reading a commercial (they were all done live at small radio stations back then) or reading the news (another task I performed to justify my princely salary of fifty dollars a week), I'd just blame it on the peanut butter sticking to the roof of my mouth. Pretty soon I became "Peanut Butter Bill."

One day during the last Christmas season I spent in Commerce, I got a phone call from the local postmaster. "Come down here right now!" he ordered. "Everybody in this town must have sent you something made out of peanut butter for Christmas. Packages are piled everywhere. This whole post office smells like Peter Pan!"

Truly, it did. I found peanut butter cookies, peanut butter cakes, peanut butter candy, and I couldn't count the jars of just plain old peanut butter (both smooth and crunchy) that the listeners had sent me. In a way it was funny, but in another way I was genuinely touched. My listeners had cared enough about me and had identified closely enough with me for them to want to send something special for the holidays. It was my first introduction to the loyalty and the closeness that develops between the people in country music and their fans.

* * *

It was while I was in Commerce that I also began seriously trying to write songs. I lived in a tiny bedroom on the top floor of the tallest building in town, the Hotel Andrew Jackson. It was all of three stories high. Every night after I signed the radio station off the air, I'd go downtown and eat supper at the Piedmont Cafe or maybe across the street at Threatt's Restaurant. Then I'd go back to my little room, study as little as I could get by with, and then I'd pick up my guitar and start strumming. I loved to write, loved to create anything, and I began to put my thoughts down on paper and to make up little tunes to go along with them. One of those "little tunes" turned out to be my magic carpet to Nashville.

It was written on the back of a WJJC radio station envelope. In pencil. And because I dated all my compositions in those days, I know I wrote it August 27, 1957. Not in my room, however, but on the roof of the hotel.

It was a stifling hot night, and the little window air-conditioning unit in my room wasn't strong enough to cut through the abusive heat and the grueling Georgia humidity. On nights like that I'd often take my guitar and retreat to the top of the hotel, flop my long legs down across their one and only lounge chair, and sing my heart out into the darkness. This particular night there wasn't a cloud in the sky. I began looking up at what seemed like a million stars above and down on what few lights there were in Commerce, Georgia, and I wrote:

> The bright array of city lights
> As far as I can see
> The great whiteway shines through the night
> For lonely guys like me . . .

My dad said later that he knew I had the imagination it took to become a great songwriter if I could look at Commerce and write about a "great whiteway." It was more like two or three traffic lights, and even they didn't work all the time. But those few words opened the doors to the world of country music for his son.

And who would have dared dream, on that hot, muggy night in August 1957, that twenty years later almost to the day the people of Commerce would erect a marble monument on a downtown sidewalk just a few blocks away from the old hotel that would read:

Bill Anderson, Country Music Hall of Fame Songwriter,
Wrote His First Hit, "City Lights," in Commerce, Georgia.

What an unforgettable occasion it was for me the day the monument was unveiled. It seemed like everybody I knew in the whole world turned out for it. They proclaimed it Bill Anderson Day in North Georgia, and Becky and I flew all night from California to be there.

By that time the little hotel where I'd lived and written my song was no longer in business; the building had been converted into a bank. The bank, along with WJJC radio, became the official sponsor of my homecoming and spared no effort in welcoming me back.

The bank lobby was filled to bursting with old friends, fans, and well-wishers when I walked in, almost two hours later than I'd been scheduled to arrive, thanks to some bad flying weather en route. But the people had stayed and waited patiently, and they cheered and applauded like mad when I finally got there. The bank officials unveiled a plaque that they said would be mounted in their lobby, marking the building as the spot where my first hit song had been written. Then, before I knew it, my old college buddy, newspaperman, disc jockey, and local entrepreneur, Billy Dilworth, grabbed me by the arm and said, "Come go with me. We've got something else to do."

I didn't have any idea what was happening, but I followed him outside the bank, down the street a couple of blocks and across the railroad tracks to the other side of the main drag where another large crowd had already gathered. I looked out and saw my mom and dad standing there, both my daughters, all my band members, Buddy Killen from Nashville; Grady Cooper, still the manager of WJJC; Bob Waters, the mayor of Commerce; and even the Lieutenant Governor of the state of Georgia, my dear friend of many years, and Becky's former employer, Zell Miller. I still didn't know what was going on, but I figured something mighty important must be about to take place.

Billy Dilworth moved to the center of the crowd, held up his hands for quiet, and began to talk, saying all kinds of nice things about me and about Commerce. Then the politicians talked, saying much of the same, and then somebody called my name and told me to step forward and untie a large rope that was holding a big piece of yellow canvas over the top of something standing five or six feet high in the middle of the sidewalk. I did as I was told, reached down and gave the cover a yank, and lo and behold beneath that canvas was the shiny marble monument paying tribute to me. I was flabbergasted.

I tried to talk, but the words wouldn't come. I was completely overcome by the excitement and the emotion of the moment. Later that night, we performed a benefit concert before a packed house at the Commerce High School football stadium, and I opened the show with "City Lights." I tried to tell the people then how much the monument and all the other events of the day meant to me. But I wonder if they ever understood how deeply I had been touched by it all.

You see, it was the people of Commerce, Georgia, who adopted me and believed in me long before anybody else did, and I've never forgotten that. I don't get to go back there very much anymore, but a big part of my heart lives there all the time. And it probably always will.

I finished writing "City Lights" the night I started it, and in a matter of just a few weeks I had made a recording of it in an unfinished TV studio in Athens and mailed the tape to Bob Tanner at TNT (Tanner 'N Texas) Music, Inc., in San Antonio. I asked him if he'd like to publish the song and perhaps release my recording of it on his TNT label. He didn't exactly do cartwheels.

Bob had published and released the first song I'd ever had recorded back in 1956, "No Love Have I," by Arkansas Jimmy Burton, on TNT, and he'd released my first record, "Take Me," with "Empty Room" on the flip side, a year later. Nothing good at all had happened with either record, but he had encouraged me to keep writing and to send him anything new I came up with. "You never know where the next big hit is coming from," he had written in response to the first letter I ever wrote him. In those days I was seeking out the names and addresses of music publishers all over the country and writing them letters, begging somebody to please just listen to a few of my songs. Bob Tanner's name was just one of hundreds on my list, but of all the companies I contacted, he was the only one who even took the time to write me back.

Not very many people remember the first record of mine that Bob put out, thank goodness. It was pretty awful. I wrote both sides, "Take Me" (which Roger Miller used to love to call "Take That"), an upbeat, lyrically bland little ditty that *Billboard* magazine called "an Elvis Presley type country-rocker sung without Preslian power." On their one-hundred-is-perfect rating system for new records, mine got a sixty-five. Somebody once told me that the worst rating any record *ever* got was a forty. "Take Me" didn't beat that by much. "Empty Room," the ballad on the other side, was recorded about two keys lower than I was capable of singing. I can't believe I ever talked anybody into releasing it.

Looking back, I guess the most outstanding thing about my first record was the engineer. I cut the songs in the studios of radio station WEAS in Decatur and used one of their local DJ's to set up the microphones and twist the knobs. He might not want it publicized, but his name was Roy Drusky. He went on to have a pretty good career in country music as a singer/songwriter in spite of the fact that his being associated with my first record could have buried him early.

Bob Tanner most definitely didn't make any money on my first release, and he was understandably hesitant about the prospect of releasing the second one. Finally, I told him I'd buy a couple of hundred copies myself if he'd just press them, because I knew I could sell that many to my radio listeners. He owned a pressing plant, so he agreed and shipped me the first box a few days later.

Naturally, I played my new release on the air the first afternoon it came in, and by that night I had sold the first copy. Well, really, I didn't *sell* it; I *traded* it to a cute little waitress at the Piedmont Café for a plate of scrambled eggs and pork chops. I didn't put any green folding money into my pocket until several days later.

It seems strange recalling it now, but "City Lights" was actually released as the B-side of my record. Remember, the music of the late fifties was not hard-core country but rockabilly and rock 'n' roll. I had written a bouncy, driving little tune called "(I've Got) No Song to Sing" that was supposed to be my A-side. I had begun singing it on a few show dates around Georgia, and it was driving the kids in the audiences wild. In fact, I worked a show in Swainsboro, Georgia, with Mel Tillis, who was then a struggling writer and performer himself, and when Mel heard the response to "No Song to Sing," he asked for a copy of my record. He took it back to Nashville and recorded the song himself on Columbia Records. It was not successful for him at all, and I tease Mel to this day because had he taken the time to listen to the flip side, he might have recorded "City Lights" and had himself a No. 1 smash!

Fortunately, a man in Nashville named Charlie Lamb did hear the B-side. At the time he was publishing a weekly trade publication called *The Music Reporter*, and I'd mailed him a copy of my record hoping to get a review in his magazine. There weren't nearly as many records released in those days as there are now, and when my record came across Charlie's desk, he took the time to listen closely. "City Lights" struck him as a powerful piece of material, and he knew my version on TNT Records wouldn't have more than limited distribution, so he took the song to Chet Atkins, the head of Artists and Repertoire for RCA Victor.

Chet listened to my record, agreed with Charlie on the commercial possibilities of the song, and in a matter of just a few days produced a great record of it on his label by a young stylist named Dave Rich. Dave was a singer like Willie Nelson, in that for many years he was simply ahead of his time. He was a tremendous singer, but the general public never quite caught on to the acrobatics he could perform with his voice. He had the vocal ability to move from one note to another in much the same sliding way as a pedal steel guitar, and he sang the living fire out of "City Lights." He took the word *array* in the first line and turned it into five syllables. He was incredible. Unfortunately, though, most people perceived him the same way as one lady who told me, "Gosh, he sure sings through his nose, doesn't he?" Dave eventually gave up on the country music business and went to preaching and singing only gospel songs, but I was thrilled to death by his recording of "City Lights," even by the sight of my name (B. Anderson) in little bitty letters on the RCA Victor label. If nothing else had happened, I'd have been satisfied.

But things were just beginning to happen. Dave Rich's record didn't set the world on its ear, but it accomplished one major thing: It got my song onto the airwaves of the leading full-time country music radio station in Nashville. And in Nashville you never know who's listening to the radio.

It turned out that Ray Price, who was just beginning to make his move into super-stardom about that time, was riding to the golf course one afternoon with the legendary Ernest Tubb when the disc jockey on WENO decided to play Dave's new record. The two of them turned up the volume and listened closely.

"That song sure sounds like one you could sing, son," Ernest said to Ray.

"Yeah, but I've already got my next record cut," Ray replied. "In fact, it ships next Monday."

"Well, if I were you I'd cancel that release and record this song," Ernest prodded. Throughout the entire round of golf that afternoon he never let up. Every time the two of them would meet on the green, Ernest would start in again. "You'd better cut that song, son," he'd say over and over until finally, and fortunately for me, Ray relented. He phoned Goddard Lieberson, the president of Columbia Records, and told him to hold up on releasing his next single. The following Thursday he called a special recording session and cut "City Lights."

I have since been told by several people who were at the session that it was a very emotional evening. After Ray and the musicians had rehearsed the song several times and had become confident that the arrangement was just the way they wanted it, Ray halted the proceedings and called all the musicians and background singers together in the center of the room.

"Now," he said, "I want you all to really think about what the ole boy in this song is going through. Listen and try to put yourself in his place. Imagine you're in Las Vegas, you're all alone, and it's cold and the wind is blowing and it's about to snow. You've just gambled and lost the last dime you have in this world. You don't know where you're gonna go, how you're gonna eat, what you're gonna do next. You pull the collar of your coat up around your neck and you walk out the door of the casino. All you see is "the bright array of city lights" as far as you can see. Now . . . let's cut the song!"

And cut it they did. "City Lights" by Ray Price on Columbia Records was an immediate smash hit, rising to No. 1 on the charts and staying in the charts for something like thirty-two weeks. Such diverse talents as soul singer Ivory Joe Hunter and Debbie Reynolds (yes, *the* Debbie Reynolds) covered the song in the pop field. In several of the year-end polls, it was voted both Song of the Year and Record of the Year for 1958.

The day I learned that Ray Price had recorded my song, I was on duty at WJJC. School was out for the summer, and I was working a split-shift, signing on at five-thirty in the mornings, working until eight o'clock, then coming back at one for my regular afternoon show. For some reason, however, this particular morning I was still at the station around ten o'clock when the phone rang. The receptionist told me it was Roger Miller calling from Nashville.

Roger and I had met a few years earlier at the old Tower Theater on Peachtree Street in downtown Atlanta when he was stationed in the Army at nearby Fort McPherson and I was a kid with a guitar wandering around town looking for someplace to play. We quickly became friends, meeting every time a big country show would come to town, standing off to the side of the stage in the darkened corners and singing each other songs we'd written, dreaming of the day each of us would become a big enough star to step out onto that stage and into the spotlight.

Roger said he was from Erick, Oklahoma, but what he wanted more than anything in the world was to say that he was from Nashville, Tennessee, and that he made his living writing and singing. Funny, I was beginning to want to tell people that's what I did, too, but for the longest time the closest either of us came to stardom was wandering through the corridors of the old building that had once been known as the Erlanger Theater, home of the famous WSB *Barn Dance,* and staring in awe at the performers who happened to be working there.

One Sunday afternoon Wanda Jackson was in town appearing as part of the Hank Thompson Show, and I nearly fainted when Roger got up nerve enough to knock on her dressing room door and ask if we might come in and talk with her awhile. She very graciously said sure, and while we were sitting there asking her all kinds of stupid questions about the music business, Roger spied her shiny new Martin guitar sitting in its case over in the corner. "Would you mind if I borrowed your guitar and sang my friend here a couple of new songs I've written?" he asked. Wanda, evidently taken back by such a request, said she didn't mind, but the look on her face told me she really did.

Roger grabbed the guitar and, not wanting to bother Wanda anymore, motioned for me to follow him out the door. He led me over to the edge of the stage where no one could see us, and he played and sang for me for about fifteen minutes. Then he handed me the guitar, and I played and sang to him for fifteen or twenty more. We were knocking each other out, telling one another how great we were, and marveling at how good Wanda's guitar sounded. Pretty soon, though, it started closing in on her time to go on stage, and she started looking around for the two clowns who had disappeared with her guitar. She couldn't find us anywhere. Finally she called her dad in on the case. He spotted me and Rog over in the corner pluckin' away. He walked over and, in a voice much calmer than mine would have been under the circumstances, asked us if we'd mind if his daughter got her instrument back. Please. Roger handed it to him like a parent giving up a baby for adoption. When her dad was out of earshot, he turned to me and said, "I'll have a guitar like that someday," and I said, "Sure, and so will I." We stood there looking at each other like a couple of lying fools and broke out laughing.

Roger moved to Nashville the day he received his discharge from the service and began to make his mark as a writer and as a performer not long afterward. He toured for a while as a fiddle player with Minnie Pearl, then became a member of Ray Price's renowned Cherokee Cowboys. Meanwhile, I went to Athens and then to Commerce. The miles came between us, but we always managed to stay in touch.

"Hey, Anderson, guess what," he roared excitedly over the long-distance wire. "Price cut 'City Lights' last night! It's gonna be his next release. I've got the other side, a new thing I just wrote called 'Invitation to the Blues'! How 'bout them apples?"

I was blown away! Roger and I hung on the phone like a couple of schoolkids, laughing and giggling and talking about how all our dreams were starting to come true. Then before I could come back down to earth the telephone rang again. This time it was Bob Tanner calling from Texas.

"Bill, I just found out Ray Price cut 'City Lights' last night. It's going to be his next release!" I dared not burst his bubble, so I acted surprised and congratulated him since he held the publishing rights to the song.

I was still bouncing off the ceiling when in less than an hour the phone rang for the third time. This time it was the head of Tree Publishing Company in Nashville, Buddy Killen. Roger had become a staff writer at Tree and told Buddy he knew this young disc jockey down in Georgia who also wrote some pretty fair songs. Buddy had no financial interest in "City Lights" but called with the news anyway. "Congratulations," he said. I acted surprised again and answered "What for?" as if I didn't know.

"Ray Price cut 'City Lights' last night, haven't you heard? It'll be his next release. Let me hear any new songs you might be writing, OK?"

I assured him that I would. Wow! Tree Publishing wanting to hear my new songs! What was going to happen next?

It didn't take me long to find out. About two o'clock that same afternoon the late Jim Denny, former manager of the Grand Ole Opry and president of the giant Cedarwood Publishing Company in Nashville, called. In his calm, understated yet very authoritative voice he said, "Bill, I think I've got something you'll be interested in."

"What's that, Mr. Denny?" I asked.

"Well, if you'll sign a contract to write all your future songs exclusively for Cedarwood Publishing, I think I might be able to talk Ray Price into recording 'City Lights.'"

Welcome to show business, Peanut Butter Bill!

7

It was approaching midafternoon when I realized that in spite of all I had already been through on this Sunday, my most important and most difficult task still lay ahead. I had to go home and tell my young son the frightful truth about what had happened to his mother.

After I was convinced that Becky was in good hands and there was nothing more I could do by staying at the hospital, I asked my brother-in-law to drive me to the condominium. All the way there I kept rehearsing over and over in my mind the things I knew I had to say to Jamey. And I thought how inconceivable it was that as little as seven years ago I had been resigned to the fact that there was never even going to *be* a James William Anderson the Fourth.

Since my dad was an only child and I had been the last male born onto our particular branch of the Anderson family tree, I had begun to assume, after having had two daughters by my first wife and seven childless years with my second, that the name would die when I did.

By 1977, Becky and I had become rather independent and set in our ways. We enjoyed our freedom—coming, going and doing as we pleased. From time to time we had talked about maybe having a child someday, but we'd usually end up laughing and saying we were getting too old for that kind of foolishness.

Truthfully, what we had become was not old but selfish. When I had to go on the road and Becky wanted to go along, she went. There was nothing at home to tie her down. Neither of us ever considered subjecting her to the day-after-day grind of the grueling one-night stands, but when a trip to Europe or a Caribbean cruise or even a tour along the west coast or a business trip to New York City came up, we always knew we were free to turn it into something we could share and enjoy together. And we often did.

At the same time I knew Becky would make a terrific mother. I had seen her interact with Terri and Jenni, I had seen her with her various nieces and nephews, and she was marvelous. It was always obvious to me that she genuinely liked kids, she related well to them, and they liked her. I used to think what a shame it was that she didn't have any children of her own, but every time I'd mention it she'd say, "Well, why don't you try staying home off the road more often?" And we'd laugh some more.

I did stay home on the afternoon of my fortieth birthday, and it turned into a unique surprise celebration. Becky had decided to give a small party for me and had invited the members of my band, my office employees, and a few close neighbors and friends to come by our house on Old Hickory Lake and share some birthday cake and coffee with us. It was a very warm but low-key, unpretentious gathering. I listened to all the "Lordy, Lordy, Bill's Turned Forty" jokes, and somewhere around five o'clock everybody congregated in the living room and I began to open a few small gifts and some birthday cards.

When I picked up the stack of cards from the table and first shuffled through them, I noticed a white envelope with the word "Dad" written on the front in a handwriting that seemed familiar. My daughters weren't there, and I casually thought, "Well, Becky's done it again. She's very thoughtfully included my girls in my birthday party and they've sent me a card." I put the unopened envelope back down in the middle of the stack and without giving it another thought began opening the cards that were on top.

Some nine or ten opened cards later, the "Dad" card surfaced again. "Well, I'll open it even though they're not here," I thought, knowing I'd probably see them later that night. I tore open the flap. On the front of the card was inscribed a plaintive "Life Begins At Forty." I smiled and opened the cover. I was surprised when I saw no printed inscription at all. I lowered my eyes to a few handwritten words:

Dear Dad:
As the saying goes, life begins
at 40 and I am beginning for you.
I don't know if I'm your son
or your daughter but . . .

My eyes came to a screeching halt. "Wait a minute," I thought. "What does that mean 'I don't know if I'm your son or your daughter'? Of course they're my daught . . ." Suddenly it hit me. No wonder the handwriting had looked familiar. I had seen it a thousand times. But it wasn't either of my daughter's handwriting at all. It was Becky's.

I looked across the room to where Becky was seated on a footstool. There was a smile on her face as wide as the channel of the lake that flowed gently outside our window. And just above the warm, loving smile a lone, solitary tear slowly appeared and began to trickle down her left cheek.

Nobody else in the room had even noticed. They'd been busy talking and eating, and they didn't pay any attention at first when I jumped up, ran across the room, and squeezed Becky so hard she had to beg me to quit. "Careful, you'll hurt the baby!" she exclaimed, and the two of us stood there laughing and crying all at the same time.

By this time heads were starting to turn all around the room. Everybody knew something was going on, but nobody had any ideas what it was. I raised my hands and asked them for their undivided attention. "I have a very important announcement to make," I said. The room grew quiet.

"I want to tell you about a very special birthday present," I began, my arm wrapped firmly around Becky's waist and a smile creasing my face from ear to ear. "This pretty lady here just informed me that she found out this very morning that she and I are going to have a baby!"

"I sure hope it's a boy!" Becky said to me at least a thousand times over the next eight months. "I've asked God to give me a healthy little Bill," she'd say, "and to please forgive me for asking for a boy. But I want him to be just like you."

"Don't pray for something you don't really want," I'd reply. "God does answer prayer, you know. Are you sure you could handle two of us around here?" She'd assure me that she could and we'd both laugh.

To be truthful, I wanted a son, too . . . I *really* wanted a son . . . but I asked God only please to make the pregnancy easy on Becky and to give us a normal, healthy child.

We knew from the beginning that the baby would be born sometime toward the end of June or in early July. As the time began to draw closer, however, our whole family began asking the question: "Is there any chance the baby might be born on June 25th?" We all began crossing our fingers and hoping there was. For we all knew that his or her entry into the world would then come on a very special day, the sixty-seventh birthday of James William Anderson, Jr., my father and grandfather to our child.

It seemed too much to ask, too much even to hope for. But when the baby hadn't come by the 22nd . . . didn't come on the 23rd . . . or the 24th . . . and when Becky woke up with funny little pains in her stomach on Sunday morning the 25th, I knew we were being blessed in a very special way. Little James William Anderson IV took his very first breath at 6:22 P.M. that afternoon.

There had never been any question as to what his full name would be, and we'd told everyone. "Great," my good friend George Hamilton IV laughed one night at the Opry. "When he grows up he can wear all my old stage coats with the 'IV' on the pocket!" But Becky and I had decided we'd wait until we actually saw our baby the first time before deciding whether we'd call him Jamey or Andy, the nickname a lot of people named Anderson end up with. I never even gave a passing thought to saddling him with Billy or Bill.

"He *looks* like a Jamey," Becky said the first morning she held her newborn son in her arms and fed him his bottle. I agreed, and Jamey it was.

From the beginning it was obvious that our prayers for a healthy baby had been answered. He had all his fingers and toes, a powerful set of lungs that made everyone ask, "Are you sure this is really Whisperin' Bill's son?" and, for better or for worse, he came into this world with a high, wide forehead, deep brown eyes, and a head full of dark brown hair. Becky got her wish. Her son was the spitting image of his father.

On the afternoon he was born, I told Becky's doctor, Dr. Joe Michael Edwards, at the last possible minute that I *had* to go into the delivery room with him and watch the birth of my child. "I don't know what to do," I confessed, "'cause I never went to any classes or anything. But I can't let y'all go in there without me. You've *got* to let me go!"

I must have played the role of Super-Dad to the hilt because Dr. Edwards looked at me for only a minute and relented. "Will you be calm and promise not to pass out?" he asked. "We'll have enough to do in there with Becky and the baby without having to stop and scrape you up off the floor." I promised him I'd stay cool as the center seed of a cucumber. He smiled and handed me a mask and a gown. "Go wash your hands," he said, "and come on. I'll trust you."

I wouldn't take anything now for the experience of having gone into that delivery room and having seen my son being born. When I heard his first little cry and realized that I truly did have a son, a newborn child to carry on our Anderson family name, it was one of the most thrilling and emotional moments of my life.

"Here, you carry him down to the nursery," the nurse said to me as soon as Jamey was bathed and wrapped in his first blanket. And she turned to hand me the warm, fragile little body that I already loved so much.

I didn't realize parents were allowed to hold their babies so soon. "Won't he get germs or something?" I asked nervously.

"Well, try not to sneeze directly in his face," she deadpanned. I reached out and took my son into my arms for the very first time.

It was only a hundred feet or so from the delivery room to the nursery, but I decided it would be as good a place as any for young James William IV and ole James William III to have their first man-to-man talk. He lay quiet and still in my arms as I carried him gingerly down the hallway and talked to him about all the things we would someday do together.

"Little man, we'll go to baseball games," I said, looking at his tiny fingers curve and wondering how and with which hand he'd grip a curve ball, "and we'll play music and we'll sing together and we'll go camping and fishing, and you'll be the most wonderful son and I'll try hard to be the best daddy in the world." And I squeezed him as tightly as I dared.

At that very special and joyous moment, I decided there should be a law prohibiting people from having children before reaching the age of forty. I was the happiest man in the world. This nightmare of a Sunday afternoon that I was now living was a million light years away.

I'll never forget the surprised look on Jamey's face when he opened the door to the condo and there I stood. "What are you doing home, Dad?" he asked innocently. "You aren't supposed to be back until Monday."

"I need to talk to you about that, son," I said, stepping inside and placing my hand on his little shoulder.

"Mom's in a meeting," he exclaimed almost gleefully. "She'll be back in a little while."

"I need to talk with you about that, too." We were interrupted by the ringing of the telephone.

"Boy, the phone sure has rung a lot today," he said. "We've really had a lot of calls."

"Come on upstairs with me, son," I said as calmly as I could. "Pam can get the phone. I need to talk with you."

We climbed the stairs holding hands. At the landing we turned left and walked into his mother's bedroom and sat close to each other on the edge of her king-sized bed. I wrapped my arm around his little shoulders and began to talk.

Slowly and deliberately I told him everything I knew. How his mom had been on the way home from the movie late last night, alone in her car, and how a man who had been drinking too much alcohol had gone to sleep at the wheel and hit her car head-on with his pickup truck. There had been a service rack mounted over the bed of the truck, and on that rack the driver had been carrying some long steel pipes. I told him that when the truck crashed into the car, the pipes had evidently shifted forward, torn through the windshield of mom's car, and crushed the top of the car much like he might crush a paper sack before he threw it in the trash. His mother's face and head had been hit by the pipes and cut open by the glass, and she was hurt awfully bad.

And, yes, Mom had on her seat belt. And, yes, she tried not to hit the man. She'd seen him coming down the wrong side of the road and had even pulled her car all the way off the road and up against a fence. She was nearly stopped when he ran into her. And I told him how a policeman who was off duty and on his way home had been following the truck and saw the entire accident. He called for help on his police radio, and he held Mom's hand until the ambulance came and the fire trucks came and the men could help get Mom out of the car and to the hospital.

I was careful from the very first word to never say Mom was or wasn't going to be well. Or come home. That she was or wasn't going to die. I didn't want him ever to come back at me and say his dad told him a lie. And I was very careful to conduct the entire conversation sitting close to him with my arm tightly around his shoulder. I wanted him to feel secure even though I was not. I wanted him to feel safe although I was fearful. And most of all, I wanted him to feel loved.

I had some experience to draw from. Becky and I had discussed as recently as a few weeks earlier how if anything were ever to happen to either of us, Jamey should be our first concern. She knew from her own childhood how important that could be. Her father had been killed by a train when she was eight years old.

Nobody had ever told her what happened. All she knew was that her daddy, whom she idolized and dearly loved, had gone to the ice house in Marshville, North Carolina, early one morning to take some meat out of a frozen food locker to bring home for breakfast. She was still asleep when the northbound Seaboard Railway passenger train crashed into the side of her father's black Chevrolet less than a hundred yards from her bedroom window. She awoke to the commotion of friends and relatives all running around in a state of confusion, and she remembers someone saying the baby was too young to be around all this. She was immediately whisked away. Nobody ever said to her, "Becky, your father is dead." Nobody ever held her close and comforted her or helped love her through this shocking tragedy. Perhaps it was because as the youngest of four daughters nobody thought she was old enough to feel the pain or understand the situation like the older girls. Maybe it was because the family doctor had come quickly and given her mother a strong sedative, and through the cloud of her own pain she hadn't been physically able to look after the children adequately. I choose to think somebody just didn't understand because what they did to her has haunted her all her life. She didn't even go to her father's funeral, and not until several years after we were married was she able to seek professional help and come to grips with her constant nightmares surrounding his tragic death.

For that reason, we had prepared ourselves for the eventuality that I was now facing. My primary concern was Jamey. I tried to explain to him everything I knew at the time as fully and completely as I could and in language I felt he could understand. I didn't try to mask my emotions either. I figured if he saw my hurt he'd know not to be afraid or ashamed of his own. He listened attentively to all I had to say but showed no emotion at all. When I finished I said, "Do you have any questions?"

"Yes," he said. "Where is that man who hit my mom?"

I answered that I didn't know for sure.

"Probably out hurting someone else," he said with a tone of both anger and disgust in his voice. Then, before I could respond, he said something I'll remember as long as I live.

"I guess there's good news and bad news, Dad," he said.

"How's that, son?" I replied.

"Well, the bad news is that mom's in the hospital. But the good news is that you and I will be spending a lot more time together."

I pulled him closer and held him tightly. Neither one of us knew at that moment just how right he was.

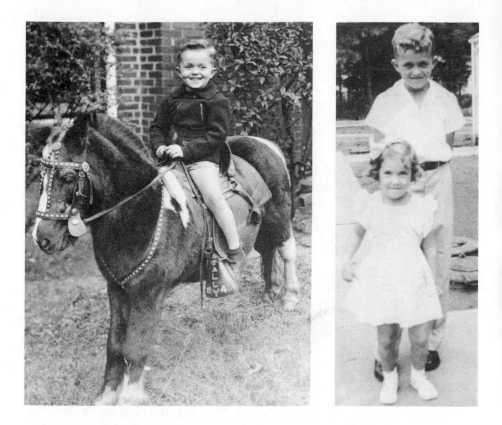

(Top left) Bill at age four in Columbia, S.C.; (top right) with sister Mary in 1946; (bottom left) the skinny slugger at age ten; (bottom right) the old lefthander as a senior at Avondale High School.

(Top left) The Avondale Playboys, clockwise from center: Bill Anderson, Jerry Jones, Billy Moore, Jim "Meatball" Bell, Charles Wynn, circa 1953; (top right) Bill as a sophomore at U.Ga.; (bottom) Bill (center) with "Meatball" Bell (left) and Charles Wynn playing on the WBGE Saturday radio show.

You win some, you lose some: (top) Bill lost a talent competition to a blind girl, but (bottom) won the Athens Lions Club talent competition, circa 1956.

Bill and Chuck Goddard on *the Ernest Tubb Midnight Jamboree,* 1958

Bill meets Ernest Tubb, 1954

First professional photo, 1957

The Po' Boys Band, 1966: (left to right) Jimmy Gateley, Sonny Garrish, Bill Anderson, Jimmy Lance, Snuffy Miller

Bill with Hank Williams, Jr., early in Hank's career

On the TV set: (left to right) Jan Howard, Bill Anderson, Loretta Lynn, Jimmy Gateley

Singing their hearts out: Jan Howard and Bill Anderson

In the studio: Jan Howard, Bill and Owen Bradley

Another duet:
Bill and
Mary Lou Turner

PART II

8

As big a hit as "City Lights" was, it went against the grain of almost everything that was happening musically in the late fifties. It was a traditional, three-chord, cryin' country song, and it stood out like a sore thumb among the likes of "Wake Up, Little Suzie," "Whole Lotta Shakin' Goin' On," and "Great Balls of Fire" on the country radio airwaves. It was almost a throwback to another era. Maybe that's why it was such a smash. The public was obviously ready for a song of that type.

Buddy Killen, true to his word, did want to hear some more of my material, and I began making frequent trips to Nashville to show him the new songs I was working on. I was falling in and out of love on a daily basis surrounded by all the beautiful coeds at Georgia and the sweet, innocent little country girls from Commerce, and I never seemed to be lacking for new ideas for songs. Some were happy, some were sad, but nearly all my early writings had two things in common: They were based on my true experiences, and most of them were written to the exact same melody.

"Anderson, everything you write sounds like you stole the tune from the Baptist Hymnal," Killen would say, and he'd sit patiently with me for hours, teaching me the art of crafting a song. He'd show me how one line had to build off the line in front of it and how a writer had to construct a song to reach a certain climax at a certain point. Mostly, though, he worked with me on my melodies. The lyrics always seemed to come easier to me, and I'd try to let the lyric "suggest" a melody. In other words, if I were writing a happy song, I'd try to come up with a happy sounding melody. The same would be true in reverse if I were writing a sad song. But I wasn't as creative melodically as I was lyrically.

I signed an exclusive songwriter's contract with Tree Publishing Company, and Buddy and I became not only business associates but close personal friends as well. I confided in him one morning about the lastest catastrophe in my love life, and before the day was over he and I had collaborated to write "I May Never Get to Heaven," a heartfelt ballad everybody from Don Gibson to B. J. Thomas to Aretha Franklin would record before Conway Twitty would finally take it to No. 1 nearly twenty years later.

And it was Buddy Killen who in the late summer of 1958 asked Owen Bradley if he'd come by the Tree offices one afternoon and listen to some songs written by the skinny disc jockey from Commerce, Georgia, who wrote "City Lights" and, perhaps, to consider this DJ as a recording artist for Decca Records where Mr. Bradley had recently been named chief of Nashville operations.

A great musician and record producer like Owen Bradley didn't need to make house calls, but out of respect for Buddy he came. And I sang, just me and my guitar, and he listened. After about a half-hour or so Owen said, "Well, son, you're not the greatest singer I've ever heard, but you sure do write some terrific songs. And your voice is different . . . you certainly don't sound like anybody else I've ever heard. If you'll keep writing songs as good as these and if you'd like to try, I think we might be able to make some hit records together." And as simple as that I became Bill Anderson, Decca recording artist.

Owen and Buddy told me my job was to get busy writing some new songs for my first recording session; they'd take care of getting all the legal documents drawn up and the paperwork in place. I went back to Commerce and back to school. Once or twice I returned to the roof of the little hotel and tried to write, but lightning never struck there again. I did write some new songs but in other places. In a few weeks my recording contract arrived in the mail. I didn't even read it. I was so excited I just signed it and sent it back before anybody had a chance to change their mind.

I flew to Nashville and cut my first record for Decca in Owen Bradley's legendary quonset-hut studio on 16th Avenue South in August 1958, and before winter quarter began at school I had become the only student in the history of the University of Georgia to have a record in *Billboard* magazine's country music charts.

Heck, I was probably the only student in University of Georgia history who had ever *heard* of the *Billboard* magazine country music charts!

Recording in Nashville with Owen Bradley for Decca Records was a far cry from recording in an empty TV studio in Georgia with a bunch of cronies and pals for TNT. I was scared half to death just looking around the room and seeing musical legends like Buddy Emmons poised behind his steel guitar, Tommy Jackson with his fiddle, Hank "Sugarfoot" Garland and Grady Martin on their guitars, Bob Moore on bass, and Buddy Harmon on the drums. These were the cream of the crop, the pickers whose music I played every day on my radio show back home, and now they were in the studio waiting to play behind me.

And the equipment! I had never even seen a gold-plated German-made Telefunken microphone before, much less ever sung into one. And the first time I heard my voice played back on the huge studio speakers, in stereo, no less, it was almost more than I could comprehend.

Owen didn't hire a vocal group to sing in the background on my first session, and I was a bit disappointed about that. Groups like the Jordanaires and the Anita Kerr Singers had become the rage in Nashville, especially on records aimed at the new, lucrative crossover market, and I had had just enough local success with my rockabilly "No Song to Sing" to have my heart set on recording for Decca in a similar style.

"No, we're going to record you straight country," Owen said when the subject came up a few days before the session. He said it in such a decisive, forthright manner that I knew there was no room for argument. I'm glad now he never allowed me to voice my opinion. What if I had been able to change his mind? I might be a washed-up rock 'n' roller today.

We cut two sides on my first session, and both were songs that I had written. One was a straight-ahead country ballad very much in the vein of "City Lights" called "That's What It's Like to Be Lonesome." The flip side was a wordy, more up-tempo love song entitled "The Thrill of My Life." Instead of "ooohs" and "aaahs" and "doo-wops" in the background, though, Owen had Buddy Killen and a newcomer to Nashville named Donny Young blend with me on some high-lonesome three-part harmony on the choruses. In later years Donny Young was to achieve a certain degree of fame and notoriety under the name of Johnny Paycheck, but on this night, for my first recording session, he was my tenor singer.

As we all gathered around the giant stereo speakers in the control room and listened to the playbacks when the session was over, everybody felt "That's What It's Like to Be Lonesome" had turned out to be by far the stronger of the two sides we'd cut. Owen said it sounded like a hit to him and that he'd ask Decca to release and promote that side. He turned out to be right. The record came out in late autumn and broke into the national charts on Christmas Day. By February it had climbed as high as No. 15. But, unbeknownst to me, Ray Price was once again somewhere listening to his radio, heard my new song, and recorded his own cover version to release as a follow-up to "City Lights." As soon as Ray's record reached the radio stations, most of the disc jockeys quit playing my cut and started playing his. Before it was over, Ray Price had his second consecutive No. 1 hit with a Bill Anderson song.

A lot of people said to me, "Gee, that's too bad," when I told them Ray had covered my record, but I didn't feel that way about it at all. Actually, it put me in a no-lose situation. I wrote the song, and I knew I'd be getting much larger writer's royalties as a result of his record than I would have off my record alone. He was, after all, an established star who had just spent over half a year in the charts with a No. 1 record. I'd be getting paid two or three cents for every copy of the record he sold whether it was on a single or in an album. In addition, I'd be receiving another few pennies from Broadcast Music, Inc., every time either my record or his was played on the radio or performed on television. It might not sound like much, but I knew a few cents here and a few cents there could eventually add up. Besides, my own record had already opened a lot of doors for me prior to Ray's cover. One of those doors came in the form of a phone call from a small booking agency in Nashville one day early in March.

"Bill, I just wondered if you'd like to go along on a little personal appearance tour I'm putting together for George Morgan in a few weeks?" the voice on the other end of the line asked. "We're going out west for about twenty-one days, and your record's done real well out there, and we'd like to have you go with us. Whatta you say?"

I was speechless. Me, a student at the University of Georgia, a disc jockey in Commerce, Georgia, going on tour with Grand Ole Opry star George Morgan! I was just a greenhorn kid who had never been anywhere outside of five southeastern states. I nearly jumped through the roof. Would I like to go on a tour? Does a five-string banjo have strings?

I told the agent heck, yes, I'd love to go. But as soon as I hung up the phone, I started wondering just how I was going to manage. I could take a leave of absence from the radio station, I knew that, but I had no idea how to get out of school. Finally I just said to heck with it, this is a once in a lifetime opportunity and I'm not about to pass it up. I've never regretted it either, even though by going on the tour I set my college graduation back a few months and ended up not earning the U.S. Army officer's commission I was only a few weeks away from receiving through the ROTC program at Georgia. I was pickin' and grinnin' somewhere the day they gave the final Military Science exams, and I learned shortly thereafter that the Army is a bit fussy about handing out officer's commissions to young men who'd rather tote a guitar than tote a rifle.

My dad nearly had a coronary, though, because he just knew I'd end up as one of Uncle Sam's buck privates someday. I never did. In fact, I was never called into the service at all, but even if I had been I honestly don't think I'd have cared. I figure I learned things out on the road on that trip that I couldn't have learned staying home and studying and taking exams for the rest of my life. Besides, to this day, the memory of that first tour serves as a constant reminder of how bad things can get in this business, and it inspires me every day to try and never let my career deteriorate to the point that I might have to go through something like that again.

The cast of the show consisted of longtime Opry great George "Candy Kisses" Morgan as the headline attraction and featured his all-star band of Little Roy Wiggins (legendary from his days with Eddy Arnold) on steel guitar, the incomparable Dale Potter on fiddle, Sammy Pruitt (one of Hank Williams's original Drifting Cowboys) on lead guitar, veteran Bill Slayman on bass, Ken "Loosh" Marvin on rhythm guitar and as master of ceremonies, and a seventeen-year-old "rookie" named Willie Ackerman (later of *Hee-Haw* fame) on drums. This group was hired not only to play behind Morgan but to play the music on my songs as well. They also were asked to back up two other young male singers and one female singer who had been invited to join the tour.

Each of the three young men on tour had had only one 45-rpm single record released at that time, none had ever recorded an album, and I dare say not one of the three attracted one paying customer to a single show. Today, however, they just might. Their names were Roger Miller, Donny Young (Johnny Paycheck), and Bill Anderson. The obligatory female was a tall, pretty lady named Wanda Jones, who never quite made it in the music business.

Morgan was one of the finest, purest singers country music has ever produced, but unfortunately had not had a big hit record in quite some time. The tour opened at a club called Rosa's in Fort Worth, Texas, then swung out through west Texas into places like Sweetwater and San Angelo, on to Hobbs and Alamogordo, New Mexico, Phoenix, Tucson, Prescott, and Flagstaff, Arizona, before mercifully ending some twenty-two days later back at Cain's Academy ballroom in Tulsa, Oklahoma. In three grueling weeks, we hadn't drawn, as "Loosh" put it, "enough people to flag a hand car." And there's nothing worse, I found out, for your ego or your pocketbook than to be thousands of miles away from home singing your heart out in an empty club, auditorium, or arena night after night after night.

But crowds or no, I was having a ball. Every day was full of new excitement, new adventure, and I came to respect George Morgan to the point of almost idolizing him. I'd stand in the wings during the shows and watch his every move, watch the way he could touch whatever audience we might have with just the right combination of seriousness and humor, and I'd yearn for the ability to be able to do the same. I was so in awe that I never spoke to him much, but he was watching me. One night after a show in a nearly empty roller rink in Alamogordo, New Mexico, he came up to me and in his most sincere manner put his arm around my shoulder.

"Anderson," he began earnestly, "I've been watching you. I've been watching all you guys, in fact, and I've decided *you* are going to be the biggest star of all three."

I beamed. I glowed. I swelled with pride. "Thank you, sir," I managed to whisper.

"Do you know *why* you are going to be a big star?" he asked.

"No sir, why?"

"Because you are different. You may be, in fact, the only guy in the history of country music who can hit an E-chord on his guitar and come in singing in the key of C!"

I was crushed for days.

A lecture in intonation, a big dose of United States geography, and the knowledge of how to survive on two cheap, thin hamburgers a day weren't the only lessons that I learned from my first tour. I also got exposed to a few things my somewhat sheltered life had thus far protected me from. In particular, those staples of the road: pills, booze, and women.

We weren't fifty miles west of Nashville riding in Miller's blue 1954 Cadillac with the clear plastic seatcovers and the four recap tires when one of the band members turned to me, opened his hand to reveal a half-dozen or so little yellow pills, and said, "Wanta bennie?"

So this was what they looked like! Benzadrine, I think, was their proper name, and I knew musicians often took them to offset the rigors of travel and the pressures of the road. I also knew they could keep you awake for days at a time. I'd never taken one, and just the thought frightened me. What if I liked them? What if I never wanted to go to sleep again? What would my conservative Methodist mother say? So I politely declined. To this day I've never taken an upper, although Miller swears that one night when he and I were en route to a show in Florida, I took a No-Doz pill with a cup of coffee, got back in the car, rolled down the window, beat out wild rhythms on the dashboard, and sang at the top of my lungs all the way to Panama City. If that's true, then I'm glad I never tried anything stronger!

Actually, I didn't need a thing on that first trip to keep me awake. The thrill of being on the road, sitting in the back seat of that big blue car, knowing I was heading for Texas was all the upper I needed.

* * *

When the tour opened at Rosa's in Fort Worth, I found myself smack-dab in the middle of a world that was as foreign to me as downtown Moscow. I wouldn't have admitted it at the time, but I had never actually been inside a nightclub until that very moment. Not only had I never performed in one, I had never been in one, period. Oh, I had played in a few American Legion halls and AMVETS clubs back in Georgia, but not in a real, honest-to-goodness Texas-style honky-tonk.

I'm sure my naiveté showed in my performance, too. I wasn't used to people drinking beer and dancing and hollering and carrying on while I was trying to sing. And the people who came to Rosa's hadn't come for prayer meeting. They said they liked our music, but I wasn't sure they even heard any of it. When it got to be my turn onstage, I sang a couple of songs and then tried telling a few jokes, but nobody paid any attention. Finally I decided to just shut up and sing. It took years for me to adjust to the audiences in Texas and some of the other southwestern states because the biggest compliment they can pay an artist there is not to applaud him but, rather, to like his music enough to stop talking and get up and dance to it.

And then there was the drinking. Liquor was something I'd never been around much either. I'd seen and smelled lots of it when I'd been in college, but drinking had never been a part of my family, and it seemed to go against all my upbringing. But they drank lots of beer and booze in Rosa's and in most all the other places we worked on that first tour. As our crowds shrank and our expenses mounted, the liquor got to flowing rather heavily among some of our cast members as well. I never was tempted to join in, though. Fact is, I was almost twenty-seven years old before I ever let my hair down far enough even to taste beer, wine, or hard liquor.

I'll never forget the first time I ordered a drink. I was in New York City, working as part of a gigantic two-day country music spectacular at Madison Square Garden. At the time, I don't think a larger country show had ever played the Big Apple. It was an exciting time, and after the Saturday night show my wife and I decided to go out to a nice restaurant to celebrate.

We found a quiet, intimate spot with a small band playing softly in the corner. The waiters were all dressed in tuxedoes, and the food coming out of the kitchen smelled delicious. I was feeling great. I decided it was time for the bashful kid from Georgia to broaden his horizons a bit. I signaled for the waiter, but when he got to our table I realized I hadn't the foggiest idea of what to order or how to go about ordering it.

"Uh, sir, you see, I've never ordered a drink before," I stammered, "and I don't really know what I want. We're here to celebrate, though, and . . . well, we'd just like something to relax. What do you suggest?"

He looked at me with that sardonic New York look on his face and said, "Why don't you try dancing?"

I ended up ordering a whiskey sour and nursing it for three or four hours. I wasn't much of a drinker then, and I've not become much of one since. Today I drink very little and never when I'm working.

Texas dance halls, clubs, honky-tonks, skull-orchards, or whatever you want to call them are not only loud and boisterous. They can also be the smokiest places in the world. It can be awfully rough on a singer when he's up on the bandstand inhaling all the fumes floating around him. Especially one like me who has never smoked himself.

Cigarettes, like liquor, have just never been much of a temptation for me. I tried them, like every kid does, when I was a teenager, but I never liked them very much. I recall vividly the last time I ever lit one up. I was fifteen or sixteen years old, about the age when a kid thinks he knows everything, and I'd gone down to radio station WEAS in Decatur to watch a disc jockey/recording artist named Texas Bill Strength do his afternoon DJ show. Bill was quite well known in those days, particularly in the South and Southwest. He'd made a few records for some of the major labels, guested on the Grand Old Opry a few times, and as such he had become one of my heroes. For no real reason he had always been extremely nice to me, inviting me to his home on several occasions, and always letting me come out on stage and sing a couple of songs as a warm-up act when he'd promote concerts by the major stars around the Atlanta area. If Texas Bill

Strength had told me to jump off a cliff, I'd probably have asked him "Which one?" and done it. I looked up to him that much.

But ole Texas Bill, as I suspected then and confirmed in later years, was quite a rounder. He smoked, he drank, he partied a lot, and he didn't care who knew it. So when I walked into the radio station with a cigarette in my hand this particular afternoon, I didn't think anything about it. I was just doing something I'd seen Texas Bill do on many occasions.

"What are you doing with that cigarette, boy?" he growled when I came into the control room, where he was seated between the turntables spinning the top country hits of the day. "Don't you want to be a singer when you grow up?"

"Yes sir," I answered timidly.

"Well, put that damn thing out and don't you ever let me catch you smoking another one, you hear me?"

"But *you* smoke," I protested.

"Yeah, and you know what? I can't hit the high notes like I used to either. And I cough a lot, sometimes right in the middle of a song. And it's 'cause I've messed up my throat with them [blankety-blank] cigarettes. Nobody ever told me like I'm telling you not to smoke. I wish they had. Now put it out!"

I did, and I was never tempted to smoke again.

I once heard a major country music star tell a disc jockey, when questioned on the air about his personal habits, "I don't take pills, I don't drink, I don't smoke, and three out of four ain't bad!" I've always assumed the fourth vice to which he could not claim abstinence was women.

I'll admit I've always enjoyed the members of the opposite sex myself. As the old stage gag goes, "I've liked girls ever since I found out they weren't boys!" By the time of my first tour, I had dated quite a bit, gone steady a few times, been "engaged to be engaged" once, whatever that is, and had my heart broken on more than one occasion.

But at the same time, I was still quite naive where the ladies were concerned. Remember, this was the late fifties and where I came from girls didn't even call boys on the telephone. So the first time a sweet young thing in skin-tight blue jeans and high-heeled cowgirl boots waltzed her curvaceous little body up to me in one of the nightclubs where we were working and said, "Dance with me!"

I didn't know whether to wind my watch or take a bubble bath. I'm not saying I didn't like it. I just wasn't real sure how I was supposed to handle it.

Since then, I've learned a lot more about the kinds of women a singer and/or musician meets when he's out on the road. I've found that they don't all fit into the same category by any means.

I've already confessed to meeting the lady I'm married to backstage at a concert, so obviously not every female who finds her way behind the footlights is a warrior on a mission to attack and destroy the morals of every young, virile guitar picker she runs into. Country stars do have their groupies, of course, who chase after their bodies just like their well-publicized counterparts in the rock field (a creative country singer, who shall remain anonymous, once nicknamed our groupies "snuff queens" or "diesel sniffers"), but the majority of women I meet at our shows are nice, decent, perfectly honorable ladies. They come in all ages, shapes, and sizes, and most of them are just big country music fans who want to get as close to their favorite stars as possible. They seek out our dressing rooms loaded down with autograph books, Polaroids and/or Instamatic cameras, and sometimes even an armful of fresh-baked homemade cakes, cookies, and pies . . . tributes to bestow upon the people whose music is pleasing to them.

For some reason, most of my fans happen to be women. Not the screaming, fainting, throw-their-panties-on-the-stage type of women, but women just the same. And, quite truthfully, I'd much rather sing my songs looking into some lady's beautiful baby blues than at some truck driver's six-day growth of beard! I'm proud to have a lot of male fans, too, and I appreciate every one, but I guess my soft singing style just appeals more to housewives than it does to construction workers. Willie Nelson may have summed up how a lot of men feel about my singing when he told Phil Donahue, "They drink beer in Texas louder than Bill Anderson sings!"

Most of the guys who do come to see my shows come to bring their ladies. That's why I've always tried to have at least one good-looking female on stage with me on my tours. That way those men who may not be into my music can at least have something pretty to look at and listen to while they're there.

I'm not a sex symbol—never have been and never will be—even though I've had women tell me they think some of my soft spoken songs are sexy. I'm glad they think so, but if you want the real truth, follow me into a crowd sometime. In almost no time at all you'll see a slinky, sexy young thing approach me with an auto-graph book in tow. Invariably she'll smile warmly and introduce herself to me, tossing her long hair back over her shoulders. Then she'll wiggle her trim little body in kind of a circular motion as if she's trying to ease just a tiny bit deeper into her clothes. This will be followed by the blinking of her dark eyelashes right in my face and a soft voice cooing, "Oh, Bill . . . may I please have your autograph?" And then just as my blood pressure and my tempera-ture start to rise and my pulse begins to quicken, she'll plead, "*Please*, Bill, it would mean *so* much. It's for my *mother!*"

To say that my first tour was a financial disaster would be to say the burning of Atlanta was a nice little bonfire. I had been prom-ised fifty dollars per working day by the promoter, and out of that I was to pay my share of a hotel room and buy all my own food. My transportation was to be furnished. It wasn't much money, but for a kid who'd been used to making fifty dollars a *week* as a disc jockey (in *cash* so that nobody in the local bank could see my check and know how little I made), I thought I'd struck gold. What the promoter didn't tell me or George Morgan or any of the others on the tour, however, was that he was depending totally upon the gate receipts from the shows to pay the talent. He had no cash reserves, and, as it turned out, most nights he didn't have any money to pay us.

Today, a booking agent would never allow his acts to leave town without the promoter having put down a sizeable cash deposit for the tour, but country music booking agents weren't nearly as sophisticated in those days as they've become in recent years. Too, in the years immediately following the rock 'n' roll explosion, long country music tours just weren't that easy to come by. It was almost a case of the artists taking whatever they were offered, and once the promoter got the acts out on the road, they were pretty much at his mercy. Every day our promoter would lie and tell us, "Boys, we've got a great advance sale building up in the next town. Hang in there with me one more day and everything will be all right." And we'd eat another hamburger and keep heading west.

About two weeks into the tour, tired, broke, and hungry, we found ourselves in Tucson, Arizona, without enough money even to buy breakfast, much less a tank of gasoline to get us to our next gig a couple of hundred miles north in Prescott. It really looked like the end of the line. To make matters worse for me, the night before I had walked into the cold, cavernous dressing room back-stage at a place called Tucson Gardens, where we were performing, and been greeted by a letter from the dean of the journalism school at the University of Georgia. He had written to tell me that he'd been trying to find me since the end of the winter term. Somehow my credits had been added wrong, and while I had been told I was going to graduate when I got home in June, in reality I was still some six hours short of having earned the required credits. Not only were we broke, not only was I tired and hungry, but now they were telling me that the college diploma I thought I had coming, and which I always figured I could fall back on in the face of disaster, was really not mine at all. I was still on cloud nine from having been on the tour, but I was confused by some parts of "big-time" show business. It made for a bittersweet time.

Fortunately, things got better. Before leaving Nashville, Roger Miller had crammed a small record player into the trunk of his car saying, "We might want to listen to our records while we're gone." I had laughed.

The record player had never been out of the trunk until Tucson. But early that morning while we were all sitting in the hotel coffee shop pondering our fate and slowly wilting from hunger, Roger hit upon the solution. "Be right back," he announced and left the rest of us sitting in a booth sipping ice water and stalling the waitress. In a few minutes he returned, proudly waving fourteen crisp new one-dollar bills in the air. "Eat up, guys, we're rich!" he exclaimed. "I hocked the record player!"

We didn't know it at the time, but there actually would be a decent crowd waiting to greet us that night in Prescott. We'd still be cutting it close, but by watching the nickels and dimes we'd be able to make it back to Nashville in just a few more days. A belly full of Rice Krispies and two cups of strong, hot coffee later, I put my college diploma way back in the corner of my mind. I walked outside with my buddies, kicked off my shoes in the front seat of the old Cadillac, propped my feet up on the dashboard, and rode off into the sunrise one more time, doing something I've been doing all of my life . . . humming an old country song and chasing a dream.

9

In a way I've always been thankful that my first tour turned out the way it did, because as soon as we limped back into Nashville riding on three skin-slick recap tires and one patched up inner-tube, totally exhausted and stone broke, I got myself back down to Georgia and back into school.

I looked for the shortest summer school session I could find and located one that lasted only five weeks at tiny Oglethorpe University in north Atlanta. The credits I earned there could be transferred toward my degree at Georgia. I paid my tuition with my second royalty check from TNT Music for "City Lights," something like four hundred dollars. (My first royalty check wouldn't have covered it. It was for exactly $2.52. I never even cashed it. I put it in a frame!) I had no intention of becoming a full-time student again, but in order to get the few remaining credits I needed for graduation, I knew I had to hit the books hard and heavy one last time. I had seen first-hand that all that glitters in show business is not gold, and I figured I was going to need all the formal education I could get. The tour had given me a large dose of the informal kind. I didn't tell anybody in Nashville about it for a long time (for reasons I'll discuss later), but I managed to graduate from college in August 1959.

While I was back in Athens for the graduation exercises, my life took another strange turn. I phoned the night I got to town to talk to my buddy Chuck Goddard, only to have his wife, LeeAnn, tell me that while I'd been gone on tour she and Chuck had separated and he had moved away. She thought he was in Swainsboro work-ing at the radio station.

"But please come by while you're here," she said encouragingly. "I'd love to see you and, besides, Bette's here. I know she'd like to see you too."

Bette Louise Rhodes was LeeAnn's youngest sister from Atlanta. Chuck had introduced us several years earlier on one of her weekend visits to Athens, hoping to spark a romance, I think, but I'd always considered her just a friend. She was still in high school, for goodness sake, and I was in college. I thought there was too big a gap between us. That is, until I went to see LeeAnn the night before graduation.

Bette had grown up. She was in nurse's training at Georgia Baptist Hospital in Atlanta, and suddenly we had a lot more to talk about than we'd ever had before. We spent almost the entire rest of the night doing just that, talking. After LeeAnn had gone to bed and we'd emptied the pantry of all the cookies we could find and drunk up all the Cokes in the house, we walked outside into the front yard, leaned up against my car, and talked some more. I told her all about the tour I had been on with George Morgan, how much fun I'd had and how little money I'd made, but how, in spite of that, just as soon as I got my diploma that next morning I was going to move to Nashville and try to get into the music business full-time. I was sincere when I told her I hoped she'd write me and stay in touch. She assured me that she would. Several dozen letters, a couple of hundred phone calls, and four months later, Bette Rhodes and I got married.

It's easy to see now that we simply weren't old enough (she was nineteen and I was all of twenty-two) and didn't know each other nearly well enough to have taken such a big step. She was an attractive girl, tall, brunette, a bit shy, and in spite of our brief courtship we made things work pretty well for a while. We even became the parents of two beautiful daughters, but Bette and I came from backgrounds that were very different. Our expectations of life turned out to be quite different, too, and we eventually grew to be two entirely different people from the kids we were in 1959. There's a line in an old country song that says, "We didn't grow together so we grew apart." That pretty accurately describes what happened to us.

Bette's father had been a city policeman in Atlanta all of his adult life. She grew up with a man-figure who left home at six-thirty in the morning, worked eight hours at his job, came home at three-thirty in the afternoon, didn't bring any of the problems of his job home with him, and built barbeque pits and poured concrete patios for his family in his spare time. A hillbilly singer-songwriter doesn't exactly keep those kinds of hours nor have the hands-on abilities of a cop. At least, this one didn't. When we bought our first house, I had a hard time digging the hole in the ground for our mailbox to sit in, and I nearly got an ulcer trying to string a clothesline between two poles.

For a long time Bette tried to understand me and my way of life, but I think show business and its high-profile lifestyle confused her. It was so different from anything she'd ever been around. I probably didn't help a whole lot myself. I was so intense and so intent on making it big that I know I often neglected to put my arms around her and guide her slowly into this strange and foreign world as I should have. There were other problems, of course, there always are, but had I not been cut out of such ambitious cloth and had I realized that life moved at any speed other than full open throttle, our marriage might have lasted a bit longer than it did. Bette and I began to drift apart around 1964, we separated in 1968, and a year later in June, 1969, our divorce became final.

Fortunately, my career was headed in a more positive direction than my personal life. I was living in Nashville full-time, and the hit songs were pouring off my pen: "The Tips of My Fingers" for me and Roy Clark and Eddy Arnold, "Riverboat" and "Face to the Wall" for Faron Young, "I Missed Me" and "Losing Your Love" for Jim Reeves, "Happy Birthday to Me" for Hank Locklin, "When Two Worlds Collide" for Roger Miller, and in 1961 a hit of my very own called "Po' Folks." I say "of my very own" because up to that point it seemed like every time I wrote a song and recorded it myself, a more well-known artist would cut a "cover" version of the same song and theirs would become the better-selling record. Owen Bradley was frustrated, saying, "We're cutting the best and the most expensive demos in town!"

But nobody tried covering "Po' Folks," thank goodness. For the first time a song finally gave me some identity as a recording artist and not just as a songwriter. And so many of the good things that have ultimately happened to me in my life and my career started with "Po' Folks." For one thing, it was the song that led to my being invited to join the cast of the Grand Ole Opry.

I was guesting as an opening act on a big star-studded Opry package in Panama City, Florida, one Saturday night when "Po' Folks" was right at the peak of its popularity. I didn't know it at the time, but the manager of the Opry, Ott Devine, was in town for a fishing trip in the Gulf of Mexico, and he had heard about our show and decided to come in off the water long enough to see us that night at the city auditorium. It was a great night for me in that the audience wouldn't let me leave the stage. I was called back time after time for "just one more verse of 'Po' Folks'" before the crowd finally stopped applauding. Mr. Devine saw it all and evidently was impressed. He came backstage after the show to congratulate me and to tell me I'd be hearing from him soon. I simply assumed he meant he'd be calling and inviting me to do another guest appearance on the Opry, since he had already been quite generous in that regard for the past several months. I thanked him but soon learned that I did not attach nearly enough significance to his remark.

I was sitting at home a few weeks later watching the All-Star baseball game on TV (they played them in the daytime back then) when the phone rang. I almost didn't get up to answer it. Who would have the nerve to call in the middle of such an important event anyhow? I finally pulled myself away from the game and caught the phone on the fourth or fifth ring.

"Bill, this is Ott Devine," I can still hear him say. And without wasting any time on pleasantries, he added, "How would you like to become a member of the Grand Ole Opry?"

Me? A member of the Opry? That was like asking me if I wanted to go to heaven when I die! I mean, this was the same Grand Ole Opry, wasn't it, that my mother and daddy had brought me to Nashville to see the summer before my junior year in high school? The one where we had the seats downstairs under the old Confederate Gallery balcony at the Ryman Auditorium and somebody upstairs spilled a soft drink on the floor and it leaked down between the cracks and dripped all over Mama's pretty new dress? The same Grand Ole Opry that I used to listen to down in Georgia by pinching the aerial on my little Arvin radio and twisting and turning the receiver until I could get the signal from WSM in

Nashville strong enough to hear Red Foley and Hank Williams and Minnie Pearl above the static. Did I want to become a part of that show? Is a G-chord made with three fingers? I hung up the phone and screamed loud enough to be heard in downtown Atlanta!

They made me the sixty-first member of the Opry onstage at the historic old Ryman a couple of Saturday nights later. There was no elaborate ceremony, no coronation of sorts, just a simple introduction by host Billy Grammer and a million butterflies in the pit of my stomach. I wore my shiny purple western suit with the gold trim and the white snowflakes all over the front and my white boots. I sang "Po' Folks" and the audience called me back for an encore. I don't think I've ever experienced a bigger thrill. Unless it was the night in July, 1986, when I celebrated my twenty-fifth anniversary as a member of the Opry cast.

You see, not just anybody can become a member of the Grand Ole Opry. It's nothing that can be achieved, nothing that can be earned. An artist has to have had a certain amount of success in the country music field, of course, even to be considered for membership, but that membership is issued by invitation only. It does not automatically come with X-number of hit records or X-amount of sold-out concerts. You must be invited to join. That's part of what makes being an Opry member something so very special.

Nobody ever forgets the first time they walk out onto the Opry stage. For me it happened almost five years before I became a member of the cast, and on my first trip across those hallowed boards I didn't even carry a guitar. I carried a camera.

My Georgia buddy, Chuck Goddard, had been invited to come to Nashville as the guest of the folks at WSM Radio to spend a weekend serving as their "Mr. DJ, USA," an honor the station bestowed each week upon a disc jockey somewhere out across the land who played country music records on his station back home. At the time Chuck played a lot of country music on WMGE in Madison, and he was thrilled to death over the prospect of plying his craft for a couple of hours on the 50,000-watt, clear-channel powerhouse in Music City. But I told him the minute he called and said he'd received the invitation that there was no way he'd be going to Nashville without me. I packed my bag on Thursday after school, drove to Athens to meet him as soon as he got off the air, and the two of us roared out of town at sundown heading for Tennessee.

We were in the hallways of WSM before the early morning announcers even logged in on Friday. We had no idea what lay in store, but we quickly learned that the station sure knew how to roll out the red carpet. Chuck was the one who was their special guest, of course, but they treated both of us to a super weekend.

On Friday night, he got to spin records and interview several country music stars live over WSM. I stood over in the corner of the studio completely awe-struck, listening, hanging on every word. Saturday evening Chuck was the special dinner guest of veteran Opry announcer, Grant Turner, at one of Nashville's finest downtown restaurants. After dinner Grant presented him with a sterling silver medallion, engraved with the date, the WSM insignia, the words "Mr. DJ, USA," and Chuck's name on the back. But the biggest moment of all was yet to come. At ten-thirty Saturday night at the Grand Ole Opry itself, Grant Turner would introduce Chuck to the audience and invite him to walk out onto the Opry stage and say a few words. From the minute Chuck found out that was going to happen, he was a nervous wreck, but when the time actually rolled around it was hard to tell who was more nervous, him or me.

"Here, Willy, take my camera," he said to me hurriedly just seconds before Grant was to head for center stage to call his name. "Go out in the audience and take my picture. I've *got* to have a picture of me onstage at the Grand Ole Opry. They'll never believe it back in Madison!"

I took the camera and started to walk toward the backstage exit and out into the auditorium when Grant grabbed me by the arm. "You don't have to go out there to take his picture," he said. "Here, follow me." And he started walking out in front of the open curtain and onto the left-hand side of the stage.

"Whoa . . . I can't go out there," I protested.

"Why can't you?" Grant asked. "Sure you can. I said it was all right."

"But . . . but that's the stage of the Grand Ole Opry!" I cried. "I can't go out there!"

Grant didn't have time to stop and argue with me. The song preceding Chuck's introduction was almost over, and Grant was about to take charge. So instead of his trying to convince me any further, he simply walked around behind my back and gave me a shove that literally pushed me from the wings out onto the most special stage in all the world. Then he calmly walked to the microphone and introduced Chuck.

I nearly broke my fingers trying to get the camera set and in focus to take Chuck's picture. I snapped it twice and took off running back behind the curtain as fast as I could go, shaking like a leaf. Never in my wildest dreams had I ever imagined that I would someday walk out on the stage of the Grand Ole Opry. And I surely never thought after that night that I'd ever go back out there again.

But I did. Less than two years later, in fact, I was back, this time as Mr. DJ, USA myself. The following year I made my first guest appearance on the Opry as a performer. Four months later I was invited back for my second visit, this time as the featured guest on the NBC network portion of the Opry that was broadcast on radio stations all around the world. And now here I was just two short years after that becoming a regular member of the Opry cast. A little less than five years from cameraman to star. Don't tell me dreams don't come true!

The Opry has provided me with some of the most memorable of all the moments in my singing career. One night at the Ryman I was in the middle of a song, went to take a deep breath, and a bug flew right into my mouth and down my throat. I began coughing, then choking, struggling to get my breath, and I know the audience must have thought I'd flipped my wig, especially the radio audience who couldn't see any of what was going on. One of the musicians from someone else's band was standing not far behind me on stage and realized immediately what had happened. "Hey, Anderson," he called out, "let the bug sing!"

Standing ovations at the Opry are about as rare as Playboy bunnies at a convent, but I've had a few and I'll never forget them. My first one came one Saturday night at the Ryman when my mother was in the audience and I did "Mama Sang a Song." I received several more when my record of "Where Have All Our Heroes Gone?" first came out. But the most memorable of all the standing ovations I ever witnessed at the Opry came not when I was on the stage performing but when I was out front watching the show from the audience.

It was in the spring of 1974, and it was one of the most emotional and historically significant weekends in the history of country music. This was the time when the Opry was about to leave its home of more than thirty years at the Ryman Auditorium and move across the Cumberland River into the sparkling new facilities of Opryland USA.

It was a move that had to be made. The Ryman, an old gospel tabernacle built in the late 1800s by a former riverboat captain named Sam Ryman, had grown too tired, too worn to keep up with the music industry's burgeoning growth and its impending charge into the last quarter of the twentieth century. For one thing, the old building could be adapted for television only very painfully. The wiring was antiquated, the production space backstage was severely limited, and there was no air conditioning whatsoever to offset the heat from both the sweltering Tennessee summers and the searing TV lights. Due to the age and the location of the building in downtown Nashville, it could be neither modified or expanded. There was virtually no convenient parking for the performers or the fans, the area immediately surrounding the Ryman was rapidly becoming overrun with seedy bars, strip joints, and adult book stores, and with country music gaining acceptance and respectability on an ever-widening front, its vanguard show had to keep pace. So on Friday night, March 15, 1974, we stood on stage, all holding hands, and sang "Will the Circle Be Unbroken?" as the tattered old curtain came together for the final time in the building that had come to be known as the Mother Church of Country Music. The following night we stood proudly but misty-eyed as Roy Acuff sang "The Wabash Cannonball" and the rich velvet curtain rose high into the rafters above the stage for the first time in the glistening new Grand Ole Opry House just a few miles north at Opryland. As a symbol of the circle remaining truly unbroken and as an assurance that the Opry would never lose touch with its past, a large circle of wood had been cut out of the old Ryman stage and implanted into the center of the new stage at the very spot where the stars would stand to perform.

There has never been a night at the Opry filled with quite as much electricity as opening night at the new Opry House. All the regular members of the cast were there, dignitaries and VIPs came from everywhere, even President and Mrs. Nixon flew down from Washington for the festivities. I was so excited I forgot for a moment that I was one of the stars of the evening. All I wanted to be was a fan.

I was scheduled to be the second person to sing on the new stage, but I didn't want to wait my turn standing in the wings. I wanted to see and hear the opening song and the inaugural cere-monies just like the folks out in the audience. So I left my comfort-able perch backstage and made my way out into the crowd. I still get goose bumps when I think about what I saw.

The auditorium was packed. There was a pulsating feeling in the air, an excitement I had never felt before, and when the house lights dimmed and the first strains of music began to filter down from the magnificent cluster of speakers hanging high above the stage, forty-four hundred people rose as one and began applauding . . . softly at first, then louder, and then louder. And I stood right out there among them and applauded just as loud as anyone.

But the first few notes of the music we heard were not being played live on the stage. A large, thin white scrim had been hung like a movie screen down across the front of the stage, and a movie projector out in the house was flashing old black-and-white motion pictures of a young Roy Acuff and his Smoky Mountain Boys off it. They were playing and singing "The Wabash Cannonball" in a scene from a movie they had made in Hollywood back in the early forties. The Opry stage itself was totally quiet and completely dark.

And then slowly but surely a few beams of light began to appear behind the scrim. Faint at first but growing brighter . . . then brighter. And the strains of the recorded music began gently to fade . . . fading . . . fading . . . as the first notes of live music started to flow, rising softly at first, then louder, then louder. The same song, the same key, the same singer. Even many of the same musicians.

And the scrim began slowly to rise. The Roy Acuff of the forties, dressed in a plaid shirt and overalls, began to disappear and the Roy Acuff of the seventies, white-haired, distinguished, dressed in a bright yellow sport coat and tie, strode to center stage and took over right where his image on the screen had left off. I'll never forget that moment as long as I live. I laughed and I cried. Mostly I just stood there and cheered.

But I had a song to sing. I stopped applauding and took off running as fast as I could from my spot out in the audience up through the backstage door and into the wings. I had only a minute to catch my breath before they introduced me. When my name was called, I bounded out into the spotlight and headed straight for the old Ryman circle. Somehow I felt that if I could just make it to there, I could relax. I'd be home.

I welcomed the crowd and told them I wanted to sing "Po' Folks" because that was the song that had been responsible for my being on the Opry in the first place. I sang it and received a warm round of applause. A short while later I came back onstage again and stood with the rest of the cast as we watched Mr. Nixon yo-yo with Roy Acuff and joke with him and talk and get caught up in the spirit of this momentous occasion. Then I joined in with everybody else and sang along as the President played the piano and led everyone in singing "God Bless America." My goose bumps were starting to get goose bumps!

The great Ernest Tubb, who had been an Opry member since the early forties, was standing next to me onstage, and it suddenly struck me to turn to him and ask him a question.

"Ernest, did you ever dream back in those early days that the President of the United States would someday come to the Grand Ole Opry?"

He thought for a minute. "No, I didn't," he replied softly, "and I'm glad he's here. But to tell the truth, I wish it had been another President."

Every interview any of us granted to the media for at least a year after that night included the question, "How do you like the new Opry House compared to the Ryman?" Most of the reporters asked it in such a way as to imply that they preferred the older setting. My answer was always the same: "If you'd ever been a member of the Opry on a Fourth of July night, tried to find a place near the Ryman to park your car, fought your way through the thousands of people lined up on the sidewalks trying to beg, borrow, or steal a ticket to the show, then once inside tried to locate even a corner where you could change into your stage clothes, rehearse a song with your band, and at the same time not die from the heat and humidity, you'd never have asked that question." I have many happy memories of our days and nights at the Ryman, but I wouldn't want us to have to go back. It's like Dolly Parton's song about the good ole days when times were bad. I've never taken an official poll, of course, but I would venture to say that ninety-nine percent of the other Opry performers wouldn't want to go back either.

I've heard people say in recent years, particularly managers and agents representing some of the industry's younger performers, that the Opry doesn't help an artist's career in today's country music market. It bothers me to hear things like that. The newer artists are the future of this business, and I want every one of them to love the Opry as much as I do, to respect what it is and what it has done for the music industry they represent. And I want every one of them to want someday to be a part of it just as much as I did.

It's true that the Opry doesn't have the impact on country music radio and country music record sales that it once had, for there was a time back in the forties and fifties when an artist could sing a new song on the Opry on Saturday night and their recording of that song would be on the airwaves of every radio station and in the bins of every mom-and-pop record shop in America by Monday morning. That's not true today. But the Opry can be very important to an artist in many other ways.

First, discounting the value of the radio and television exposure for a minute, an artist can appear on the Opry for one week during the summer and perform *live* for over thirty-five thousand people from all over the world! The Opry House seats over forty-four hundred people, and they fill it eight times (a Tuesday matinee, a Thursday matinee, two Friday night shows, a Saturday matinee, two Saturday night shows, and a Sunday matinee) every weekend from Memorial Day to Labor Day. There aren't many country artists out on tour playing to as many as thirty-five thousand people a week!

Second, millions of people still stay home to watch and listen to the Grand Ole Opry. Currently, it's broadcast in its entirety live over WSM, whose clear-channel signal blankets North America, and over sister station WKY in Oklahoma City. In addition, the Nashville Network sends a half-hour segment each Saturday night into more than forty million additional homes via cable television. When a performer walks onto the Opry stage, it's staggering to think of both the number and the scope of the people he's reaching.

I'm ashamed to admit it, but there were times earlier in my career when I used to wonder if anybody was listening to the Opry anymore myself, only to go out on tour somewhere and have dozens of people come up to me at a concert and tell me the only way they knew I was coming to their hometown was because they'd heard me announce it on the Opry. Say something stupid on the Opry (like I did one night not long ago when I was hosting a portion of the show sponsored by Beechnut Chewing Tobacco and I announced, "We'll be right back after this word from Red Man!") and see how quickly your mailbox fills up. The listeners are still out there, believe me.

Sure, the Opry is yesterday . . . that's part of its charm. It's a reflection and a reminder of a simpler, easier day and time. The Opry is also family. It's home. It's a place to come back to, a place to hang your hat, visit with old friends, sing a few songs, have a few laughs, and relax from the pressures of the business. Besides, the Opry looks after its own.

The day before Thanksgiving following Becky's accident, I was at home with her and Jamey at the condo when the doorbell rang. I answered it and there stood a messenger from the Opry holding in his arms a fully cooked turkey dinner, complete with all the trimmings, for me and my family. Up to that point I hadn't even considered what we might have for Thanksgiving dinner, but it wouldn't have been much. On top of the turkey was a small card. I opened it and read:

"Happy Thanksgiving from Your Friends at the Grand Ole Opry."

Me ever leave the Opry? They'll have to run me off!

A few months after having had the hit record "Po' Folks" and having joined the Grand Ole Opry, the biggest things of all began happening in my career. In early 1962 I wrote and recorded a semi-autobiographical recitation (the first of many talking songs I'd be doing over the years) called "Mama Sang a Song," and it surpassed anything I had ever done, climbing all the way up to the top of the national country charts. It was my very first No. 1 record. It was such a smash hit that it even entered the pop charts, not only my version but a cover version by jazz legend Stan Kenton (he might have been a great bandleader, but he did a lousy country recitation) and later by Walter Brennan, who put all the emotion and feeling into the song you'd expect from an actor of his stature. There were several weeks when all three of our records were high in the pop music charts despite the song's heavy religious overtones. I didn't know it at the time, but the stage was set for the big explosion in my career.

Owen Bradley, however, clearly saw what was going on and put it into words. "Well, Bill," he said after "Mama Sang a Song" had reached No. 1 and had begun to slide back down the charts, "we've finally had a No. 1 country record, and I'm happy for you. But, because you're primarily known as a country artist and because 'Mama Sang a Song' was so religious in nature, your record couldn't go any higher in the pop charts or sell any more records than it did. But now we've got some momentum going for us. If you can write a *love* song that fits the same formula as "Mama Sang a Song" . . . you know, a little singing and a little talking . . . I honestly believe you're ripe to bust the country charts *and* the pop charts wide open."

I listened intently. "Now, don't make this song you're going write religious," he emphasized. "Make it about a man and a woman. We want the appeal to be as broad as we can get it."

"Gosh, Owen," I said, "that's a big order. I don't know whether I can do it or not."

"Sure, you can," he encouraged me. "You can do it and it'll be the biggest thing you've ever done." He was prophetic and one hundred percent right.

Fortunately, the song I needed to write almost wrote itself. The best ones often do. And like most of my best songs, it was inspired by something that actually happened.

I had gone back to Atlanta to visit my folks in the fall of '62, and while I was in town the producer of the leading local morning television show phoned the house and wanted to know if I'd come by the station sometime during my visit and do a live interview. Sort of a "local boy makes good" type of story. I said sure, I'd be glad to, but it wasn't until after I'd accepted the invitation and hung up the receiver that I remembered one of my former girlfriends from college worked at that very station. I hadn't seen her for several years, and I wasn't too sure I wanted to.

You see, there had been a time when I had been crazy about her, but she had jilted me—a small-town country disc jockey in Commerce—to run off to Atlanta, take a job at the city's largest TV station, and marry the station's top-rated local weatherman. I mean, how cruel can you get?

Yet, just a few years earlier, she and I had almost run away together ourselves. In those days when you "ran off together" you usually got married, so I guess we'd have probably done that too.

Because of the regional success of my record of "City Lights" on TNT, I'd had a feeler from the *Louisiana Hayride* in Shreveport concerning the possibility of my joining the *Hayride* as a performer and joining the staff of the *Hayride*'s originating radio station, KWKH, as an announcer and disc jockey. Being terribly in love and not wanting to go all the way to Shreveport alone, I considered making the move only if this lovely woman-child would agree to go with me. She worked in radio as well, and I figured she could get a job somewhere in the market herself and bring in a few extra bucks to help put groceries on the table. It sounded too good to be true. Turned out it was. Enter the weatherman and a long spell of cold, rainy weather for me. I never did get to check out the climate in Shreveport.

And now, four years later, I was agreeing to go to the television station where she and ole Partly Cloudy himself both worked and do an interview? My first thought was to call the producer back and cancel my appearance. Then common sense and pride took over. "Hey, dummy," I said to myself, "she's probably not even working there anymore. And what if she is? All that stuff was over years ago. Act like a man. Go!" So I went, but all the way to the studio I wondered how I'd feel and how I'd act if I did happen to run into her.

I didn't have to wait very long to find out. I pulled my car into the parking lot and, not being familiar with the layout of the building, began searching for anything that looked like an entrance. Suddenly my eyes came to rest on a double-wide plate glass door behind some high shrubbery, and I eased my car closer in order to get a better look.

And there she was, standing right behind that very door peering out. I learned later that she'd been standing there for nearly an hour waiting for me to arrive.

I stopped and stared at her through the window of the car, through the glass door, and I could tell every inch of her was still the beautiful, vibrant young woman I remembered. Then I thought of how quickly the worm had turned and how I was now a much bigger star than her darned ole weatherman. And I smiled as I pulled my Cadillac into the parking space next to her Chevrolet.

Up to that point, everything was fine. But I had my car radio on, and, as fate would have it, just as I went to get out of the car and stride confidently into the television station, the disc jockey on the station I was listening to decided to play George Jones's record of "Just a Girl I Used to Know":

> Just a girl I used to spend some time with
> Just a friend from long ago
> I don't talk about the nights I cry without her
> I say she's just a girl I used to know.

I came bounding back down to earth in a hurry. That song had always moved me, but this time it was like an earthquake. I started thinking, started remembering, and I wondered if I was as over my old girlfriend as I had thought I was.

But I took a deep breath and walked right on in through the wide double doors. I smiled, we said hello, made a little small talk, and she led me to the studio where my interview was to take place. The show came off without a hitch. I made it through the interview just fine, made it through seeing her again with no problems—I made it through everything—everything, that is, except the night.

I drove back to Nashville late that afternoon, went home and tried to pretend the whole day had never happened, but when it came time to try and fall asleep, I couldn't do it. Finally, around three o'clock in the morning with my brain racing ninety miles an hour down a dead-end street, I climbed out of bed, walked into my little pine-paneled den, and in almost less time than it takes to tell it I sat down at my old manual Underwood typewriter and wrote the words and music to a song called "Still":

> *Still . . . though you broke my heart*
> *Still . . . though we're far apart*
> *I love you still*
> *Still . . . after all this time*
> *Still . . . you're still on my mind*
> *I love you still.*

I've been asked a thousand times over the years who I wrote "Still" for and I've always carefully dodged the question. Actually, I didn't write "Still" *for* anybody. I wrote it *because* of somebody and because of a situation I found myself in. I was not still in love with my former girlfriend, but I had experienced the *feeling* of being in love with her again, and that's what I wrote the song about. It's a thing called empathy, and it's the greatest friend a songwriter can have. I'll discuss it in more detail later.

To be honest, in the beginning I didn't think "Still" was all that great of a song. Even today I think I've written several songs that are a lot better. But somehow I was able to write into this very vanilla lyric ("Remember, vanilla still outsells all those thirty-one other flavors of ice cream," Owen Bradley loved to say) the feelings, the thoughts, and the emotions of hundreds of thousands of people. I can't begin to tell you how many people have come up to me over the years and said, "My husband and I fell in love to your song 'Still'" or, "We were about to get a divorce and he/she sent me a copy of that record and we got back together," or, "That was our song while I was in Viet Nam . . . it kept us going." Somehow my song struck a nerve with virtually every segment of the population, every age group. If I knew how to do it again, I'd do it every time I write a song. So would every writer. It's that magical little something that you search and search for, and if you're lucky you find it once in a lifetime.

If "Still" was a good song, then Owen Bradley turned it into a great record. First, he encouraged me to slow down the tempo. I had originally written it a bit brighter, but he knew it needed to be a more mellow ballad. Second, he added a few passing chords to the melody that I didn't even know how to find on my guitar. And they were beautiful. Third, he worked and worked the day of the session with both the engineer and the Anita Kerr Singers to get that bright little ringing sound every time the group sang the word *still*. He called it "like a little bell," and nobody before or since has been able to duplicate it. Many have tried but none has succeeded. The secret lay in the fact that Owen didn't really have the group *sing* the word as much as he had them *say* it on pitch and then let the echo chamber take over and make the word ring. If you think that I think Owen Bradley is a genius, you're one hundred percent right!

"Still" did exactly what Owen had predicted it would do. It streaked up the country charts all the way to No. 1 in almost no time and it stayed there. Then, because of that just-right combination of elements he'd gone searching for and found, the record slowly began to be accepted by the pop audience as well. At first it was just a city at a time. Today Toledo, tomorrow Cleveland, the next day Pittsburgh, the next day Philadelphia. Then one day somebody at the powerful WMCA Radio in New York City got turned on to the record somehow and decided to air it on that station. From then on it was Katy-bar-the-door. By the time the dust settled some eight or nine months after the record had first been released, "Still" had reached No. 1 on the country charts, No. 5 on the pop charts, sold a million copies, been translated into several foreign langauges, inspired both parody and answer records, and had changed my life forever. After all this time, the one song people around the world most closely associate with Whisperin' Bill Anderson is still "Still."

When the song was at its peak, I was running back and forth across the country like a madman promoting it everywhere I could. I was booked onto every major country music tour I could possibly be a part of. I toured the South with a big rock 'n' roll review featuring many of the top pop stars of the day. I went with movie star James MacArthur to Rochester, New York, to perform at another rock extravaganza, and he and I stood backstage and wondered how two fish like us managed to get so far out of our native waters. While some teenaged be-bop group was blasting away on stage, we gave up, snuck out a side door, and went back to our hotel.

The crowning jewel for a singer with a pop hit in the late fifties and early sixties, however, was to be booked for an appearance on Dick Clark's *American Bandstand* television show. There was no bigger show anywhere for a recording artist to be on (with the possible exception of the *Ed Sullivan Show*), and I was thrilled the day the *Bandstand* producer called and said they wanted me. But the week they'd be using me, he said, Dick would not be doing the show from his customary studio in Philadelphia. Instead, he would be on location outdoors on Miami Beach. That sounded even better to me. Lie on the beach, soak up a little sun, and appear on national TV. What else was there?

ABC flew me to Miami, put me up in a big, swanky hotel, and I went out and bought a new sport coat to wear. I mean, this was major league, and I didn't figure the purple suit with the snowflakes was exactly what I needed for a teenage dance party by the sea.

I was scheduled to be the last artist to appear on Dick's final show of the week on Friday afternoon, and I was some kind of pumped up. The cameras were set up outside around the swimming pool at the hotel, the Atlantic Ocean rolled gently in the background, and as we rehearsed that morning the bright blue Florida sky glistened overhead. There couldn't have been a more beautiful setting.

The show went on the air live, coast to coast, around four o'clock that afternoon. I stood off to the side and watched the other performers who went on ahead of me, my heart pounding loud enough to wake up people sleeping in Fort Lauderdale. Finally there was nobody left to go on but me, and I stepped from the shadows out onto my mark. Dick spent what seemed like five minutes introducing me, saying all kinds of nice things. Finally he called my name, the recorded music started rolling, and I was on.

"Still . . . though you broke my heart . . . Still . . . Though we're far apart" . . . everything was going perfect. But suddenly from out of nowhere came a sound that I'd never heard on the record before. Then I heard it again. What was that? I wondered as I struggled to maintain my concentration and my composure. But in less than a heartbeat I knew exactly what it was. It was thunder.

I wasn't two lines into the recitation on the first verse of my song when the heavens opened up and the bottom fell out. It rained like I had never seen it rain. Rain on my face, rain on my hair, rain all over my new sport coat, rain on the cameras, rain everywhere. And we were on the air live. What was I supposed to do?

Dick Clark provided the solution. Pro that he is, he quickly motioned to one of the cameramen to swing his camera off of me and turn it instead on him. He was just as soaked as I was, but as the camera picked him up he took off running madly away from the swimming pool and directly toward the open waters of the ocean, slinging water everywhere. The rain was coming down in sheets by now, and here was this nationally known TV celebrity streaking wildly over the sands toward the Atlantic . . . still dressed in his dark, conservative suit and tie.

He never broke stride. He dove like a porpoise headfirst into the breakers, came up for air, waved good-bye to the camera, and the credits rolled and the show went off the air. I stood dripping wet back by the swimming pool, bewildered, wondering if my career had also just gone out with the tide.

But Dick was marvelous. He came back up onto the patio area wringing wet and apologized to me like the rain had been his fault. And he promised me that when my next record came out, my follow-up to "Still," whatever it might be, he'd have me back on his show from drier quarters in Philadephia. And it wouldn't matter, he said, whether the song was in the pop charts or not. He'd still have me back.

He kept his word. The following winter I had a song out called "8 X 10," and I flew to Philadelphia and performed it in a nice warm, dry *American Bandstand* studio.

Back in 1963, there was no such thing as a country music awards show on network television. There was not much country music on television, period, particularly at the network level, which was another thing that made my two appearances with Dick Clark so very meaningful. When it came time to pass out the plaudits for achievement in the country music field each year, everybody just gathered in Nashville in late October or early November for the annual Disc Jockey Convention and Grand Ole Opry birthday celebration. That's when the performing rights society, Broadcast Music, Incorporated, the organization that collects the monies and pays the songwriters and music publishers for the radio and television performances of their songs, held their small annual banquet open only to a few composers, publishers, and invited guests, and handed out their Citations of Achievement to the people responsible for creating the biggest hits of the year. The various music trade publications like *Billboard*, *CashBox*, the *Music Vendor*, and the *Music Reporter* banded together during that time as well to present their trophies and plaques. These were the only country music awards back then. The Country Music Association wouldn't enter the awards business for another four years. I've often wondered what the impact would have been on my life and my career had "Still" come along after the nationally televised CMA Awards became the career-making event they are today.

The best you could hope for back in 1963 was to have your name called out at a breakfast for convention participants held in the cavernous Nashville Municipal Auditorium. If you won an award, you walked on stage in front of a few hundred folks who put down their sausage and biscuits long enough to applaud politely, you posed for a few snapshots, talked into a few tape recorders, and that was about it.

The breakfast and awards presentation that year happened to fall on November 1, my twenty-sixth birthday. And because of "Still," I won just about everything they gave away. *Billboard* named it Song of the Year and Record of the Year. *CashBox* said it was the Most Programmed Country Record of the Year on radio stations. *Music Vendor* saluted me as Male Vocalist of the Year, and the *Music Reporter* honored me with their most prestigious award, The No. 1 Award, for being as they called it, "The No. 1 Artist of the Year." "Still" also won for me as a composer both a country citation and a pop citation from BMI. I had never had a birthday party quite like it, and even though I've had three or four extremely memorable birthdays, nothing will ever quite match that one as far as gifts are concerned. I left the auditorium carrying so many prizes I looked like I'd just robbed a jewelry store.

The ever jolly and always acerbic Faron Young spotted me as I was leaving the breakfast struggling to make it out the door and to my car with all the loot. In the midst of all the well-wishers and right into a battery of open radio microphones, his voice loud enough to be heard in Memphis, he bellowed, "What's the matter, Anderson? Is that all you could win? Hell, I thought for sure you'd figure out a way to win Female Vocalist of the Year, too!"

10

There was no doubt in my mind, nor in anybody else's, that the key to my budding success in the music business was my songwriting. All my early hit records— "Po' Folks," "Mama Sang a Song," "Still,"—were songs I had composed. As a recording artist, I'd begun to develop a bit of a style, but I knew I wasn't a great singer. Chet Atkins once told me the world is full of great singers but the only ones who are successful are those who have a supply of great songs to sing. He was right.

For some reason there seems always to have been a universal fascination with the business of writing a song. It has often seemed to me that every housewife who ever stood over a sink washing dishes or walked behind a vacuum cleaner, and every man who ever dug a ditch, built a house, plowed a field, drove a truck, or sat on a creekbank with his fish hook dangling in the water has, at one time or another, tried to write a song. It appears to be an easy enough thing to do, and if you're not too picky about the end result I guess writing a song is relatively easy. But writing a good, solid, commercial song with the potential to become a bestseller is not very easy at all.

The two questions I've been asked more than any others over the years are (1) How do you write a song? and (2) Of all the songs you've written, which one is your personal favorite? I've also been asked nearly every day of my professional life by an aspiring songwriter somewhere "How can I get my song published?" but that's another story for another time.

There are as many different ways to write a song as there are different songs to be written. There's no formula, no roadmap. I can speak only for myself and from my own experience, but I find that writing from a lyrical idea or from a catchy phrase or hook line is the best place for me to begin. If I have real-life inspiration like "Still" or an experience similar to the one on the hotel roof that produced "City Lights," then I'm that much farther ahead of the game. But I've never been the kind of songwriter who had to get drunk to write about getting drunk.

To me, the greatest asset a songwriter can have is empathy, the ability to put himself in another person's place, to think like another person thinks, to feel what that other person feels. The biggest compliment I can be paid as a songwriter is for somebody to come up to me and say, "You must have written that song *just* for *me*. Your song says exactly what I feel but I didn't know how to say." That's when I know I've hit home.

When John D. Loudermilk was writing some of the best songs and biggest hits coming out of Nashville in the sixties ("Waterloo," "Then You Can Tell Me Goodbye," "Tobacco Road") he'd often go downtown and hang around the blue-collar bars or spend the night just sitting in the local bus station talking to the winos in search of that very thing, empathy. I guess it worked for him, but I always preferred to close my eyes at home and imagine myself in those places. I got more rest that way, it was cheaper, and with a little creativity I always felt I could transport myself mentally to the places I needed to visit.

When you write songs from an idea, you find that the whole world becomes one big constant song idea flowing through your mind. A talented painter looks at a gorgeous sunset and sees brilliant yellows, bright oranges, soft pinks, and vivid blues dancing in front of his eyes. And by simply picking up his paint brush he is able to transfer those images beautifully to canvas. That's his world, colors and images, captured by the touch of a master's hand. As a songwriter, however, I could look at that same sunset and not be able to draw even a good broomstick cowboy but I might write:

> I watched the sun go down this afternoon
> And paint the city's face all red
> Then I wished upon a silver star
> That crept into the pink sky overhead . . .

The painter and the songwriter saw the very same sunset. We were both moved to want to preserve the beauty of the moment forever, and each of us attempted to do so in our own way. He painted with colors and I painted with words. Maybe it's called having "songwriter's eyes." To me, it simply means looking at everything that you see, hear, and feel in the world around you and thinking at least subconsciously how those things might fit together in a song.

I was having dinner in a restaurant one night at a big round table packed with friends when suddenly one of the guys pushed back his chair, tossed his napkin onto his plate and announced, "Well, gang, I've enjoyed as much of this as I can stand." And he got up and walked away. Everybody else at the table roared with laughter, but I simply reached into my coat pocket, took out a pen, and scribbled the words he had just spoken onto the back of a scrap of paper. Before the night was over I had composed a song that would soon become a No. 1 record for Porter Wagoner called "I've Enjoyed as Much of This as I Can Stand." Any one of the other people at that table could have written down that same phrase, but nobody else heard it in the same light that I did. I was just accustomed to listening with songwriter's ears and observing through songwriter's eyes.

I went into a small dry cleaning establishment out on my end of town one day to pick up some clothes. When I walked in the door, I noticed the owner of the shop standing there with a bewildered look on his face. "What's the matter?" I asked.

"You won't believe what just happened," he said, his eyes glazed over in bewilderment. "This guy walks in here about five minutes ago and asks to pick up his cleaning. I bring it to him . . . it was a pretty large bundle . . . and he turns and walks outside to put it in his car. I assume he'll put it down and come back in here to pay me. Instead, he gets in his car and roars out of the parking lot. Stiffs me on the ticket. I can't believe it."

"You know the guy?" I asked.

"Never seen him before in my life," he answered. Then he shook his head, shrugged his shoulders and said, "Well, I guess if he can live with it I can live without it."

Bingo! Right between the eyeballs it hit me. What a great title for a song, except not about a guy stealing his laundry but about a

man-woman relationship where one of them breaks off the marriage or the commitment and splits. And the one who's left behind
says, "Well, if you can live with it I can live without it . . . If you
can face your conscience I can face my pride." I have a plaque on
my wall that says it was a pretty good idea. I wrote the song,
recorded it myself, and it went to No. 1 in the charts.

When you look at and listen to the world constantly thinking
song, song, song, you find that ideas for songs are all around.
They're in advertisements for products, in the scripts of television
shows and movies (the daytime soaps are a great source of material . . . of course, these days you have to clean most of it up
before you can use it!), they're in newspaper articles, magazine
stories, and sometimes ideas for new songs are even buried deep
inside the lyrics of old songs.

I got the idea to write "I Love You Drops," one of my best-
known songs and biggest hit records from the mid-sixties, by picking out an obscure phrase in Chuck Berry's classic rocker
"Memphis." There's a line hidden deep in the words of that song
where he talks about "hurry home drops on her cheek," and when
I listened closely and realized what he was saying, I thought to
myself, What an unusual way to describe tears. He called them
"hurry home drops" and it stuck with me. There was nothing
illegal or immoral about my using that one phrase and writing a
totally new song called "I Love You Drops." I didn't have to split
the copyright with Chuck Berry, nor would he have expected me
to.

I've had people write songs from phrases and thoughts I've put
into my own songs many times. You can copyright a song, but you
can't copyright a song idea. And a song title is not exclusive to
only one musical work either. A few years ago the pop group, the
Commodores, had a big hit with a song called "Still." It was the
same title as my most famous song, but all I could do was hope
maybe I'd accidentally get some of their royalties. I couldn't stop
them from putting it out. One of Billy Joel's biggest hits was titled
"My Life." I had the No. 1 Country Record of the Year by that
same title in 1969. (I really did get some of his performance royalties by accident, but somebody caught on and I had to give them
back!) And a rock group once cut a song with the title "Wild
Weekend." In country circles that title is synonymous with Bill

Anderson, but again there was nothing I could do but wish them well.

I once wrote another hit for Porter Wagoner called "I'll Go Down Swinging." Baseball nut that I am, I had heard that phrase all my life, but it wasn't until I heard a tag line at the end of a Hank Snow record called "Breakfast with the Blues" that I realized "swinging" didn't necessarily have to involve a ball and bat. My song had nothing to do with our national pastime.

The Charlie Louvin No. 1 hit "I Don't Love You Anymore" was inspired by a joke I heard Ray Price pull on one of his band members during a show one Sunday afternoon at the Queen Elizabeth Theater in Vancouver, British Columbia, Canada. I was standing in the wings watching his show when I heard Ray tell the audience that one of his band members didn't drink anymore. "Of course," Ray added, "he doesn't drink any less!" My songwriter's antenna went up instantly, and I transposed the drinking to loving and went back to my room at the Georgian Hotel and wrote a song about a guy who says he doesn't love his lady anymore. "Trouble is," the lyric goes, "I don't love you any less."

One of my very first fans and dearest friends over the years, Mrs. Margaret Patterson, was taking me to the bus station in her hometown of Roanoke, Virginia, late one night following a show I'd done there early in my career, and she got to telling me a bit about her family. She'd gone through a long list of sons, daughters, aunts, uncles, and cousins when she came to a person she said was the black sheep of the family. "Oh, he'd probably be all right," she said, "if he wasn't afraid to go out and get a little dirt on his hands."

Again, whammo, home run! I asked her if I could borrow a piece of paper and a pencil, and in the back of a dark, rockin', rollin' Greyhound between Roanoke and Bristol, midnight and dawn, I wrote "Get a Little Dirt on Your Hands," a song I recorded once as a solo and once as a duet with David Allen Coe. It was a reasonably successful song in the United States, but it was recorded in Australia by a pop group called the Dell Tones, and in that country the song is legendary.

Becky and I were having dinner one evening in a little restaurant across the street from the church we attend, and we were enjoying a glass of wine with our meal. Suddenly I looked up, and several of the church members were coming in the door. My first inclination was to slide my glass of wine behind the menu propped up on the table. I wasn't sure I wanted the elders and the deacons to know I was imbibing.

Becky refused to be a partner in my little act of subterfuge. "Hey, the Lord knows I'm drinking," she said. I got mashed potatoes and gravy all over my elbow falling across the table reaching for a paper napkin. Becky calmly finished her meal. I totally lost my appetite. I was too busy writing on the napkin the words to a song about an ole boy who was having a few drinks in a little neighborhood bar one night when a "self-righteous woman" from the church came in and started preaching to him about his sinful ways. He told the lady, just as Becky had told me, "Hey, the Lord knows I'm drinking." That was the hook line, the title of the song, and I've got all kinds of awards hanging on my wall today attesting to the fact that a lot of people identified with the message. The song was a No. 1 country hit for Cal Smith and even earned me a pop award from BMI due to the tremendous amount of airplay it received from all formats of radio.

Not everybody writes songs the same way. Some writers compose a melody first and then add lyrics to it. I'm sure that works fine for them, but it's never been comfortable for me. Then again, melodies have never been my long suit.

I've heard people who knew Hank Williams say that he believed if a song couldn't be written in twenty minutes it wasn't worth writing. I agree up to a point. Sometimes when an idea strikes, it hits so hard the song almost seems to write itself. One minute you're staring at a blank piece of paper, the next minute the words to a song are staring back at you. Nearly every successful writer I've ever talked to has at one time or another experienced the overwhelming phenomenon of suddenly having a song appear and not being able to recall writing it. Yet nobody has ever been able to explain how it happens. In my religious song "I Can Do Nothing Alone," I wrote, "I held the pencil, but He wrote this song." How else can a writer explain a song suddenly arriving on an empty sheet of paper? I believe there are definitely times when a composer's thoughts and inspirations come from a Higher Power.

Mel Tillis, who has written some of the greatest country songs ever composed, evidently agrees. When I asked him recently if he'd been writing any new songs, he shook his head and said, "No, I haven't."

"Why not?" I asked.

"I'm not real sure," he replied. "It could be that the Lord only gives you so many. Maybe He's already given me all of mine."

Of course, not all good songs or successful songs are written in twenty minutes. Many are just as much perspiration as they are inspiration. I have written songs in *less* than twenty minutes, and I once agonized over a song for three years before I was finally able to finish it. And it was one of the simplest songs I've ever put together in terms of the silly idea and the plaintive sing-along chorus.

The song was called "Peel Me a 'Nanner," and it was an award-winning song for me thanks to the fine recording of it by Roy Drusky. For three years I carried these lines around in my head, unable to add anything to them:

Peel me a 'nanner . . . Toss me a peanut
And I'll come swinging from a coconut tree
Peel me a 'nanner . . . Toss me a peanut
'Cause you sure made a monkey out of me.

As you might expect, I've been teased and kidded about that song for years, but if you knew all the trouble I had writing three verses to go with that crazy little chorus you wouldn't laugh at all. It nearly drove me nuts! First, the chorus and the idea are both so ludicrous that the temptation was to try and write nonsensical verses. But I'm no comedian, and how much "silly" can one song stand anyhow? So I tried writing the verses in a serious vein. But how serious can you be when you're writing about monkeys swinging from trees? After struggling with this thing off and on for over three years and not being able to get it off my mind or come up with a solution, one day I was driving along in my car when *zap!* out of the blue I hit on the way to connect the chorus and the verses. The result was part serious, part foolishness, but it worked:

There I was in all my innocence
Loving you with all of my might
Come to find I didn't have any sense
You had a different darling every night.

Although nobody will ever confuse "Peel Me a 'Nanner" with Beethoven's Fifth Symphony, I was happy with it when I quickly added two more verses and realized all the pieces finally fit. I tell people it's a song that took me three years and twenty minutes to write!

I've never worked very much with cowriters. Most of the songs I've written over the years have started and stopped with me. There were a few exceptions along the way, however, the most notable being a song written years ago in the back seat of Roger Miller's bright green Rambler station wagon in the middle of the night somewhere between Nashville and San Antonio, Texas.

Roger had seen the science-fiction movie *When Worlds Collide* not long before and had become convinced that the title of the movie could and should be transferred to a country song. "You know," he'd say, "it'll be about the separate worlds of a man and a woman being on a collision course." And I would argue, "But we can't steal the title of a movie and make it into a song!"

"OK, so we'll change it a bit," he agreed, and we did. When the song came out, it was called "When *Two* Worlds Collide," and it became a big hit for Roger himself and later for several other artists, including Jim Reeves.

The night we finally got it written, we were travelling to a string of personal appearance dates in Texas and had a young singer named Johnny Seay in the car with us. Roger was under the wheel, Johnny was riding shotgun, and I was in the back seat directly behind the driver when the juices began to flow. Roger immediately stopped the car and told Johnny to slide under the wheel and drive. He reached into the back of the wagon and pulled out his guitar, climbed into the back seat with me, and I grabbed a piece of paper and a pen. The only light we had was from the headlights of an occasional passing car and a big silver moon high in the sky overhead. Roger would come up with a line and I'd write it down. Then I would think of a line and feed it to him, and he'd keep singing it over and over for fear he'd forget the melody. We couldn't afford the luxury of a portable tape recorder in those days, and since neither one of us actually composed music, we just wrote down the words and hoped we wouldn't forget the tune before we reached a place where we could record it. We were so knocked out with what we were writing that even though we finished the song somewhere around midnight, we didn't dare go to sleep for fear we wouldn't remember it when we woke up the next morning. When we pulled into San Antonio around eight A.M., neither one of us had closed our eyes all night. But we knew our new song awfully well!

We checked into the old Gunter Hotel, Roger singing the song over and over—in the lobby, on the elevator, all the way up to our floor. As soon as we reached our room, he got on the telephone and called a disc jockey buddy of ours in town named Neal Merritt (who was later to write a hit song himself called "May the Bird of Paradise Fly Up Your Nose") and instructed him to "come over quick and bring a tape recorder!" Neal did, and there in that little hotel room Roger and his guitar cut the original demo of "When Two Worlds Collide." Only when we were finally assured that the machine had worked and the song was safely on tape did we allow ourselves to fall limply across the beds and go to sleep.

Cowriting songs is the big thing in Nashville songwriting circles these days, but back then it was rather rare. There were only a few people I felt comfortable enough around to want to share my very heart and soul and guts with. And that's exactly what you do when you compose a song. You pour it all out, and it's not easy working on a song, creating your own little "baby," only to have somebody listen to what you've written and say, "Hey, your kid is ugly!" You've got to have a special relationship with someone to open yourself up that far. And they've got to trust you as well.

Jerry Crutchfield, who has in recent years become one of Nashville's top record producers, wrote some songs with me in the early sixties, the most memorable of which was a Brenda Lee hit called "My Whole World Is Falling Down." We intended to write that song to the tune of "London Bridge Is Falling Down," but we got our nursery rhymes mixed up and it came out to the tune of "Mary Had a Little Lamb" instead. Jerry and I wrote mostly what I'd call "light" songs and nothing very heavy lyrically, but we had a few hits.

Buddy Killen and I wrote several songs together, usually combining my lyrics with his melodies. "I May Never Get to Heaven" was probably our most successful. Most of the other songs on which I'm listed as a cowriter were one person's idea (usually the other person's) and my actual composition.

Steel guitarist/record producer Walter Haynes brought me a song in 1964 called "Just an Old 8 X 10," a story about a child finding a faded photograph of his parents. I didn't care for the song very much, but the phrase "8 X 10" really caught my eye, especially the way it was written with the letter X being used for the word by. I took that germ of an idea and wrote my hit "8 X 10," which by the time I finished it had become not a song about mom and dad but a lament of lost love. I figured it was more commercial that way.

A lady named Jerry Todd, a fan of mine from Cleveland, Ohio, later brought me a song called "3 A.M.," but there was nothing whatsoever in her lyric that I could use. But, again, as with "8 X 10," there was something about "3 A.M." that jumped off the page and hit me square in the face. I wrote my own song from her idea, and it, too, was a big record for me. Jerry and Walter are each listed as cowriters on the songs for which they supplied the ideas, and they have, over the years, shared in the royalties the songs have earned.

There is a difference, however, between the case of somebody who deliberately sets out to give a writer an idea for a song and that of someone who casually makes a comment in passing and the songwriter later takes that comment and turns it into a song. The former should definitely be listed as a cowriter and expect to participate in whatever monies the song might bring in. But a person who casually says "Boy, it's a beautiful day," to someone who then goes home and writes a song called "Boy, It's a Beautiful Day," should not necessarily expect to be rewarded with a cowriter's percentage of that song. The writer might be generous and offer a share to the person, but that's up to the writer's discretion.

I was once in the right place at the right time and got partial writer's credits on a song that I had nothing to do with conceiving but which turned out to be an award-winning smash. Don Wayne had written the first two-thirds of a clever story song called "Saginaw, Michigan," but as he began to reach the end of the song, he didn't know how to bring his story to a conclusion. The idea was that a young couple lived in Saginaw and fell in love, but the girl's father was very much against the boy and against the relationship. So in an effort to impress the father with both his resources and his ingenuity, the young man left Saginaw and went to Alaska in search of gold. It was Don's idea that the young man return from

Alaska to face the father and claim the girl, but at that point he hit a stone wall. He just wasn't sure how to make it all come together.

I suggested the idea of having the boy come back and tell the father that he'd found this tremendous amount of gold up in Alaska but for a price he'd be willing to sell the rights to his claim to the father. The old man fell for the lie hook, line, and sinker, and took off to Alaska himself "looking for the gold I never found." While he was gone, of course, the boy and girl got married and began to live happily ever after.

In the beginning I didn't even consider my being listed as a cowriter on the song because I had intended to record it myself. I figured the work I had done on it would be more than justified if my recording turned out to be a hit. But I made a big mistake. I took the song to my next recording session but never got around to cutting it. Instead, I recorded a song I had written about another town, "Cincinnati, Ohio." Before I could set up another session, Don pitched "Saginaw, Michigan" to Lefty Frizzell and the rest, as they say, is history. It became the last No. 1 record of Lefty's illustrious career.

After Lefty cut the song, Don Wayne did a very kind and honorable thing. He offered me a percentage of the song and had my name added to the copyright as cowriter. Unfortunately, the first copies of Lefty's record had already begun to ship to the radio stations and record stores by this time . . . without my name on them. I received credit on later pressings of the single, and my name was always listed on the album copies, but for a long time I had trouble convincing some people that I wrote part of "Saginaw, Michigan." If you have a copy of Lefty's original single, you might want to check and see if there are two writers listed or only one. If there's no "B. Anderson" on the label, it could be that you have one of those rare early pressings. Hang onto it. Someday it might just be a collector's item.

It's not always easy to write an ending to a song. Many's the time I've written myself right into a corner with a song, much like a painter might back himself into a corner while he's painting a room. And there have been times when there has appeared to be no exit.

That's exactly what happened when I was writing one of my favorite songs, "The Cold Hard Facts of Life," a third composition of mine which Porter Wagoner took to the top of the charts in the late sixties. I began the song by telling the story of a man who had been out of town, presumably on business, but had come back home a day before he'd planned to. He thought about calling his wife to tell her he was home but decided to surprise her instead. The surprise turned out to be on him, however, when he found her at their house having a wild party with lots of friends and "a stranger."

In my lyric, the hero of the song stops in "a little wine store on the corner" to buy a bottle of champagne to take home for his wife. While he's there he overhears another man asking the clerk for "two bottles of your best." The man tells the clerk, "Her husband's out of town and there's a party. He winked as if to say 'you know the rest.'" Our hero leaves the store "two steps behind the stranger" and realizes as he's following the man in his car that the stranger is headed to *his* house to see *his* wife. The story was gripping and spine-tingling as I was writing it, until I suddenly realized I didn't have the foggiest idea how my little soap opera was going to end. I had exactly sixteen bars of music, about four lines of lyrics, and possibly a tag line with which to wrap the whole thing up, and I wasn't sure quite frankly if it could even be done.

I tried every angle I could think of, then finally decided to have my hero burst into his own home and confront both his wife and her lover face to face. Throughout the story the singer had been referring to the entire scenario as his "witnessing the cold hard facts of life." So, I felt it only fitting in the climax of the song to write:

> Lord, you should have seen their frantic faces.
> They screamed and cried "please put away that knife"
> I guess I'll go to hell . . . Or I'll rot here in this cell
> But who taught who the cold hard facts of life?
> Yes, who taught who the cold hard facts of life?

Where in the world I came up with the "who taught who" line I'll never know, but it was perfect. It was my payoff. And it got me out of my corner. But it's also a lot easier telling it here than it was coming up with it then. It was just one of those fortunate things that happened when I needed it to happen most.

When a young, aspiring songwriter comes to me for advice on how to perfect his craft, I stress three things. First, I talk about empathy, but I've about decided over the years that empathy is something you either have in your psychological makeup or you don't. I'm not sure it can be taught or acquired.

Second, I tell would-be writers, "So what if you can't be great? You *can* be original. And, who knows, that originality might just be your key to greatness." They didn't understand Willie Nelson around Nashville for years, but it wasn't because he wasn't just as great then as he is now. He was just so very original that the rest of the world needed more time to catch up to what he was doing and join in his parade.

I saw firsthand Roger Miller's struggle for acceptance, writing those crazy little "Do Wacka Do" type songs. When the world finally caught on to what he was up to, they said, "Gee, how original!" But it took time. And Roger and Willie and all the others who've been successful with their originality also never gave up. That's the third thing I stress—total dedication and commitment. Without that, you may as well hang it all up.

I've often wondered if a song lyricist's craft isn't more difficult to perfect than, say, a newspaper columnist's or a novelist's, because a songwriter has such a limited number of subjects he can write about. Whereas a writer of prose can go on forever writing about nuclear waste dumps and old men chasing whales at sea, a songwriter must operate inside much more restrictive and confining barriers, both in terms of subject matter and style. Nobody tells a novelist, for example, that he can only write X-number of pages that can be read in X-amount of time. But a songwriter has three or four minutes at best in which to get his entire point across. Plus, his words have to rhyme and conform to some kind of meter and cadence.

Still, the *greatest* challenge a writer of songs has is to say what he wants to say in a way that it's never been said before. His primary objective must always be to *think* original, *write* original, and *be* original. It's tough, but if it's any comfort, it's exactly what every successful songwriter before him has had to face as well.

I once had a young soldier in uniform bring me a song he had written which, he said, "would be perfect for you to record." I played his tape and read along with his handwritten lyrics. It took only the first eight lines or so for me to tell it wasn't anything I'd be interested in. But I kept on listening, nonetheless, because there was something about his melody that struck me. That's really a nice tune, I began thinking, and then suddenly I realized I'd heard the melody before.

"Hey, that's the tune to the old Hank Williams song 'You Win Again,'" I said.

"It sure is," the soldier beamed proudly.

"But you can't use that," I informed him.

"Why can't I?" he asked defensively.

"Because," I replied, not sure this conversation was actually taking place, "it was Hank Williams's melody. It belongs to him."

"Hell," the soldier answered. "If it was good enough for ole Hank it's good enough for me!"

Obviously, no one had taken the time to preach him my sermon on originality.

I never got into the songwriting business for the money or for the glory, even though I confess I've enjoyed what bits of both I've been able to attain. I'm particularly proud of my induction into the Nashville Songwriters' Association Hall of Fame. In fact, that may just be the one thing in my whole career that means the most to me.

But I never sat down to write a single song with the idea of making money from it or winning an award because of it. Why then, you wonder, do I write? I've asked myself that very question on many occasions, and I don't think I could put it into more revealing, more insightful words than did the author who wrote the following. I clipped this from a newspaper years ago, pasted it into a scrapbook, and it's so yellow and faded now I can hardly make it out. I have no idea who wrote it, but it says:

If you have the stuff of which artists are made, you cannot be discouraged. You will continue to produce work, not because you like to but because you must. The artist's compulsion is very much like the addict's.

Nor does the artist require a slight push. He is self-propelling; he cannot be torn away from his mission. He will write, paint, or compose, whether his children are starving, his wife has deserted him, or the world treats him like a lunatic.

I am not saying that these are optimum conditions for the artist; I am not making the foolish and insolent middle-class assumption that such scorn and sacrifice are actually "good" for the artist; I am simply pointing out that these are the dynamics of his nature.

I was out of town on the Sunday night in October, 1975, that the Nashville Songwriters' Association announced they had voted me into their Hall of Fame. When Maggie Cavendar, executive director of the association, learned that I'd be gone, she'd called and urged Becky to come to the awards dinner and represent me. Naturally, Becky went.

Harlan Howard, a Songwriters' Hall of Fame member himself, asked to be the one to announce my induction because, as he put it, "Bill Anderson inspired me to be a better songwriter. Every time he'd write a great song, I'd try that much harder to write a great song myself." Harlan read my credits to the crowd and presented my "Manny" (short for "manuscript") to Becky.

I was on stage at the Veterans' Auditorium in Des Moines, Iowa, in the middle of singing a song, when one of the emcees from the local radio station walked up beside me and pulled the microphone right out of my hand. "Ladies and gentlemen," he announced to the stunned audience, "I hate to interrupt Bill's show like this, but we have just received a very important phone call backstage from Nashville, Tennessee." I could hear a big gasp rise up from within the crowd. It was like they expected to be told of some great tragedy.

"It seems that while this man has been here on this stage singing his songs for you tonight," the emcee continued, "back in

Nashville he has been named the newest member of the Nashville Songwriters' Hall of Fame!"

I stood there totally speechless. Twelve thousand people rose to their feet and began to cheer and applaud wildly. I looked around behind me and every member of my band was standing and applauding too. I tried to talk, but I wasn't able to do a very good job of it. A big tear welled up in my eye and trickled slowly down my cheek.

And I stood there thinking that this wasn't what I'd had in mind at all that night up on the roof of the hotel in Commerce when I'd written "City Lights." Nor was it what I'd thought about the afternoon I'd wheeled my car into a filling station in some little town in Michigan, grabbed a paper towel that was supposed to be used for cleaning windshields from out of the dispenser, and leaned over onto the roof of my car and written a song called "Then and Only Then," a hit for Connie Smith. I hadn't thought about Mannys or BMI Awards or the Songwriters' Hall of Fame then or on a single one of the hundreds of other days or nights that I'd stopped in the middle of whatever I was doing, wherever I happened to be, and begun to write a song. I had written for all the other reasons . . . the musts, the self-propulsion, the dynamics of nature. But I had to admit that it sure was a nice, warm feeling to be standing there on that stage in Des Moines and be told in such a meaningful and lasting way that what I had done had been recognized. And appreciated.

There are two of my compositions that I feel deserve a little more attention, even though I've referred to them earlier. One is "Po' Folks" and the other is "Mama Sang a Song." Both of these songs have been extremely important in my career.

People have asked me for years, "Were you really as poor as you sing about in your song 'Po' Folks'? And if you weren't, how could you write about it like you did?"

The answer is no, I did not grow up as poor as the lyrics of "Po' Folks" might suggest. But I know people who did, and I called on that feeling again—empathy—and I tried to write those lyrics with the same feelings and sensitivity I would have felt myself had I grown up that way.

When I first started writing the song, it wasn't even called "Po' Folks." My working title was "The South Side." I had written:

> There's a whole lot of people lookin' down their noses at me
> 'Cause I didn't come from a wealthy family
> There was ten of us living in a two-room shack
> On the banks of the river by the railroad track
> And we kept chickens in a pen in the back
> 'Cause that's how it is on the south side . . .

I liked the first few lines but somehow the title didn't seem to click. There was no snap to it. I decided to keep working on it, though, and carried the idea with me on tour to California. One day I was visiting Johnny Cash at his home in Encino, and I picked up his guitar and sang him the first few lines. "What do you think?" I asked him. "Is there anything here?"

He smiled and said he liked it. He took the guitar and fooled around with it a while and said we ought to call it "One Mule Farmer" 'cause it reminded him of back home in Arkansas where a lot of people had to work big farms with no machinery at all and only one ole mule to plow. We kicked that idea around for most of the afternoon, but somehow it didn't really seem to work either.

One day after I got back to Nashville, I was singing the first few lines around the house, still trying to make them connect, when my mother-in-law overheard me. "Sounds like you're singing about po' folks to me," she said innocently. My search for a title was over.

I wrote much of "Po' Folks" with my tongue planted far over into my cheek. The part about "If the wolf had ever come to our front door he'd have had to brought a picnic lunch" was only my exaggerated way of trying to inject a little humor into the song while attempting to illustrate a point. The real objective of what I wanted the song to communicate was, "Hey, it doesn't matter one iota about the material things we may or may not have in this life. What matters is how we feel about ourselves and about each other." So when I ended the writing, "We patched the cracks and set the table with love," I summed up everything I intended for the song to say.

(A fan once sent a handwritten note to me on stage at a concert wanting me to sing "Po' Folks," but she couldn't think of the title. "Do that song," she wrote, "where you sing about if the fox had ever come to the back door he'd have brought a bucket of chicken!")

"Mama Sang a Song" is probably my favorite of all songs I've ever written, and for years I've introduced it on stage by saying it's a page out of my life. And it is. Actually, it's more than that. It's many pages out of many different parts of my life.

Perhaps the lyrics bear repeating here:

Mama Sang a Song

God put a song in the heart of an angel
And softly she sang it to me

I get to thinking lots of times about back when I was a lad
Of the old home place where I grew up . . . Of the days
*   both good and bad*
My overalls were hand-me-downs, my shoes were full of
*   holes*
I used to walk four miles to school nearly every day
Through the rain, the sleet, and the cold . . .
I've seen the nights when my daddy would cry
For the things his family would need
But all he ever got was a bad-land farm
And seven hungry mouths to feed.
And yet . . . and yet our home fire never flickered once.
'Cause when all these things went wrong
Mama took the hymn book down . . . And Mama sang a
*   song.*

What a friend we have in Jesus . . .

Oh, I've been rocked to sleep many a night to the tune of
*   "What a Friend"*
And then come morning and "Rock of Ages" would wake
*   me gently once again*

And then I remember how Daddy would reach up and he'd
    take the
Bible down . . . And he'd read it loud and long
And I always felt our home was blessed when Daddy would
    say
"Mama, sing a song" . . .

Sister left home first I guess . . . And then Bob, and then
    Tommy, and then Dan
By then Dad's hair was turning white and I had to be
    Mama's little man
But, you know, it seemed that as Daddy's back grew weak,
    my mother's faith grew strong
And those were the greatest days of all . . . when Mama
    sang a song.

Rock of Ages . . . cleft for me
Let me hide myself in Thee.

I guess the old house is still standing . . . I don't get to go
    home much anymore
No voice is left now to fill those halls . . . And no steps to
    grace the floor
For you see, my mama sings in heaven now . . . Up around
    God's golden throne
But I'll always believe this old world is a better place
Because one time . . . My mama sang a song

Precious memories flood my soul.

Again people are always asking, "Is that song really about your mother?" And the answer is yes. But it's also about my grandmother, both my grandfathers, my father, and perhaps even one or two other people who have touched and influenced my life. And it's only about one side of my mother.

I am very blessed by the fact that my mother is still living, which makes the last part of "Mama Sang a Song" not true. Also, Mama would be the first to admit that she never was what you'd call a very good singer. To be honest, she couldn't carry a tune in a bucket! But anytime she sang, you always knew it came from deep down inside her heart. When she'd sing, "Just as I am . . . without one plea," you knew she was honestly and sincerely bringing herself and her problems to the Lord without any pomp or frills. She came just as she was.

Having grown up as the daughter of a minister, Mama has always had a deep and abiding faith in God. At the same time, it would be very unfair for me to give the impression that all my mother ever does is walk around with an open Bible singing hymns. She's one of the most fun-loving, full-of-life people I know. Life to her is a treasured gift and she lives every day of it to the fullest. I've heard her say many times that she doesn't believe the Lord wants his children to walk around with long faces. He wants us to be happy. And even though life has dealt her some tough blows, like losing her mother when she was in her teens, leaving Mom to raise her baby sister as if she were her own daughter, Mama has always managed to be a positive, upbeat lady.

People always seem to be surprised to learn that one of her true loves in life is sports. Whatever sport is in season—baseball, football, basketball—it doesn't matter. Mama will watch it on TV, listen to it on the radio, and keep up with it in the newspapers. I guess I'm to blame for much of her addiction, because when I was growing up if she wanted to communicate with me she had to talk about either sports or country music. She learned a lot about both, I'm sure, in self-defense.

One year when I was about ten years old, I decided the greatest gift I could give her on Mother's Day was to take her to a baseball game. Heck, that's what I'd have wanted someone to give me. It never dawned on me that the reason Mama had never seen a baseball game in her life might be because she had never wanted to. I saved my money and bought us two box-seat tickets right behind first base to see the Atlanta Crackers play the Nashville Vols at old Ponce de Leon Park in Atlanta. I bought her a scorecard and told her who all the players were, and during infield practice the Nashville shortstop threw a ball over the first baseman's head and it landed squarely in Mama's lap. It wasn't thrown hard enough to hurt her, thank goodness. She quietly picked the ball up and looked at it, much like one might inspect an egg if a bird suddenly flew overhead and laid one on an unsuspecting soul below.

Not having a lot of use for a baseball, not even an official Southern Association model, and knowing her son and his friends often played with a ball held together by large globs of black tape, plus just being the sweetheart she is, Mama gave the ball to me.

Today she's the biggest baseball fan you ever saw. And come football season, she and Dad travel all over the country following the University of Georgia Bulldogs. They have season tickets to the games in Athens and always seem to have some kind of business that needs tending to in the very same towns where the Dogs just happen to be scheduled for their road games. Every two years Becky and I know they'll be coming to see us in October, not because we're high on their list of favorite people, mind you, but because Georgia will be in Nashville to play Vanderbilt. When I think of all the gifts my parents received on their fiftieth wedding anniversary, I believe the one they enjoyed the most was the trip Mary and I gave them to California to see the Rose Bowl.

Mom stays in great physical condition, too, and has kept her figure trim by following a strict self-imposed exercise regimen and carefully watching her diet. Hardly a day goes by that she and Dad don't walk at least a couple or three miles, and the routine never varies, not even when they travel.

Travelling to new places, seeing new things, meeting new people are all things my mother loves to do. When Mary and I were growing up she never went anywhere, seldom even downtown to the movies, but over the past few years, and particularly since Dad retired, they've travelled to just about every state in the union and visited all kinds of exciting places overseas. It amazes me sometimes just to have a conversation with my mother. She talks to me in one breath about riding to town in a horse and buggy when she was a girl and living in a house with no electric lights, and then in the next breath she'll tell me about flying across the Pacific Ocean in a 747 and visiting the Royal Palace in Tokyo. I constantly marvel and am continually thankful for the scope, the depth, and the fullness of the life my mother has lived.

When Mom and Dad got married in the early 1930s, the years following the Great Depression, things weren't easy. They both had to work long and hard for what they achieved, and they sacrificed constantly so that my sister and I might have a few of the advantages in life that they had never enjoyed. I know now that it was Mama's faith that got her through many of her most trying hours.

Mary tells of coming home one night not long after we'd moved from South Carolina to Georgia and seeing Mom standing on one leg in the tiny kitchen of the small apartment where we lived, shelling beans, for supper. Her other leg was draped over an open cabinet door, the varicose veins bulging so badly that she couldn't bear to put weight on the leg at all. Dad had quit his job, lost the medical insurance coverage he'd had through his company, and his new business wasn't yet bringing in a dime. The last thing our little family could afford was an operation for Mama. She knew that. So she endured.

Many nights as a boy I watched Mama stand over a sink full of dirty dishes, washing and drying by hand, masking her anxieties by singing "What a Friend We Have in Jesus," or "Rock of Ages" or "Amazing Grace," songs she had literally rocked me to sleep with when I was a child. Those songs seemed to calm her fears, sustain her hopes, and restore her strength. And they made a deep, lasting impression on me.

My dad is a fine Christian man himself. His integrity, his loyalty, his honesty are a shining example to everyone who comes in contact with him. He started his own business on a shoestring when he was thirty-five years old with not much more going for him than a dream and a heart full of persistence. He had to work hard, he had a wife and two children to support, but he always seemed to find time to serve in the latest county-wide Red Cross campaign or the Lions' current drive to raise money to aid the blind, or any of a number of other local campaigns and causes. And he always found time to take me to the Sunday afternoon double-header baseball games at Ponce de Leon Park. My dad is one of the most patient and unselfish people I've ever known; in fact, when people ask me who my heroes are, he is always at the top of my list.

At the same time, he was not in reality the one who "took the Bible down and read it loud and long," as I wrote in my song. That would have been my grandfather, the minister. And many's the time when I, as a little boy, was sure I was going to starve to death at mealtime waiting for him to quit praising the Lord and blessing the food. Once when I was very young, I even interrupted his Bible reading one morning.

"Grandaddy," I said with all the innocence and guile of a four-year-old. "You read the Bible at the table. My daddy reads the newspaper!"

I was actually inspired to write "Mama Sang a Song" while sitting around my house one afternoon not long after I'd moved to Nashville, thinking back on an old-time camp meeting revival we'd once had at our church when I was in my early teens. The Reverend Homer Rodeheaver, a well-known evangelist, songwriter, and singer, had been in town all week conducting the services, and a big part of what he did every night before preaching his sermon was to break out his big, loud trombone and lead the congregation in singing the old gospel-type hymns.

The sanctuary of the church my family attended at the time was shaped like a capital letter T. When you walked in the rear door, you were standing at the bottom of the T, and the pulpit was directly in front of you. That meant that as the minister faced the congregation there was a section of the church off to each side of him that could not be totally seen by others seated in the back of the building. There was also a small balcony above the main floor in the rear.

The Reverend Rodeheaver always made a big issue out of dividing the congregation according to where the people were seated and having each section of the church try to "out-sing" the others. And he was in rare form this particular night.

I had gone to the services with some of my teenaged friends, and we were seated off to the right-hand side of the pulpit on the back row. From where we were, I could not see around the corner and into the rear of the church very well, and I could not see the balcony at all. Therefore, I had no way of knowing that my mother and my sister had come into the services late and were the only persons seated in the balcony.

The hymn Reverend Rodeheaver had picked out for us to work on was the old favorite "Brighten the Corner Where You Are."

"Let's just see which corner of this church we can brighten the most!" he cajoled us. "Let's see which group can sing the loudest!" And with that he began blowing his trombone, the organist joined in, and the rafters really started to ring.

"OK, we'll start with the left side," he said, and everybody over there opened up with "Brighten the corner where you are" at the top of their voices. "Now the right side," he said, and my buddies and I let fly. "Now the main floor," and finally, "Now the balcony!"

Well, you can imagine what it sounded like after all the big booming voices filled the church with their rich baritones, basses, altos, and sopranos, when my mother, the only adult seated upstairs, came out singing by herself about four keys flat: "Bry-tun thuh caw-nuh (I forgot to mention her deep Southern drawl!) whah-uh you ahhh!!" My buddies fell to the floor laughing. I wanted to crawl under the pews and never come out. Mary said everybody in the main sanctuary suffered whiplash from turning around to see where that awful voice was coming from.

But thinking back on it years later as an adult, I realize that my mother had simply done what she'd always done. She had brought her faith and her love to the Lord the only way she knew how. There were dozens of people there that night who sang that song right on pitch but didn't have any idea what they were singing or why. My mother did, and the corner where she sang was truly brightened.

I've got to believe that God probably laughed a little bit at the time, but I'll bet later on He gave her an E for effort. That's why I ended my song by saying, "This old world is a better place . . . because one time . . . my mama sang a song." There's no doubt about it. It truly is.

11

I've always felt that I got into the country music business at the best of all possible times. The late fifties marked the end of the hillbilly era, the end of the "Let's tie the big upright bass fiddle to the top of the car and go out and hit the road" mentality that had ruled country music since day one. (Actually, on our famed western tour, we did tie the big upright bass to a luggage rack mounted on top of Roger's faded blue Cadillac. That worked fine until it started to rain and we had to bring Big Bessie inside the car to ride with five cramped and extremely irritable musicians. I'm convinced the two greatest inventions in the history of show business have been the electric bass and the blow dryer!) The early sixties turned out to be the formative years of both the art form and the country music industry as we know it today. I got to Nashville just in time to see it from both sides.

I never thought about it at the time, but my compadres and I had come to launch a whole new generation of country music. The torch was about to be passed from the legends of the thirties, forties and fifties to a totally new group of players. Within a matter of just a few years Nashville became home to Bill Anderson, Roger Miller, Harlan Howard, Hank Cochran, Willie Nelson, Mel Tillis, Tom T. Hall, Loretta Lynn—all energetic, creative young people who came to town and changed the face of the music they composed and performed. It was the new day of the singer-songwriter, the creator who wrote the song then went into the recording studio and out onto the stage and performed it. It was a fun time, innocent in a way because none of us were very sophisticated musically, yet the words we wrote and the melodies we sang in those days have more than withstood the test of time.

I'm sure the young entertainers who come into our business today—the *new* new generation—would find a lot of the things we did back then strange, awkward, and hard to believe, particularly those of us who tried to build careers as singers as well as song-writers. For example, today a record company offers a new artist a recording contract; then either the company or some wealthy group of investors puts up money for tours, buses, bands, and all the rest. In 1964 I was coming off my third consecutive No. 1 record, "8 X 10," and I was struggling to make ends meet with a two-piece band.

Can you imagine a major country star attempting to tour with a two-piece band today? But back then that was all I could afford. Nowadays if an artist had had three consecutive No. 1 hits, one of which was a gigantic crossover smash in the pop field, he'd have six or seven musicians touring with him, two or three pretty female backup singers, and he'd be commanding upwards of twenty-five thousand dollars per performance. At least! He'd probably have two tour buses, a sound and lighting truck complete with crew, a separate truck and crew to merchandise his souvenirs, at least one manager on the road with him, a half-dozen or so gophers and flunkies to cater to his every whim, and he'd be working more or less when and where he chose. I was so excited that I threw a party in 1964 the night I worked my first gig where I got paid as much as five hundred dollars!

Actually, five hundred dollars a day in 1964 was really pretty good money. The top acts in the business were only making $750 to $850 per working day. That would have been the headline attractions like Faron Young, Ferlin Husky, Carl Smith, Kitty Wells, Marty Robbins, and others. I think I heard someone say once that Jim Reeves had cracked the one-thousand-dollars-per-day barrier at some point before his death in August of that year, but Don Helms, the great steel guitar player with Hank Williams's Drifting Cowboys, told me that so far as he knew Hank never made as much as a thousand dollars for any one show he performed his entire life.

I realize that five hundred dollars a *day* sounds like an awful lot of money to someone making two or three hundred dollars or less per *week*, but let me break that down a bit. First, an artist has to pay at least ten and possibly fifteen percent of his or her fee to a booking agent for arranging the performance. Let's say it's ten percent to the agent and another ten percent to the artist's manager, who stays home and handles all the various details of the artist's life and career. On a five-hundred-dollar appearance, that leaves only four hundred dollars of "real" money. Now, let's say the musicians are making forty dollars a day, which is about what the American Federation of Musicians union scale was in the early sixties. With a four-piece band, that brings the artist down to $240 or less, depending on whether or not one member of the group gets paid a little extra to serve as band leader and/or road manager.

Now, the artist has to furnish both the transportation and the lodging for his musicians. That means a car, car insurance, gasoline, oil, tires, maintenance, and all that goes with providing transportation, including the possibility—no, the probability—of two or three breakdowns during the year and the artist's having to rent cars or furnish airline tickets. Hotels can run anywhere from the top of the line to the bottom, but stars aren't going to put their musicians nor stay themselves in fleabag hotels. Putting four musicians into two double rooms and himself into a single costs another seventy-five to a hundred bucks. And we're talking 1960s dollars, remember. Today it's a whole lot more.

Musicians are responsible for their own food on the road but not their own stage costumes. Unless you let your group work onstage in the same clothes they've been travelling in all day (and I've never allowed that), there goes some more of the profit. You can readily see that while the artist working for five hundred dollars a day might clear a few bucks, at the end of the day he's going to be a long way from being rich.

But I don't know of a single artist in the entertainment business who got into this line of work to make money. I certainly didn't. In fact, a friend of mine once said that planning to get into the music business to make money is about like planning to go to a monastery to meet girls. Most people play music for one reason and one reason only: because they love it. And the money, as somebody else once said, is just one way of keeping score. At the same time, if we lost money every time we went out to sing, none of us could afford to stay in the business very long.

One key to the tremendous difference between what country stars made in the sixties compared to what country stars make today lies in the fact that what it cost a fan to see a country concert back then was a drop in the bucket compared to what it costs today. Somebody recently sent me a poster advertising a tour I worked through Iowa and Minnesota in the late sixties. I was the headline attraction, Hank Williams, Jr., was my opening act (that in itself shows how the times have changed!), and the ticket prices topped out at four dollars for the best reserved seat in the house. General admission tickets were $2.50 and children's tickets cost one dollar. I thumb through *Amusement Business* and *Performance* magazines today and routinely see country concert tickets selling for anywhere from $17.50 to twenty-five dollars. Plus, the arenas are much larger now and can accommodate many more people.

But, of course, it's not just country music that's more expensive, it's life. What did a loaf of bread cost in 1967? A tank full of gasoline? A sideman (a musician working in an artist's band) only made $18.75 per working day when I first came to Nashville in 1959. Some salaried players working the road now pull down as much as fifty thousand dollars a year or better. Ted Williams was the highest paid baseball player of his time, and people cringed with disbelief when he signed a contract in 1957 guaranteeing him $100,000 for the season. A ballplayer making $100,000 today is among the lowest paid on the team.

Even though I'd gladly work in this business for free if I could afford to, I look around me and wonder sometimes if I wasn't born about twenty years too soon!

When I hired my first two musicians in the summer of '63—Weldon Myrick, recognized today as one of the premier steel guitar players in the world but at that time a newcomer to Nashville fresh off the police force in Big Spring, Texas, and a young lead guitar player from near Steubenville, Ohio, named Jimmy Lance—I put them on a weekly salary. I honestly don't remember how much I paid them, but I do remember hoping every week that I'd be able to meet the payroll.

I wasn't yet able to afford the luxury of hiring a bass player or a drummer and, as you might suspect, that made for a lot of fun-filled and exciting evenings on the bandstand. Weldon, Jimmy and

I would roll into a strange town, and if we weren't working as part of a package show with other Opry stars where we could borrow a couple of pickers from out of their bands, we'd have to get on the phone and try to pull a couple of musicians out of a local group someplace. More often than not these guys would be God-awful bad. Maybe it was my material. My songs were not the type many local bands included in their repertoire like they did the Buck Owens and Ray Price songs of the day, and when we'd start into songs like "Still" with all its passing chords and "Mama Sang a Song" with its intricate arrangement, the local players would usually throw their hands up in horror. Finally, after almost a year of trying to make it with only two musicians, I had no choice. Extra expense or not, I knew if I was going to survive in this business I had to have my own band. In self-defense if nothing else.

I started out by adding to Weldon and Jimmy a chubby, reticent former record salesman from Atlanta named Len Miller to play drums and a guy I had grown up watching on Red Foley's *Ozark Jubilee* TV shows, Jimmy Gateley, to play bass, fiddle, and front the band. ("Fronting the band" is country for "emceeing the show.") Because of my 1961 hit and another real lack of creativity on my part, I cleverly named my newly formed group the Po' Boys. They said based on the way I paid them in the beginning, the name was fitting.

At the start, the five of us travelled in my car pulling a luggage trailer behind us loaded down with our costumes and instruments. I was proud of that little trailer (I bought it used from former Opry great Carl Smith) because having it meant we no longer had to tie anything to the roof of the car. I had my name and the name of the band painted on the sides of the trailer and across the back in big black letters that glowed when hit by the headlights of a following car: BILL ANDERSON & THE PO' BOYS . . . GRAND OLE OPRY . . . NASHVILLE, TENNESSEE. I thought I was the king of the road until we pulled into our very first motel to check in.

"We're Bill Anderson and the Po' Boys from the Grand Ole Opry," Jimmy Gateley said proudly to the lady at the front desk. "That's our trailer out there!"

"What'cha got in it?" came her caustic and uninterested reply. "Ponies?"

* * *

You've never lived until you've taken off on a thousand-mile journey across North America in a car packed with five itinerant musicians. It sounds glamorous in the beginning—seeing the country, riding the wind, singing your songs—but it's amazing how quickly it turns into mile after boring mile of sitting upright in one uncomfortable but fixed position, the radio blaring loud enough to clear your sinuses and cure your grandpappy's gout ("We don't want the driver to fall asleep, now do we?") and you so exhausted that you finally nod off to sleep on the shoulder of the guy sitting next to you, only to be awakened by the slamming of the brakes, the screeching of the tires, and the screaming of the driver: "Damn, I almost hit that pig!" And it slowly dawns on you that you're a slave to the habits, idiosyncrasies, and manners of the others cooped up inside that tiny, ever-shrinking vehicle with you. If they smoke, you inhale. If they pass gas, you hope you're sitting by the window.

There's rarely any time built into your travel schedule to stop and eat a meal at a decent restaurant, so it's usually a lap full of fast food on the run and catsup running down your pants leg. There's no such thing as pausing en route between towns to shave, change a shirt, or take a shower. It's hurry up and get to the next place you're playing so you won't miss the show . . . and miss getting paid. The most exciting part of your day comes when you see a sign reading "Rest Area Next Exit" and you know the driver needs to "rest."

When you add to that mix one band member, the drummer, who is so jittery he talks nonstop mile after mile, day after day, who screams in fear every time you meet a passing car, and who keeps his drumsticks lying loose in the area up behind the back seat so that every time the car goes around a curve they r-r-r-roll to one side and then on the next curve they r-r-r-roll back to the other, your father's insurance agency back in good ole Decatur, Georgia, or your Uncle Cyrus's feed 'n' seed store down in Gumlog, Arkansas, starts looking better and better all the time.

From the very beginning Len Miller was a nervous wreck. He couldn't relax no matter where he sat in the car or what time of the day or night it happened to be. He was constantly afraid we were about to have a wreck.

And he'd try to cover up his anxiety by talking. He would jabber nonstop at the top of his voice mile after mile after mile. For the rest of us there was no place to hide. A car doesn't exactly come equipped with private soundproof compartments. One night the other guys in the band decided none of them would talk at all, not even respond to anything Len might say, just to see how long he'd babble on. They put a stopwatch on him and timed him talking without interruption for twenty-two minutes and twenty-five miles.

"Look out!" he'd cry every time we'd pass a side road. "That car's gonna pull out in front of us and we're gonna be snuffed out!" And then he'd pick up his drumsticks, which I could never talk him into putting in a stick bag and stashing in the trunk of the car, and he'd beat nervous rhythms on the back of the front seat. I'd tell him to cool it, but in thirty seconds he'd be turned around doing the same thing up behind the backseat. All the time yelling every time we'd meet a car or truck, "We're gonna be snuffed out, I just know it! Snuffed out!"

I finally backed off the accelerator driving somewhere through the Dakotas late one night, turned around and told him, "Len, I am sick and tired of hearing you run your mouth. And I'm telling you if you say 'snuffed out' one more time I'm gonna dock your paycheck. And that's not all. I'm gonna introduce you on stage tomorrow night as 'Snuff' Miller!" Sure enough, he did, sure enough, I did, and nobody has ever called him Len Miller since.

"Snuff" soon became "Snuffy," and the heretofore shy, pudgy little drummer quickly began to take on a whole new extroverted personality to match his colorful new nickname. He used this new persona as the basis from which to launch a fresh, spontaneous comedy act that he and I developed together. I ended up playing the part of Snuffy's straight man for more than six years.

We built our stage routines around his constantly agitating me, which was typecasting at its finest. Snuffy was marvelous at getting under my skin both on the stage and off. At certain points in the show he would deliberately goof up playing the drums and I'd light into him. From then on he was liable to do anything to me and I was liable to say anything to him. And the more we fought, the funnier it usually became and the more the audiences loved it.

He'd sit behind me at the drums and mimic my facial expressions while I was singing. He'd hide a pair of custom-made drumsticks about the size of baseball bats behind his stool, and when I'd stop and accuse him of not playing right, he'd wait until I had turned back to face the audience, pick up the sticks, and act as though he were going to bring them crashing down across my head. After a while our timing became impeccable and the act which started quite by accident became a highlight of our stage show.

We eventually found certain routines that worked so well they became a permanent part of the show, but everything Snuffy and I did in the beginning was strictly ad-lib. I never knew what he might do next, he never knew how I might respond, and that was a big part of what made it funny.

The routine we became best known for occurred near the end of our show when Snuffy would say to me in mock disgust, "Whisper, you're just not with it tonight. I've been watching you real close and you're just not putting enough feeling into your songs. Let me come up there and show you how to do it." He'd unhook his snare drum and, before I could stop him, he'd be standing center stage. "Now, this is how you're supposed to do it," he'd say, and the band would break into "Still." Snuffy would stand there with a pained expression on his face, kick his right leg back behind him like I used to do when I played guitar and sang, and with an exaggerated whisper in his voice he'd make fun of the way I recited the second verse of my biggest hit song:

This flame in my heart is like an eternal fire
For every day it burns hotter and every day it burns higher
And if this flame burns any hotter or any higher
You'll come home and find that I've made an ash of myself!

And the audience would roar! Later, when Jan Howard joined our show as the featured female vocalist and my duet partner, Snuffy would tie a ladies' scarf around his head, come up front with the two of us, and play the role of "the other woman" in a song about a three-sided love affair called "The Game of Triangles." He could be hilarious and the crowds at our shows loved him. Even one of the major newspaper critics in hard-to-please New York City once reviewed our show at the Taft Hotel in Manhattan and called our routines "cornball humor done well." The "done well" part is underlined in red ink in my scrapbook.

Snuffy could be funny in ways the audience never saw or heard too. On a night when I might be having trouble getting the crowd warmed up and into the flow of the show, he'd call out encouragement from his perch back on the drums: "Hang in there, Willy, you'll get 'em. Just rare back and whisper!"

In addition to his being a pretty fair country drummer (he was good enough that Owen Bradley hired him to play on most of my recording sessions) and a crowd-pleasing comedian, Snuffy was also not a bad singer at all. I'd try to let him sing on our concert dates when time permitted, he sang frequently on our syndicated television shows, and he sang at least one solo on each of the record albums the Po' Boys cut in the late sixties. He enjoyed the center spotlight and decided one day in the early seventies that he wanted to get serious about perhaps launching a full-time singing career. His voice was good enough that Pete Drake, the great steel guitarist and record producer, signed him to his label, Stop Records. I wrote what I thought was a solid, commercial song for him to record called "I Sure Do Enjoy Loving You," encouraged him to sing it on stage, and smiled when the fans applauded and told him how much they liked it. But with each round of applause, each bit of critical acclaim, Snuffy the funny-man, the comedian, the goofy-acting drummer that everybody loved, began to take himself more and more seriously.

He went from being comical and lovable to being uptight and difficult to deal with at times. He seemed to lose all interest in playing the drums and in playing comedy. He wanted to be a star, and he started acting like one. One Saturday night in Tulsa, he laid the crowd in the aisles with his antics and his singing, so much so that he decided it would be all right if he rested up for the next night's performance in Oklahoma City by sleeping through the Sunday afternoon matinee. I had to go to Merle Haggard, who was working the dates with us, and ask him if he'd let his drummer, Biff Adams, back me up that afternoon, which he graciously did. When Snuffy showed up for the night show all fresh and ready to go, I took him out to the bus and told him I thought it might be best from that point on if we went our separate ways.

It was really a hard thing for me to do because deep down inside I've always loved ole Snuffy, and he had become an important part of my act. For the first few months after he was gone, in fact, I felt like a lost little puppy out on stage without him.

Snuffy's singing career lasted only a short while. He played drums briefly for Dottie West and later for Nat Stuckey, then finally decided to get off the road entirely and pursue other interests. Thousands of people who saw us work together, though, still remember the routines we used to do and are always asking me where Snuffy is now and what he's doing.

A few years ago at the country music Fan Fair in Nashville, I held a Bill Anderson Reunion Show and invited back all the pickers and singers who had been associated with me down through the years. Snuffy came, and he and I performed the old routines for the first time in over fifteen years. We didn't rehearse at all, and I was amazed at how much of our timing was still intact and how well our comedy bits had stood the test of time.

These days I seldom see Snuffy. I know he produces record albums for comedian Jerry Clower, and in the summer he occasionally drives the bus for the Nashville Sounds baseball team. I just hope he doesn't sit up under the wheel late at night and keep the players awake yelling, "Help! . . . we're gonna be snuffed out!"

In the beginning, I never quite believed I could hire Jimmy Gateley to be a part of my group. After all, he'd been in the music business for years in and around his hometown of Springfield, Missouri, and along with his duet partner, Harold Morrison, had been a big part of the cast on the Red Foley shows on ABC television in the early fifties. I just couldn't imagine anybody with that kind of background wanting to play bass in my fledgling band.

But he did, and it was my lucky day when I hired him. He had moved to Nashville from Springfield after the *Ozark Jubilee* had folded, and in the beginning he was primarily interested in working as a songwriter. He'd written a couple of pretty fair country hits, "The Minute You're Gone" for Sonny James and "Alla My Love" for Webb Pierce, and from all outward appearances his career was in good shape. But he missed the excitement of performing live, and I just happened to be in the right place at the right time. He heard I was looking for a bass player, gave me a call, and joined the Po' Boys in April 1964. He stayed with me for thirteen years.

Jimmy (we all called him "Gate" or "J.G.") wasn't a great bass player, and as soon as I could afford to expand the band to five members I let him out of that job. What I primarily wanted him to do onstage was to open our shows, welcome the people, relax them, sing a song or two and get them in a good receptive mood for the rest of the evening. And he was great at that.

When the curtain would go up, he'd come out and get things moving by singing a good peppy song, then slow it down with a pretty ballad or two, tell a couple of funny stories, and finally he'd tear into his rousing version of "Orange Blossom Special" on the fiddle. And Jimmy was an excellent fiddle player.

I heard him play "The Blossom" so many times over the years that sometimes I can close my eyes and almost hear him . . . dragging that big, resined bow across the finely tuned, tightly stretched strings, filling the night with the sound of the whistle of an onrushing steam locomotive; plucking a couple of the open strings with his fingernail to emulate the sound of a ringing cowbell, daring Snuffy and the rest of the band to play fast enough to keep up. Even if nothing else in the show had clicked up to this point, by the time that old train sped around the last bend and headed for home, Jimmy had the crowd in the palm of his hand. While they were still applauding him, he would introduce me. All I had to do was hit the stage running. Gate had already made sure the audience was on my side.

During my part of the show, he would step quietly to the rear and play either rhythm guitar or fiddle behind me, depending on which song I was singing. And he'd sing harmony with me. And we'd check out the good-looking ladies in the audience and laugh and have a ball.

Jimmy Gateley meant a lot to me onstage, later on records, and then on television for several years, but it was offstage where he came to mean the most. He was the only band member I've ever had who was older than I. In those days I was not only young, but I could also sometimes be extremely impatient and moody. Occasionally I'd become so intense that I'd let my feelings overrule my better judgment. I know now that I just had a very large case of insecurity. I was afraid I'd wake up one morning and find this had all been just a dream and I was back in Georgia somewhere picking peaches.

But Jimmy Gateley, more times than I could ever begin to count, was the calming force that cooled me down. He never seemed to get upset himself, and he always seemed to know just what to say to me and how to say it when I'd let my emotions get the upper hand. He could smile his way through any situation and was one of the funniest people offstage that I've ever been around.

His humor didn't run to the side-splitting, rib-tickling style of a comedian but was rather the heartfelt, soft-spoken wisdom of someone who'd been down a few roads and learned a few lessons along the way. I'll never forget how he'd stop right in the middle of something he was doing and, with a serious, almost pained expression on his face, say to me, "Willy, I'm really worried."

I'd fall for it every time and take him seriously. "What's the matter, Gate?" I'd always ask, truly concerned.

"It's nothing really," he'd reply. "I'm just worried. I'm afraid I won't ever be this happy again!" And I'd crack up.

On the rare occasions when we were able to eat a big meal in a nice restaurant out on the road, he'd inevitably lean back in his chair after dinner, pat himself on his full, round belly and sigh, "Boys, I'm sufferin' in comfort!" Or he'd smile and say, "I wonder what the po' folks are doin'? I know," he'd reply to his own question. "They're playin' rock 'n' roll!"

And he'd tell stories about the country people he grew up around in rural Missouri, like the ole boy who thought the shiny metal inlay on the front of his car was called the "hood ointment," and the farmer who wandered into the local radio station one morning while Jimmy and Harold were taking a break from their show and a newscast was on the air. Peering into the studio through the glass-enclosed partition in the hallway, the farmer became very upset and called Jimmy over. "Hey," he said indignantly, pointing to the newscaster on the other side of the glass. "That news-teller is *readin'* that news!"

But my favorite story Jimmy used to tell concerned an elderly, almost blind musician who once toured with the Foley show and was constantly begging someone in the group to let him drive the car. "We can't let you drive," Gate told him. "You can't see well enough."

"Sure I can," the old man answered. "Just give me a chance."

Finally one night when he'd stayed awake driving about as long as he could, Jimmy relented and let the old fellow under the wheel. Jimmy slid over by the window and immediately fell asleep. He woke up suddenly just before dawn when he realized the car was stopped. He sat up with a start just in time to see the old man roll down the window, lean out, and ask directions from a mail box!

Jimmy Gateley and I had more than an employer-employee relationship. We had to for it to last almost thirteen years. Most musicians are gypsies at heart and not many are willing to stay in one job for that long. And, quite frankly, not many employers want people around that long. But Jimmy was special. We wrote songs together, the most well-known of which I still use as my theme song at the Grand Ole Opry, "Bright Lights & Country Music," we fished together, played golf together (once on an unfamiliar course in Durham, North Carolina, he got a hole-in-one only to learn later he'd hit the ball into the wrong hole!), and our wives became good friends. Jimmy had a swimming pool built in his backyard when his son and daughter were growing up, and Becky and Jimmy's wife, Esther, spent a lot of time lying out beside it working on their tans. During the time we lived on the lake, the Gateleys lived on the banks of the Cumberland River, and we'd often take our boat through the locks at Old Hickory Dam and cruise down to see them. We'd tie up to a tree in their backyard, swim in the pool, and cook burgers on the grill. Jimmy and I would sit for hours and just talk. He loved baseball and we'd argue for hours over the Cardinals, his favorite team, and my favorites, the Reds and the Braves.

The last conversation we had was on the telephone in early 1985. Jimmy had just returned home from a stay in the hospital, and I was confined to my bed with back pain. We must have spent an hour one Sunday night lying flat on our backs, laughing and talking about old times. His heart had been causing him some problems, but he felt sure the doctors had everything under control. He sounded happy to be back with his family and assured me that he'd be up and around again in no time. Less than two weeks later Mary Lou Turner called and told me Jimmy had died. I cried like a baby.

It still hurts to think about it because Jimmy was so young and still had so much life to live. His daughter, Teresa, had made him a grandfather, and he worshipped his grandkids. But his heart, which was probably larger and warmer than just about any I've ever known, finally gave out on him. He had become a devout Christian several years earlier, devoting the last few years of his life to writing and singing mostly gospel music. He left behind a treasury of good songs, country and gospel, much of which has never been heard. Someday, I hope, the world will discover some of it. But more than that, he left behind a lot of beautiful memories. I miss ole Gate tremendously.

Jimmy Gateley and Snuffy Miller were probably the two people more responsible than anyone for getting the Po' Boys out of the car we travelled in and into our first bus. Looking back, I don't know if I should have thanked them or blamed them.

The trip that convinced me there surely must be a better way to travel than by car was when we had to drive and pull our trailer all the way from Prince George, British Columbia, Canada, about four hundred miles north of Vancouver, to New York City in slightly over three days. It was the most brutal trip imaginable. When the guys came to me a few days later and told me they'd located an old bus for sale in Mansfield, Ohio—cheap!—I listened.

Actually, they made me an offer I couldn't refuse: "Willy, if you'll get us a bus, we promise you'll never have to drive on the road ever again!" Up to that time I had been driving a regular shift in the car just like everybody else. We'd each get under the wheel for three hours at a time and then we'd rotate our sitting places in the car. The worst spot of all to ride was in the middle of the back seat. Right over the hump, with somebody sitting next to you on each side. There was no place to stretch your legs and very little padding beneath your bottom. We affectionately nicknamed that most miserable of all saddles "Big Sid."

"And you'll never have to ride 'Big Sid' again, either. We promise! If you'll get a bus we'll do all the driving. We'll clean it, we'll take care of it, everything. Please!" I should have made them put it all down in writing. In blood.

But for something like forty-five hundred dollars, they finally convinced me to purchase what was left of an old GMC Silversides, the bus Greyhound ran on the road for years, the one that had the picture of the big leaping dog down the side. That particular model was also referred to by many as "Ole Frog Eyes" because of the weird appearance of the two small rear windows above the engine. Before I was through with my particular Silversides, however, I called it a lot worse things than "Frog Eyes."

Not many country stars were travelling in buses back then. The larger bands, like Hank Thompson's and Ernest Tubb's, were in them, and I think maybe Johnny Wright and his wife, Kitty Wells, transported their large family entourage via bus, but basically it was still a relatively new way for entertainers to travel. There weren't, therefore, many companies experienced in converting buses from coaches full of seats to travelling houses on wheels complete with beds, baths, and many of the conveniences of home. We found a carpenter to strip out the seats, nail together a few bunks, put in a toilet and a door or two and that was about it. It wasn't much better than a car for travelling—it wouldn't even go as fast—but at least we could get up, stretch our legs, and not have to stop as often at "rest" areas.

The people who sold me the bus had said, "Sure, she has heat and air conditioning!" And she did. Lots of heat in the summer and plenty of cold air in the winter. Once, right after I bought her, we had to take her up east for a couple of days. It was in January and during the time after the bus seats had been taken out but before the bunks had been put in. Everybody had agreed it would be no problem, we'd just bring sleeping bags and pillows and sleep on the floor. Kinda like a rolling Boy Scout campout.

Well, we should have brought some sticks to rub together. The morning we headed back to Nashville I woke up frozen to the floor. There was a sheet of ice about a half-inch thick covering the entire floor of the bus. It's a good thing I didn't have any matches. I'd have probably tried to start a bonfire right then and there and blown Ole Frog Eyes to bits!

Because of the color the bus was painted when I bought it, we immediately nicknamed her "The Green Goose." Actually the green-and-white paint job didn't look too bad, but when Snuffy decided to surprise me one day by having "The Bill Anderson Show" painted down the sides in brilliant red lettering, the ole Goose lost a bit of her charm. I never wanted to choke anybody as bad in my life as I did Snuffy when I first saw the paint job. And to make matters worse, he had the sign painter send me the bill.

Buses today are a far cry from the old Green Goose. I've owned four of them in my lifetime and had a couple of them outfitted pretty fancy. But still it's hard to explain to someone who's never been inside an entertainer's bus exactly what they're like.

"Oh, you mean it's like a van?" they usually say.

"No," I reply, "it's like a bus. Except it doesn't have any seats in it and it sleeps twelve."

And then they say, "Yeah, I gotcha. My Uncle Wilbur has one of those except he calls his a camper!"

I guess it is hard for normal folks to understand that somebody would actually take a bus—a forty-one passenger Silver Eagle bus like many of the major bus lines run on the highway—rip out all the seats, and spend upwards of a quarter-million dollars putting in things like wall-to-wall carpeting, a couple of color TV sets with VCR's, a refrigerator, AM-FM stereo sound systems with the latest state-of-the-art equipment, private bedrooms, showers, baths, closets, desks, wall safes, burglar alarms, intercom systems, trash compactors, microwave ovens, and built-in vacuum cleaner systems. Uncle Wilbur's twenty-one-foot Winnebago is pretty fancy, but you just carry a broom and sweep it out whenever it gets dirty.

And I guess there really is something that just doesn't sound romantic about saying you travel in a bus. I remember the crusty old man in overalls who knocked at the door of our bus one time when we were parked behind the stage at a fairgrounds in North Carolina.

"You boys come over here in that thang?" he asked.

Fighting the temptation to say, "No, we stopped by the rent-all and picked it up after we got here," I answered, "Yes, sir."

"Ernest Tubb was here a few weeks ago, and he come in a Cadillac."

"Is that right?"

"Yep, a gold Cadillac. I thought you was doin' at least as good as Ernest Tubb. Why ain't you got a Cadillac?"

"I do," I answered, "but it's at home. Besides, you can buy a dozen Cadillacs for what it cost to buy this bus."

"Yeah, but I thought you'd a-come in a Cadillac."

"Well," and I was getting a bit testy by this time, "we prefer to travel by bus."

"Hell," the old man said as he spit the juice from his plug of chewing tobacco at my right front tire. "Stars are supposed to ride in Cadillacs. *I* can ride in a bus!"

And then there was the time we were travelling through Georgia and I saw a young kid hitchhiking by the side of the road carrying a sign that read "Athens." Thinking he was probably a University student on his way back to classes, I told the driver to pull over and pick him up.

"Oh no," the boy exclaimed when I opened the door and invited him to come aboard. "I can't afford to ride on a bus."

"It's not gonna cost you a thing," I laughed, realizing he thought we were a commercial vehicle. "Come on . . . it's free!"

He stood there a bit dazed and looked the bus over thoroughly from front to back. Finally he couldn't think of any good reason not to climb aboard, and he began to ease himself slowly into the doorway.

At the time I was the only one awake other than the driver, and the bulkhead door just behind the front lounge was closed. This meant our new passenger couldn't see past the tables and chairs in the small lounge area up front and didn't know there were bunks and closets and a bath and large stateroom to the rear. All he could see was the front one-third of the vehicle.

"Wow!" he exclaimed staring wide-eyed at his new surroundings. "From the outside this bus sure looks a lot longer!"

Of course, I don't go everywhere on the bus. If we're opening or closing a tour in Portland, Oregon, for example, I can guarantee you this cowboy is going to hop an airplane. That's just more miles than I care to see through a windshield, one at a time. Besides, I figure my time is one of the most valuable assets I have, and I can use the hours I would be spending riding across the country on a bus doing something much more productive back in my office in Nashville. But on a trip, say, east of the Mississippi, travelling by bus is often by far the best way to go.

Let's say we're working a show in Cleveland, Ohio, on a Saturday night. We can work the Friday Night Opry in Nashville, load the bus around midnight, pull out of town at one o'clock in the morning, and arrive in Cleveland some ten hours later. I can get on the bus, relax with the band members for a while, crawl into my bed between clean sheets, prop up on my pillow and read awhile, watch a little TV, and still get eight good hours of restful sleep. When we get to Cleveland the bus delivers me right to the door of the hotel or motel where we're staying. And when I get to the auditorium or the fair or the park where we're performing, my clothes are there hanging neatly in my closet. I have a place to dress, to eat, and to relax. The bus really becomes a home on wheels.

But let's say I send the band to Cleveland on the bus and I decide to fly. I can go home after the Friday Opry and sleep in my own bed, but I have to get up no later than eight o'clock Saturday morning, pack my bag, get dressed much nicer than I'd have to dress if I were riding the bus, and be at the Nashville airport no later than ten. I have to check my bags and walk halfway to Cincinnati searching for my gate. My flight leaves at ten-thirty, which is eleven-thirty Cleveland time, and arrives there just before one. No lunch is served en route, so I have to grab a bite to eat at the airport snack bar when we get in.

Then I have to round up my baggage and hope it all arrived in one piece. I have to catch a cab or rent a car or depend on someone to pick me up at the airport and take me to the hotel. By this time it's midafternoon and I'm already feeling like I've put in a full day's work. I still have to get from the hotel to the gig, lugging my suitcase and wardrobe bag all the way. By the time I walk on the bus and greet the group, I'm ready to plop down on the sofa and take a nap. But there's no time. I've still got a show to do.

I'm often asked, "Isn't it hard to sleep on a bus rolling down the highway?" Sometimes it is, like maybe the first night of a tour after you've been off the road for a while. By the second night, though, you're sleeping like a baby. After a long tour, night after night, travelling mile after mile, it's sometimes hard to come home and sleep in a bed that doesn't move.

"Get up and shake the bed for a while, will you, honey?" has been the plea of many a musician in from off the road. "And, darling, if you really want to make me feel at home," he adds, "how about spraying some diesel fumes around the bedroom!"

12

Robert Sheldon of the *New York Times* once wrote, "Vaudeville never died, it just moved to Nashville." In a way, I guess he was right, because those of us in the country music business do keep a lifestyle similar to that of the old vaudevillians of the early 1900s. We pack and unpack a lot of suitcases, eat meals at places we probably wouldn't be caught dead in if we were at home, sleep everywhere except in the comfort of our own beds, and ply our craft in far-flung places with strange names like Ottumwa, Oshkosh, Oneonta, Oneida, and Opelika. We are gypsies of a sort and not everybody understands. Many's the time I've been asked, "Why do you work the road? Why don't you just stay home and write songs?"

Sometimes I'm not too sure of the answers myself, but the bottom line is probably that in spite of all the hardships and inconveniences of such an existence, I still love it. I don't know of anything else I could be doing that I would enjoy as much. And any entertainer will tell you the same thing: There's no feeling in the world quite like the feeling you get when you're up on that stage performing for an audience. When I'm clicking on all the right cylinders and the crowd is responding, it's a high like no other high I've ever experienced. And even after all these years, the excitement is still there. On the other hand, nobody applauds when I write a song. Maybe I just haven't come to the point yet where I've been ready to make that trade.

Besides, I'm lucky to be able to entertain people for a living. Not everybody who wants to can do it. It's what I've worked for, what I've strived for. There are thousands of people in the world who would gladly swap places with me in a minute. I know that, and I guard my opportunities jealously.

The travelling and the touring are just part of the dues one pays for the privilege of being an entertainer. If I'm going to make phonograph records, appear on television, and work to have a career in show business, then the unwritten portion of the contract I make with the world says that I will also make myself available for personal appearances. That I won't go hide in a closet, but rather I'll ride up and down the highways and byways thanking my fans for their support and singing personally for them the songs they've heard me sing on the radio and on TV. It's not much to ask, and fortunately for me I've built up a long and varied list of songs over the years that people have wanted to hear.

Following the success of "8 X 10" in 1964, my next hit was a sad, somewhat prophetic song about the inspiration a father received from his child following the death of his wife, called "Five Little Fingers." We knew when we cut it that this song didn't have the crossover potential of a "Still" or an "8 X 10," but it was a solid country success just the same. Next came a couple of even more traditional country offerings, "Three A.M." and "Bright Lights & Country Music," followed by another crossover success, "I Love You Drops." The flip side of "I Love You Drops" was also a top-ten country hit, the poignant "Golden Guitar." Written by a young Texan named Curtis Leach, "Golden Guitar" was my first hit recording of a song I didn't write.

The first up-tempo record I ever had to go to No. 1, "I Get the Fever," came in 1967 and was the first in a chain of hits I wrote and set to a musical beat that was quite different for that day and time. Musicians around town called it "the Fever beat" or "the Bill Anderson beat" for years, but it was simply music played four beats to the measure with equal emphasis given to both the downbeat and the upbeat. In effect, that made it sound like eight beats to the measure.

Today it's commonly called "straight eights," and it's a rhythm pattern used on both up-tempo songs and ballads as well. I used straight eights or some variation thereof on subsequent hits like "Get While the Gettin's Good," "Wild Weekend," and my country version of the First Edition's "But You Know I Love You." For a while this unusual rhythm pattern became almost as much a part of the Bill Anderson signature as the soft-sell talking and singing sound that preceded it.

By the late sixties and early seventies I had had hit records of several different types and began feeling secure enough as an artist to begin experimenting musically and reaching out a bit. In 1969 I got caught up in the emotion and turmoil of my personal life, and in answer to my wife's charges that I'd be throwing away my life if I allowed our marriage to dissolve, I wrote the biting "My Life (Throw It Away If I Want To)," the humor and poignancy of which was totally lost on both her and her divorce lawyer. *Billboard* magazine liked it, however, enough to name it the No. 1 country record of the year. In a 180-degree turnaround just one year later, I stirred up nationwide feelings of both patriotism and anger when I coauthored and recorded "Where Have All Our Heroes Gone?"— interpreted as a flag-waving anthem by some but in my mind, at the outset, simply the posing of a social question.

The song was born quite innocently. I was sharing the concert bill with Merle Haggard one Sunday afternoon at mammoth Cobo Hall in Detroit when his "Okie from Muskogee" was at the height of its popularity. The huge auditorium was packed to the rafters, and when Merle broke into the opening line, "We don't smoke marijuana in Muskogee," the place nearly came apart. Spotlights danced across the gigantic American flags draping down from the ceiling, eighteen thousand people leaped to their feet screaming and applauding their approval, and tears of patriotic pride welled up in every eye in the house. We were in the heart of a city, remember, that had only a few months before been racked by dissension and strife, fire and bloody riots in the streets, and Merle's politically conservative message was exactly what the white, blue-collar Detroiter wanted to hear.

I was standing off to the right-hand side of the stage visiting with a Detroit newspaperman named Bob Talbert when the eruption took place. Bob, who is originally from Columbia, South Carolina, as I am, turned to me and said, "Boy, this is exactly what these people need right now—a real hero. Look at that . . . Merle is their hero. Where have all our heroes gone, anyhow?"

We started talking about the people we admired and looked up to when we were kids going to the movies and to ball games and listening to the radio back in South Carolina. Bob started rattling off names like Joe DiMaggio, Stan Musial, Roy Rogers, Gene Autry, Eisenhower, MacArthur, and I said, "Whoa! Wait a minute! You're going too fast. But this is a great idea for a song. Take all that you're saying, put it down on paper, and send it to me in a letter. I believe I could sort it out and make a song out of it. Whatta you think?"

Bob liked the idea and went right to work on it. In just a few days I received from him sheet after sheet of single-spaced typewritten thoughts at random about America's heroes of the past, our lack of modern-day heroes, and even the presence of the anti-hero in our current society. Within a few weeks I had condensed Bob's rambling thoughts into a narrative for a song, written a melody and sing-along chorus, and prepared a speech designed to convince Owen Bradley that I should record it. Owen didn't even put up a fight. I sang it for him one time, and we cut it immediately.

I have never, before or since, released a song that created the impact of "Where Have All Our Heroes Gone?" Radio stations started playing it the day the record came in. When people heard it, they jammed the phone lines at stations all over the country wanting to hear it again. Record stores couldn't get copies in stock quick enough to meet the demand. The first week the record was out it came in on the Hot 100 chart at No. 37. The second week it was No. 12 and the third week it hit No. 1. And it stayed and it stayed.

The story of the song was built around a man who overheard a group of young boys talking about the contents of a magazine they were reading one day while out on the playground. Supposedly the youngsters were enamored by the pictures and stories of the long-haired, hippie, headline-grabbing anti-heroes that our society seemed to be producing in abundance back in those days. As the man listened to the boys' comments and heard their professed adulation for the people whose behavior he abhorred, he was shocked into wondering out loud how our society had managed to sink to such depths. "Are these the people these young boys look up to?" he asked. "Are these their idols? Are these the heroes of the 'now' generation?"

To me, my thoughts and musings weren't anything all that shocking. I had read numerous newspaper and magazine articles that said virtually the same thing I was saying. Youth leaders all across the country were voicing similar concerns. So were ministers and teachers and guidance counselors. Everybody was wondering where the admirable people in our society had wandered off to. All I had done, to my way of thinking, was condense their thoughts into a three- or four-minute narrative and put some music behind it. For that reason, I was totally unprepared for the reaction my record received.

I was called to be on the *Today* show, and all the other talk shows wanted me, too. Suddenly my political views were being sought out, people were labeling me everything from "super patriot" to "super idiot," and most of America was missing the entire point of what Bob and I had been trying to say. It was such a time of polarization in this country—the Viet Nam war, the riots in the streets, the emerging drug culture—that people saw themselves and others as either liberal or conservative, either right or left, black or white. There was very little patience with anything gray. We hadn't been trying to make a political statement but rather a social statement. Kids were looking up to the free-living Joe Namaths, the rebellious Joan Baezes, the angry Huey Newtons, and we were simply saying, "Hey, where are the John Waynes and Gary Coopers and Lou Gehrigs when we need them?" But very few people bothered to hear it that way.

My record was strictly a love-hate record. People either loved it or hated it. Fortunately, most of my fans loved it. We started selling out concert appearances everywhere we went and receiving five- to ten-minute standing ovations every time we performed the song. Promoters were bringing American flags into the coliseums and theaters where we were performing, and while I was singing they'd have the spotlight operators focus one pin-spot on me and the other one on the flag. The crowds would go into a frenzy. I had never seen anything like it.

But on the other side of the coin, the program director of a radio station in Aspen, Colorado, wrote MCA Records and said, "Don't ever send us another MCA Record and expect us to play it. Any company who would release such a piece of maligning bulls--t as Bill Anderson's 'Where Have All Our Heroes Gone?' doesn't deserve our support." At the same time a right-wing organization from Florida petitioned me to go back into the studio and overdub my voice on the record to include the name of Lieutenant William Calley, of My-Lai massacre fame, among my list of heroes. I couldn't win for losing.

A friend of mine helped me put it all in perspective, though, one Saturday night backstage at the Opry. I started telling him how unsettling it was to be written about in the press nearly every day, how hard it was to have to listen to all the criticism that was being dished out, even though I could also hear the cheers ringing in the background. "Are they spelling your name right?" he asked. I said they were. He reached out his hand and touched my arm. "Then don't worry about it," he smiled. And from then on I didn't. Today I'm proud to say that Bob Talbert's original letter to me and my original lyrics to "Where Have All Our Heroes Gone?" are on display in the songwriters' section of the Country Music Hall of Fame and Museum in Nashville.

I thought it best, however, that I return to more traditional themes for the subject matter of my songs that were to follow. I warbled such noncontroversial lines as, "Always remember I love you," "Don't she look good in the new dress I bought her," and "We called it magic . . . then we called it tragic . . . finally we called it quits." The *Today* show wasn't calling, but I wasn't getting any hate mail either. And I was working the road to the tune of some two hundred dates nearly every year.

When people realize how much I've travelled and the places my travels have taken me, their first reaction is, "Boy, I wish I had a job like yours. You get to go to so many exciting places and see so many interesting things. That must be the greatest life in the world!" In a lot of ways they are right.

But two hundred days a year is hard work. That's two hundred *working* days, so you add in at least another fifty to seventy-five days or part-days for travel. That's more than seventy-five percent of a year spent away from home. And on the days at home, an entertainer doesn't exactly get to loaf. If he did, when would records get cut, publicity photos be taken, television appearances be taped, and all the other thousand-and-one things that go to make up an artist's career get accomplished?

But the travel *can* be enjoyable, particularly if you look at it as part of the overall learning experience. That's how I've tried to approach it over the years, particularly the times I've had the opportunity to travel outside the United States.

Some entertainers don't like to travel overseas. It's tiring and often difficult to adjust to the time change, the food is different, the hotels aren't what they are at home, there's no twenty-four hour room service, no McDonald's right outside the window. But I've enjoyed seeing other countries, other lifestyles. Had it not been for the music business, I'd probably still think the world started and stopped at the city limits of Commerce, Georgia.

I've had the opportunity during my career to perform in Germany, England, Ireland, Scotland, Holland, Norway, and Sweden, as well as every state in the union and every province of Canada. I've found in my travels that people are people wherever you go and that music is an international language. It can cross a lot of boundaries.

By that I mean, people might not always understand the words you say to them, but they can always *feel* the music you sing and play for them. For example, once in the early seventies I was touring Europe with Conway Twitty and Loretta Lynn, and we ventured north into Scandinavia where none of us had ever been before. It was our opening night in Bergen, Norway, which is probably the most beautiful place I have ever been, and our concert was being televised live all across the country. I was the first act to go on stage. After my opening medley of songs, the audience applauded generously. Then with no warning at all their applause turned into a loud, rhythmic foot-stomping. It began softly at first . . . and slowly . . . then it became more staccato . . . then louder . . . and louder . . . until all I could think of was pictures I'd seen of German soldiers in World War II marching in that high-kicking, goose-step motion. I didn't know if the audience was organizing into a mob about to storm the stage and lynch me or not. They just kept on stomping and clapping louder and louder.

Finally, I held up my hand for quiet and I said to these people in my slowest and most deliberate English "I . . . do not . . . understand. What . . . does . . . this . . . mean?"

The auditorium grew strangely still and quiet. Then a young man seated by the aisle about halfway back in the house stood up and said in halting English, "It means . . . we love you!"

With that, I turned to the band and motioned for them to join me, and we started clapping and stomping our feet right back at the audience. "We love you too," I shouted, and the crowd went berserk. I don't know of another single moment in my career when I've felt so much love fill one hall. And it was all because of the music. The music spoke to everyone there regardless of their nationality or their native tongue. There has been only one other night in my career that could possibly have matched that one for me emotionally. That came several years later in Belfast, Northern Ireland.

People seem surprised when I tell them that I have performed in Belfast. Actually, I've gone there twice, and I'll admit both times it was scary. The first time I went I had never been any place where people were fighting a war, and it wasn't exactly what I'd call a Sunday stroll in the park.

Becky went with me, and when we arrived at the Belfast airport from London, we had nothing in our possession but the clothes on our backs. The authorities had confiscated our wallets, the ladies' purses, everything. In fact, before the flight ever boarded in London, they had taken us all, one at a time, behind little privacy curtains and frisked us from head to toe. They were afraid we might be trying to smuggle in weapons or ammunition or something. Then on the bus ride into Belfast from the airport, we rounded a big curve in the road and were suddenly face-to-face with an armored tank rolling in the opposite direction. Soldiers with guns were peeking out the top, looking all around. I remember thinking, "Boy, I hope those guys like country music!" but they passed us right on by.

Things were so bad between the Catholics and the Protestants on that first trip to Belfast that our tour promoters wouldn't even let us stay at a hotel in town. They feared for our safety. They put us up in a little inn way out in the country where they said we'd be less likely to have any trouble. As soon as we checked in, I went to the room and sacked out, but Becky wasn't tired at all. She took a shower, got dressed, and went down to the restaurant to get a bite to eat. When I woke up she told me, "Boy, this sure is a nice hotel. Everybody downstairs was dressed so nice."

"What do you mean?" I asked.

"Well, when I was down there eating, there were all these men sitting around the lobby in three-piece suits reading newspapers. Several others were in the dining room, and they were all dressed real nice, too. Even the men walking outside in the garden were all dressed up."

I pulled the curtains back and looked out the hotel window. Sure enough, Becky was right. Well-dressed men were walking around everywhere, but I knew immediately what they were. "Those aren't just hotel guests," I told her. "Those guys are detectives or policemen or something like that. Lord, I hope they're on our side!"

Turned out that's exactly who they were and what they were. They were there to protect us, to make sure no incidents took place while we were there. It was scary.

On my second trip to Northern Ireland, we stayed right in downtown Belfast, but our hotel was completely surrounded by barbed wire and was staked out twenty-four hours a day by uniformed, armed security guards. A week after we left, I read in the paper where that very hotel had been bombed. I don't know about anybody else, but the night we were there I slept with one eye open!

The emotional part came at the show itself. You see, they don't get much entertainment there, as you might imagine, and people came from everywhere to see our show. They walked, they rode bicycles, they came anyway they could just to be there. There was a curfew on how late they could be on the streets in their cars, so most people just left their cars at home. The concert hall was packed, and I didn't find out until long after the show was over that in addition to all the fans, there had been over sixty armed guards, plainclothesmen wearing bulletproof vests, scattered throughout the audience. They, too, had been there, we were told, for our protection "just in case." Fortunately, everything came off without incident.

It was the opening night of our tour and the promoter, Jeffrey Kruger, was anxious to see our show and time the individual segments. This was because there were to be future dates on the tour where the amount of time we'd spend on stage would be critical. Some of the theaters we were to play were only in the two- to three-thousand seat range, and in order to accommodate the crowds there would have to be both an early and a late show the same evening. So on this particular night in Belfast he sat in the audience with a stopwatch to clock our numbers.

As we were told to do, we stayed on stage for exactly sixty minutes. I sang a variety of the songs I figured they'd heard over the years—a few of the fast ones, a few of the slow—and the reaction was incredible. When we came off, I met Jeffrey in the hallway backstage. He was staring at his stopwatch as if he didn't believe what it was telling him. "Do you know that ten minutes and thirty-seven seconds of your sixty minutes was taken up by applause?" he asked. "I've never seen such response in my life! Go back out there and sing them a few more songs," and we did. Again the applause was deafening.

I came offstage the second time emotionally drained and out of breath. And then I learned why they had accepted us so warmly. "Most entertainers won't even come here," an elderly man said to me softly as he stopped me outside my dressing room, deep lines creasing his brow. "We're so thankful you came," and I noticed a tear beginning to form in the corner of his eye. He reached out his burly arms and gave me a big bear hug. "Thank you," he said. "Thank you for helping us forget our troubles for a while. May God bless you and keep you safe," and then he broke down sobbing. Many of the other fans followed suit, coming up to embrace us, shaking our hands warmly, and begging us to "Please come again!" I was very touched to think that all I had done was something that I loved to do—play and sing my music—and in the process I had made so many people so very happy.

The ladies who cooked in the kitchen of the little country inn where we were staying baked us a rich layer cake and a fresh fruit pie to take with us on the return flight to London the following morning. "You must come again," one of them said to me, "when things are better." I thanked her and assured her that we would. But the look in her eye told me she expected that to be a long, long time.

13

Life on the road can be very tiring, very draining emotionally, but it can also be very funny. I've probably laughed harder, longer, and louder over things that have happened on the road than over things that have happened anywhere else. And some of the warmest memories I have are woven around this nomadic existence I've enjoyed for over a quarter of a century.

I've never seemed to attract the really wild, roaring-crazy musicians to my band, and I guess some of the fun we've had over the years probably pales in comparison to tales other groups could tell. Sure, I've had some guys (and a few gals, too) who liked to take a drink or two after a show and party and cut up a little bit, but I've never employed anybody who was on drugs, anybody who had a serious drinking problem, or anybody whose behavior was of a destructive nature. I have had many musicians with me on the road, however, who were extremely attracted to members of the opposite sex.

Once years ago we were working a week-long engagement at a nightclub in a major northern city, and one of my band members had invited a female acquaintance from another state to come see some of our shows. She arranged her work schedule so that she was able to accept his invitation. She flew into town and checked into the hotel where we were staying. At the same time another acquaintance of this same musician found out she could get off work that week, so she, too, hopped on a plane, buzzed into town, and checked into our hotel. Neither lady was aware of the presence of the other. One lady had a room on the third floor, the other a room on the twelfth. My buddy's room was on the fifth floor.

The rest of us tuned in to what was going on right away. Musicians learn to spot pretty ladies sitting alone in a crowd about the same time they learn to go from a G-chord to D. Maybe sooner. We'd see both these young ladies sitting in the audience night after night, both very attractive and both apparently unescorted. Then between sets we'd watch as our pickin' pal would go to their separate tables and visit first with one and then the other. He would then table-hop all around the room and visit with our other fans so that nobody got suspicious. Each lady thought she was the one and only special lady in this guy's life. The masquerade went on for days.

We all began to wonder about the fourth or fifth day, however, just how our friend was managing to juggle things so as to keep each lady ignorant of the fact that the other one was there and had come specifically to see him. And I was starting to wonder if and when this guy was getting any sleep. The mystery finally began to unravel late one afternoon when I overheard him on the house phone in the lobby of the hotel taking to one of his companions.

"Honey, I won't be able to get with you tonight after the show," he said. "Would you believe Bill has called a rehearsal for midnight? You go on back to your room after we get through tonight and I'll check with you as soon as I get in. Don't wait up, though, because it may last a long time."

Then I heard him hang up the phone and dial another room number. The conversation sounded a lot like the first one with one major change: "Honey, I won't be able to be with you very long tonight," he said. "Would you believe Bill has called a rehearsal for six o'clock tomorrow morning? We can be together for a little while after the show, then I'll have to leave. But I'll call you the minute I get back in." And the sly ole fox hung up the phone.

I've often wondered what the ladies must have thought of me. They no doubt figured I was the slave driver to end all slave drivers. Of course, I had called no rehearsals at all.

We were all getting a big kick out of watching what was going on, though, and we marvelled at our friend's ingenuity, skill, and stamina. But his luck ran out the very last day we were in town.

The club where we were working had a policy of opening its doors on Saturday afternoons for a matinee performance designed for families and children. A special section of the club was roped off where no alcoholic beverages were served, and a nice lunch was offered. It was a very popular feature, and the house was usually packed. This particular Saturday afternoon was no exception. When we took to the stage for our show, there wasn't an empty seat in the house.

In fact, while the band was tuning up, the hostess was working her way in and out among the crowded tables making sure that no seat was left unfilled. People were being asked to make room for strangers at their tables and . . . you guessed it. Our musician-buddy walked to the stage, looked out into the crowd, and turned as white as a ghost when he saw one of his two lady friends being escorted to sit at the table of the other. I'd have given anything to have had a camera to capture the expression on his face.

When the show started, the rest of us couldn't hold it in. We laughed until we ached. We could see out into the audience and tell that the ladies were conversing with each other across the table. We could only imagine, however, what they must be saying. Up on stage our pal squirmed, he fidgeted, and the more he suffered, the more we rubbed it in. I lied to the audience at one point and said I had a special request to sing "Three Hearts in a Tangle." The band cracked up. I didn't sing it, but if I had, he'd never have made it through the first verse. I told every joke I could think of about love triangles. If the song "Trying to Love Two Women" had been out then, I'd have sung it a half-dozen times. The guys in the band and I were having a ball. We deliberately stretched the show and made it last as long as we could. Our buddy was in agony.

As soon as the show was over, he left the stage like he'd been shot out of a cannon. The ladies calmly got up from their table and left the club together. We didn't see our friend again until showtime that night, and we never did see either one of his companions again . . . ever. We kidded our Don Juan unmercifully for days, and for a while we almost had him believing that the girls had gotten together, compared notes, and were coming after him with a gun in the next town we were headed for. We thought it was hilarious. He threw a crick in his neck looking over his shoulder.

Travelling musicians form something of an unspoken fraternal bond among themselves, sort of a modern code of the Old West.

They do for each other . . . and they often do *to* each other as well. Guys who share bumpy bus rides, lousy restaurants, crummy motels, long hours, days, weeks, and months together away from their families sometimes become closer than brothers. And brothers, as you know, often have no mercy on one another.

One night in Wichita, Kansas, for reasons that will forever go unknown, Snuffy Miller decided he'd put some soap on Jimmy Gateley's fiddle bow. He knew if he put enough of the waxy substance on the hairs of the bow they couldn't rub against the strings of the fiddle and the fiddle couldn't make a sound. He also knew I'd had a hot record in Wichita with "Bright Lights & Country Music" and that it had a fiddle intro. And he knew I'd be awfully upset if Jimmy stepped up to the microphone to kick off that song and no sound came out of his instrument.

Which is exactly what happened. I gave the song a powerful introduction . . . "Folks, here's a song you made a big hit here in Wichita. I hope you remember it, and I hope you like it." Jimmy strode into the spotlight at center stage, placed his fiddle under his chin, and dramatically raised the bow. He brought it crashing down against the strings and . . . dead silence. He tried it again. Again no sound. Believing the third time to be the charm, he went through the whole exercise again and still nothing happened. I looked at Jimmy, not understanding exactly what had happened myself, and there was a horrified look on his face. Suddenly he took his fiddle out of his left hand and switched it over into his right. He began pounding his left ear with the palm of his hand. It never occurred to him that his bow had been tampered with. The poor guy thought he had gone deaf!

Everybody laughed like the dickens. That is, everybody but Gate. He was too bent on revenge. He got it, too, in short order. I had used a trumpet to play the introduction to my recorded version of "But You Know I Love You," and on stage Snuffy had become quite proficient at playing his snare drum with one hand and the intro on a trumpet with the other. Never quite forgetting or forgiving Snuffy for the soap-on-the-bow incident, Jimmy decided to stuff the horn of Snuffy's trumpet with Kleenex. The effect was the same as with the fiddle. No sound could come out. In fact, no air could pass through the instrument at all. This time when I cued the intro for my song, Snuffy took a big deep breath, raised the trumpet to his lips, and nearly blew his brains out!

(Not long ago I ran into my buddy of many years, Johnny Western, who is now a disc jockey at KFDI Radio in Wichita. At the time of the soap-on-the-bow and the tissue-in-the-trumpet episodes, Johnny was a recording artist and touring performer himself and had been a part of the tour where these monkeyshines took place. He remembers the incidents well but contends that all these years I've been blaming the wrong persons for what happened. He swears the true culprit was the show's comedian, Don Bowman, who actually instigated both incidents. If so, I apologize belatedly to Gate and Snuffy. I can't wait to talk to Bowman and hear his side of it!)

Fun on the road comes in all shapes and sizes. I once organized a softball team among the members of my group, and for a while we almost forgot we were travelling musicians. We thought we were The King and His Court, Eddie Feigner's touring softball-playing legends. We'd get ourselves booked into a town for an evening's concert and then arrange an afternoon softball game pitting our band against a team of local disc jockeys, musicians, or the local chapter of Little Sisters of the Poor. We weren't too choosy about our competition. We just wanted to play.

We'd come bounding off our bus at the local ball field, sometimes with several thousand people in attendance, wearing our black-and-white softball uniforms trimmed in gold, trying our best to hold our stomachs in and let our athletic prowess hang out. The games were always played for a local charity, so in addition to providing us with an outlet for our pent-up energies, we raised a lot of money over the years for a lot of worthwhile causes.

Once in Hattiesburg, Mississippi, the immortal Dizzy Dean served as our umpire. And Ronnie Milsap, the great blind singer and musician, snuck up behind me without my knowing it at a game in Nashville dressed in full umpire's regalia. I was at bat, and the pitcher threw a pitch that sailed at least five feet over my head. I heard the ump yell, "Strike one!" The crowd roared, and I turned around to jump all over the umpire. When I saw Ronnie standing there in his umpire's uniform and wraparound dark glasses, I yelled "Hey, what's going on?"

"Don't you scream at me," he barked, "I calls 'em like I sees 'em!"

Ball playing at our ages was sometimes more dangerous than I had realized. Prior to a game one night, I was hitting some fly balls to our outfielders when my piano player, Monty Parkey, walked right in front of a blistering line drive hot off my bat. It hit him square in the face and blood came gushing from everywhere. It scared me to death. I thought I had killed him. I rushed him to the hospital, and he ended up missing several concert engagements suffering from a broken nose.

Rounding third base at Tim McCarver Stadium in Memphis one night, I got tangled up in my own feet and did a triple somersault right across home plate. I lay there in the dust and the dirt afraid to move, frightened that I might have separated the shin bone connected to the ankle bone. The crowd was evidently afraid that something much worse had happened, for they grew quiet as a mouse. When I caught my breath and realized I was all right, I jumped to my feet, dusted off my uniform, and trotted to the dugout to the tune of a standing ovation. I politely tipped my cap just like I'd seen the big boys do on TV. I thought I was Ty Cobb reincarnated.

I not only played softball, but once I even got back into playing baseball for a while. A group of country music stars, musicians, songwriters and others who worked in our industry decided in the mid-seventies to form a team. They called it the Nashville Pickers and rounded up some sponsors to furnish uniforms, others to furnish equipment, and an ex-major league player, Dick Sisler, who lives in Nashville, to serve as manager. They came up with a unique way to promote and market the team and at the same time have a lot of fun.

They would sign contracts each season to bring the ball team to a half-dozen or so major league cities on the day of a regularly scheduled game. An hour or so before the big league game, the Pickers, many of whom were well-known country stars, (Charlie Pride, Roy Clark, Johnny Duncan, Bob Luman, and Charlie McCoy among them) would challenge a team made up of local radio, television, and newspaper personalities to a baseball game. They'd play three or four innings, or as much as time would allow, then turn things over to the real ballplayers. After the major league game, the stars would come back out and give an hour-long concert.

It was a tremendous concept, and there were very few big league clubs who weren't receptive to the idea. Some of the larger cities with minor league clubs went for the idea as well. Over the years, there weren't many baseball parks of any size around the country that didn't receive at least one visit from the Nashville Pickers.

When the team was first organized, I was working so many dates on the road every summer that, even though I wanted badly to be part of it, I just couldn't fit it into my schedule. Finally one year things eased up a bit, and I made it to a few of the games.

I'll never forget the Sunday afternoon I got to play first base in the Astrodome in Houston. The Montreal Expos were in town for a game with the Astros, and I was like a kid at the circus. I guess I might have been a bit too nervous because I came to bat twice in the game and both times hit weak little rollers back to the pitcher. I was thrown out at first base by twenty yards each time.

When the game was over, my longtime friend, Tommy Helms, who had played for years with the Cincinnati Reds and was finishing out the last days of his career as a member of the Astros, called me over to the Houston dugout and gave me one of his custom-crafted Louisville Slugger baseball bats. I guess he figured I needed something to help me hit the ball better than I had done that afternoon. I was thrilled with the bat and could hardly wait to get it back to Nashville and show it off.

But there was one rather pertinent question: How was I going to get the bat home? It was too big to fit in my suitcase, I'd have felt like a fool carrying it on my shoulder through the Houston airport, and besides I figured they wouldn't let me on an airplane carrying a ball bat anyhow. What was I going to do?

Finally, I hit on a solution. I was carrying my stage costume in a leather hang-up garment bag. Why couldn't I just slide the bat down into the garment bag and carry it on the plane with me? Sounded like a good idea to me.

The next morning Johnny Duncan and I caught a cab to the airport, and I told him what I was doing. "I'll bet they stop me at security, though," I said. "They'll think I'm gonna use the bat to hit the pilot over the head and hijack the plane or something."

But, surprise, when I put my bag on the conveyor belt to be x-rayed the security guard let it pass right on through.

I picked up my bag as it came off the far side of the belt and was about to walk on to my gate when the guard tapped me on the shoulder. "I'd like to take a look inside your bag, please, sir," he said.

"Uh oh, here it comes," I thought. "He'll never let me take this bat on board. Guess I'll have to leave it in Houston."

The guard never said a word. He unzipped my bag, reached in behind my clothes, and pulled out the shiny Louisville Slugger. He looked at it carefully, rolled it around in his hands once or twice, then put it back in the bag and zipped it up again. Then he handed the garment bag to me.

"Aren't you going to confiscate my bat?" I asked him, puzzled by his actions. "I could use it to hit the pilot over the head, you know."

He looked at me and never changed his expression. "I saw your game at the Dome yesterday," he said softly, "and I'm not worried. In your hands that bat is no weapon!"

I got so serious about playing ball there for a while that it began to affect my business. I signed our team up to play in a city league in Nashville and found myself cancelling and moving show dates around so we could play softball every Wednesday night. In a double-header league no less. One night it dawned on me that while I was having tons of fun playing ball, I was really starting to neglect my career. I had chosen years ago to be an entertainer, not a ball player. I began to rethink my priorities and decided I'd best put my bat and ball back in the closet and get back in the music business where I belonged.

I've never been much of a card player, but there didn't used to be a band in the business that didn't play a lot of poker or other card games while riding down the highway looking for a way to pass the time. I once had three or four extremely serious poker players in my group who would break out the cards the minute the bus was loaded after a show ("You wanta look at a few?" was their byword invitation to one another) and still be playing when we'd pull into the next town the following morning. I don't think the stakes were ever very high, but evidently they were high enough to attract poker players from some of the other bands we'd be touring with. I remember one tour when Del Reeves, Jack Greene, and Kenny Price rode more miles on my bus than they did on their own just to play cards with my band. Today the younger musicians are into video games, and they often sit before the TV set on the bus and play for hours.

I miss the old package show tours where several artists would travel together for long periods of time. It was always fun to have other singers and musicians climb on our bus, and I'd often ride with them on theirs. Today I might work a show with two or three other artists and never even get a chance to speak with them. They come into town from one direction, we come in from another, they check into one motel, we check into another. They'll then stay secluded on their bus until showtime, and our paths never cross. I don't like that. We're all missing out on a lot of fun.

I especially used to love to work in the Sunday package shows with George Jones and Tammy Wynette when they were married. Tammy would put a pot of beans on the stove in their bus and a ham in the oven prior to the matinee performance and let them cook slowly while she and George were on stage singing. Between the matinee and the night show, she'd mix up a pan of cornbread and invite the other entertainers on the show over for dinner. I used to tease and tell them their bus was one of the best truck stops on the circuit!

Some of the best socializing among entertainers can take place on the tour buses. Grandpa Jones, one of my favorite people in the world and one of our business's greatest characters, was once visiting on my bus at a little county fair. We were sitting around swapping stories, waiting for the time for us to go onstage. The bus was parked directly behind the stage, and when the local band opened the show and began to play, the noise from the power generator running the lights and air conditioning on our bus began drowning them out. They turned to the promoter of the show, who was standing off in the wings, and asked him to ask us if we'd either turn the generator off or move the bus a few feet away from the stage.

Since the day was a scorcher and we didn't want to sit there with no air conditioning, we decided on the latter. Our driver cranked up the big diesel engine and backed up a good hundred yards from the stage. In about ten minutes here came the promoter again telling us the generator was still too loud on stage. So we backed up another hundred yards or so. Believe it or not, this still did not satisfy the musicians who must have had supersonic hearing, so for the third time we were asked to back the bus up even farther. All this time Grandpa hadn't said a word. He'd just sat there watching and listening.

Finally we had moved the bus as far away from the other band as possible without leaving the fairgrounds. Grandpa looked out the front window at the other performers who were now just a small spot on the horizon. "Well," he said in his patented nasal tone, pronouncing *well* as if it rhymed with *pail*, "we'll have to book a date between here and the stage!"

For several years in the late seventies and early eighties, I placed in back of me and the band on stage a backdrop comprised of three large movie screens, behind which we mounted up to as many as nine computerized slide projectors, and at various times throughout my concerts I would show pictures on the screens to illustrate the music the band and I were performing live. Several artists carry screens and slides today, some even show video tapes, but at that time my slide show was something quite innovative. As you might suspect, in those days there was still a lot of room for improvement in the equipment.

When our slide show worked right, it was one of the most effective and stunning presentations imaginable. But when it didn't, it could be disastrous.

I used it only at certain strategic points in the show, one of which was when I sang a medley of songs from the sixties. I would pull out one of my old custom-made rhinestone suits from that era and put on the jacket, talk about the sixties and ask the audience to remember the music that went with the times. As we played and sang our songs, slides would appear illustrating the current events of the decade.

Later in the show I did a tribute to the history and the roots of country music with a different set of slides. My opening line was,

"In the beginning, there was just a man and a guitar," and an old black-and-white picture of a farmer sitting on the front porch of a little log cabin picking his guitar would slowly fade up on the screen. It was quite dramatic. As the slide slowly eased into focus, the guitar player in my band would begin picking out the melody to "Wildwood Flower" on his acoustical guitar.

By now I'm sure you're ahead of me. We were working at a big fair up in New England and I was about to close the show with the country music medley, when somehow the computer and the slide projectors got their signals all crisscrossed. The lights went down, and I began talking about how country music began, saying slowly and dramatically, "In the beginning, there was just a man . . . and a guitar." The guitar player went into his soft, emotional version of "Wildwood Flower." But suddenly I noticed the audience shifting nervously in their seats. A couple of them were looking at the screen with puzzled looks on their faces. One or two were even snickering.

"What's so funny?" I thought, and I turned to look at the screen behind me. But instead of seeing the picture of the old farmer quietly strumming his guitar, I found myself looking directly into an eight-foot-high picture of the sneering face of Spiro Agnew! It was no doubt the only time in history that the former Vice President of the United States had ever been credited with founding country music.

My audio-visual show was such a hit with audiences all over the country, though, that I was once invited to showcase it before one of the most influential and prestigious groups of all, the National Association of Fair Buyers at their annual convention in Las Vegas. These were the ladies and gentlemen responsible for booking most of the acts into the biggest fairs around the country, and it was an honor to be asked to appear before them. I knew if we did a good job we'd get booked at a large number of major fairs the following season.

The showcase was set for the large auditorium inside the beautiful Aladdin Hotel. We got to town the day before the showcase, and our technical crew spent all the next day making sure everything was in perfect working order. But, alas, when I went to wrap up my performance with "In the beginning, there was just a man

. . . and his guitar," a field of beautiful yellow flowers appeared behind me on the screen.

I stopped and told the fair buyers that something had malfunctioned, and we started over again. This time, the "man and his guitar" turned out to be the silhouette of two lovers rubbing noses in the twilight. The buyers roared. They had all been through the experience of a ferris wheel breaking down or a merry-go-round that wouldn't work at their fairs. They knew what I was going through, and they were laughing because this time it was me suffering instead of them. When on my third attempt at getting it right still another wrong slide appeared on the screen, I turned to the audience and said, "Aw, to hell with it. If you want to see this thing work right, you'll just have to book me!" And I walked off the stage to a standing ovation!

I've had the opportunity to meet many people, see many places, and witness many special events in my lifetime that I'd never have gotten the opportunity to be a part of were it not for the fact I was an entertainer travelling the road. I've been invited to the White House, I've been to two Super Bowls, to the World Series, to the bottom of the Grand Canyon and to the top of Pike's Peak. I've been able to go on seven Caribbean cruises, and I've taken my band members and their spouses with me. We've seen shows on Broadway, been to both the baseball and the pro football Halls of Fame, watched them make beer at a brewery in Wisconsin, manufacture maple syrup in Vermont, make cereal in Battle Creek, and build guitars in Kalamazoo. I've have fans take my picture, ask for my autograph, and pay their hard-earned money to sit in the audience and applaud my music and laugh at my jokes. One night at Memorial Hall in downtown Dayton, Ohio, a lady dressed in a full-length dress and a mink coat walked up on stage in front of several thousand people while I was singing "Still" and started taking off her clothes. And I've had people say to me just about every conceivable thing imaginable. Like the lady who told me after a concert just recently, "I would have been at your show the last time you were in town, but I had something else to do." And another one who said, "Oh, Bill Anderson, it's such a thrill to meet you. I've liked you ever since back when you used to be popular!"

My favorite may have come last winter, though, when I was driving a new four-wheel-drive vehicle I had just bought in Florida back to Nashville and had to stop and check into a motel in northern Alabama to avoid an oncoming ice and snow storm. (I bought the car to help me navigate the icy, snowy hills in the section of Nashville where I live, then I couldn't even get it home because of an ice and snow storm!) I signed the guest register at the motel and handed the lady behind the counter my credit card. She looked at my card, looked down at the name I'd just written, glanced back at my card, then looked up at me.

"Bill Anderson," she said slowly as if trying to remember where she'd heard that name before. "Bill . . . Anderson. Bill . . . ? Say, didn't there used to be somebody famous named Bill Anderson?"

I looked at her and smiled. "Yeah, I think there did," I said. "But it was a long time ago."

"Really? What did he do?" she asked seriously.

I just laughed. "I don't know, but I bet he had a lot of fun doing it, don't you?" She stared at me blankly.

I winked at her, picked up my key, and headed for my room. "I'll *guarantee* you ole Bill Anderson, whoever he was, had a lot of fun, lady," I mumbled under my breath. "Yes m'am. He had a heckuva lot of fun!"

14

The young entertainers today may travel in faster, more expensive buses, sing into more sophisticated and more elaborate sound systems, and employ bigger and better bands than I ever did, but most of my cohorts and I from the 1960s put the newcomers to shame in one area of the business: We bought much gaudier wardrobes to perform in!

I've never been in favor of country artists rolling out of their bunks and going directly onstage wearing wrinkled T-shirts and dirty jeans, but, Lord, I wish I had back all the money I sent to Nudie's Rodeo Tailors of North Hollywood, California, to purchase custom-made stage wear for me and my band. I wish I had *half* the money back. I could quit working and go fishing for a couple of years!

I've always believed in dressing my band to look the part of showmen. And I feel a certain obligation to the fans not to walk onstage myself dressed like the guy sitting in the second row. Trust me, for years I never did!

"Nudie Suits," named after the man who made them, Nudie Cohen, and not because they were made out of see-through material, were the ultimate in stage wear in the fifties and sixties. Nudie made a few outfits for Elvis and some of the other rock 'n' rollers, but his costumes were mostly for country singers and silver-screen cowboys. They were western-cut and decorated with embroidery and rhinestones until they almost glowed in the dark. And the Po' Boys had pink ones and green ones and yellow ones and blue ones, and I had contrasting white ones trimmed in gold, black ones trimmed in silver, purple ones with snowflakes, red ones embroidered with flowers, and just about any other lavish combination you might name. In true show-biz fashion, I figured anything worth doing was worth overdoing.

By the time I was able to afford to get the Po' Boys into Nudie suits, the band had expanded to six members. I had added a full-time bass player and a piano player. At somewhere around $750 a pop, plus the boots, the neckties and other accessories, that meant it would cost me well over five thousand dollars for just one set of outfits. The suits were mostly made from wool and mohair, which meant they were heavy and hot, and there was no way to wear them beneath the bright stage lights without perspiring like crazy. That meant we always had to have three or four complete sets in good shape just to be able to stand next to each other the last few nights of a long tour. There's never any time on the road to go to the dry cleaners.

My own outfits were naturally fancier than the band's, and that usually meant somewhere between twenty-five hundred and three thousand dollars apiece for mine. I've even paid higher. My white boots were always custom-made, and they cost an additional several hundred dollars (I once went crazy and had a pair covered completely with rhinestones!), most of my shirts were custom-tailored, and when I'd rip the seat out of my britches, like I did one night jumping down off the stage to sign autographs after a show in Providence, Rhode Island, and again a few weeks later doing the same thing at a fair in Hopkinsville, Kentucky, there would go another couple of grand slip-sliding away.

I began easing out of the flashy but costly costumes and into more casual and less expensive stage wear in the early seventies. But I'll confess: I have never felt as much like a star in what I have worn since as I did in the old rhinestone suits. Once my manager made a deal for me to endorse a line of J.C. Penney's sportswear by wearing it on my personal appearances. The clothes were lighter weight than the Nudie suits, and it didn't cost me a dime to outfit myself or the band, but one day I stood on stage and counted four people sitting out in the audience dressed just like I was. Penney's loved it. But I hated it!

After he'd hired a band, bought a bus, and outfitted all the band members in the most ornate costumes imaginable, the next thing any self-respecting touring country music star would do back in the sixties was add a girl singer to his entourage. I was no exception.

By the end of the decade, I was playing more and more places where the promoters of my concerts expected me to provide the entire evening's entertainment, and there was no way to please everybody in the audience all night long (especially the men) by giving them nothing but a half-dozen hairy-legged ole boys to stare at the whole time. Porter Wagoner faced the same problem and hired "Pretty Miss" Norma Jean to tour with him. The Wilburn Brothers introduced to the world a young girl from the coal mining regions of Kentucky named Loretta Lynn. And thanks to an unusual sequence of events, my female counterpart became a talented but feisty little redhead from West Plains, Missouri, named Jan Howard.

I had started a weekly syndicated television show in early 1965 called, oddly enough, the *Bill Anderson Show*. The original cast consisted of myself, the Po' Boys band, singer-comedian Grandpa Jones (this was a couple of years before *Hee-Haw* came along), and country songstress Jean Shepard. Our show was videotaped in Charlotte, North Carolina, at the facilities of Jefferson Productions, where we'd gather once a month to crank out four thirty-minute programs. "Syndicated" meant our show was sold to television stations all across the country on a station-by-station basis rather than being offered to them as part of a network. It was my first regular television exposure to a nationwide audience, so in spite of the hardships of having to tape the shows five hundred miles from Nashville, I was thankful for the opportunity of doing the show, period. I didn't really care where it was done.

Jean and Grandpa, however, weren't exactly as thrilled about it as I was. Jean was consistently in the country charts with her recordings in those days and could work all the personal appearance dates she wanted to with or without the exposure from the TV show. Grandpa had always been an outstanding act on any country show, especially at the fairs and the outdoor festivals, and while I think he enjoyed television, those dreary ten-hour rides from Nashville across the mountains to Charlotte (no interstates then, remember?) seemed to get longer and longer each time. Jean and Grandpa made the trips for a year with no complaints, but when their paychecks from the producers began taking longer and longer to come in, they began to grow more and more unhappy. Finally, when the checks stopped coming in at all, they each decided that there had to be a better way for them to spend their time. In January, 1966, they somewhat angrily quit the show.

Grandpa, in particular, had a short fuse back in those days, and I'll never forget one of his last taping sessions with us when he was getting fed up with the whole situation. My band was attempting to play an instrumental following a song Grandpa had just sung, and they couldn't get it right for anything. At that time there was no such thing as editing videotape, so every time the band would make a mistake, the director would yell "Cut!" and stop the tape. This meant we had to go back to the point of the last commercial break and start over. So Grandpa, who'd sung his song perfectly every time, had to come back on the set and sing his song again. And again. And again and again. I thought if I heard "Methodist Pie" one more time I was going to change my religion. Or give it up altogether!

And if you think I was upset, you should have seen Grandpa. Finally, after at least a half-dozen attempts, the band played their song well enough for the director to be pleased. But then the guitar player said he didn't like his part and asked if he could play it "just one more time." Whereupon I looked over into the corner of the studio and spotted Grandpa. He had shoved his banjo down in its case and had picked up a broom from back in the prop room. And he was moving like a madman ninety-to-nothing across the studio floor with that broom.

"What in the world are you doing, Paw?" I asked.

He shot back, "I'm a-sweepin' me off a place to have a fit!"

I wasn't getting my paycheck most of the time either, but the exposure from being on a hundred or more television stations all across the country each week was helping me in a lot of ways that veteran performers like Jean and Grandpa didn't necessarily need. The show was helping country fans to put a face and a personality with my name. People who had only heard me sing on the radio or jukeboxes up until then could now invite me right into their homes and watch me as well. And I learned real fast that no medium in the world creates closeness between performer and audience like television.

I also realize that I look better on the radio than I do on television, but I weighed my options and decided I'd be better off in the long run by continuing to do the TV show than by pulling out. Occasionally the producers would toss a nickel or a dime my way and I'd buy some gasoline and keep on trekking across the mountains.

During the year we had been taping in Charlotte, Jan Howard had appeared on our show two or three times as a special guest. The producer liked her singing and her personally, so when he got wind of Jean's planning not to return, he offered the permanent female singer's job to Jan. She asked me what I thought about it, and I told her not to plan on spending all the money she'd be making in one place. She got the message. But at the same time she had made a new commitment to her career and was as anxious as I was to add to her exposure. She accepted the job eagerly. Funnyman Don Bowman, who had just begun recording a series of comedy albums for RCA, signed on in Grandpa's place.

With our new cast and new look, we continued to tape our programs in Charlotte until the fall of 1966. Quite a few new stations began to carry our show, and more and more artists with records to promote began asking me if they could come to Charlotte and tape guest appearances with us. I was always glad to welcome my friends to the show, but I invited one artist that, had his appearance not been a smashing success, could have cost me my job.

Charley Pride was new on RCA Victor records and had just begun to promote his songs and work on his career. There weren't many people who had even heard of him at this point, and I doubt the ones who had, had the slightest idea that he was black. At that time there had never been a black singer in the field of country music.

Charley had also never been on television. When I realized I had a chance to be the first person in the country to present him to a TV audience and found out how badly he wanted to come guest on my show, I extended him an invitation. And he accepted. Only trouble was I didn't tell the producers he was coming.

The morning of the taping I figured I'd best tell somebody that I was about to have the first black country singer in history on my show, so I went upstairs to the Jefferson Production offices and decided I'd go right to the head man. No use beating around the bush with the peons. I told him everything.

"You've done *what?*" I can still hear him yell. "You can't have a black man on your show! We just went on the air in Meridian, Mississippi . . . Jackson, Mississippi . . . Alexandria, Louisiana . . . for God's sake! We'll lose all those stations, don't you know that? You just tell him you're sorry, that you made a mistake. But you can't put him on. It'll be the end of your show!"

"No, sir, I'm not going to tell him that," I answered. "You'll have to tell him. But I don't think it'll hurt the show at all. In fact, I think it will help it. He's never been on TV. We've got a chance to have him first. Don't you think that's worth taking a chance for?"

Mr. Boss Man didn't like it one bit, but after giving me all of his reasons and listening to all of mine, he finally gave in. After all, Charley was already in the dressing room downstairs and getting ready to go onto the set and rehearse with the band. When the tape started to roll early that afternoon and Charley Pride walked on camera to sing his first song, everything in that entire building came to a standstill. Every executive, every secretary, every person who could crowd into the little viewing room high above the studio was there, looking down through the thick plate glass, watching something they didn't understand and could scarcely believe—a black man singing country music. And Bill Anderson committing professional suicide.

Fortunately, Charley never knew until I told him years later that anything out of the ordinary was going on. He was nervous enough just standing in front of the camera. He certainly didn't need anything else to worry about. He sang both sides of his first release, "The Snakes Crawl at Night" and "The Atlantic Coastal Line." And he sang them well, even though he has told me many times since that he was scared to death.

The show began to air on stations around the country about three weeks after we taped it, and the reaction from our viewers was unbelievable. Whereas in a normal week our show might have generated a couple of hundred letters nationwide, this week they brought mail to me in a bushel basket. Hundreds upon hundreds of cards and letters, all with something to say about that new singer, Charley Pride. They loved him. Mississippi loved him, Louisiana loved him, every single letter but two said, in effect, that they thought Charley Pride was fantastic. We didn't lose one station or one single viewer that I ever knew of. The only negative letters I received were one postmarked Chicago and another from Milwaukee. I threw them both in the trash.

It had nothing at all to do with Charley Pride's appearance on our show, but before the year was out we left Charlotte and moved the production of our show to the studios of CKLW-TV in Windsor, Ontario, Canada, just across the river from Detroit. We had a new producer and new syndicators by this time, and the new folks had promised us if we'd make this move they could get our show onto stations all across Canada as well as keeping us on all the stations that were already carrying the show throughout the United States. It sounded like a good idea to me. Besides, we could get to Windsor about as easily as we could get to Charlotte, and CKLW-TV saturated the metropolitan Detroit market on Channel 9. Plus, they wanted us to add another ninety minutes of prime-time programming every week in the nation's fifth largest market to the coverage we already had for our weekly half-hour in the rest of the country. That meant we'd have two hours of TV exposure every week in Detroit alone as well as the exposure across Canada. I figured we couldn't lose on a deal like that, and even though the Canadian part never fully materialized, I was right. In addition, once or twice we even got paid!

About the same time Jan Howard was asked if she'd like to join our television show, she was in the process of dissolving her recording affiliation with Capitol Records and had begun negotiating a move to the label where I was recording, Decca Records. As soon as she came with us on TV, it seemed like the natural thing for us to begin singing duets together. Our voices had a unique blend, and we began to receive a lot of extremely favorable mail from our viewers. The next thing I knew Jan had signed her contract to record for Decca, and we were badgering Owen Bradley to let us record together. He agreed that it might work, it did, and a whole new career was born for both of us.

Jan's and my first duet release was a remake of the old Reno and Smiley classic, "I Know You're Married (But I Love You Still)," and as soon as people heard it they began to whisper that some kind of wild offstage romance must be going on between us. Otherwise, why would we be singing a song like that? Then when our second release, "For Loving You," turned out to be an even mushier, gushier ballad, the tongues really started to wag. Especially when we'd perform the song live and I'd say to Jan:

> For loving you . . . My life is so much richer
> You've given me so much to live for
> And I never really lived before . . . Before loving you.

And in return she'd say to me:

> And for loving you . . . My faith is a little stronger
> For a world that could give you to me
> Couldn't be as bad as it's made out to be
> There was good there I just could never see
> Before loving you.

Neither one of us composed those words, but when we recorded them and our record started racing up the charts toward No. 1 many people began to assume we were actually *living* all the things we were saying and singing. Nothing could have been further from the truth.

For some reason, folks seem to have a hard time believing that a man and a woman can travel together and sing together and work together as closely as Jan and I did for seven years without there being something sexual going on between them. Jan wrote in her marvelous autobiography, *Sunshine & Shadow*, that "Bill never appealed to me as a man," which hurt my feelings, of course, but which was also the truth. Jan and I became good friends, but the basis for that friendship was always our professional relationship and our music. And we worked hard to keep it that way.

I first met Jan in the early days of my career when she and her songwriting husband, Harlan Howard, lived in a modest little house in Gardena, California, long before they ever moved to Nashville. At the time my impression was that Jan was much more interested in being a good wife and a good mother to her three sons than she was in becoming a singing star.

I had gone to California early in 1960 to work a few club dates, a few radio and television shows, and to try and get my name known a bit on the west coast. I had come to know and admire Harlan through his terrific songwriting and a few phone conversations I'd had with him from Nashville, but we'd never met face-to-face. He'd already written such hits as "Pick Me Up on Your Way Down," "The Key's in the Mailbox," and "Mommy for a Day," and I wanted badly to meet this man whose work I admired.

Jan had made a couple of records at the time, including a hit called "The One You Slip Around With" and a successful duet with Wynn Stewart titled "Yankee Go Home," records I had played on my DJ shows back in Georgia. She primarily looked upon herself, though, as someone to help Harlan make demonstration tapes of the songs he had written and someone to cook supper for him and the boys when they got home. When Harlan would write a song he thought would be right for a female singer to record, he'd teach it to Jan and she'd sing it on the demo session, but I honestly don't think at that point Jan cared one iota about being an entertainer herself.

I was a couple of thousand miles away from home and living alone in a small motel in what were then the far reaches of the San Fernando Valley when Jan and Harlan called one day and asked me if I'd like to join them for dinner at their home the following Sunday afternoon. I told them I'd love to come, and I drove out in my rented car.

There were six of us there, the three adults and Jan's three sons, Jimmy, Corky, and David, whom Harlan had adopted. Jan was, and still is, a great cook, and she sat us down to a delicious roast beef dinner with all the trimmings. I gorged myself. I think it was the only home-cooked meal I had the entire three months I was in California.

Harlan and I hit it off immediately, and after dinner we sat up until the wee hours of the morning passing his guitar back and forth, bouncing our newest song creations off one another and swapping lies. I ended up spending the night in a small bedroom in their home, sharing bunk beds with the three boys. It was a happy and innocent time. I've thought back to that night many times, especially since Jimmy's death in Viet Nam and David's suicide. Back then they were both so young and full of life and full of energy . . . just boys being boys. In a way it's a shame they ever had to grow up and become men.

The professional coming-together of Bill Anderson and Jan Howard in the late sixties provided me with some of my most memorable times in this business. Good friends or not, we had ups and downs like anybody would have living and working so closely together all the time, but I've always figured if Jan hadn't liked me a little bit she wouldn't have saved my life one night on the bus in Fort Worth, Texas.

We were working a Saturday night gig at the infamous Panther Hall in Cowtown, and I was alone on our parked bus in back of the building a few minutes before showtime. Jan had gone inside with the rest of the group to get ready. I was brushing my teeth when somehow I became choked on the toothpaste. I could not catch my breath.

I tried raising both my arms over my head, then dropping one arm and pounding myself on the back with it as hard as I could, but nothing would unclog my windpipe. I was becoming frantic and began stumbling toward the front of the bus to try and go for help when, for some reason, Jan just happened to walk back on board. She immediately sensed my problem and came running toward me, hitting my back with her fist. She liked to have beat the living daylights out of me, but whatever was stuck in my throat soon dislodged and I caught my breath. I doubt that I could have made it up the tall stairs and inside Panther Hall before passing out had Jan not come along. I might have become the late and not-so-great Whisperin' Bill long before my time!

(In Jan's book she says she was sitting in the front of the bus filing her fingernails when I became choked. I distinctly remember that no one was on the bus when I first made my way to the front lounge. I guess that proves that even after all these years she and I still can't agree on everything!)

One of the things that made Jan and me different from the other male-female duets of the day was the fact that when we performed our songs onstage or on television we'd always look directly at one another rather than looking out into the audience or staring head-on into the TV camera. Much of our material was the intimate boy-talks-to-girl, girl-talks-to-boy type, and somehow it always bothered me to perform it staring away from the person I was supposed to be communicating with. But more times than not, it was extremely difficult for me to look directly into Jan's eyes and keep a straight face while reciting or singing those highly personal songs. I'd always think about something that had happened on the bus on the way to the show or some goofy thing we had been talking about backstage, and I'd start laughing. Jan was just too much of a buddy for me to be very serious with her. Finally, after far too many times of my cracking up and laughing in the middle of our serious songs, I hit upon what I thought would be the perfect solution. I'd pick out a spot on Jan's forehead and stare at it rather than trying to look her directly in the eyes when we sang. It was the only way I knew to act serious and not break into uncontrollable laughter.

From the audience no one could tell I wasn't looking Jan directly in the eyes, but she could tell it. Try sometime talking to a person just a few feet away and look at their forehead instead of into their eyes while you're speaking to them. It'll drive them crazy. She'd beg me every night, "*Please* look me in the eyes," but I couldn't do it.

Finally, on the last day of a long Canadian tour, she couldn't take it any longer. She went out that afternoon and bought a copy of *Mad* magazine and found a picture of the most repulsive, disgusting bloodshot eye you could ever imagine. And in her dressing room before the show she cut the eye out of the magazine and glued it to the spot on her forehead where I usually stared. Then she combed her hair down over the paper eye, and I never knew it was there.

About halfway through our closing song, "For Loving You," when I was staring at her forehead and reciting the part about how much I loved her and how much I needed her, she slowly started to move her hand up to her face and gently began sweeping her hair off to one side. And then in a soft whisper that only I could hear she said slowly, "I said, 'Look me in the eye, dammit!'"

Well, I totally lost it. There I stood staring into the most hideous picture of an eye I had ever seen. Right in the middle of Jan's forehead! I knew immediately what she had done and why, and I went into convulsions right there on the stage. The audience, of course, hadn't noticed a thing, and they were totally stunned to see this long-legged hillbilly all of a sudden begin to flop and fall all over the stage. But I honestly could not help it.

I finally began to gather my composure enough to explain to the silent crowd what had happened. Once they understood, they laughed as hard as I did. Jan had made her point. From that moment on I was afraid *not* to look her in the eyes ever again.

Following the success of "For Loving You," we had several more hit duets together, including "If It's All the Same to You," a country version of the Supremes' "Someday We'll Be Together," and a song we cowrote with her son Corky called "Dissatisfied." We even recorded the original version of "Satin Sheets" as a duet long before Jeanne Pruitt hit big with it as a solo, but we didn't have enough sense to release it anywhere except in an album. We recorded a gospel album together, and our TV show grew to become one of the most widely seen of all the country shows in syndication. On several occasions the various country music fan magazines and trade publications around the country named us country music's Duet of the Year.

People have asked me for years why Jan and I broke up and stopped singing together, and I've simply said that Jan wanted to pursue her own solo career. That's only partly right. Actually, Jan and I split after the death of our manager, Hubert Long, in 1972. We disagreed deeply over who should handle our careers at that point, and it turned into something we simply could not resolve. I felt strongly one way, and she apparently felt equally strongly another way. We decided it was best to part professionally while we could still be friends. It was a good decision because today I don't have a better friend in the world than Jan Howard.

In many respects I didn't want to try and find a replacement for Jan after we split. I wanted to tour with just the band for a while. But the promoters of our concert dates had become so used to my show's being a complete package that my agent was afraid if I didn't continue with myself, the band, Jimmy Gateley (who had become a featured act himself), and a girl singer, it would hurt our bookings. Plus I did need to add a new girl to the TV shows. So I launched a nationwide talent search, complete with tons of publicity, to try and locate the best female artist available.

As soon as the word got out that I was looking for a singer, hundreds upon hundreds of applications began pouring in from female singers all over the world. I sifted through every single one of them, but I ended up hiring someone who didn't even know the search was going on.

Mary Lou Turner was performing in relative obscurity on the *Jamboree USA* show in Wheeling, West Virginia, when I saw an album review of her newest release in *CashBox* magazine. The review, which was superb, reminded me that I had seen and heard Mary Lou on several occasions when I had appeared as a guest in Wheeling and that I had been impressed with her talent. I phoned Glenn Reeves, talent director at the *Jamboree*, and asked if he'd mind my talking to her about the job. He said no, even gave me her telephone number, and I gave her a call.

"Why haven't you applied for the job?" I asked when I got her on the line.

"What job?" she replied.

I explained that Jan and I had decided to go our separate ways, and I told her I was looking for someone to take Jan's place. We'd be working a show in Vero Beach, Florida, in a few days, I explained, and if she'd like to go along and sing a few songs and let me listen to her, I'd be glad to let that serve as her audition. That is, I said, if she were interested in working with me at all.

She said she was most definitely interested and took me up on my offer. She came to Nashville, had dinner with Becky and me in our home, asked a million questions about the job and all it might involve, then rode to Florida with me and the band on the bus. When we got to the show in Vero Beach, however, she walked out on stage and promptly forgot the words to the song she'd come all that distance to sing. She thought for sure she'd blown her big chance, but I thought she covered it up so well and handled the situation in such a professional manner that I hired her right on the spot.

Mary Lou stayed with our show for six years. She was a delightful lady to work with, pleasant to be around, and my fans liked a lot. When I first hired her, I envisioned her singing only on the television shows and touring with us on the road. I hadn't intended for us to make records together, thinking it might not be fair to all concerned for her to come along so close on the heels of my recording career with Jan. ("Mary Lou broke you and Jan up, didn't she?" was a comment I'd already heard more than once during those days.) But I wrote a song while we were on tour in England in 1975 that I knew was a smash. It was one of those songs that didn't care who sang it, it was going to be a hit anyhow. I figured Mary Lou and I might as well have the hit as anybody, so when we got home we cut it. I was right. The song was called "Sometimes."

In the lyrics I would say to her:

Hello beautiful . . . Are you married?

And she would reply:

Sometimes . . .

The plot thickened from there. Not only did the song go to No. 1 on the charts, it put a lot of Bill-and-Jan rumors to rest for good!

Mary Lou and I followed "Sometimes" with another hit duet called "That's What Made Me Love You," a song that nobody remembers by that title. Everybody calls it "Champagne in a Dixie Cup" or "Motel in Dallas," two of the key phrases from the lyrics of the song. Later, we had some chart success with "Where Are You Going, Billy Boy?" and after that with "I'm Way Ahead of You," a clever song in the same vein as "Sometimes," but one where we each anticipated and interrupted what the other had to say.

But Mary Lou didn't just record the duets with me. She signed her own recording contract with Decca/MCA and a couple of times she came real close to having a hit record herself. Her version of my song "It's Different with You" got high in the charts but never managed to get over that hump that separates minor hit records from major ones. Everybody in the business, disc jockeys, show promoters, newspaper critics, believed in Mary Lou, though, and figured it was just a matter of time before she'd hit big on her own. But it never quite happened.

There came a time when she finally began to wonder, as Jan had sometimes wondered before her, if being primarily known as "Bill Anderson's girl singer" wasn't more of a detriment to her than it was an aid. Eventually she decided that if she were ever going to make it on her own in a solo career she needed to give it a try while the opportunities gleaned from our years together were still there. She left me in 1979 and went out on her own. She recorded some good records, but they never were quite commercial enough to help her turn the corner. After a while she quit singing country and turned to gospel music. Then one day a couple of years ago she decided that maybe it might be best if she moved away from Nashville altogether. She and her husband, David, and their two children packed up and moved to Branson, Missouri, where she began singing during the summer months with Boxcar Willie's show. David hired on as Boxcar's full-time piano player. It must be agreeing with her because the last time I saw Mary Lou she looked happier and seemed to be more at peace than I had known her to be in years.

I've had a couple of other interesting experiences with female singers in my lifetime.

In August 1963, when "Still" was at its peak and people figured anybody with a record that big must know the answer to everything, I was asked to help judge a talent contest at a country music park called Frontier Ranch just east of Columbus, Ohio. The deal was that I'd appear on the show myself that afternoon, sing a few songs, and then take a seat alongside two or three local dignitaries out in the audience and help them decide who among the area's hopeful young artists was the most talented. The winner would then be invited back to sing on our night show and would be richer for her efforts. The promoters of the contest spared no expense. First prize was five shiny silver dollars.

But it turned out to be no contest at all, not after a tiny, young lady with long blonde hair and sparkling blue eyes walked out onstage wearing a white-fringed homemade cowgirl outfit and white boots, playing a guitar almost as big as she was, and singing like nothing that I or any of the other judges had ever heard before. Three notes into her song, the five silver dollars had a home.

The song she sang was one Jean Shepard had made popular called "I Thought of You," but it was the singer and not the song that turned all the heads. None of us could believe such a big voice was coming out of such a petite lady. I actually wondered for a minute if she were pantomiming somebody else's record. She sounded that good.

Her name was Connie Smith. Constance June Meader Smith, to be exact, and I told her backstage after the contest was over that if she ever wanted to come to Nashville and try to make it in the music business I'd be there to try and help her. I knew instantly she had the talent it took to be successful, and I told her so.

But no, she said, she didn't think that was what she wanted to do right then. She hadn't been married very long, she had a new baby boy, and she was happy just being a housewife and a mother. She travelled once a week or so over to West Virginia to sing on a television show, and that was about all she cared to involve herself with right now, thank you very much. And I told her if she ever changed her' mind to let me know.

That was about it. In fact, I didn't even see her again until one Sunday afternoon in January of the following year. I was performing at the Municipal Auditorium in Canton, Ohio, and she and her husband, Jerry, drove through a blinding snowstorm from their home in Warner, Ohio, to come see me. They had been thinking more and more about my offer to help Connie launch a singing career, and they wanted to talk with me about it. That is, if I were still interested. I assured them that I was, and the three of us sloshed our way through the snow to a small nearby restaurant between the matinee and evening performances to have dinner and continue our discussion. Connie confessed that she'd been thinking a lot about my offer, and if it were still open, then maybe now was the right time for her to give the music business a full-time shot. I told her it wasn't going to be easy, but I was game if she was. We trudged back to the auditorium through more snow, making plans for her and Jerry to come to Nashville in the spring.

(I've often thought it somewhat ironic that Connie and I reached our decision where we did and when we did. The auditorium I was working that day was the same one Hank Williams had been en route to on New Year's Eve, 1952, when he'd died in the backseat of his car near Oak Hill, West Virginia. And the very same day Connie Smith came to Canton to see me, a group of four young singers calling themselves the Kingsmen had driven up from southwest Virginia through that same snowstorm to audition as background singers for Johnny Cash. When Connie and I got back to the auditorium after dinner, we stood in the wings and watched these four young men tear the audience apart with their unique vocal harmonies and hilarious comedy routines. Johnny hired them right there. Today they're known as the Statler Brothers.)

I left Canton and went back to Nashville to begin concentrating on writing some songs for this new female discovery of mine to sing. My first step had to be to find her a recording contract, and I knew that her having good songs would be the key. I came up with three new ones that I believed in and went to talk with Owen Bradley about the possibility of his recording her for Decca.

"She sings great, Bill," Owen said after listening to the demo tapes she'd made, "but you know I've just signed this new girl the Wilburns brought me named Loretta Lynn, and I think I need to concentrate on her right now."

"Well, I just wanted to give you the first chance at her," I replied, "and I hope you won't mind if I take her to somebody else." Owen assured me that he didn't mind at all and thanked me for my loyalty. The next move was already calculated in my mind. I wanted Chet Atkins to listen to her at RCA.

There was no way Chet could not have been impressed when he heard Connie sing, but after my manager and I played him the tapes he expressed concern about her ongoing supply of good song material.

"We've got more girl singers already than we've got good songs for them to sing," he said. "Our people are constantly looking for songs for Skeeter Davis and Norma Jean and Dottie West. If this girl hits, where are the rest of her songs going to come from? I don't have time to go looking for them."

I assured Chet that I could write hits for Connie, and those I couldn't write I'd help to find. It wasn't like me to make rash promises, but I believed in her that much and I believed in myself. I felt like the two of us were a winning combination. Chet agreed to let me give it a whirl.

We began to lay the foundation. Connie took her first airplane trip and flew to Nashville in March to appear on the *Ernest Tubb Midnight Jamboree*. In May she came back to town to record some demos, in June she returned to sign her RCA contract, and in July she came to sing. To *really* sing!

Connie's first recording session for RCA Victor Records took place July 16, 1964, not even one full year after the talent contest at Frontier Ranch. True to my word, I provided three of the first four songs she recorded: "I'm Ashamed of You," "The Threshold," (cowritten with my friend Chuck Goddard), and "Once a Day." She cut them in that order. The fourth song, written by Willie Nelson and Hank Cochran, was called "Darling Are You Ever Coming Home?"

Weldon Myrick, Jimmy Lance, and Snuffy Miller from my band all played on the session. The producer, Bob Ferguson, was on staff at RCA, but he said since I knew Connie better than he did at the time and since the songs she'd be singing were mostly mine anyhow, he'd allow me to have a good deal of input into what went onto the tape if I wanted to. It turned out to be a collaborative effort on everybody's part. We all got excited and pitched in. Then when the session was over and the tapes began to circulate among the RCA executives over the next few days, the whole company started to grow as excited as we were about the future of the little girl with the big voice.

There was no doubt in any of our minds but that the most commercial record we'd made was "Once a Day." RCA agreed, coupled it with "The Threshold," and released it to the disc jockeys in late August. Most of them loved it and put it on the air immediately. Listeners started calling in and asking to hear it again. It began to play like crazy on jukeboxes, and it was making cash registers ring at record shops all across the country. It raced up the charts like wildfire and the week of the annual DJ Convention and Grand Ole Opry Birthday Celebration in November "Once a Day" became the No. 1 song in the nation. And Connie Smith was suddenly the hottest new act in country music.

From that point on things broke fast and furious. I signed Connie to a management contract, arranged for the Wil-Helm Agency to handle her concert bookings, and the career which she hadn't even been sure she'd wanted only a few months before, shifted into high gear.

Looking back on it now, I guess a lot of it happened too fast. One day this immensely gifted, beautiful young lady is a wife and a new mother and in less than a year she's got the No. 1 record in the country and people are saying she's the greatest thing since sliced bread. George Jones, who had always been Connie's idol as a singer, was going around saying Connie Smith was *his* favorite singer. It often became more than the shy little housewife could cope with.

Connie says now that she never had time to learn, never had time to build her career one brick, one step at a time like most artists do. She had hit the ground running before she even knew what track she was on.

"I didn't have any idea what was happening," she confessed to me one night not long ago sitting in my dressing room backstage at the Opry. "I even started feeling guilty because I felt like here I was having all this success and I hadn't earned it. I hadn't paid any dues. It really messed my head up, too. I'd go onstage and see somebody like Loretta Lynn standing over in the wings watching me, and I'd forget the words to songs I had sung a thousand times. Then I'd start to withdraw, to hide because I felt guilty and I was so insecure. People started thinking I was stuck up but really I was just scared!"

I helped to get her guest spots on the Grand Ole Opry and eventually an invitation to join the cast as a regular. She began to appear on national television, starred on the *Jimmy Dean Show* when it was the hottest country program on television, and flew to California several times to appear as a guest on the *Lawrence Welk Show*. She was once even offered the chance to become a regular member of the Welk cast but turned it down. I had trouble understanding why.

"The show's not country enough," was her answer at the time, "and they make me sing standing too far away from the band. I can't hear." I thought she was making a mistake and told her so. It was years before she finally admitted the real reason she didn't take the job was because it nearly killed her to leave her young son and fly all the way to California.

She began to tour, taking her husband and her boy with her whenever she could, but often having to leave them behind for days, weeks, even months at a time. This was a part of the business she hadn't counted on, and she didn't like it at all. Even as the world was beating a path to her doorstep and calling hers the Cinderella story of the decade, Cinderella herself was slowly beginning to grow very confused and very unhappy.

From the beginning I liked Connie a lot personally and tried to help her, to talk with her, to explain this crazy business to both her and her husband as best as I could, but I didn't ever seem to get through. I'd tell her how she had the opportunity millions of people would die for, and she'd just shrug. I'd make suggestions as to how she might better balance her family life and her career. I'd talk to her about saying and doing the right things with the fans and with people in the industry, but nothing worked. She was quickly gaining a reputation of being short and snappy with the fans and uncooperative with the media. I'd talk to her about it until I was blue in the face, but most of the time it was like talking to a stone wall. She says now it was just a major case of insecurity, but I'm not sure I'd have believed that at the time. I didn't see how anyone with a voice like hers could be insecure about anything. The lady could flat-out sing. Lord, how she could sing!

By the time her second record was released, another song of mine called "Then and Only Then," she was booked constantly. The world was literally her oyster, yet she seemed to dwell in perpetual frustration. "I was stubborn," she says now. "I don't know why. I guess I was just born that way."

I remember clearly the day she was about to leave on a long tour to sing her first record and promote her second one, and I handed her a stack of several hundred postcards.

"Here, these are addressed to disc jockeys all over the country," I told her, "and they're all ready to mail. All I want you to do is send a few of them each day wherever you are on the tour. Just write a couple of short lines . . . you know. 'Thanks, Tom, for playing "Once a Day." Sure hope you like my new record. "Then and Only Then." Love, Connie Smith.' And drop them in the mailbox at the hotel. That's all there is to it, and the guys will love you for it. You'll have another No. 1 smash before you know it!"

I thought she'd be thrilled, but she looked at me as if I'd just told her she had to go to Alaska without an overcoat. "I'm not going to do that," she snapped. "If I have to do that, I'll just quit this business and go back to Ohio." You could have blown me over with a feather.

Looking back on it now I realize I probably should have told her to go on back to Ohio. There was no way she'd have gone, and deep down I knew it.

"I just didn't have any concept of the business," she admits today. "I thought something like mailing those postcards would be like trying to *buy* the dj's approval. I didn't have the sense to know it would be showing them I appreciate their help. I didn't have a fan club for years because I didn't want the fans to feel like they were obligated to buy my records or come to my shows. I never wanted to consider myself a product. But I know now that I am a product. I just have to be able to separate where Connie Smith the product stops and Connie Smith the person begins."

As Connie's manager, my idea was to try to help her build a career that would last, one that would be more than a flash in the pan, and I knew that kind of a career needed roots, it needed a foundation laid not only in good music but in good will. And I continued to try and help her until her attitudes finally became more than I could handle. One day I just said to heck with it. I took the contract I had with her and tore it into tiny little pieces, laid the pieces in the palm of her hand, wished her well, and walked away.

It might sound funny after all I've just written, but Connie Smith is still and will probably always be my favorite female country singer. And she's one of my favorite people. She's more than paid me back for any help I might have given her in the beginning. At last count she had recorded forty-something songs of mine, including one entire album entitled *Connie Smith Sings Bill Anderson*. I saw her go through the unhappy phase of her life, two failed marriages, repeated bouts with depression, and although she never knew it, I hurt right along with her. Then when she turned to her faith and sang nothing but gospel music for a while, I rejoiced with her. I hoped every day she'd somehow be able to find the peace she was looking for.

Today I think she's there. She's back singing country music at the Opry, carrying a six-piece band and travelling the road on a limited schedule. The little boy she was holding in her arms that day at Frontier Ranch has now made her a grandmother. He lives in Holland, is married to a lovely blonde from Norway, and works as a missionary. Her third marriage is closing in on twenty years and seems to be rooted in solid ground.

Sometimes, though, I look at Connie and I wonder if she appreciates my getting her into this business or if she hates me for it. She says that over the years she's done a little of both. "For so long I blamed the business for all my problems," she says, "but that was before I had the guts to look at myself."

I hope she's happy because to me she's a remarkable lady. And I'll promise you there's not a one of those hotshot new female singers in country music today who can wrap their voice around a country song any better.

Not long after my experiences with Connie Smith, I tried to help another female singer break into the music business. The story didn't turn out quite the same way.

A friend of mine had just taken over an important producing job with a major record label and was looking for a girl to record. He called and asked me if I knew where there might be another Connie Smith out there somewhere. I remembered a girl I had seen while out on tour not long before, and in an effort to help my friend I called the girl and asked her if she'd be interested in recording and perhaps even relocating in Nashville. She sounded thrilled, and I suggested she come to town as soon as possible.

She did, and the night before I was to introduce her to my buddy, the record producer, I thought it might be best if I talked with her a while about everything that was going to take place. She was very young, totally inexperienced in the business, but I knew if she played her cards right she could be well on the way to having all her dreams of a career in music come true. I wanted to make certain she understood that.

I took her out to a nice, quiet dinner, and we talked. I tried carefully to explain to her how she needed to say and do all the right things, how she was about to have the chance some girls would kill for.

After dinner we walked back to the lobby of her hotel and I continued talking, more like a big brother than anything else. "You've got to keep your nose clean in this town and earn their respect," I emphasized. "You've got the talent . . . just sing your songs and you can be a big star. But once you start hopping in and out of bed with every producer, singer, musician, and executive in this town, they'll write you off in a minute. Do you understand that?"

She looked me right in the eye and said, "I sure do. And I appreciate you telling me that, too." And then she got up from where she'd been seated, walked over to where I was standing, reached out, and touched me on the arm. She looked seductively up into my eyes, a look on her face as serious as cancer.

"Now," she whispered softly, sighing as if the weight of a heavy burden had been lifted off her shoulders, "you wanta come up to my room?"

15

I read somewhere once that Anderson is the sixth or seventh most common last name in the United States. I know that in nearly every telephone book I've ever opened I've been able to find at least one Bill Anderson or William Anderson or John William or James William Anderson. I don't have an unusual name.

In the beginning of my show business career I thought that was an asset. I wouldn't have to try and come up with a stage name. My real name was easy enough to pronounce and easy enough to remember. But I have found out over the years that it's also easy to forget and easy to get confused. I've been called Bill Alexander, Bill Andrews, or Bill Henderson more times than I care to remember, and once in Wisconsin a lady from a local TV station was introducing me onstage and forgot my name completely.

"You folks are gonna love this next act," she told the crowd, nervously peering over at me in the wings trying to get some kind of clue as to who I was. "He's real handsome, ladies," she stalled, "and he's wearing a gorgeous black suit." Finally, she realized she had no idea what my name was and it was not going to come to her. With a big sweeping gesture she turned toward me and said, "Come on out here, boy, and tell 'em who you are!"

Somehow I don't think that would have happened had my name been Engelbert Humperdinck, or Cleofis Thigpen, or Ferdly Crumpacker. That's why I'll always be grateful to Don Bowman, the little silver-haired comedian who joined my syndicated television show after Grandpa Jones departed. Don was the first person ever to call me "Whisperin' Bill."

In the spring of 1968 we had moved the production of our TV

show again, this time from Canada to the General Electric Broadcasting Company facility in Nashville. G.E. had taken over ownership and syndication of the show, and since they also owned WNGE-TV, the ABC affiliate at the time, it made sense for them to bring us all together under one roof. And it didn't take me long to appreciate the fact that their studios out on Murfreesboro Road were a lot closer to my house than the studios had been in Charlotte or in Canada!

On taping days we'd usually begin wandering into the station around four o'clock in the afternoon, videotape two half-hour programs before a live audience that evening beginning around eight o'clock, and by ten or eleven o'clock that night we'd be through. Don was single at the time, he slept during the daytime, and he'd usually be wide awake and raring to go when our tapings were over. Many nights after we'd finished he would wander up to the studios of WSM Radio where Ralph Emery was the all-night country music disc jockey. He'd join Ralph on the air over the fifty-thousand-watt, clear-channel station, and Ralph would ask him what he'd been up to.

"Oh, I've been out taping TV shows with Ole Whisper," Don would reply.

"Who is 'Ole Whisper'?" Ralph would ask.

"Oh, you know Ralph, Ole Whisperin' Bill Anderson. The one who *says* all those songs!"

And in those days I guess I did "say" a lot of my songs. Actually, I sang on most of them, too, but the sing-a-little, talk-a-little format that we began to develop on "Mama Sang a Song" and "Still" distinguished me from the other country singers of the day. I'd used it on "8 X 10" and on "Five Little Fingers," and I spoke all the lyrics on "Golden Guitar." I never made a concerted effort to whisper, but neither did I want my records to sound like I was doing a commercial for a used car lot. I mostly wanted them to sound believable, and for me to do that it had to come out soft.

In those days, every disc jockey in the country listened to Ralph Emery late at night to find out what new songs he was playing (he often had advance releases from the major companies) and to listen to his personal interviews with the stars. And whatever Ralph played and whatever he said at night was repeated by the local DJ's on the smaller stations all across America the next day.

Therefore, when Ralph Emery began calling me "Whisperin' Bill," so did everybody else.

In the beginning I was sensitive to it and wasn't quite sure how to handle it. I figured maybe if I'd ignore it, it would go away. Then several of the major stars took to impersonating me in their stage acts, and I had no place to hide.

I remember well a tour when I was opening for Ferlin Husky. I'd go out on stage every night and do my bit, then retreat to the side of the stage to watch him do his. And there has never been an artist in any form of musical entertainment who could entertain an audience like Ferlin Husky could when he was right. He'd sing his hits like "Gone" and "Wings of a Dove" and then launch into his alter-ego character, Simon Crum. And Simon would do impressions of other country stars. He'd sing like Ernest Tubb and Red Foley and even Kitty Wells. But his biggest hand and his biggest laughs always came when Simon imitated Whisperin' Bill. Ferlin would slide his right leg back behind him in an exaggerated imitation of my stance on stage and whisper real breathy into the microphone and do his own rewrites of my songs. And the people who had been applauding me just a few minutes before would then be sitting out there laughing their heads off. I laughed a lot myself because it was truly funny, but down deep inside it stung me a little.

I'll always love Ferlin for picking up on my sensitivity. He came to me one night after a show and he said, "That bothers you when I imitate you, doesn't it?"

I admitted that yes, sometimes, I guessed I did.

"Well, let me tell you something," he said. "In the first place if you weren't different I wouldn't have anything to imitate. Think of all the singers who are just plain singers, and there's nothing that makes them stand out enough for anybody to imitate them. You're different and you've got your own style and people recognize it. You should be grateful for that.

"And in the second place," he continued, moving swiftly from the deep, sincere voice of Ferlin Husky to the whimsical, whiny tones of Simon Crum, "hell, if I didn't like you, I wouldn't give you the publicity!"

My attitude changed from that moment on. I became proud to be "Whisperin' Bill." It gave a special name and unique identity to someone with a very common name. It gave me a hook . . . a handle. There wasn't another Whisperin' Bill in a phone book anyplace that I knew of. I loved it. Nowadays when they imitate me, I laugh louder than anybody. In fact, if I'm on a show with someone who I know does a Bill Anderson impression when I'm not around, I'll do everything I can to get them to do it with me looking on. I once walked onstage behind Billy "Crash" Craddock with a baseball bat cocked high above his head, daring him to leave his impersonation of me out of his show. If they're going to mock me behind my back, I figure the least they can do is mock me to my face. And most of them will.

A distinctive voice like mine can also be a liability, as I have found out on more than one occasion. I lost my cool and snapped at a long-distance telephone operator out on the road one night when she couldn't get my call right. I didn't figure she knew me from Adam, but when the call finally did go through she said, "Thank you, Mr. Anderson." I had no idea she'd recognized my voice. I wanted to leave town on the next fast freight.

My face is pretty recognizable these days, too, due primarily to all the television exposure I've had over the years. But when people recognize me walking through an airport or a shopping mall, I'm never sure just where it is they know me from. Most people, of course, know me from country music. But nowadays some know me only from game shows. Others as a performer on a soap opera. Still others from my endorsements and commercials.

One of my favorite being-recognized-in-public stories occurred on an airplane when the stewardess on my flight knelt down very quietly by my seat and said, "I don't want to embarrass you, but may I please have your autograph?"

"Sure," I smiled. "What's your name?"

"Cindy," she replied.

I began to scribble on the slip of paper she handed me . . . "To Cindy—With Love—Bill Anderson."

"I have a lot of your records," she said.

"Thank you." I answered.

"And I love to watch you on TV!"

"You're very kind," I said, as I handed her the autographed paper.

"Oh my goodness!" she exclaimed when she saw what I'd written. And I could see her pretty face begin to redden.

"What's the matter?" I asked with a wide grin. "Didn't anybody ever write 'with love' to you before?"

"Oh, no, that's not it," she blushed. "It's just . . . uh . . . I thought you were Roger Miller."

I was recently checking into a large big-city hotel when the bellman helping me with my luggage decided he'd seen me somewhere before. "Did anybody ever tell you that you look like a country music singer?" he asked on the way up to my room.

"Oh, some people will tell you anything," I smiled.

"Well, I'm a big country music fan," he confessed. "and I know who you are. You're Mel Twitty, ain't you?"

Every entertainer who's been around the business a while has dozens of stories of this type, but I still enjoy collecting them and sharing them. Like the one that happened not too long ago when I stopped by a Nashville restaurant dressed in an old pair of jeans, a sweatshirt, tennis shoes, and a baseball cap, my favorite offstage wardrobe. A lady who was obviously more accustomed to seeing me on television wearing a coat and tie eased over to my table a bit hesitantly.

"Are you Bill Anderson?" she asked. I admitted that I was. "Well, I wasn't sure," she blurted out. "This is the first time I've ever seen you with clothes on!"

And then there was the lady who came down front at the Opry one night during the recent Christmas season. I was hosting a half-hour portion of the show and had just cued the announcer on the side of the stage to take over and read a commercial. I was standing quietly at center stage waiting for him to finish so I could introduce the next act when I saw her standing there with her camera poised and pointing up toward me. She looked for all the world like she was about to take my picture. Since nothing else was going on in that area of the stage at that time and since I'm a big ham anyway, I stretched out my arms, put one foot dramatically in front of the other, and shot her a big grin about a foot wide. I expected to see her flash go off at any minute. Instead she looked up at me real disgusted, dropped her camera down by her side, and said, "That's real nice, but would you mind getting out of the way. I'm trying to get a picture of the Christmas tree!"

And I'll never forget the mother who brought her eight- or nine-year-old son to see me one day at an autograph session. There had been a long line, and they had been patiently waiting their turn. When they reached the spot where I was signing pictures, I looked up and said, "Hi."

"Do it, Jason," the mother immediately said to the boy. "Do it!"

I assumed she meant for Jason to ask me for my autograph, and, figuring he might be a bit shy at that age, I reached down and roughed up his hair a little bit and said, "How you doin', Jason?" Jason never said a word. He just stood there staring at the floor.

"Do it, Jason," the mother prodded. "If you don't do it right now, I'm taking you home. Now do it!"

With that, the little boy, still looking down at the floor, began whistling. No tune, no melody, just whistling loud and rather aimlessly. I wasn't sure exactly what I was supposed to do when his mother solved the puzzle for me.

"See there," she said proudly. "When he grows up, he's going to be just like you, *Whistlin'* Bill!" I didn't have the heart to tell her she'd missed the point.

Fans, however, aren't the only people who zing me from time to time. Not long ago a "friend" pulled this one:

A waitress was pouring coffee for several of us who were killing time in a little restaurant in the town where we were to do a concert later that evening when she handed me a paper napkin and asked me to sign it. I saw her nametag and wrote, "To Nancy—Love Bill Anderson" and handed it back. She broke into a big smile and said, "Oh, thank you so much. I just love your singing. I have all of yours and Tammy's records!" And with that she walked away.

I was stunned. Suddenly it hit me, and I turned to the guy sitting next to me. "Good Lord," I said. "She thinks I'm George Jones!"

"No she doesn't," he replied. "She thinks you're Jim Bakker!"

While on the subject of mistaken identity, let me bring up another matter that never seems to go away—my relationship to country singer Lynn Anderson. For some reason, no matter how many times each of us announces that we are not kin to each other in any way, shape, form, or fashion, somebody picks up that we are man and wife, brother and sister, or—good grief!— father and daughter. Actually, we are none of the above. The next time somebody mentions it to you, please show them this page where it's written in black and white:

Lynn Anderson and Bill Anderson are not related to each other at all!

And neither of us is related to John, although the other day an airline pilot knelt down beside my seat on a flight to Nashville and asked for my autograph. "I just love your music, Mr. Anderson," he said. "Sign it 'Just-a-swinging'!"

I smiled. "That was John Anderson," I said. "My name is Bill Anderson." He didn't hear a word I said.

"Yessir," he went on. "I believe that 'Swinging' is my favorite record that was ever made. Sign it now 'Just-a-swingin', John Anderson.'"

I started to try and explain to him one more time just who I was, but then I remembered a story Burl Ives had told me one time several years ago. Seems he was having dinner in a restaurant in New York not far from the theater district when a lady who had obviously just been to see a play spied him sitting at his table. She rushed over, thrust a piece of paper and a pen onto the tablecloth in front of him, and said, "Oh, Mr. Ustinov, you were just marvelous in the play! May I please have your autograph?"

Like me, Burl started to explain. "No m'am, you see I'm . . ."

"I just believe you are my favorite performer in the whole world, Mr. Ustinov!" the lady continued, and Burl realized that nothing he could say was going to make her change her mind about who he was. So he graciously reached out, took the pen, and wrote "My best wishes, Peter Ustinov" and handed it back to her. The lady was absolutely thrilled. She thanked him profusely and walked away, never knowing she'd gotten an autograph from the great Burl Ives.

I decided I wasn't going to try and change the pilot's mind either. Besides, he liked John Anderson so much, what the heck. I signed the paper just like he told me to, "Just-a-swingin', John Anderson" and handed it back to him with a smile. He never knew the difference. But I'll bet the next time he sees ole John on TV he's going to turn to whoever is there watching with him and say, "You know, that ole boy don't look the same on TV as he does in person!"

I've been told by some people in this business that I don't have enough of the temperament of a star, that I don't have a big enough ego. They suggest I should put more distance between myself and the public, that I sign too many autographs, meet too many of my fans up close, that I'm "too available." Maybe they have a point. But I have one as well.

First, I don't ever want to be so big a star that I can't go shopping at Wal-Mart, take my family out for a hamburger, or ride the ferris wheel at the state fair without being besieged by an adoring public to the point where I'd have to retreat to my privacy elsewhere. Elvis's life was sad to me in many respects because he was a prisoner of his own success. If he wanted to go to a movie, he had to rent the whole movie theater to keep his fans away. I've heard Dolly Parton often has storekeepers come to her hotel room to fit her with clothes and shoes because she can't so much as go into a store and shop like ordinary folks. To me, that's not glamorous. It's sad. I have just enough recognition to feel good about it and to be proud of it, but I honestly don't think I would want any more.

Second, long before I was a "star" I was a "fan," and I still remember what it feels like. I've stood in line for autographs only to be brushed aside by somebody I admired, and it hurts. I've written fan letters and watched my mailbox for days on end just to get a simple reply and have been crushed when none ever came. Once when I was in the seventh or eighth grade I wrote a letter to Hank Williams and asked him to send me a list of all the records he had ever made because I wanted to be sure I had them all. Maybe he never got my letter. Maybe I sent it to the Opry at a time when he wasn't even with the Opry. Maybe my dad forgot to mail it. I don't know. All I knew was I never got an answer from my idol, and I was hurt. So hurt, in fact, that I traded all my Hank Williams 78 rpm records to a friend for all his Spike Jones records. Wonder what those Hank Williams originals would be worth today?

I don't want to sound like I'm trying to be some kind of super-hero or anything, but I've tried hard never to break anybody's heart like some of the people I admired broke mine. I'm sure I've probably slipped up somewhere along the way, and there's probably somebody out there who thinks I'm the biggest jerk in the world because I didn't cotton to them like I should have. If that's true, I'm sorry. All I know is I've signed autographs until my hand ached so bad I had to go soak it, and I've stayed at my office until long after midnight many times signing fan mail and sending out pictures. Especially to kids. I don't know that I've ever proved a thing by it, but I've done it this way far too long to think about changing now.

Having been both a disc jockey and a newspaper reporter, I have probably also had more of an understanding of the press and the electronic media than many entertainers. I've always tried to cooperate with them, too, realizing they have a job to do. Overall, the media have been good to me, but I was once burned awfully bad.

It was in the mid-seventies just after John Denver and Olivia Newton-John had won some major CMA awards, and several of the more traditional country artists were upset. In a move that was totally unrelated but awkwardly timed, George Jones and Tammy Wynette called a large group of us together at their big Franklin Road mansion one night not long after the awards show to discuss the music business in general and to socialize a bit. Out of this meeting was born an organization called ACE, the Association of Country Entertainers. We decided we needed to be closer as a group and have some picnics and parties during the year, there was some talk about our trying to start a retirement home for country entertainers, and that's about all there was to it. However, the press was not invited nor allowed to attend our gathering. They had no idea what was going on, but some of them got together and decided we must be perpetrating some kind of evil against the pop stars who had won country music awards. And they had a field day.

They wrote that we were bitter and angry and that we'd had this secret meeting to discuss boycotting the Country Music Association, maybe even pulling out of the CMA to start our own organization. There was no foundation whatsoever for the things they were writing, but they began to get attention and attention sells newspapers. So they didn't let up. In an effort to combat the lies they were writing and saying about us, we met at George and Tammy's again and decided to hold a press conference the following day to set the record straight. The other entertainers elected me to be spokesman for the group.

I faced a battery of microphones and cameras early the next morning and read from a statement prepared by a lawyer who had been at our meetings as the invited guest of a major performer. I don't remember everything I said or exactly how I said it, but it was something to the effect that we weren't mad at anybody and we weren't bitter and we just decided this was a good time to organize all the entertainers into a group. After all, the music publishers had an organization and the talent agents had an organization, why couldn't the entertainers themselves have an organization? It was as simple as that.

After the press conference was over, however, a couple of reporters cornered some of the other stars who were there and asked them their personal opinions about the recent CMA awards. One of the artists, and I honestly don't know which one, supposedly made the statement, "Outsiders are coming in here and trying to take our music away."

When the papers hit the streets that afternoon, it was quoted all over the country that, "ACE spokesman Bill Anderson says, 'They're coming in here and trying to take our music away.'" Nothing could have been further from the truth. Not only did I not *say* it, I didn't even *feel* that way. And even if I *had* felt it, I wouldn't have been stupid enough to *say* it. You cannot imagine how upset I was.

I stayed up half the night calling the papers and the wire services pleading with them to print a retraction. Nowhere on any tape recorder (and there had been dozens of them at the press conference) could they produce a copy of my saying the words I was supposed to have said. But they realized immediately that they had created a newspaper-selling monster, they were getting tons of publicity from it, and they loved it. They weren't about to let something as relatively insignificant as the truth interfere with their fun.

But for me it was too late. By the next morning I was getting phone calls from people all over the country calling me everything from a fool to a pinko commie pig. Paul Harvey talked about me on his newscast. At the time I had a record that was No. 5 with a bullet in the national charts, the "bullet" signifying that the song was still strongly on the rise. The next week it fell to No. 11 with no bullet. The following week it disappeared from the charts forever.

A columnist for *Billboard* magazine wrote a lengthy piece taking me to task within the industry, and there were actually radio programmers who read her garbage and said they'd never play another Bill Anderson record. I wrote a personal letter to every major station in the country telling them *my* side. Most of them, once they heard the truth, believed me.

Tom T. Hall wrote me a very nice letter in which he said he really felt sorry for me "in the controversy over the good work you did with ACE and the bad publicity you received in return." He went on to say, "I am sure there are people who must look after their own interests in writing these press releases, but it's a pity that they must make someone else look small in order to make themselves look big." I appreciated his sensitivity to my plight and, more than that, the fact that he took time out to write and let me know.

In time it all blew over and things returned to normal, but I learned in that one episode how powerful and how vicious the press can sometimes be. And how helpless most of us really are to fight it.

Because I have never deliberately isolated myself from the public and because of my well-publicized role in the establishment of Connie Smith's career, I have also been for years a target for every would-be singer and songwriter in America. They all seem to think if they can just get a tape and a picture and a bio into my magic hands, I can wave a wand and make them all stars overnight. It ain't so, Joe.

In the first place, if I listened to every song I receive and tried to help every aspiring artist who asks me, I'd have no time for my own life or my own career. It pleases me to have been able to have helped out a few folks over the years, but that's something I've done as a sideline to my other activities and not something I ever intended to make a career out of. But still the requests keep coming.

"Please help me," a man wrote recently. "I want more than anything to be a songwriter but I only write the words. Can't you please take my words and write lyrics to them?"

Another gentleman cornered me one night at a rodeo in Texas and shoved a couple of copies of his new single record into my hand. His name was something like John Smith and his record was on the J.S. label, which was a dead giveaway that he'd paid for his session and his record pressing himself. But he had an unusual angle.

"I want you to help me," he pleaded, "because, you see, this record was almost on RCA. Yes sir," he said in a whisper as if Chet Atkins were listening at the door, "it was almost on RCA."

"What happened?" I asked.

"Well, they said they'd release it except I was too well unknown!"

As far as I know, he still is.

The late Tex Ritter, as kind, gentle, and benevolent a man as I've ever known, was like me in his attitude toward the press and the public. But like all of us, Tex also had his limits. Once he was approached during a private moment by a well-meaning fan who said, "Mr. Ritter, I hate to bother you . . ." whereupon, before the fan could finish, Tex snorted, "Then why *do* you?"

On the other hand, I often saw Tex display the patience of Job. Once he was being interviewed for a newspaper story while he was backstage getting dressed for a performance, and he invited the reporter to make himself at home. This he did, following Tex to the mirror as he tied his tie, sitting beside him on a wooden bench as Tex shined his boots, and finally trailing him right up to the urinal in the men's room. As "America's Most Beloved Cowboy" reached for his fly, the reporter asked, "Tex, what's the main difference between country music stars and pop music stars?"

Before Tex could answer, a fan burst into the room waving a piece of paper and a pen and demanding, "Hey, Tex, gimmee your autograph."

Undaunted, Mr. Ritter calmly let go of his zipper, took the pen, wrote his name on the paper, affixed the date of the occasion underneath, and returned it to his admirer. He then turned back open-flied to the reporter and said, "In answer to your question, sir, we are *accessible!*"

16

Most of my life I've been lousy at keeping secrets, but until about the time "Still" became a big hit, I didn't tell anybody in Nashville except my very closest friends that I had been to college. Never mind that I had paid most of my own tuition with money I had earned playing music and working in radio, I just didn't want the subject brought up. It wasn't that I was ashamed of it, but rather I was afraid my college degree might keep me from being accepted by others in the music business. Most of the pickers and singers from the late fifties and early sixties simply had not had the opportunity I'd had to attend college. Most of them came from rural or small-town backgrounds, many had no formal education past grade school or early high school, having had to drop out in order to work and help support their families. Music had been their magic carpet off the treadmill to oblivion, and I didn't want anybody thinking that I thought I was better than they were just because I happened to have been lucky enough to finish sixteen years of school.

In fact, when I first got to Nashville I didn't talk very much about my background at all. Besides my insecurities about my having gone to college, I was also very sensitive to the fact that I had not grown up on a farm. Or even in the country. Except for the short time we had lived with my grandparents in Griffin, I had been a city boy all of my life. How honest would they think it was in Nashville for a kid from the city to be trying to write and sing country music? Today it wouldn't matter at all, but back then I didn't want to take any chances. I figured the less that was known about me and where I had come from, the better off I'd be.

I don't know what role, if any, my education had to play in my initial approach to show business, but from the very beginning I was able to recognize this industry as being just what the name implies: half show and half business. And in my early days I spent whatever time I wasn't spending trying to absorb the show part attempting to learn all I could about the business itself.

I was left somewhat to my own devices, however, because for several years after I got into the business I did not have a manager. And in show business a good manager is almost a necessity.

An artist can't go around telling people how good he is, but his manager can. Besides, a creative person should be free to create and let his manager worry about the day-to-day dealings with the business world, the contracts, the lawyers, the accountants. And, as my first manager told me, a good artist-manager relationship has to be almost like a marriage. It requires a lot of faith in the other person and a lot of give and take on both sides.

In the beginning I had a hard time finding very many people who believed in me as an artist. There was no doubt I could write hit songs and all the music publishers went out of their way to court me, but as a performer I was someone with a unique style as opposed to someone with a technically great singing voice. I was different, and sometimes difference has to grow on people.

Buddy Killen helped guide me in my early career decisions, introducing me to talent agents and promoters and helping me obtain my first appearances on the Opry, but Buddy was not in the talent management business. He was a music publisher. Roger Miller and I both tried long and hard to convince Buddy to open a talent agency division at Tree Publishing because we both wanted to make a home there for all facets of our careers, but Buddy, probably very wisely, declined.

In those days in Nashville one person often functioned as both an artist's manager and his booking agent, and one of the most successful and well-respected of these was a gentleman named Hubert Long. Hubert was a protégé of Colonel Tom Parker, having worked for the Colonel long before the Elvis days when Parker had managed country stars Eddy Arnold and Hank Snow. Hubert had left Colonel Tom to start his own talent management firm and booking agency in the early fifties, and when I arrived on the scene he was the guiding force behind the super-successful careers of both Ferlin Husky and Faron Young. Unlike most of the other talent agents in town, however, he didn't try to sign every artist who knocked on his door seeking representation. He was very particular about his artists, deliberately keeping his roster and his office staff small and manageable. It was almost an honor for an artist to say he was represented by Hubert Long. By late 1962 I had knocked around town working in and out of the various agencies long enough to know that I wanted Hubert Long to manage me and guide my career. But how was I going to be able to convince him to do it? That became the $64,000 question.

I knew Hubert was never going to sign to represent me based on my singing ability alone. But two other things caught his eye. First, my songwriting contract was about to expire at Tree, and Hubert was in the process of starting a new company called Moss Rose Publications. Obviously he wanted me to write songs for his company. In fact, in true managerial style he told me early on that if he were ever to agree to manage me he would want to manage every phase of my career. Translated, that meant he wanted to publish my songs. I wasn't too sure about that for a while. The second thing that worked in my favor, however, was the fact that Hubert Long was very attracted to my attitude toward country music as a business.

I remember well the day it all came to a head. I had been sitting in his office since early afternoon listening to him work his magic on the telephone, booking concert dates right and left for Faron and Ferlin.

Between a break in his phone calls, we started talking about what we'd each done the night before. Hubert, a confirmed bachelor who never spent very many dull moments in his life, was telling me about a party he'd attended and a special new lady in his life. He then asked me what I'd been up to.

"I stayed up until after midnight writing disc jockeys," I told him.

"What do you mean 'writing disc jockeys'?" he asked.

"Oh, I just drop short notes to all the radio guys I've met in my travels and thank them for playing my records. And then if I've got anything new coming out, I'll ask them to give it a special listen when it comes in. That's all."

"Who pays for all that?" Hubert asked.

"What do you mean?"

"Well, who pays for the postage?"

"I do."

"And the letterheads and the envelopes?"

"Same person."

"And who does the typing?" he asked, not sure of what he was hearing.

"I do," I told him truthfully.

"Boy, you sure must want to be in this business awfully bad," he said.

"More than anything else in this world," I confessed.

He sat there a minute and just looked at me. "Well, I've got a feeling anybody who wants it that bad is going to make it," he smiled. "And I think I'd like to be your manager!"

Before I could thank him, laugh, faint, or jump up in the air, he reached into his desk drawer and pulled out a big roll of postage stamps. "Here, use these next time," he said, tossing them into my lap. Then he stood up and we shook hands. That handshake was the only contract we ever had, and it lasted for ten years until Hubert's untimely death from a brain tumor in 1972. He was only forty-eight years old.

I'm not sure Nashville will ever see another Hubert Long. He was a big man physically, standing well over six feet tall and at one time probably tipping the scales at close to 250 pounds. He had slimmed down to around 185 or 190 by the time I met him, however, after having been diagnosed as diabetic and told by his doctors that he had to rid himself of the excess baggage. He had only a few strands of sandy hair left to comb across the top of his perpetually tanned head, but his quick smile and genteel, almost chivalrous warmth charmed everyone who ever met him. He was a shrewd businessman, but more important than his business acumen, Hubert Long brought *class* to our business at a time when many people looked upon us all as a bunch of hayseeds. He was impeccably honest, he'd bend over backwards to be fair to his artists and his clients alike, and he had a genuine affinity for the people he represented.

We artists were Hubert's family, and he was available to each of us twenty-four hours a day, seven days a week. Many's the time I called him in the wee hours from some tiny dot on the map with a problem of some sort, and he never failed to help me solve it. When I separated from my first wife, it was Hubert who scouted and found me a place to live on Old Hickory Lake. "Being close to the water will be good for you," he declared. Because he had lived high upon the banks of the Cumberland River for years himself, I knew he spoke from experience. "The water will help you relax and give you a good frame of mind so you can create," he said. He was right, and I lived in the house he found for me for twelve years. Some of my biggest hit songs were written inside those walls.

When Becky and I married, Hubert was my best man. But he didn't stop there. I always accused him of "producing" our wedding because he knew we needed dishes and silverware, and he told each of the invited guests just what gifts to bring. Had it been anybody but Hubert, such actions might have been considered gauche or ill-mannered, but everybody just laughed and went along.

Hubert, along with me, George Hamilton IV, and Bud Wendell, was in on the original conversation that eventually led to the establishment of the country music Fan Fair, the annual pilgrimage that now draws some twenty-five thousand country fans to Nashville each June, an event which has replaced all others as *the* major gathering of our industry. The four of us were standing in a stairwell at the old Capitol Park Inn in downtown Nashville during the yearly Disc Jockey Convention complaining that we couldn't get close enough to the disc jockeys to talk and visit with them because of all the fans who'd come in. "Maybe we need to have a separate convention just for the fans," one of us said. Bud's eyes lit up. "You know, that's actually not a bad idea," he said. "Maybe we should give it some thought." Less than two years later Fan Fair was a reality.

Hubert served as both president and chairman of the board of the Country Music Association and was one of the primary sounding boards used by the management of WSM in the planning and building of Opryland. He didn't live to see Fan Fair become a reality or to see the doors to the new Opry House swing open, but he left an indelible mark on this business and on me personally. The night he was named posthumously to the Country Music Hall of Fame in 1979, I stood on the front row of the Opry House with tears in my eyes and cheered louder than anybody.

When Hubert died, I lost not only my manager but a business partner (I finally had signed to write for his Moss Rose Publications, and we also had gone into some other music publishing ventures together, including the establishment of my own publishing firm, Stallion Music, Inc.) and a dear friend as well. How would I ever be able to replace such a loss? Fortunately, someone was looking over me again.

In 1970, my close friend, Dean Booth, a brilliant young attorney from Atlanta, had been in New York representing ABC Television in some kind of legal capacity. One night over dinner with one of the vice presidents of the network, Dean casually mentioned my name and my work in the music business around Nashville.

"Bill Anderson is one of the most successful artists in the country music business today," Dean told the executive, "and he has one of the top syndicated television shows on the air. But everything he does comes out of Nashville. He very seldom appears on the networks. He needs to be seen on some of the bigger shows. I'd like to help him find somebody up here in New York, where all you heavyweights in the industry are located, to work with him and advise him and help him expand his career. Do you know of anyone here who might be able to help him?"

The ABC representative, who didn't know Bill Anderson from Bill Monroe, recommended that Dean contact a man named Bobby Brenner. Bobby, he said, had been a major talent agent in New York for years, working with large companies like Music Corporation of America and Ashley Famous Artists, and representing such clients as Ed Sullivan, Eddie Albert, Peter Duchin, and others. But he had recently turned his back on the corporate life and gone into business for himself as an entertainment consultant. He might be just what Dean was looking for.

So Dean gave Bobby a call, arranged to go by his office in Manhattan the next day to talk with him, and then scheduled me to fly to New York in a couple of weeks to meet with Bobby myself.

From that very simple beginning came not only a whole new world of television exposure for me and a dozen or more new avenues for my career, but this energetic, brilliant little man from

New York ended up becoming my manager, my business partner, my very close friend, and eventually even godfather to my son.

But when Bobby and I met for the first time and discussed my objectives and my career goals, there were a lot of unanswered questions on both sides. He didn't just automatically jump in and agree to manage my career. In the first place he'd never even seen me perform and knew very little about me in general. He had once been Ed Sullivan's representative in Nashville, responsible for booking the country artists who had crossover hit records onto the *Ed Sullivan Show*, but even with the success of "Still," somehow our paths had never crossed. He needed to know much more than he did in regard to what Bill Anderson was all about.

Likewise, I knew very little about him. I'd spent more than ten years living in Nashville and listening to all the horror stories of "those terrible New Yorkers who come down here and rip off the poor hillbillies," so my approach to him was a cautious one, too. I kept my eyes and ears wide open.

Finally I realized after several rounds of verbal sparring that if we were ever going to get anywhere in this relationship we'd have to quit tiptoeing around each other and get down to business. So I crossed my fingers, plunged in and did what he asked me to do.

First, Bobby said, he wanted to see me onstage. So I arranged for him and a press agent friend of his, Bernie Ilson, also from New York, to fly to western Pennsylvania and join me and my band for a county fair date we were to be working in the little town of Clearfield. Bernie came along because Bobby had said that if he did decide to represent me, one of the first things he would want me to do was to hire a press agent. He figured if he'd never read about me in the national magazines and newspapers, the chances were that millions of other people hadn't either. Before he could begin to make some connections for me in the world of television, he said, we'd have to generate some publicity. It all sounded mighty big-time to me, but once I decided to make the move I became anxious to get started.

On the morning of the show in Pennsylvania, I caught a plane in Nashville and met Bobby and Bernie at the small airport in Altoona, where we rented a car and drove to the fairgrounds in Clearfield. I tried to say and do all the right things, but I was excited. I couldn't wait for Bobby and Bernie to see our show. I had told the band I was bringing these two hotshot New York agents to see us, and they were climbing the walls too. Maybe, just maybe, this was the big break we'd all been waiting for.

We were all so hyper and pumped up with energy that when I hit the stage that night and ripped into my first song, I could just see Ed Sullivan falling at my feet. As it turned out, however, fate had a plan of its own.

About two-thirds of the way through my very first number, for a reason I still don't know to this day, all the electricity on the entire fairgrounds went out. There I stood, a big smile on my face, every little hair on my head combed perfectly, dressed impeccably, with two powerhouse New York agents looking on, and I was suddenly surrounded by nothing but pitch-black darkness. Surely they'd get the power back on in a minute, I thought, but one minute became five and five minutes became ten and there I stood. The audience, a large, impressive crowd just like I'd hoped for, couldn't see us because the lights were out. They couldn't hear us because, of course, the sound system was out as well. We couldn't play our electrical instruments because there was no power to the amps. We just stood there dying a little more with every ticking second. The length of time Ed Sullivan might be willing to grovel was beginning to prey heavily on my mind.

There was a dirt racetrack between the stage where we were standing and the covered grandstand beyond. Suddenly I looked up from out of my misery and saw that a car was being driven onto the track, its headlights shining brightly up onto the stage. In a few minutes here came another car, then another, then another. Pretty soon the entire stage was bathed in the light from these six or seven automobiles.

Then I looked out and saw that the several thousand people who had been seated in the grandstand were now up and walking toward the stage. "They're gonna lynch us," I said to a fair official standing nearby. "No, they're not," he said. "They just want to come closer where they can hear."

"Hear what?" I asked him. "We don't have any power to our amplifiers. The only instruments we can play are the accoustical guitars and the banjo and the piano. And there's no P.A. system for us to even sing into. We can't do a show like that!"

But I was wrong. All those people wanted was to see us make an effort, to show them that we cared for them enough to play a couple of songs as best we could under the circumstances. They knew it wasn't our fault the power had gone out any more than it had been theirs. So with the headlights of a half-dozen automobiles providing the light and two flat-top guitars, one banjo, and a badly out-of-tune piano making the music, I stood in front of two or three thousand country music fans and two New York agents, looking sadly out of place in their neatly tailored three-piece suits, and sang my heart out into the night.

It was called making the best of a bad situation. Bobby and Bernie excitedly called it "showing them you're a pro!" They left Clearfield with us on the bus and rode to Binghamton, New York, as fascinated with us and our lifestyle as we were with them and theirs. It was the beginning of a marvelous association with each of them that lasts to this day.

To look at Bobby Brenner and me together you'd immediately call us the odd couple. I'm about six-foot-two and weigh close to 190 pounds. Bobby stands no more than five-foot-three and weighs about 135. He is Jewish, a New Yorker by way of Scranton, Pennsylvania. I'm a WASP, a Nashvillian by way of a whole bunch of wide spots in the road in the Deep South.

Because of the nature of my business, I have to be reasonably fashion- and style-conscious. I shop often for new clothes. Bobby has been known to have new collars and cuffs sewn into his old dress shirts. My hair is medium length, Bobby wears a crew-cut. I drive a late model car, Bobby drives a 1962 Ford Falcon. I love air conditioning. Bobby wears thermal underwear in the summertime and sleeps with the heat on. You can usually set your watch by my punctuality. Bobby will be two days late to his own funeral. Yet, in spite of our differences, perhaps even *because* of some of them, we have an incredible personal and professional relationship. I shudder to think what might have happened to my career following Hubert's death had Bobby not come along.

At first, he was not my manager but only a consultant in the area of television and worked closely with Hubert. Later, when the responsibility for my entire career came to rest on his shoulders, he devised a brilliant master plan.

"Your basic appeal, Will," (he never calls me Bill . . . it's always "Will" or "Kid" of if he's mad at me it's "James William") "is to women. Women buy most of your records, women are the ones who come to your concerts. Now, when do women watch television?"

I wasn't real sure what he was driving at.

"Women watch television in the daytime," he said. "Now, here's my idea: Let's let all the other country stars keep chasing after guest spots on the *Tonight Show* and on the the prime-time specials, and let's us go after getting you onto daytime television. I think it will work." I wasn't too sure.

But work it did! By this time Bernie had generated enough publicity for me to sink a battleship. Tons and tons of articles with my name, my picture, my dog's picture and my mother's favorite recipes—anything to get Bill Anderson's name into circulation. I was having other country artists tell me that they'd go into a town for a concert and pick up the local paper to read about their show and instead all they'd find was a story about me. It was a bit embarrassing, but our mission was being accomplished.

It was only a matter of a few weeks until I appeared on NBC's *Today* show. I was the first country artist to appear on the *Mike Douglas Show* ("This will set our show back ten years!" I overheard one of the staff band members mutter when he saw me and the group coming into the studio lugging our guitars), and I probably appeared with Mike as much or more than anybody from Nashville during the years his show was on the air.

Bobby booked me on all the top entertainment-talk shows with all the top hosts—David Frost, Dr. Joyce Brothers, Dinah Shore, Della Reese, John Gary, and so many others I can't remember them all. And then one day he really snuck up on my blind side.

"Will, I want you to start doing guest appearances on some of the daytime game shows," he said.

"*Game* shows?" I exclaimed. "What for, Bobby? I don't even *watch* game shows!"

"Well, *start* watching them," was his answer.

"But I don't even *like* game shows!" I protested. "I mean, all they are is a bunch of people coming to a studio dressed like pepperoni pizzas and acting like they have about as much sense as one. Yukkk! Do I have to?"

"No, you don't have to, but I've booked you a spot next week on *Match Game* at CBS in Hollywood. It's for six shows, five of the daytime programs and one nighttime shot. I think you should take it, but if you don't want it, I can probably switch them over to Tom T. Hall."

Bobby has always had a way with words.

I started watching *Match Game* and decided it really wasn't so bad after all. Gene Rayburn, the host, seemed like a nice enough guy, and with a supporting cast that included actor-not-yet-turned-game-show-host Richard Dawson, the quick-witted Charles Nelson Reilly, and Jack Klugman's bubbling ex-wife Brett Sommers, it came across like a bunch of zanies throwing a big afternoon party and having a good time. I found when I flew to California and taped six episodes that the cast did, indeed, to put it mildly, enjoy their work.

Match Game was the show where a contestant was asked to fill in the blank in a question ("Marshall Dillon said, 'Miss Kitty's real name isn't Kitty. We call her Kitty because she eats *blank!*'") and a panel of celebrities tried to anticipate and match the answer the contestant would give. It was a serious game in that the contestants had a chance to win some big bucks, but it was played in a none-too-serious manner by the panel. They told us to try our best to match the contestants but to have fun doing it. And if we could throw in something halfway witty in the process, feel free to do so. I don't remember how many matching answers I came up with that first time but it must have been a few and I must have acted semi-insane doing it, because they asked me to come back. And then back. And back again.

And then Bobby, having gotten *my* foot inside the Hollywood game-show circuit door, carried his madness one step further. He turned *Becky* into a TV star. He booked us an appearance together on another CBS show called *Tattletales*, a program where three celebrity couples would try to match the answers their spouses or partners might give to personal questions about themselves and their relationships. The couple who matched the most answers in each daily half-hour segment was declared the winner. As with *Match Game*, we were contracted to six shows.

The questions were sometimes silly but provoked some interesting responses. ("You're staying with friends in a house with two guest bedrooms. There is one single bed in each. Husbands, will your wife say that you would want to sleep in separate bedrooms or in the same single bed?"). The ad-lib answers, as you might imagine, could sometimes get rather personal and pretty crazy.

Becky was a little nervous before we went on *Tattletales* the first time, but it didn't take her long to relax and fall right into the flow of things. After about two questions and a couple of small giggles from the audience when she'd come up with a cute answer, she got to feeling her oats and didn't really care what she said. "Hey, it's not *my* career," she'd laugh, and then give some outlandish response to whatever the question happened to be. The more the studio audience and host Bert Convy would laugh at her answers, the more turned-on she'd become and the crazier she'd act. Most of the time it was funny and I'd laugh too, but once we got into a terrible argument over something she said.

The question had been, "Ladies, which one of the two of you will your husband say eats more junk food, you or him?" Well, Becky has always been a junk-food junkie and I can either take it or leave it. Naturally, I answered that she ate the most. She had said that I did.

"Why *I* don't eat junk food!" I exclaimed on nationwide TV. "*You're* the one who's always reaching your hand down in a sack of potato chips or into a can of cashew nuts. And you're always drinking a Pepsi!"

"Oh, no, you've got that all wrong. You're always making a turkey sandwich at midnight or eating an extra piece of lemon pie for dessert," she squealed.

"But that's not *junk* food," I protested. "That's nourishment!"

The crowd in the studio roared and the producers were loving it. Convy was egging us on, and the more we argued the better they liked it. But I was becoming more and more irritated. I felt like Becky was sacrificing the truth in an effort to get the audience on her side. In the dressing room after the show I confronted her and asked, "Why did you have to say something so wrong and so stupid just to get a laugh on TV?"

She said, "Well, you know good and well you eat more junk food than I do," and the argument started all over again. I couldn't believe what she was saying. We ended up going back to our hotel in separate cabs.

Becky enjoyed her "celebrity" status as a frequent guest on *Tattletales*. Her favorite moment came in a drugstore in Miami when she and I were doing some last minute shopping prior to leaving on a Caribbean cruise. A lady walked up to her—not to me, but to her—and said, "Hey, aren't you on television?" Before Becky could answer the lady said, "Yeah, I've seen you on *Tattletales*. You're Becky Anderson. You're the wife of the one they call 'Whisperin' Somebody.'" Becky has teased me about that for years!

We've also had some good laughs over another incident that took place on *Tattletales*. Again the question was to the ladies: "Girls, what will your husband say was his most embarrassing moment?" The panel that day consisted of author Mickey Spillane and his wife, Sherri; game show host Allen Ludden and his wife, the marvelous Betty White, and us. When it came Becky's turn to answer, she launched into the story she'd heard me tell of the time in high school when I went onstage with my pants unzipped. However, when she came to the punch line about my having held my guitar in a rather unique position, she said, "He held his guitar down around his knees." The studio audience howled, whereupon Betty White flashed the camera one of those patented astonished, dry looks of hers, raised her eyebrows, leaned forward and said, "Well, Becky, I have just gained a whole new respect for your husband!"

Becky was good on television because she was herself. She was honest, she was funny. They call it being "real." We announced to the public for the first time that we were expecting a baby on one of our appearances on *Tattletales*. For a couple of years following her automobile accident, I couldn't bring myself to watch the tapes of those old shows because Becky was so far from being that wonderful, full-of-life person she was back then. But now, as I've watched her fight back, so determined to regain that which was taken away from her, those shows are an inspiration to us both.

Tattletales isn't on the air right now, but I hope someday a show will come along that the two of us can do together again. I'm prejudiced, of course, but I think we made a pretty darn good team!

17

I had no way of knowing it at the time, but my appearances on *Match Game*, *Tattletales*, and later on *Password*, *Hollywood Squares*, and other daytime game shows were leading to something else— something a whole lot bigger—that was ultimately to have a pro- found effect on both my life and my career. For I found out in the early spring of 1977 that I was about to be asked by Mark Good- son, the king of the game show producers, if I'd like to audition for the role of *host* of a new game show he'd just devised, the pilot for which he had sold to ABC. When I first heard about it, I was told the show was to be called *The Stronger Sex* and would feature a male and a female as cohosts, something that up until this time had never been tried in game show television.

"Lord, Howard," I said to Howard Felsher, a longtime friend of Bobby Brenner, one of the top producers at Goodson-Todman and the man who had brought me to Mr. Goodson's attention in the first place, "I'm just a guitar-pickin' hillbilly singer and songwriter from Nashville. What do I know about hosting a Hollywood game show?" But the idea both intrigued and excited me, even though it frightened me a bit as well. I knew if the opportunity actually did present itself that I'd have to give it a try.

(I often use the term "hillbilly" in referring to myself and my friends in the country music business. I realize that to some readers that term might seem inaccurate and perhaps even derogatory. Let me explain:

First, "hillbilly" is a perfectly acceptable, almost flattering term for one country musician to use in referring to himself or another person in this business. Over the years we've always called ourselves hillbillies or 'billies. We haven't always liked it when out-siders, such as newspaper and magazine writers from New York, for example, have called us hillbillies because they've often used the word as a put-down. But in calling ourselves that it's almost like saying, "Hey, we're part of a very special club or fraternity. We're hillbillies and you're not!"

A public relations man from the East once took me out on a promotion tour to visit radio and television stations as well as several major newspapers and magazines in a half-dozen major northern cities, and he'd get angry every time he'd take me into a prestigious spot like the *Washington Post* and I'd refer to myself as a "hillbilly." "Don't call yourself that," he'd say. "You are *not* a hillbilly!"

"Oh yes, I am a hillbilly," I answered, "and I'll call myself that all I please. Just be careful when *you* call me a hillbilly!")

"Understand now, the show isn't yours to host by a long shot," Howard Felsher emphasized. "All you're being offered is an audi-tion, a chance for you to see and us to see if you can handle it. And all you'll win if you pass the audition is a chance to cohost the pilot, not the series, if in fact there's even going to *be* series. At this point *that's* not even for sure. But what do you say?"

The whole scenario was full of *if*, *perhaps*, and *maybe*, but I knew Howard was one of the very top people in the whole game show profession—at the time he was the producer of ABC's top-rated *Family Feud*—and I had all the confidence in the world in his judgment and his ability. If he felt strongly that I should do it, then maybe I should. Too, I've always loved a challenge, and hosting a game show would most definitely be a challenge.

People ask me all the time why I involve myself in so many careers aside from my primary career in country music, and I tell them it's because I'm a lot like the guy in the TV commercial who comes down from climbing the high mountain and his friend asks him, "Why did you climb that mountain?" And he answers, "Because it was there." Many times in my life I've gone chasing after something simply "because it was there." Why should this be any different? "Sure, coach," I said to Howard, "I'll play your game. Send me in!"

I was told that before any new show goes on the air at a major network a test program or pilot episode has to be taped. The idea is to give both the producers and the network officials a way to look at the show and judge how well all the elements blend together prior to committing to invest hundreds of thousands of dollars in actual production costs. Sometimes audiences are even brought into the studios and shown tapes of the pilot programs to test their reactions. Not all pilots that are taped get on the air, and many shows reach the air only after many revisions and changes are made. Sometimes those changes include even the stars of the shows themselves.

But at least I was going to get a chance. Me and twenty-seven other would-be male hosts. Before it was over, Goodson-Todman would audition everybody they could pull in off the street in an effort to find not only, as they put it, "some fresh new faces," but a host and cohost who could work well together and blend the elements of the male-versus-female concept of the game into a cohesive unit. I was warned that when a producer said he wanted a "fresh new face" that usually meant he would try out a bunch of people who'd never worked in this particular area of show business before and then at the last minute retreat to a trusted game show veteran like Bill Cullen or Tom Kennedy when the tape began to roll and the chips were on the line. But my attitude was still, "What-the-heck, let's go for it. It's a chance to learn from and be critiqued by the best minds in the business." I figured when it was all over and I was sent packing back home to Nashville I could at least look back upon the experience as my having taken advantage of a once-in-a-lifetime opportunity. Like the old country song says, "I'd rather be sorry for something I did . . . than for something that I didn't do."

The first thing I had to do after saying yes, I'd like to try, was to promise the producers I'd spend every available minute over the next few weeks in southern California learning the premise of the new game and how I might best negotiate the move from country singer to game show host. I caught a lot of red-eye airplane flights in and out of the Los Angeles International Airport, and I put in many long and tedious hours in the Goodson-Todman offices under the watchful eye of executive-producer-to-be, Ira Skutch, learning just what it is that a game show host is supposed to do.

I couldn't have had a better teacher than Ira, a lanky, bespectacled, transplanted New Yorker who had worked around game show television ever since he was employed as a page at NBC as a teenager. I had worked with Ira when I'd been a member of the celebrity panels on *Match Game* and *Tattletales*, since he produced both shows, and I had come to love his sense of humor and to respect his knowledge of game shows and the game show business. But this was different. Here he was training me to be in charge, to run the show myself. If I were to get the job, a large part of the success or failure of the entire show was going to be resting squarely on my shoulders. Ira knew that and brought me along slowly, showing me step-by-step how to execute each move, patiently explaining to me as we went along just why each piece of business had to be handled in a particular way and why it was necessary for me sometimes to speak in specific scripted language.

The use of that specific language turned out to be one of the toughest things for me to learn. Not having come from a background in the theater, I was a lot more used to ad-libbing my way through certain situations than I was memorizing lines. But on a game show if you say just one word out of context, you run the risk of changing the entire meaning of what you're trying to communicate. That's a luxury a host can't afford. He might end up giving away a million dollars to a contestant who just missed a question all because he got his tongue tangled up. These little nuances were confusing and hard for me to master at first, but the whole thing was also extremely fascinating. And there was no doubt that I was being tutored by some of the masters of the art.

Finally, after several weeks, when Ira and producer-to-be Bobby Sherman thought I had a good enough grip on the basic mechanics of the game to attempt some actual run-throughs, they began teaming me up with the various ladies they were considering as cohosts. I hosted a mock version of the game with a former Miss America, Nancy Fleming, and she was very pleasant. In fact, I flew back to Nashville thinking she and I might make a good team, only to be called back to California almost immediately to try out with another potential cohost, author Joanna Barnes. Before it was over I must have done run-throughs with at least a dozen ladies, including Patty Duke, who was never considered as a cohost but who came by one afternoon to help out as a favor to Ira. It took less than five minutes in her presence for me to know I was in the company of a real pro.

The procedure as a whole was exhilarating, but at times it could also be very rough on my nerves. We'd play the game on a simulated set built in the Goodson-Todman offices with office staff members posing as contestants. After each half-hour run-through the production staff would leave without a word and disappear inside their private offices down the hall to talk about what they'd just seen and heard. Then they'd come back into the rehearsal room and give us their critiques, sometimes pages upon pages. Each time they'd return I'd feel like I should stand and address them as "Ladies and gentlemen of the jury." They were mostly kind in their remarks, but I never received from them any indication of how my performance was stacking up against the others in the running. That only added to the intense pressure I was beginning to feel.

Periodically when things would reach the point where the brain trust of the show (producers, writers, directors, etc.) thought I was ready for the next step, they'd call in Mark Goodson himself, and I'd have to perform everything I had learned thus far for him. Sometimes he'd make suggestions and offer me invaluable criticisms. Other times he'd decide there were some little changes he wanted to make in the game itself, and I'd have to spend hours after he left the room *unlearning* things I had been struggling so hard during the previous hours to learn. Every few days, just to add to my load, I'd look up and not only would Mark Goodson be scrutinizing my every move, but Fred Silverman, the head of the entire ABC-TV network, would be standing there glaring at me as well. At the time Fred Silverman was the single most important man in American television, and I had to pinch myself the first time I realized he'd come to watch and listen to me. He made me nervous, probably because I never saw him smile.

More than once I wondered if being the host of a network game show was really worth all the effort I was having to put into it, all the tension, all the stress. I'd sometimes close my eyes there on Sunset Boulevard in the middle of Hollywood and pretend I was back in Nashville listening to the ringing of an open E-chord on my ole flat-top guitar. And I'd think about writing a song or climbing on the bus and heading out somewhere to perform for people who put no pressure on me at all. "I don't need to be a game show host," I'd tell myself. "I've already got a pretty good job." But I stuck with it, and I've lived to be extremely glad that I did.

Given the fact that I knew over two dozen other men had tried out for the job as cohost of this new show, including several who'd had network game show experience, I figured when it came time for Mr. Goodson and his staff to choose the host for the taping of the pilot my chances of landing the role rested somewhere between slim and none. I had, in fact, about given up hope of being chosen when my phone rang at home late one night and Ira gave me the surprising but happy news.

"Now, this doesn't mean you'll get the series," he cautioned, "but they do want you to host the pilot. And that's the first step." I knew Ira had been in my corner from day one, and I thanked him profusely.

Even though I was more than a little surprised when the call came, there had actually been several things working in my favor from the beginning, not the least of which was the political climate of the country at the time. Jimmy Carter, a southerner, had just been elected President, and southern lifestyles and southern people were very much in vogue. More than once I had heard Mark Goodson say, "Bill has that soft, southern manner about him, he's a 'fresh new face,' and I think the timing might just be right." After having been in show business for nearly twenty years, I hardly considered myself a "fresh new face" (I'd look in the mirror sometimes and swear I could see the road map of the world imprinted there!), but I was fresh and new to the world of game shows. Now at least the pilot, if not the series, was mine.

I was determined not to worry about the series and whether or not it would ever get on the air. I planned just to relax and have a good time taping the pilot. And I did. My cohost turned out to be none of the ladies I had worked with in the run-throughs, but rather a tall, striking blonde who at the time was hosting *Good Morning, Los Angeles*, sort of a local version of *Good Morning, America*, on KABC-TV in L.A. Her name was Sarah Purcell.

Sarah had never worked on a game show either, so in that respect we started out even. In fact, at that time, Sarah hadn't been working in front of a TV camera very long, period. She was a former secretary at a television station in San Diego who got pressed into on-the-air duty one night when the local TV weather girl didn't show up. The show-biz bug bit her so hard she never returned to her typewriter and steno pad. Mark Goodson hadn't met Sarah when he first spotted her either, but he liked what he saw on the local show and called her in for an audition.

Sarah and I more or less inherited one another, but we hit it off immediately and I can't tell you how relieved I was. I'd had visions of having to share the stage with some air-brained Hollywood ego-head, and Sarah was the complete opposite. She was lively, witty, just flaky enough to be real cute, and above all she was a lady. When she found national, prime-time stardom as one of the hosts of *Real People* a few years later, nobody was happier for her than I was.

In spite of my resolve to relax and have fun, there was a tremendous amount of tension in the air the week we taped the pilot. Large amounts of money and several jobs were at stake, not just mine and Sarah's, but the dozens of staff positions that would need to be filled if the show went into production. It might not seem like it watching at home, but a game show requires many people working behind the scenes to make it click—writers, contestant coordinators, production assistants—each performing intense, specialized tasks. Each of these people had his or her own special reasons for wanting the pilot to succeed, and since I had gotten to know quite a few of them during the run-throughs, I wanted to do a good job for their sakes as well as for mine.

I had to mark off an entire week on my schedule to tape the pilot. I flew into Los Angeles late on a Sunday afternoon, and on Monday morning we moved from our tiny make-believe studio at the Goodson-Todman offices into the honest-to-goodness real ABC-TV studios on Prospect Avenue. There we set up shop on a shiny new stage that I was told was the most expensive, elaborate set ever constructed for a game show. They said it cost over three-quarters of a million dollars just to build. And then, with real cameras beneath real lights and with real contestants for what seemed like a hundred days and nights on end, I practiced making the rest of my transition from being a country music singer to being the host of a network game show.

After the first few days I thought I could begin to feel the pieces slowly but surely falling into place. I wasn't sure, but I thought I could feel myself relaxing. I could feel Sarah and me becoming more and more used to working together. I could feel the show becoming more and more a part of me and me a part of it. Somewhere around the third or fourth day in the studio we actually videotaped one of the rehearsals and gathered around the studio monitors afterward to watch the playback. I was happy, but I could sense Mr. Goodson wasn't totally pleased with what he saw.

What he turned out to be unhappy with had nothing at all to do with me or with Sarah, but rather with the game itself. There was a small part of it that he felt just wasn't jelling. I don't know if it was brashness or naiveté on my part, but I sensed his mood and spoke up and offered him a suggestion I thought might help. As soon as the words were out of my mouth, though, I wanted to draw them all back in.

The studio grew strangely quiet. Every head in the room turned toward me, every eye focused on the Tennessee hillbilly who hadn't been around Hollywood long enough to know that you didn't tell Mark Goodson how to repair his creation, no matter how badly it might be sputtering. I learned later that everyone fully expected Goodson's renowned wrath to come crashing down on the top of my head. But instead he paused, puffed on his pipe a time or two, and said, "That might just be a good idea. Let's try it once that way and see how it works." Luckily, it worked well, and he incorporated my idea into the permanent structure of the show. From that moment on I felt this legendary man began to look at me in a different light. I felt that perhaps for the first time he was *truly* on my side.

We taped three half-hour pilot episodes of our new game show on Friday night before a live, jam-packed studio audience. I was so pumped up with excitement and fear that I barely remember it, but I assumed by all the handshakes and pats-on-the-back I received when it was over that I must have done a fairly good job. At the very least I was convinced beyond any shadow of a doubt that I had made the right decision to have gone for it because even if the show didn't sell or even if it sold and somebody else became the host, I knew I'd gotten to siphon knowledge off the top of some of the greatest minds in the television business. And even if I never appeared on another game show in my life, I knew I could take this experience and transfer it into whatever other areas of show business I might someday find myself involved in. As I dressed, left the studio, and headed for the airport to catch the midnight flight back to Nashville, I smiled, comfortable in my belief that I had done the best I could do. Besides, I told myself, if I approached it casually rather than pinning all my hopes on becoming a game show star, it would make it a whole lot easier to take when the proverbial ax came swinging down across my neck. Which is exactly what happened.

"I'm sorry, Bill," Ira Skutch said to me over the long-distance wire from L.A. one Sunday afternoon about three weeks after the taping of the pilot. "We all thought you did a helluva job, all of us did, but Silverman just won't buy you. He doesn't think you're right for the show. Mark, all of us, we've talked 'til we're blue in the face, but he won't budge. ABC likes the show and wants it to go on the air in July, but I'm afraid we're going to have to go with someone else."

"Who's going to get it?" I asked, trying to hide my disappointment. I had been chasing the dream so long by this time that I had really begun to want to capture it.

"Probably Wink Martindale."

"And Sarah?"

"Silverman likes her."

"Well, give her my love and tell her I wish her the best. And, Ira, thanks for the chance. I learned a lot from all you guys and I'll never forget it. Please thank Mark for me, too. It's really been great getting to work with the best there is!"

I hung up the phone and called Bill Goodwin, my booking agent. I told him to get busy booking me some concert dates for the summer. My brief career as a game show host was over.

A few weeks later, I was signing autographs inside my fan club booth at the country music Fan Fair in Nashville, the world of Hollywood and game shows a million miles from my mind. Suddenly, above the noise and commotion generated by ten thousand country fans who'd come to Nashville from all over the world to see and meet their favorite stars, I could hear my name being called over the loudspeaker system. Someone was paging me to come to the telephone.

Being totally surrounded by humanity, flashbulbs, and autograph books, unable to move more than a few steps at a time, I turned to Becky and asked her if she'd mind going to find out what it was and bring me any message.

She came back in about five minutes out of breath and pale. "You'd better go to the phone quick," she said, and I conjured up all sorts of images of tragedy.

"What's the matter?" I asked anxiously, pushing the crowd aside.

"It's from California," she panted. "Silverman has changed his mind. You've got the show."

18

By the time our show got on the air in July 1977, the name had been changed from *The Stronger Sex* to *The Better Sex*, but for some reason the general public always seemed to want to call it *The Battle of the Sexes*. I never cared what they called it as long as they watched it. Today I meet people who only vaguely remember the show who'll come up to me and ask, "What was that 'sex show' you used to do on TV?" I smile and tell them I was the original Dr. Ruth!

ABC gave our show a good time slot, the half-hour following the highly rated *Family Feud*. That meant we were on at noon on the east coast, however, and many of the stations in the larger cities preempted us for their local noontime news. In the other time zones we were carried by virtually all the ABC affiliates.

The ratings on the show started off high, the result of a barrage of advance publicity and promotion. After the initial honeymoon period, however, they tapered off a bit before starting to build slowly but steadily back. We had been guaranteed only that we'd be on the air for thirteen weeks at the outset, which I learned is standard fare at the networks, but our first option was quickly picked up by ABC and we launched our second thirteen-week cycle. Everybody felt good about the future of the show, and I was having a blast. At first I missed my guitar, but I soon forgot it wasn't hanging around my neck and concentrated on trying to make *The Better Sex* an entertaining television show.

If you never saw the show, you're probably wondering just what this whole thing was all about. Basically, *The Better Sex* was a trivia game, and the premise was to see whether a team of five women captained by Sarah Purcell or a team of five men captained by yours truly could answer the most trivia questions. The winning team could then boast, "We are 'the better sex'!"

Trivia of all kinds was hot in those days, and our subject matter knew no bounds. We asked everything from "Which U.S. President once got stuck in the White House bathtub?" to "Who broke Babe Ruth's home-run record?"

A player was "knocked out" of the game and had to take a seat on the bench if he or she gave an incorrect answer. The team with a player or players still standing at the end of a round was declared the winner. The winning team would then move downstage and match trivial wits with thirty selected members of the opposite sex in the studio audience. If my men's team had won the round, for instance, and they could then "knock out" or stump in five questions all thirty women they were matched against in the studio audience, the men would win five thousand dollars. If there were audience members, however, who didn't miss a question of the five they were asked, they would then divide five hundred dollars among themselves. We gave away many thousands of dollars to both contestants and the audience during the time we were on the air, and never once did we lack for people coming to see the show. Unlike most game shows, the audience knew they had a chance to leave the studio richer than they were when they came. They came in droves.

Once we swung into production, I found that hosting a five-day-a-week game show, while perhaps not in the same league as laying concrete block or performing brain surgery, can nonetheless be very taxing, both mentally and physically. Most of the time we taped five half-hour programs in one day, although once or twice we got in a bind and had to tape as many as seven. A taping session would usually last three or four consecutive days. At the end of some of those sessions I didn't know what planet I was on! The shows were taped, as most game shows are, back-to-back in the order in which they would be played on the air with only time enough in between shows for Sarah and me to change clothes. If you've ever noticed that most game shows seem a little goofier on Fridays than on other days of the week, now you know why!

Many times I was also having to face this grind on three or four hours sleep a night. I was living in Nashville trying to maintain a career in country music, which meant nonstop touring in the summer (remember, when I thought I hadn't gotten the game show I'd asked my agent for a heavy work load), and I had to hop many midnight flights to and from California.

I hadn't rented an apartment or a house on the west coast either, because I never had more than a thirteen-week guarantee of employment at any one time. I figured as soon as I signed a long-term lease on living quarters somewhere my show would get cancelled. There weren't any rental properties out there that I knew of that were available in thirteen-week cycles, although that might not be a bad idea. (Watch some real estate sharpie pick up on that and make a fortune!) I would fly out for each taping session, rent a car for my transportation around town, and check into an all-suite hotel in the little village of Westwood. Had the show stayed in production longer, I had already decided to concentrate on finding some type of permanent living arrangement in southern California.

Several interesting, memorable, and funny things happened during the grand and glorious twenty-six weeks we were on the air. Just about the time the show was set to go into production, there was a big strike at ABC and all the cameramen, technicians, and many of the support personnel walked off the job. That left vice-presidents of the network to run the cameras and anybody else they could pull in from management to do all sorts of other odd jobs. One group of people who walked out were the make-up artists.

Due to the way television lights reflect off human skin, a person can't go on TV without make-up. I've always said I need camouflage more than make-up but, lucky for me, at that time Becky was a licensed television make-up artist. She had gone through extensive training in Nashville and worked on many of city's locally produced music shows, gospel music shows in particular, but she had only once or twice ever done *my* make-up. That is, until someone at ABC learned of her background. From that day until the day the strike was settled, Becky flew to California every time I did and served as my personal make-up artist. We often joked that we made it to the big-time together!

The strike made it difficult as far as the show itself was concerned because it took place when the show was still in its formative stages. The producers had to call extra rehearsals, set aside extra days for us to tape, and move at a much slower pace in general because the regular crews weren't there. But aside from the inconvenience, and speaking purely on a personal level, I was sort of glad it all happened like it did. Otherwise, Becky would never have gotten to become as big a part of it all as she became.

Having her around sure kept the days (and nights) from being so long and lonesome. Often we couldn't fly out to California together because I'd be coming in from a show date somewhere and she'd be leaving out of Nashville, but we'd meet at the hotel or at the studio. Once we got there she'd have to keep the same hours that I did because before we'd begin to tape each new half-hour show, she'd have to put some powder on my nose or touch up Sarah's eyeliner or something. That meant we could usually have all our meals together and sleep on a somewhat similar schedule. Much of the time we couldn't even do that at home.

Becky made a lot of friends in California, too. She and Sarah became big buddies, and she struck up friendships with some of the production assistants and some of the wives of the executives at Goodson-Todman as well. They'd go shopping together after work, or we'd stay over on a weekend sometimes and see a show or just visit. Sometimes I'd fly out after a taping session and she'd stay in town. I'd work a couple of shows someplace then fly back to Los Angeles. It was nice having her there waiting for me.

Once the shows got rolling on a regular schedule, I began really to enjoy my work. I met a lot of interesting people, many of them contestants, and some of them turned out to be very strange and unique characters. We had one giant of an ole boy come in to play on the men's team one day who must have stood about six-ten and weighed close to three hundred. He told us to call him "Big Jim." I mean he was *huge*, and never once did I ever see him smile. He seemed to have a permanent scowl chiseled onto his face, a decided contrast to the typical Hollywood game show contestant who always seems to be auditioning for a toothpaste commercial.

The first game this big dude happened to play was on the fifth show of the day, and the women's team skunked the men. The women then went downstage and played against the men in the audience, after which our taping day was finished. Since a team had to lose twice in order to be eliminated, the men were all told to be back at the studio at ten o'clock the following morning.

Well, they all showed up that next day except Big Jim. He was nowhere to be found. Finally, with taping time rapidly approaching, one of the contestant coordinators decided to try calling him on the phone. Much to her surprise, he answered.

"Jim, aren't you coming to the studio to tape *The Better Sex* again today?" she asked.

"Hell, no!" he answered emphatically.

"Why not?"

"'Cause ain't no damn woman ever beat me at nothin'," he growled, "and they ain't about to start now!"

And that was the last we ever saw of Big Jim.

There were many very nice and extremely talented people on our production staff, but from the beginning a very beautiful, vibrant young lady who researched much of the question-and-answer material that we used on the air caught my eye. Somehow she just seemed to sparkle above the rest. I had been introduced to her during some of my very first run-throughs at the Goodson-Todman offices, but the only chances I had had really to talk with her had come during the commercial breaks on taping days when she would come bounding up onto the stage from her seat at the control center out in the audience to hand me my question cards for the next round. She was extremely attractive, but there was something else about her—some type of elusive quality I couldn't quite put my finger on—that impressed me as well.

One day when we weren't taping shows I went by the Goodson-Todman offices to pick up some mail, and she happened to get on the elevator with me as I was leaving. We exchanged a little small talk on our way down, and when we reached the ground floor she reached out to shake my hand. "I probably won't be seeing you at the studio anymore," she said.

"Why not?" I asked, very surprised and missing her already.

"I'm leaving Goodson to go to work for Chuck Barris," she said.

"Don't tell me you're going to work on *The Gong Show*," I gasped, knowing this was one of Barris's many productions.

"No," she smiled, "what I really want to be is an actress. He's promised to help me move in that direction."

I thought, Honey, every girl in California wants to be an actress. If I were you I wouldn't give up my day job! But I kept my thoughts to myself and wished her well.

I guess it's a good thing she didn't ask for my advice. She might still be researching trivia questions for game shows. Instead she's gone on to star in a TV drama called *The Fall Guy* and more recently seems to have really found her niche as an actress on one of my favorite comedy shows, *Night Court*. I haven't run into her on any elevators recently, but I do see pictures of her and read articles about her in virtually every magazine I pick up. My intuition about her being special turned out to be right. Her name was, and is, Markie Post.

My favorite story from *The Better Sex* days, however, involved Sarah and something that never got on camera. Maybe it should have. We were taking a longer than usual break one afternoon taping shows, and Sarah had not had a particularly good day. I wondered sometimes how she kept up the pace anyhow. She'd get up before dawn, go on the air with her local show for two hours, and then come to our studio at eleven-thirty and tape game shows until long after sundown. She was young and energetic and did very well most of the time, but anybody working those hours would be entitled to a bad day occasionally.

This particular evening Sarah's husband, Joe, had come by the studio prior to the taping of our last half-hour show. Sarah was in her dressing room changing clothes, and Joe could sense that all was not well. He tried to cheer her up.

"Would you like a little drink, honey?" he asked, opening the small refrigerator in her dressing room and taking out a bottle of chilled white wine. "It might make you feel better."

At that precise moment Sarah, in the midst of dressing for the next show and putting her wireless microphone in place on her blouse, accidentally hit the switch that turned her microphone on. Tape wasn't rolling, of course, but the sound engineer had not turned off the monitor speakers in the audience. The crowd was sitting there patiently waiting for our final show to begin when suddenly they heard Sarah's voice come booming into the room.

They had not heard Joe ask her if she wanted a drink. All they heard was Sarah saying in a somewhat loud and agitated voice:

"Not now, honey, I've got one more show to do!"

When she walked out onto the set moments later, they gave her a standing ovation. And she never knew why.

I really enjoyed working in Hollywood despite the inconveniences of having to live out of a suitcase all of the time. And I'd enjoy having the opportunity to work there again someday. But I can tell you for sure that there are a lot of differences between taping a show in southern California and taping a show in Nashville.

For one thing, in L.A. they give you the "star treatment" all the way. There is somebody at hand constantly to attend to your every need or whim, and they act like you've insulted them if you don't let them take care of you. At the studio it was constantly, "Mr. Anderson, may I get you a pillow?" or "Would you like some Perrier in your fridge?" or, my favorite, "There's a bit of lint on your trousers; may I remove it for you?" I wasn't used to that, especially from the wardrobe guys who kept hanging around wanting to help me get dressed and undressed. I didn't like the look in most of their eyes, and I told 'em real quick that where I come from men learn early how to dress and undress themselves!

The star treatment didn't exist just at the studio, however. While we were on the air—and I mean ours was just a daytime game show, for goodness sakes—I could walk into almost any restaurant I might choose in Los Angeles or Beverly Hills and get the best table in the house and usually a bottle of complimentary wine or champagne sent over from the manager. And people would speak on the street and in the shops, and even in L.A. where there's a big movie or TV star every half-block, I'd get asked to sign autographs and impart my wisdom about show business. They treat you nice in Nashville but this . . . it was wonderfully bizarre.

I got treated the same way when I went over to NBC in Burbank a few months after *The Better Sex* was cancelled at ABC. I had been called in by Mark Goodson to work on a pilot for a new series, another game show called *Spellbinders*. On this show I was to be the sole host, and celebrities from television and the movies were booked to come in and play on teams with the regular contestants. I thought it was a good show, and I was excited about being chosen to host it. All of us who were hired to work on the show, and that included Ira Skutch and several staff members from *The Better Sex*, were under the impression for quite some time that it would be going on the air, but for some reason it never did. We did get three pilot episodes on tape, but that was as far as things ever progressed.

Everybody treated me super at NBC, but the whole time I was flying in and out of L.A. working on the new show I could sense myself becoming "Bill Who?" in the minds of the people in southern California real fast. Although I had a new series in development, I couldn't be seen on the air everyday, and that seemed to make a big difference. I once went back to a restaurant where only weeks before I had been the apple of the maitre'd's eye and gotten free champagne sent to me and my party at the best table in the house, and this time, honest to Pete, the same guy led me without so much as even a smile to a cramped little table in the corner. The guy who had fallen all over himself trying to sell me some shirts at an exclusive men's store was suddenly busy when I walked in. It was frightening. From the penthouse to the outhouse with one fell swoop of somebody's pen. It made me realize how easily some of the people in Hollywood who are duped into believing their own publicity and who fall into the trap of thinking they are something special just because they work in the mass media can have so much trouble adjusting to life in the real world when the merry-go-round quits turning. I never took Hollywood all that seriously myself. I think if a performer can somehow accept the town for what it is—a land of enchantment and fantasy and make-believe—it can be wonderful. As long as he or she realizes everything there is an illusion, they'll be OK. Trouble is, so many young aspiring entertainers, actors, and actresses aren't able to separate the real from the pretend. That's when they lose all perspective, and before they know it the place turns on them, jumps up on their backs, and claws them to death.

The Better Sex stayed on the air until the early part of 1978 and was cancelled then not because of bad ratings but because ABC had a lady named Jackie Smith in charge of daytime programming. Her crystal ball could see clearly into the future. Jackie saw that game shows in general were declining in favor with the public and that daytime dramas (affectionately known as "soap operas") were getting hotter and hotter every day. There were two soaps on ABC then, *General Hospital* and *One Life to Live*, which were only forty-five minutes each in length, and Jackie felt the rising tide for the soaps compelled her to extend those programs to one hour each. In order to do that, she had to recapture thirty minutes of program time from somewhere.

She couldn't cancel *Family Feud* because its ratings were the highest of any game show on any network. All the other ABC daytime shows were already soaps and she wasn't about to cancel any of them. She didn't want to cancel our show, but it turned out to be the only place she could find the half-hour of time she needed, so she took it. Her decision turned out to be the right one for the network because within only a few months ABC became No. 1 in daytime television for the very first time. It was all due to Jackie Smith's soaps and her foresight.

But for me and Sarah and all the rest of the people who had worked so very hard to try and make *The Better Sex* come alive, it was a tough pill to swallow. The network gave us a little party backstage after we taped our last show, and there were a lot of us walking around the room wearing long faces. Jackie came to the party and moved graciously among us trying to console our collectively wounded pride. Shows are born every day and die all the time in California, but when a group of people works as long and diligently as we'd all worked, faces the hardships of a strike, creates a successful show, and then gets only a pink slip for the effort, it hurts just the same. Many of us had become close friends both on and off the set, and nobody wanted to see it end.

"Bill, you've just been marvelous," Jackie said to me, sensing, I'm sure, the disappointment in my face. "But you'll be back. In fact, if you don't come up with another game show, which I feel sure you will eventually, I want to use you in one of my soaps. How would you like that?"

"Me? In a soap opera?" I almost laughed. "Doing what?"

"I don't know right now. Let me think about it. I promise you'll be hearing from me, though."

Sure, and the Russians are going to dismantle their nuclear weapons and take up tiddlywinks. Right?

But dad-blamed if the lady didn't keep her word! Before I could say American Broadcasting Company real fast three times in a row, I was in New York on the set of *One Life to Live*, script in hand, ready to launch a whole new career as an actor in a daytime television drama. Show business had totally amazed me one more time.

"I don't know one thing about acting," I told the director the first morning I showed up at the studio to tape *One Life to Live*. "I mean, you are going to have to show me *everything*. But I'll do my best to learn."

"You don't have to act," the kind and very patient man told me. "You're playing the part of yourself, Bill Anderson, the country singer. Why do you have to act? Just be natural and do what you'd naturally do under these circumstances. The great actors don't act anyhow, they react. Just calm down and let's have some fun." And we did.

(Many times in these pages I've referred to my work as being fun. I've carried a clipping in my wallet for years that reads:

Find something you like doing so much you'd do it for nothing. Then learn to do it so well that they'll pay you. And you've got it made.

That's pretty much been my philosophy of life within the scope of show business. I love what I do so much that I'd probably do it for nothing if I could afford to. Getting paid for it is just the icing on the cake. I feel sorry for people who have to get up every day and make a living at something they don't enjoy. And all the time I encourage people to make a career change if they are unhappy and can afford to take the financial risks involved. Life at best is short, and unhappiness shouldn't have to be a partner on the journey.)

More than one professional actor has told me that the most difficult dramatic role of all is playing oneself, but somehow I didn't find it hard at all. After all, I've been playing me for years. The only change was that on *One Life to Live* they gave me a whole set of new friends.

In the story line I was an old pal of a man who ran a small nightclub in suburban Philadelphia. This man had supposedly befriended me early in my career, and anytime I was on tour in the Philadelphia area I stopped by to see him. When the *One Life* viewers first saw me, I was presumably en route to a nearby concert engagement and popped into the club for a few minutes to chat with my old buddy.

My friend asked me to pull up a chair and started telling me about this young girl who'd just moved up from North Carolina and who was singing part-time in his club. "Her name is Becky Lee Abbott, and I think she's got real potential, Bill," he said. "I'd appreciate it if you'd take a listen to her and maybe give her some advice."

The director was right. This wasn't acting. This was doing something I'd been doing every day of my life for nearly twenty years. "Do I have to stick right to the script?" I asked, noting that the language they'd prepared for me seemed a bit contrived and stilted.

"Shoot, no," he said. "Just put it into your own words. We want this thing to be as realistic as possible."

So I sat backstage in the little club and told Becky Lee all about show business. How she needed to try and develop her own style of singing, how it would be helpful if she could write some of her own songs, the very same things I tell aspiring performers every day of my life. And I just happened to have my guitar with me, and we just happened to sing a song or two together.

It must have come off all right because almost as soon as the first two episodes I taped hit the air they called me back for a couple more. In a few weeks they wanted me back again, and this time they said for me to bring my entire band. We all went and played a concert in the little club and had a ball. Suddenly I began to realize the writers were not only weaving me in and out of Becky Lee's life but slowly turning her into a major star as well. The next thing I knew they were telling me that I was going to bring her to Nashville and invite her to appear with me on the Grand Ole Opry. Except, not to worry, they were conveniently going to move the Grand Ole Opry to New York.

And they did it! Right there in a television studio on West 67th Street they built a replica of the Grand Ole Opry stage that gave me chill bumps the first time I saw it. It was that realistic. And for days Becky Lee moved in and out of crisis after crisis as the script built toward that magical night when the little girl from North Carolina would walk onto the most famous stage in all of country music to perform for the first time.

Not only did they construct a replica of the Opry stage and backstage area in New York City, but they also flew in Minnie Pearl and singer Jeanne Pruett for even more realism. They hired square dancers to dance and people to come and just sit on the stage and eat popcorn like they do at the real Grand Ole Opry. The atmosphere looked and felt so much like back home that a newspaper writer who'd flown up to New York to cover the tapings for Nashville's morning paper swore she'd never left Nashville. "I am in New York," she kept repeating to herself over and over as if she needed constant reassurance as to just where she was.

There was really nothing to the "acting." We all just did the things we'd naturally do at the Opry any Friday or Saturday night. I'd introduce the acts, including, of course, Becky Lee, pick and sing a few songs, and cue the commercials. When the episodes went on the air, we were told that they brought in the highest ratings in the show's history. I was on cloud nine. Everybody knew we were onto a good thing, and nobody wanted it to stop.

Following the Opry scenes, the writers wrote me and the band into the script again, this time as featured entertainers at a big party thrown at a mansion out on Long Island. There was no make-believe involved here, however. We actually went to the mansion instead of their bringing the mansion to us. Even our bus and our bus driver, Joe Rose, got into the act this time, delivering us in style to the front door of this multimillion-dollar estate. These episodes took a week to tape, ran on the air for nearly three weeks, and once again the ratings went through the roof. From there they called us back into the studio almost immediately, and we started all over again.

The following spring, ABC flew several key members of the cast and crew into Knoxville for several days shooting in and around the city's annual Dogwood Festival. It's a wonder those episodes ever got taped, though, because the night before the first day's work Becky and I (my wife Becky, not Becky Lee) took the whole gang out to a little southern-style restaurant we were familiar with on the outskirts of town and stuffed them all full of fried chicken and vegetables and cornbread and all kinds of goodies. Many of them had never eaten our down-home style of food before, and they loved it. But nobody wanted to get out of bed and go to work the following morning!

Next came a real, honest-to-goodness trip to Nashville for the cast and crew where the real Becky Lee Abbott, played by Mary Gordon Murray and her singing partner from the show, Johnny Drummond, played by Wayne Massey, actually did appear on the Opry and on *Hee-Haw*. It was life-imitating-art-imitating-life at its finest. I wasn't sure half the time if we were acting or really doing all these things, but I didn't care. Just as long as we kept on doing it.

It did finally all cool down, however, and the writers married Becky Lee off and sent her down to Memphis to live and do whatever newlyweds do in Memphis. By the time she left and the country music storyline began to subside, though, I had spent a large portion of nearly three years of my life appearing on *One Life to Live*. The promise I hadn't put very much faith in at the beginning had turned out to be a major reality. And it surely had opened my eyes.

I had no idea until this experience how many people watch soap operas. I was mistaken about soaps in the beginning very much like I'd been about game shows. I didn't watch them, so I figured nobody else did either. Wrong!

One of the first concrete signs I had of people's knowing and recognizing me from the soap was the large number of blacks who began coming up to me in public and knowing who I was. For the most part, blacks aren't really into country music, but thanks to my appearance on the soaps, and even the game shows, I now meet quite a few blacks in my travels who are fans of Bill Anderson. It pleases me tremendously.

Another group of people who discovered me through *One Life* was the kids, the teenagers who wouldn't be caught dead listening to a country station on their radio. I was standing outside a hotel in Lake Tahoe, Nevada, one morning with Charlie Pride and Barbara Mandrell (prior to her television series) when my episodes on the soap were airing. Three or four teenaged girls spotted us standing there and came running over squealing and giggling. I was astounded when they ran right past Charlie and Barbara and shoved pieces of paper into my hand asking for autographs. "We see you on our favorite show!" they exclaimed, grabbing their souvenirs and disappearing without so much as a glance toward the two superstars. Charlie and Barbara, not big daytime television watchers, were floored. But not any more than I was!

People who watch the daytime dramas often refer to their favorite program as "my" show. The characters are "my" friends, this is "my" story, and they become very possessive about it. They want to know everything they can possibly learn about the actors and actresses who play the roles. "What is so-and-so *really* like?" I get asked all the time. "What was it *really* like being on that show?"

I can truthfully say that the cast and crew of *One Life to Live* treated me and all my people like royalty. I was apprehensive in the beginning because we were outsiders playing on foreign turf, and you never know how people are going to react to something that might appear to them as posing a threat of some kind. But I never saw one indication of any kind of jealousy, any pettiness, or anything but genuine affinity from all the stars toward us.

Judith Light, who won several Emmy awards for her work on *One Life* and who has since gone on to prime-time stardom on the popular sitcom *Who's the Boss?*, was one of the top stars in all of daytime television in the days when I was first there, and she was marvelous. During my first afternoon on the set when I had the dressing room scene with Becky Lee and I had to deliver quite a bit of dialogue, Judith stood off to the side and watched intently as I struggled to do it the best I could. When it was over and we had evidently pulled it off to everyone's satisfaction, she jumped up and down and applauded like a high-school cheerleader. I could have hugged her neck. From that moment on I felt at home.

Michael Storm, who plays Dr. Larry Wolek on the show, turned out to be as big a baseball nut as I am, which gave us plenty to talk about. He loves the New York Yankees, and they were in the playoffs one year while we were taping. He had box-seat tickets. He'd be doing his scenes at the studio and looking at his watch hoping we'd finish the show in time for him to get to the stadium and see some of the action. I think he did get to catch a couple of games.

Mary Murray and Wayne Massey, who played the singers, were and are both excellent vocalists. People used to say to me, "They're not really doing their own singing, are they?" assuming that actors can't be singers too. But they both did their own vocals and did them well. Wayne, in fact, is now in the music business full time. He is married to and singing with country star Charly McLain.

Philip Carey, the great character actor who plays the evil Asa Buchanan on *One Life*; Bobby Woods, who plays his son Bo; Clint Ritchie, who plays the other son, Clint Buchanan; Erika Slezak (Vicky); Brynn Thayer (Jenni); Robin Strasser (Dorian)—all these people were so great to us. One night the band and I were booked into a new country music nightclub in Manhattan, and I'll never forget the feeling I got when I walked out onstage and saw the whole cast of the soap opera sitting out in the audience whooping it up for us. These were people who had been in the studio working since before sunrise, people who had scenes to study and lines to learn for the next day's taping, which would again start at daybreak, and here they were spending their valuable time coming out to a nightclub to watch our show. It was like we'd found a whole new beautiful family.

I have nothing but the utmost respect and admiration for the people who ply their trade in daytime television drama. For some reason soap opera stars in general never seem to get the credit that people in other areas of show business receive. I know this much: The ones I worked around are super-talented and super-professional.

They (and we) had to be at the studio between six and seven o'clock every morning. With a cup of coffee in one hand and a script in the other, we'd read through our lines and learn our paces for the day under the watchful eye of the episode's director in a small, completely mirrored room in the basement of the studio. (Because the soaps tape so much drama every day, it requires that more than one director be on the staff. At the time we were there, *One Life* was rotating three people in and out of the director's post, each person working on the set every third day. On the two off-days, the director would be reading over his next assigned script and planning his every move.) Around nine o'clock they'd move us upstairs, and we'd go through it all again, this time actually on the set with the cameras and microphones in place and the technicians learning their roles as well. After a short lunch break, we'd go through a complete, on-camera dress rehearsal. Around four o'clock on a good day and five o'clock on a slow day, tape would actually start to roll. When the director and the producer were satisfied that they had a quality sixty-minute performance in the can, then and only then would everybody get to go home. I've seen taping days end by five-thirty and I've seen them last well into the night. It's not an easy way to make a living. I appeared on the show only part-time, and I learned real fast how draining it can be. These people do it every day, five days a week. I can't tell you how greatly I admire them.

I did come to learn, however, that my newfound family, those wonderful, nice, hard-working folks that I've been saying all these nice things about, possessed a seamy side. They once stole an employee away from me. And I couldn't do one single thing to stop them.

Well, the actors and actresses didn't actually steal anybody, but the network did. Marty Slutsky had been the audio engineer on all my tours for several years, and naturally I took him along to *One Life* to mix sound for us. Marty was a super audio man, so good in fact that the engineering staff at ABC watched him work with me, recognized his talents, and offered him a job. I knew I couldn't begin to match the salary and the benefits they offered him, and although I hated to lose him, I told him he'd be crazy to pass up the opportunity if it was something he thought he'd like to do. He took the job.

He's still working there today, living in Nashville and commuting every week or so to New York. I occasionally see his name on the credits of various ABC-TV shows, including even the prime-time news. Last year he gained some nationwide notoriety as the sound man who put the microphone close by the bench of the U.S. hockey team at the Winter Olympics and picked up a few well-chosen words from one of the coaches. I'm glad he never tried hiding a microphone in the back of the bus while he was working with me!

People ask me nearly everywhere I go even today, "When will you be back on *my* show?"

"I did a small part on *General Hospital* recently," I tell them.

"Yeah, but that's not my show," they complain. "*One Life to Live* is my show."

"Well, I'll be back whenever they write me into the script again," I say, and I guess that's true. It would be fun to do the soaps some more, to see and work with my friends there again, and who knows, maybe someday I will. But for right now I'm just enjoying the memories of the shows I did work and not holding my breath.

19

At the same time I was flying back and forth to California trying to be Bob Barker, and up to and back from New York in hopes of getting my picture in *Soap Opera Digest*, some subtle winds of change were beginning to blow across the music business in Nashville. Even though I had been busy chasing new dreams, I hadn't detached myself from the old ones at all, and I was very aware of what was going on. It forced me to make two of the toughest decisions I've ever had to make in my life.

The hit records and hit songs had kept on coming. Songs like "All the Lonely Women in the World," "If You Can Live with It (I Can Live Without It)," "World of Make Believe," and "The Corner of My Life" all went to the top of the charts. Jan and I had gone to No. 1 with "Dis-satisfied," and Mary Lou and I had two smashes in a row, "Sometimes" and "That's What Made Me Love You." On the surface, my recording career appeared to be in good shape.

Yet underneath it all I was growing anxious. Country music itself was beginning ever so slowly to change. New artists were coming on the scene. New songwriters. The competition was beginning to stiffen. Nothing was as certain as it had seemed to be for so long.

And some strange things started happening to me. My follow-up to "Corner of My Life" had been a beautiful, modern country ballad called "Can I Come Home to You?" which I had recorded with high hopes. But MCA somehow mastered the tapes and pressed the records with too much bass on them. When the song was played on the radio, it sounded muddy and garbled. I was extremely upset. We asked the label to notify the radio stations that the pressings were faulty and assure them that a new pressing was on its way, but instead of solving the problem, that only seemed to intensify it. Some stations who had started playing the record as soon as they received it and probably had never noticed the muffled sound got nervous and pulled the record from their playlists. Other stations never got around to adding it, saying they were waiting on the new pressing. By the time the confusion settled down, we had lost three or four valuable weeks and the record never regained its momentum.

My next release after that was the ill-fated "Everytime I Turn the Radio On," the record that was killed by the ACE controversy. The next record, "I Still Feel the Same About You," just simply was not a hit. We pulled "Country DJ," an autobiographical ode to small-town radio announcers, out of my current album for the next single, and while it was a big hit with the DJs who could relate to all that it said, the general public didn't exactly throw their babies up in the air when they heard it. I next tried a song I'd found in England called "Thanks," and I quickly realized I should have said "No thanks" and left it over on the other side of the ocean. Five releases in a row without a killer. I was nervous.

Up to this point, Owen Bradley had produced every record I had ever recorded, and I knew I owed him more credit than I'd ever be able to give him in one lifetime. He had taken my simple recitation of "Mama Sang a Song" and created a musical masterpiece around it. I've already recounted how his meticulous production on "Still" made it so different, so unique, and so inimitable. And it was Owen Bradley who first helped me rewrite the melody and then created the signature "raindrops" sound on "I Love You Drops." And he who made Jimmy Colvard tune the big A-string down two frets on my old flat-top Martin guitar and pick out the melody over and over and over again until he got it just right on "Golden Guitar." "You've got to make it *sound* golden!" Owen said relentlessly, until in fact it did.

I thought there was no record producer in the world who was in the same league with Owen Bradley, and time has certainly proven that to be the case. But at the same time it had been five record releases in a row since a Bill Anderson record had really clicked. That was more than a year's worth of records without a hit. Had we lost something? Had I lost something? Owen was like a father to me, but had time begun to pass us by? Was the magic not there anymore? Could another producer bring it back? And if so, who? I didn't know, and I began to agonize over it constantly.

I wasn't the only artist on the label asking these questions. Owen had been virtually the only producer on staff at MCA for years and at one time had something like forty artists under his guidance. Some thought his time and his talents were spread too thin. He had produced over twenty big country hits for Conway Twitty, but one day Conway decided he wanted a new producer and left. Several other MCA acts were talking about making a change, too, and that doubled the pressure on me. I didn't want to leave Owen when everybody else was running out, but at the same time I feared my own career was on the verge of growing stagnant if I stayed. In the music business, if you're standing still, you're going backwards.

In addition, my trauma was compounded by the fact that Owen and I had not only our artist-producer relationship of nearly twenty years, but we had developed a very close personal friendship away from the music business as well. We lived in the same part of town, we were often together at the Vanderbilt football and basketball games, and Owen had been the person who first got Becky and me interested in boating.

He and his wife, Katherine, owned a big houseboat, which they kept on Old Hickory Lake not far from his legendary Bradley's Barn recording studio, and many's the time we'd break away from the pressures of recording and slip away down to his boat to relax. Sometimes we'd just sit in the lounge chairs out on the boat's spacious front deck and talk, other times he'd crank the engines and we'd go out for a ride on the water. Owen and Katherine spent all their weekends and whatever other time they could manage together on or around their houseboat. It seemed to be a relaxing way of life for them, and Becky and I couldn't help but notice. One day we decided we had to have a houseboat, too, and we bought one. Ours wasn't nearly as big and fancy as Owen's (his was named *Studio A* and ours was called *The Po' Boat*), but that boat turned out to be our refuge from the world many times and provided us with some of our happiest moments together. I'd get home from a weekend road trip on Monday afternoon, and by Monday night Becky and I would be out on the water. We'd carry a sack of groceries, and she'd put a ham in the oven and a pot of beans on the stove; we'd each carry a good book to read, maybe a game of Scrabble, and we'd anchor down in a little cove and just sit there, sometimes for days. Owen helped us obtain membership in the same boating club he belonged to, and spending time with him and other friends on and around the water became a big part of our lives. No matter what professional decision I might have felt myself being forced to make, above all I did not want to jeopardize my friendship with this marvelous man.

I also need to point out in fairness to Owen that he was under a tremendous amount of pressure from the parent MCA company in California about this time. There had been a lot of changes in the corporate structure out there, and his bosses were suddenly a whole new group of players. And as so often happens when changes are made, the new folks came in with their own sets of rules. Owen had not been in the best of health, either, and I think his mind was often on things other than producing phonograph records. I felt bad that I couldn't be part of the solution. Therefore, I guess I was part of the problem.

It finally reached the point where I knew I had to make up my mind one way or the other. Who would produce my records if I left Owen? Would I just be trading one set of problems for another? I was about to drive myself crazy with worry when I remembered something George Hamilton IV had said to me nearly twenty years earlier.

At that time I had been debating whether or not to leave Tree Publishing as a writer and sign with Hubert Long's Moss-Rose Publications. I had been successful for over three years at Tree, and Moss-Rose was a new, unproven company. At the same time I wanted Hubert to manage my career more than anything else I could think of, even though he had made it plain that his signing me as an artist would be contingent upon my also writing songs for his company. "You need to put all your eggs in one basket," he kept saying, even as he had tossed the postage stamps into my lap. But still I was having a hard time making up my mind. One day I would feel one way about it, and the next day I'd feel just the opposite. In the midst of my dilemma, I asked George to go to dinner with me between Opry spots one Saturday night and help me figure out what I should do.

Over a hot hamburger steak and a plate full of crispy french fries at the old Flaming Steer restaurant on West End Avenue, I explained to George as best as I could the rock and the hard place I felt like I was caught between. He listened carefully to all I had to say then said, "Well, here's how I've always tried to make major decisions in my life: I take a long time making up my mind about something. I try to look at all the angles, weigh all the pros and cons of whatever decision it is that I'm trying to make. And then when I've gathered all the evidence and examined it as carefully as I can, I make up my mind. Then—and this is the most important part—I never look back!"

"I never look back!" There's no telling how many ulcers and how many gray hairs that one little piece of advice has spared me over the years. "I never look back" has probably been one of the two or three most significant things anybody has ever said to me in my life. Because up to that point in my life I'd no sooner make a decision that I'd be right back stressing myself out over whether it had been the right decision or not. I guess I saw my dad do that to himself a lot during the years I was growing up, and I copied him. But that was wrong. George's advice was much better, and I continue to heed it today. It's the only way I've found to make decisions and keep from driving myself insane.

I told Owen the following week that I felt it was best for everyone concerned if I made a change. It was one of the hardest things I've ever done. I hurt me because I know it hurt him, but once I made up my mind I didn't, I couldn't, look back. I had to go on to the next step.

Buddy Killen had wanted to produce records for as long as I had known him. Although he was basically a music publisher, he got a kick out of moonlighting as a record producer and had actually produced quite a few hits. Perhaps the best known of these had come in the early sixties when he talked a bunch of studio musicians and background singers into helping him record a song he had written called "Forever." He got the record released on a small label, invented the name the Little Dippers for the group, and set out to have himself some fun. But suddenly the record started taking off around the country, and before Buddy knew what hit him he found himself with a pop smash on his hands.

I was hanging out around Tree a lot in those days and was there the day Dick Clark's office called and said they wanted the Little Dippers to fly to Philadelphia and appear on *American Bandstand*. "Lord, there's no such *thing* as the Little Dippers," Buddy moaned to me as he tried frantically to come up with a solution. In those days you just didn't turn down an appearance on *American Bandstand*. He ended up hastily putting a group of singers together, sending them to Philadelphia, and ultimately I think they even worked a few rock 'n' roll tours. And it whetted Buddy's appetite to produce more records.

He helped on nearly all the Roger Miller hits, he produced several million-sellers by soul singer Joe Tex, he cut country records by Dottie West, Diana Trask, Jack Reno, and several others, and when I decided to make my change, Buddy was the first person I knew to turn to.

"You really need to do some new, exciting things," Buddy said to me when I first brought up the subject of wanting to revitalize my recording career. "What you've been doing has been all right, but it's gotten stale," he said and I agreed.

"But would you help me?" I asked.

"If you'd like to reach out a bit and try something different, I would. In fact, I think I'd really enjoy working with you."

"Hey, I'll try anything once," I answered, not knowing or really caring just what Buddy had meant by "reach out . . . and try something different." At that point I was ready and willing to try anything. We shook hands, and as simply as that, nearly twenty years after our first meeting and our first successes together, Bill Anderson and Buddy Killen were back working on the same team again.

I have never seen a record producer work as hard as Buddy worked in selecting the material for our first session together. We must have listened to a thousand songs—"No, this one's not quite right" . . . "This one is OK, but we don't need one that's OK. We need one that's *great!*"—until we settled on the four best pieces of material we could find. Then and only then did he book the musicians and head me into the studio.

I was nervous recording with Buddy for the first time. I had been used to Owen's laidback approach, and Buddy was much more intense, maybe because we had something to prove. He spent hour after lengthy hour getting the musical tracks just the way he wanted them, then he made me sing the songs over and over and over again until I had them exactly the way he felt like they ought to sound. The more he'd push, the more uptight I'd become. Once or twice I began to wonder if I'd done the right thing by signing with Buddy, but I finally calmed down and gave him something he could keep. Looking back, there's no doubt that he knew exactly what he was doing.

The first release to come out of those sessions was a Bobby Braddock song called "Peanuts and Diamonds." It was definitely different from anything I had ever attempted before. It also went to No. 1 on the charts. Our second release, "Liars One, Believers Zero," came off that same first session and it went to No. 2. We cut a country version of Orleans' "Still the One," and it clicked. Buddy produced the entire second duet album with Mary Lou, and in a 180-degree turnabout, it was his idea to ask Roy Acuff to sing with me on a song about an old-time musician seeking one last moment in the spotlight, the touching "I Wonder If God Likes Country Music." No matter what direction we tried to go in, the Anderson-Killen chemistry—music from a pair of Scorpios—seemed to be working.

But our biggest success and our ultimate statement to the world was still ahead of us. It came about as the result of a very simple question I asked Buddy one day in conversation. Disco music was just beginning to take the country by storm, and the disco beat felt very exciting to me. I couldn't really relate to very many of the songs themselves, but those hard-driving, pulsating rhythms made me want to get up and move. I thought it felt sexy.

"Tell me something, Bud," I said innocently one afternoon in his office. "Is there any reason you couldn't take a country song and put a disco beat to it?" Frankly, I couldn't think of one.

"I don't know," Buddy answered. "I never thought about it. I guess you could. Why?"

"Well, I've just been thinking that it might make a pretty exciting sound. It might be something I'd like to try."

"You got any particular song in mind?"

"No," I said, "but I might just try to write one." And I left his office with the thought firmly planted in my mind.

I don't honestly remember how many nights later it was that I was sitting around in my den, strumming on my guitar, when I began trying to write a country lyric and a country melody that I thought would lend themselves to a disco beat. I knew the lyric had to be just right. I couldn't sing about Mama or trains or kids or gettin' drunk. It had to be a song about love, and the lyric had to be as pounding and as sexy as the beat behind it. I had never before set out deliberately to write a sexy song.

I don't know where the idea came from or how I happened to start writing it, but in a few minutes I was sitting at my typewriter, guitar strung across my shoulder, singing, "I can't wait any longer . . . This feeling's getting stronger . . . Satisfy my hunger . . . You're the only one who can . . ." And the melody was as country as country could be. But in my mind's ear I could hear a hot, rapid-fire disco beat electrifying the words I was singing, and I knew the two would fit. I got excited. This was what I wanted. I kept on writing:

> *Where do I have to go*
> *What do I have to do*
> *Who do I have to lie to*
> *So I can lie with you*
> *I can't wait any longer.*

I called Buddy the next morning and told him I thought I had come up with a country lyric that would match with a disco beat, and he got as excited as I had been. I said, "I've gotta come down there and sing it for you!" and he said, "Come on!" but when I got to his office I suddenly got stage fright. Or whatever kind of fright it is that a songwriter gets when he's not sure his new song is really worth showing to anybody. Buddy almost had to beat me over the head to get me to sing it to him.

Finally I got up the nerve. "You'll have to use your imagination," I said as I sat there on a stool with just my guitar. "Imagine all the instruments, that disco beat . . ."

"Willy, I've been using my imagination on your songs for twenty years," Buddy smiled. "Now *sing* it!" And I did.

He loved it. He walked over to his piano and began playing along with me. Then he started adding some chords I hadn't written. "It's going to need a little bridge of some kind," he said. "See how you like this." What he played sounded super to me. Suddenly I had a cowriter.

"Can we cut it?" I asked.

"How much nerve you got?"

"What do you mean?"

"I mean, have you got the guts to take the flak we're gonna get if it's a bomb? Heck, we'll probably get flak even if it's a *hit*," he said.

"I'm game if you are," I answered, and Buddy booked the session.

It's a rule of thumb in our business that if the musicians and background singers on a record session like the records you're making, then chances are you're cutting a flop. Pickers and singers who make records for a living hear so many songs day in and day out that nothing moves them. When something does, it's usually something that's way over the head of the record-buying public. That's why I got doubly scared when we cut "I Can't Wait Any Longer." All the players on the session loved it.

Buddy outdid himself on the production. He hired some of Nashville's most capable and versatile studio musicians and then supplemented them with players from Joe Tex's rhythm-and-blues band. Janie Fricke was still singing background vocals in those days, and Buddy used her, both to sing along with me and to sing answer lines to some I was singing. Nobody knew if a country song set to a disco beat would sell two copies or not, but we knew when it was finished that we'd done what we set out to do. That was to give it our best shot.

"What else does it need?" I asked Buddy after all the overdubs had been laid down and the mixing was in its final stages.

"Willy," he answered, resting his arm on my shoulder, "this record don't need nothin' 'cept *out!*"

Becky was well into her pregnancy with Jamey when I recorded "I Can't Wait Any Longer," but she didn't let a little thing like a puffed-up belly and swollen ankles stop her from coming to my sessions the way she had always done. She sat quietly in the control room and listened and smiled and tapped her toes . . . and let me know simply by looking at me in her own special way that she thought what we were doing was some kind of fantastic.

We laid down all the musical tracks and most of the overdubs. Everybody was getting anxious to hear what this strange combination of country music and disco music was starting to sound like. Pretty soon Buddy called us all into the control room and told the engineer to cue up the tape.

For some reason all musicians, most singers, and many producers like to listen to the playbacks of the music they create at full volume, especially when the music is still new and fresh and exciting to them. I am no exception. As soon as everybody had gathered around, the engineer slid the faders on the control board up as high as he could get them to go without blowing the speakers and he turned on the tape. Everybody stood there listening, smiling, grooving out on the music we'd just made.

Becky was sitting on a small sofa in front of the recording console, directly underneath the giant studio speakers when the music started to play. Within seconds the whole control room started to vibrate.

Suddenly, above the loud roar of the music, I heard Becky start to laugh. And she laughed louder . . . and louder. Finally I walked around to where she was seated to see what in the world was so funny. "Come here," she said, "and put your hand on my stomach. You won't believe what this baby is doing."

"What's he doing?" I asked, already referring to my child as "he" and not being able to imagine an unborn baby being able to do much of anything.

"Here . . . right here," she said, guiding my hand to a spot on her swollen tummy. "Feel that?"

I pressed my hand gently on Becky's stomach, and I couldn't believe it. Thump—thump—thump. That little baby inside her body was kicking or flinging his arms about or dancing or something, and he was doing it almost exactly in time with the music!

"Good Lord," I exclaimed. "The kid's got perfect timing! What do you reckon you've got in there, a drummer?"

* * *

I swore after "Where Have All Our Heroes Gone" that I'd never record anything controversial again, but "I Can't Wait Any Longer" made "Heroes" look like "Mary Had a Little Lamb." From the minute it hit the market, everybody and his brother had an opinion on it.

"It's the greatest, most original thing I've ever heard," some of the DJs were screaming.

"We'll never play that trash on our station!" others said with equal determination. "That's the filthiest, most suggestive song I've ever heard. Our listeners would run us out of town if we played it!" And every time I answered the phone or opened the mail, somebody was either praising me or lambasting me.

Surprisingly, a lot of people at my own record company were laughing at me and putting me down, especially some of those in the promotion department who were on the receiving end of many of the complaints. "Who does he think he is, coming out with all that heavy-breathing stuff?" they'd say. "A forty-year-old sex symbol? Don't make me laugh!" But while they were putting me down on the one hand, with the other hand they were writing orders from dealers buying as many copies of the record as they could get their hands on.

The fact that we'd taken a country song and set it to a disco beat, however, seemed to be lost on most people. Most of the ruffled feathers were from people who didn't like the plain-spoken lyric. "Our lives have touched . . . our minds have touched . . . and I can't wait any longer for our bodies to touch . . . and our souls to touch" seemed to turn off the people who had loved it when I whispered "My mama sang a song." But it sure seemed to turn a lot of other folks on.

"We get more requests for 'I Can't Wait Any Longer' than any other record we play," more than one perplexed disc jockey told me when the record was at its peak, "but we also get more complaints on it than any other song we play. One minute I say I'll never play it again, and the next minute the phones are ringing off the wall from people wanting to hear it. I don't know what to do!" I wasn't too sure what to do either.

I didn't want to offend people or upset people who had been fans of mine for twenty years, but at the same time this was fresh, it was new, and it was exciting. MCA pressed up a twelve-inch version of the record that lasted nearly seven minutes and shipped copies to every disco nightclub in the country. Bobby booked me on a nationally syndicated disco television show from an old warehouse in New Jersey called The Soap Factory, where I was singing and dancing and laughing with some of the loveliest ladies imaginable. And the record went to No. 1 in the country charts.

The reaction to the single caused MCA to call for an entire album of similar material, which they titled *Ladies' Choice*. It was a solid seller, but to this day people will tell me that it's either (a) their very favorite album or (b) their most un-favorite Bill Anderson album.

In the fall of the year, *Billboard* magazine presented me with their Special Breakthrough Award for 1978, recognizing my bringing country music and disco together as "the most outstanding creative musical achievement of the year." Buddy and I were on top of the world, but we made one big mistake. We jumped down off our horse before the race was over.

We listened to what some of the promotion people at MCA who didn't like the record were saying, what a small handful of old-line, hard-core Bill Anderson fans were saying, and we allowed them to influence the songs we chose and the type of records we cut the next time we went into the studio. As soon as we finished *Ladies' Choice*, we began to back away from the very thing that had made us successful. The momentum we generated with "I Can't Wait Any Longer" and the follow-up, "Double-S," began to slip away. Within two years we had removed ourselves so far from it that we had allowed it to die out completely.

Buddy became totally frustrated with MCA. Here he had breathed new life into an artist who had been on their label for twenty years, given my career a whole new shot in the arm, and instead of appreciating it and building upon it they were standing on the sidelines laughing at both of us and, in effect, telling us not to do it anymore. So Buddy quit. He didn't need the hassle. He quit producing my records; he quit producing any records at all for MCA. Instead, he took what we had started together and transferred it to the records he began producing for T. G. Shepard on Warner Brothers. The same type songs, the same musicians, the same type arrangements. Warner Brothers didn't laugh, they believed in the concept, and T. G. became a star. I tried cutting a

few more records for MCA under the direction of Jim Fogelsong, a
wonderful man who became the head of the company's Nashville
operations following a big shake-up at MCA and their subsequent
purchase of the ABC-Dot label, but nothing clicked. My contract
expired at the end of 1982, and the label where I had hung my hat
for twenty-three years put me out to pasture.

I have always prided myself on having a good band. From the
early days of the Po' Boys to my current edition of the Po' Folks
Band, there has rarely been a time since the mid-sixties when
people couldn't truthfully say that I carried one of the best back-up
groups in the country music business.

It hasn't been by accident. I've always chosen my people carefully. I figure as closely as we all have to live, travel, and work that
it's tough enough with good people. It would be impossible with
bad ones. But in the late seventies, with a band full of good people
working behind me, I found myself being forced to make an almost
impossible judgment: Should I or shouldn't I fire my entire band?
It was a scenario that nearly destroyed me, becoming the second
half of the hardest decision I've ever had to make.

I've been told by some people that they think I'd be difficult to
work for. Over the years there have probably been times when I
was. I once had a member of another Opry star's band tell me,
"Anderson, I could never work for you." I answered, "You're right,
you never could." But he meant his remark one way. I meant mine
another.

What he meant was that he felt like I expected too much of my
people, that I was too demanding, that he could never fit into my
scheme of things. What I meant was that he was too sloppy in his
approach to music, that he didn't treat his job like it was a business, that his attitude and mine would clash before we were halfway through our opening song on opening night. I've hired one or
two losers in my time but not very many. Most of the people I've
hired have ended up staying with me for long periods of time.
Compared to most country bands, my band has, over the years,
experienced very little turnover. If I were too bad a guy to work
for, I don't think most of the players would have bothered to hang
around.

I've always tried to treat the people I hire like I'd want to be treated if I were in their shoes. I've never said that people work "for" me. I've always said they work "with" me. We both know who signs the paycheck, but I've never seen any point in rubbing it in. I am a bit of a perfectionist but not nearly as bad as I once was. I like things done a certain way within my organization, but I'm certainly not a tyrant. I tell my employees what I expect of them when I first bring them on board, and I try to hire people who are mature enough to understand and accept what few rules and regulations I do have. I'm not on their backs harping about things constantly. I don't have time for that. I've even been accused by some onlookers of being too lenient and treating my people too good. I'd like to think I fall somewhere in between.

There was a time in my early days, though, when I'll admit I had a tendency to be too strict, especially about little things. I remember on one of my first overseas tours I told the band I wanted them to wear coats and ties on our airline flights. "We are representing country music to people all over the world," I reasoned, "and we need to put our best foot forward." My guys did as they were told, but when all the other groups on the tour travelled in T-shirts and blue jeans we stuck out like sore thumbs. I don't have that rule anymore.

I don't have very many rules, period. Show up on time, be sober, and be prepared to do a good job. That's about it. What you do on your own time is your own business except for one thing: You need to remember always that so much of the time, especially when we're on the road, you are not Joe Jones. You are Bill Anderson's guitar player. Everything you say, everything you do, good and bad, reflects on me. You have, as a result of your position with me, the capability of both helping my career flourish and grow and the power to tear down in five minutes a reputation I've spent nearly thirty years building up.

So be careful.

I remember exactly where I was when the thought that I might soon have to fire my entire band first crossed my mind. The Po' Boys and I were working for a week at the rodeo in Camdenton, Missouri, in the heart of the Ozarks. By day we swam and fished and went boating with our families (once or twice a year I try to arrange trips where the musicians can bring their spouses along), and at night we put on our Nudie suits and climbed up on the back of a flatbed truck, rode out into the middle of the rodeo arena, and picked and sang for forty-five minutes or so. It was a real tough tour of duty, but somebody had to do it.

It was the third or fourth night we had been in town, and I was standing back by my bus listening to the band play their opening songs. David Byrd, Mary Lou Turner's husband and an excellent musician himself, was standing beside me. I thought the band sounded particularly good that night, and I said so to David. Something like, "Boy, that's *some* band, isn't it?" I stood tall with pride.

But his response knocked me for a loop. "Yeah, they're good," he said, "but they sure are starting to sound dated."

"Dated?" I said. "What do you mean 'dated'?"

"Well, it's just the same old country sound that's been around forever," David replied. "Fiddle, steel guitar, lead guitar. Music is changing today, and it's going to be changing a lot more in the next few years. If I were you, I'd start thinking about changing a little myself."

"What kind of changes? How?"

"Well, for one thing synthesizers are the coming thing. Everybody is gonna be using them before much longer. You can get all kinds of string sounds and keyboard sounds with them. Your band is great, but they really didn't sound enough like your records. Plus, you need some real backup singers, not just guys in the band singing harmony. Now with some of this new technology . . ."

Before David had a chance to finish, I could see Mary Lou coming off stage, down the rear steps of the truck, and I could hear Jimmy Gateley across the arena starting to introduce me to the crowd. I had to stop the conversation and head for the stage, but David's words burned a hole in my mind the rest of the night. I wasn't sure exactly what he'd meant, but the seed was planted. I had to find out more.

When I got back to Nashville, I broached the subject with Buddy Killen. "David's right," Buddy said, "this business *is* changing. And if we're gonna be making these new records that stretch you out a bit, you need to have a band that can go on the road and recreate the sound of the records on stage. From what I've seen, the band you've got right now can't do that."

But couldn't I just take the group I had and make a few changes? Couldn't we make some adjustments here and there and get the same results? Did I have to hire a whole new group? Surely not! I mean, this had been one of the best bands in the business for years, hadn't it? What would my fans say? I couldn't just run everybody off. But it soon became apparent that I didn't have much choice.

I began by talking with some of the members of the band about changing a few things. Surprisingly, I met a lot of resistance. The piano player didn't have a synthesizer and didn't seem to be very excited about the possibility of getting one. The people in the group who could sing background harmonies, but who hadn't been asked to do so up to that point, balked when I mentioned that perhaps, with a little work, we could broaden our vocal sound. Nobody seemed the least bit anxious to change the status quo at all.

I know now that it was because of one reason and one reason only: The band wasn't hungry. Everybody was making a good salary, living in a nice house, driving a new car, and quite frankly they had gotten lazy. They didn't see any need whatsoever to exert themselves working on something new. I wasn't aware of just how complacent they had become until we began having these conversations and until one weekend toward the end of the year when we were booked into a nightclub in Austin, Texas.

I hadn't worked in Texas very much for quite some time, and I knew why. In Texas, people who come to see and hear country bands and country stars also come to dance. I said earlier that the greatest compliment an audience can give you in Texas is to get up and dance to your music. Texans aren't big on applause, and they're not big on sitting still and listening to a concert. But they *love* to dance. Over the years I just hadn't given them enough of the right kind of music for them to dance to. For stage show purposes in other parts of the country, I had grouped many of my hits together in medley form, singing only a few lines of each one and moving on to something else. Have you ever tried to dance to a medley? One minute we were playing up-tempo straight-eights rhythm on "Wild Weekend," and the next we were doing a slow shuffle on "City Lights." You could break a leg in a dance hall trying to keep up with foolishness like that! As a result, my trips to the Lone Star state had become fewer and farther between.

A week before the date in Austin I called a meeting of the band. "Guys, we've got to come up with a few new wrinkles when we go to Texas next weekend," I told them. "I want us to forget the medleys this time and sing all our songs all the way through. They wanta dance, and it's up to us to give 'em something to dance to! You guys work up some nice long intros and turnarounds.

"Gate," I said to Jimmy Gateley, "I know you haven't wanted to amplify your fiddle all these years and I've never pushed you to do it, but I think it's time. I want you to get a little pick-up of some kind and play through an amp this trip. That's what they're used to in Texas." And to Gregg Galbraith, my guitar player and band leader, I said, "I want you guys to work up a 'Cotton-Eyed Joe' too. You know they always ask for that in Texas." And I entrusted him with the responsibility of calling a rehearsal and working on the things I had mentioned. He assured me that he would.

I don't remember what I had to do the rest of that week, but I had to take care of some kind of business and never checked in with Gregg or the band. I just assumed everything was on track. I didn't ride the bus to Austin, but I flew down and met the group onstage at the club in time for sound check late on the Saturday afternoon of our gig.

"Well, did you work up some arrangements on the songs we've been doing in the medley?" I asked, anxious to hear what the band had accomplished while I'd been away.

"No," came the reply, "we didn't."

"How about the 'Cotton-Eyed Joe'?" I asked.

"Nope, didn't have time," I was told.

I looked toward Jimmy's fiddle to see if the pick-up had been purchased and put in place. It wasn't there either.

"Why haven't these things been done?" I asked, more than a little bit irritated.

"We all had a lot of other things to do," somebody said in a totally disinterested tone of voice. I stood there stupified by what I was hearing. Nobody had done one single thing I had asked them to do. I clenched my teeth, turned, and walked out the stage door of the building and up onto the bus. With a show coming up in just a few hours, I didn't want to get in an argument and all bent out of shape, so I just locked myself in my stateroom and glared at the wall.

But my mind was made up. I hadn't wanted to believe that it was true, but my band — the great Po' Boys band, voted one of the best bands in all of country music for umpteen years in a row — didn't care anymore. And if they didn't care, then why the heck should I? The decision I had been destroying myself over— the day-after-day agony of "Should I let this group go and modernize the band?"—was made for me. And I never looked back.

After the show in Austin was over, I stood outside the bus and called each band member to come out one at a time. I gave each of them a time to meet me at my office on Monday afternoon, each appointment an hour apart. I was going to tell them individually that I was letting them go and exactly why. I assumed they could tell by the events of the evening and the tone of my voice and the look in my eye that I was highly upset.

But I actually found out later that at least two members of the band thought they were being summoned to my office to be given a *raise*! I could hardly believe that when I heard it, but it was the honest truth. I guess I had been so good to them and so lenient with them that they thought by then they could get away with anything. I'm afraid being fired jolted a few of them back to reality.

Letting Gate go was the hardest thing of all. He had been with me for thirteen years, and the Good Lord never put a kinder man on the face of this earth. But the time had come. I had to plow ahead without him. Out of respect for his loyalty and all our years together, I structured a generous financial settlement for him and took him and his wife on a Caribbean cruise with me and the new group the following year. I don't think Jimmy was ever bitter toward me, and I certainly was never bitter toward him. It was a business decision that had to be made, and I like to think each of us was man enough to look at it and accept it that way.

It was mid-November and the Po' Boys and I were still booked for two or three more weekends on the road before we'd be knocking off for Christmas. There was no way I could get a new band together, rehearse them, and get them on the road in time to cover these last few dates, so I asked the guys I had fired if they'd stick it out and stay with me through these few remaining concerts. I wasn't sure whether they would or not. And I was definitely not sure how they'd act and what their attitude would be if they did hang around. To their credit, they agreed to work the rest of the dates and did so in a good mood, possibly even the best mood I had seen them in for a year or two. Maybe they were relieved to be out from under the pressure, I don't know. But I do know that on our very last date together, a couple of them had the chance to zap me real good, and they didn't do it.

The final concert booked for Bill Anderson and the Po' Boys was in a little theater in Cornwall, Ontario, Canada, quite a long bus ride from Nashville. On the way to the date we pulled into a truck stop near Syracuse, New York, to fuel the bus and get a bite to eat. Everybody got off the bus, but two of the band members, my bass player Larry Fullam and the drummer Randy Hauser, somehow didn't get back on. The driver didn't know they weren't on board and accidentally drove away and left them at the truck stop.

We were more than a hundred miles on up the road before we realized Larry and Randy weren't anywhere on the bus. There was no time to turn around and go back after them. We'd have been late for the show. We were already cutting it close.

The thought crossed my mind that maybe the guys had planned this little surprise for me. As a going-away present perhaps. They wanted to see how I'd do onstage without any bass and drums. I was beginning to wonder how I'd do it myself, and I wasn't too excited about the prospect.

But I knew there was nothing I could do about it. We moved on up through upstate New York, crossed the border into Canada minus two of the people whose names were on the contract, and just as the sun was going down we pulled into Cornwall. And I got the surprise of my life.

When we walked into the lobby of the little theater to ask where to park the bus and unload our equipment, there lay Larry and Randy asleep on the carpet. They had hitched a ride with somebody at the truck stop and beat us to the gig.

They didn't have to do that. I knew it, and they knew it. What could I have done if they hadn't been there, fire them? I had already done that. It made for an emotional night. When I introduced the band members to the audience that night, knowing I was doing it for the final time, in spite of everything that had taken place, I got all choked up. I loved these guys, and I told them so. I just couldn't live with them anymore.

I had no idea whatsoever about how to go about putting together a new band. I hadn't had to start from scratch in nearly fifteen years. What kind of band did I want anyhow? What kinds of changes did I need to make? Where did I even begin?

Turnover in band personnel was something I had never had to face on a grand scale. Even today, after twenty-five years of employing musicians, I have actually had very few different players working with me. I've had only five steel guitar players, for example, and every one of those was great: Weldon Myrick, who left me after only two years but who went on to become the steel player in the Grand Ole Opry staff band as well as one of the top session players in all of country music; Bob Lucier, who followed Weldon for a brief time before returning to his native Canada, where he has worked behind such top Canadian stars as Anne Murray and Tommy Hunter; Bruce "Sonny" Garrish, who came with me when he was barely out of his teens and stayed for almost ten years. He created a great deal of "the Bill Anderson sound" with his masterful speed-picking on records like "Wild Weekend" and "Get While the Gettin's Good" and countless others. Sonny left in 1975 only because he was in such demand to play on record sessions that it had started costing him money to be out on the road with me. He is probably considered *the* top steel player in Nashville today.

Jack Smith followed Sonny and was with me until mid-1979 when my current steel man and band leader, Mike Johnson, came along. Jack has since been in the bands of Johnny Paycheck, Gene Watson, and Connie Smith. Mike is in the same league with Sonny and Weldon and the other great ones. He's not only a super picker, though; he's a great band leader, musical arranger and record producer. He has produced or coproduced nearly all of the phonograph records I've cut in the eighties.

But I haven't had only great steel players in my bands. Guitarists like Steve Chapman, who worked for years as a part of Ernest Tubb's renowned Texas Troubadours, and Gregg Galbraith, considered by many today to be one of Music City's leading guitar players, were both Po' Boys for a while. So was Doug Renaud, the drummer who took Snuffy Miller's place and who, had he not been tragically killed in an automobile crash in 1975, would have undoubtedly gone on to become one of the top drummers in all of country music. When Randy Hauser left the Po' Boys, he became Chet Atkins's drummer; Jimmy Lance became Eddy Arnold's guitarist, and the list goes on. I'd hired some great players over the years. How was I ever going to top what I'd already done? And where was the starting place?

Buddy Killen and David Byrd had both emphasized to me that I needed to begin sounding more like my records on stage. But what were my new records going to sound like? And would the same band be able to duplicate my new records and then go back and perform my earlier ones as well? Help!

I finally decided to begin by sitting down and listening to a stack of my older records. I seldom listen to my own work after I've finished recording. Usually when the release date arrives, I've spent so much time working on the songs I'm sick of them anyhow. Besides, after they've been out awhile, I tend to cringe every time I hear them. I always focus on all the places I know I could have done so much better. Faron Young told me once, "I hate to listen to my old records. I sound like a girl!"

But I played the records anyhow and analyzed what was on them. Most were heavy with background voices, and most of the background groups were heavy with female voices. Maybe I needed to hire some females.

I listened further and noticed many of my biggest hits like "Still" and "I Love You Drops" and "8 X 10" were lush with the sound of strings. Over the years I had used the sustaining steel guitar sound to play the string lines that the violins, violas, and cellos had played on the records. Now, with these new synthesizers, maybe I could come closer to the original sounds. There was certainly no way I could hire a complete string section to travel with me. Maybe a synthesizer was the next best thing.

I started writing down the instruments I knew I had to have. I'd need a steel guitar, of course, because Weldon Myrick and Sonny Garrish had played so many great steel licks on my records over the years that their sound was a necessity. I'd need a lead guitar, naturally, and a piano and bass and drums. That was five people already. The Po' Boys had been six. I figured at least two girls to sing, that would make seven. What about the synthesizer? And a sound man? I had decided I needed to buy some good new sound equipment and hire a professional sound man to run it. After all, we were selling "sound," and it had to be the best we could possibly give. But, good Lord, my band was starting to look like the Nashville Symphony Orchestra! How was I going to transport all these people? And, more importantly, how was I going to pay them?

I worked it out in a strange but very functional way. David Byrd knew of a keyboard player working in a small club up in Ohio who played the piano with his right hand and keyboard bass with his left. "Hire one man, get two instruments," David encouraged, but I was skeptical. A quick trip to Ohio, however, showed me I had nothing to fear. I hired Monty Parkey.

Next I decided if one of the girls I hired could play a synthesizer I could kill another two birds with one stone. I found a set of twins, Kay Sutton and Karen Klinger, who could *both* play keyboards and could *both* sing. I hired them, but not before I renamed them Kay and Karen Stacy.

I had heard about a versatile young guitar and banjo player named Randy Bethune working with Doc Williams at *Jamboree USA* in Wheeling, West Virginia. I hired him to play, sing, and emcee the shows. From LeRoy Van Dyke's band came the drummer, Mike Streeter, who is still with me today. I asked Jack Smith, my steel player from the Po' Boys, if he'd stay on, help me make the transition, and become the leader of the new group. He agreed, and the Po' Folks Band was born.

We rehearsed, got to know each other, and began to feel comfortable during most of the month of December. After the Christmas break we came back and rehearsed and rehearsed and rehearsed some more. Our first concert together was booked for a little high-school gym in Sterling, Illinois, toward the end of January. There was a lot to accomplish and so little time.

I was as nervous as I ever remember being at a show that cold, snowy Sunday afternoon when we pulled into Sterling. Word had gotten out among the fans that I was making some big changes, and a lot of people who had followed my career for years were pretty upset about it. They had gotten to know the Po' Boys over the years and considered many of them to be friends. They were skeptical about these new people they didn't know, this new sound they weren't familiar with, and they came in droves to Sterling to see what I had done.

I told the audience right off the bat that this was a new group, we were working our first show together, and to please be patient with us if we messed it all up. But they didn't have to be patient. The show came off like clockwork, and the crowd loved everything about it. They applauded, they laughed, they tapped their toes, they sang along. Then they honored us with a prolonged standing ovation. I breathed easy for the first time since November. It was going to work. I felt like a kid with a new toy.

In some ways I guess that's exactly what I was!

20

Have you ever noticed that there's something inside nearly all of us that drives us to want to succeed in an area of life where we have no expertise, no experience, and, more often than not, no talent?

A rich oil magnate invests his profits in the career of a country singer. A rich country singer invests in oil. A ball player buys a restaurant. A wealthy restaurateur buys a sports franchise. And on it goes, the common denominator usually being that each person would have been well-advised to stay within the boundaries of his own knowledge.

My venturing out from country music into the worlds of game shows and soap operas turned out well, but I probably should have quit right there while I was still ahead.

You see, I'm basically an entertainer. A creator, perhaps, but my creativity has for the most part revolved around the business of entertainment. Maybe I can entertain in more ways than one, but I'm still an entertainer. Or a singer. Or a performer. Nowhere in the book does it say Bill Anderson is a businessman. Nor should it.

But I've tried to become a businessman a couple of times when I should have kept right on pickin' and grinnin'. And I've paid for it.

Back in 1975 I heard of a little radio station in Provo, Utah, called KIXX that was for sale. Now, anybody who has ever worked at a radio station thinks he knows how to run a station better than anybody he's ever worked for. And every lowly disc jockey sits in the control room where he works and dreams of the day when he will own his own radio station. I was no exception. Owning a station had been my dream ever since the days back in Commerce, and I was determined to someday make it come true. Besides, not only was this station for sale, it was for sale cheap. That really caught my attention.

But not nearly as much as the sun caught my attention the first morning I saw it rise above the Wasatch Mountains overlooking Provo. I'd have bought anything they were selling that day—filling station, radio station, I didn't care. I'd never seen anything so beautiful in my life. It was September and the mountains were, as the natives say, "in bloom." From off the stark brown, rocky mountainsides bounced brilliant reds, bright greens, and dancing yellows, combining to give the appearance of a ten-thousand-foot-high rainbow hovering over the Utah Valley. Someone many years before crossed those same mountains a few miles to the north and exclaimed, "This is the place." I knew exactly how he must have felt.

Dean Booth, my attorney friend from Atlanta, had actually been the one who heard about KIXX's being for sale. He knew I wasn't going to be happy until I tried my hand at owning a station and, being a bit of an adventurer himself, he decided he might as well come along for the ride. I purchased eighty-five percent of the stock in the station, saving the remaining fifteen percent for him.

We found out quickly why the station had been on the market so cheap. It had a terrible reputation in the community. "KIXX is for hicks" was the rhyming local expression I kept hearing over and over after my name was on the dotted line. Robert Redford's father-in-law owned the land on which the studios sat, but even his presence didn't help. From day one, people popped up everywhere telling me how this person or that person previously connected with the station had mistreated them or left town owing them money. It didn't take me very long to realize our little radio station needed a king-sized face-lift.

I started by changing the name. We were a full-time AM station at 1400 on the dial, and it was my idea to call us K-14. So I applied to the Federal Communications Commission for the call letters KFTN. Get it? FTN, short for fourteen. I thought it was brilliant, never realizing that when you say "FTN" real fast the listener wonders if you said "XZM" or "SDM" or what. We finally settled on just "Radio-14" as our handle and used the official call letters only when the FCC required us to.

The small concrete block building that housed the offices and studios a couple of miles south of downtown Provo was a disaster. The station had been on the air since 1947, and I honestly believe they were still using some of the original equipment. In fact, there were actually some 78-rpm records in the control room. I started the remodeling procedure by directing that all those old records be taken to a storage room in the rear of the building. And left there.

Next I went down to a local paint store and loaded up on paint, paint brushes, rollers, and all the accessories. Both the inside and outside of the building were in dire need of a face-lift. Becky put on some old clothes and grabbed a paint brush. So did the off-duty announcers. So did the salesmen. So did the husbands and the wives of the announcers and the salesmen. The unspoken orders were that anybody who wanted to make their living working at KFTN had to pitch in and help make KFTN a nicer place to work.

The outside of the building was awful. There were potholes in the driveway so large that I didn't know, as Grandpa Jones once said about his driveway, "whether to have them repaired or stock them with fish." Windows on all sides of the building were broken out, the result, no doubt, of the studios being located just off the tenth tee of the Timpanogas golf course. We repaired those, covered up the dingy white paint and faded red lettering on the outside of the building with an attractive beige paint trimmed in dark brown, then put our slick new logo across the top in bright orange. I went down to a local advertising agency and bought twenty-five or thirty outdoor billboards around town advertising our "new" radio station, then sat back and waited for the listeners to beat a path to our frequency.

Having come out of the programming side of radio myself as opposed to being from sales, I was more concerned in the beginning with how my little radio station sounded than I was with how many advertisers we had. I thought if we sounded good the sponsors would stand in line to advertise. Since the selling of ads pays all the bills around a radio station, however, I would say I put the cart slightly before the horse. If I had it all to do over again, I'd have hired a crackerjack sales manager to bring some sponsors on board and then used the advertising money to hire some good programming people. But what did I know? I was just a hillbilly singer trying to rekindle the fire of an old love from his youth.

The format of the station was, of course, country music, but a lot of people in Provo, Utah, home of Brigham Young University and quite a bit of rather high-toned culture for a town its size, didn't exactly jump up and down over Porter Wagoner, Conway Twitty, and Loretta Lynn. At least not at first. But by doing our job on the air in a professional manner and by a lot of good station promotions, we slowly but surely began to feel the tide changing in our direction.

We did anything we could to try and get attention. One of our disc jockies once broadcast live from the window of a downtown appliance store for nearly a week without ever sleeping. I came to town one time and gave away free gasoline to every listener who would drive into our sponsor's filling station and say they heard about it on KFTN. That particular promotion was a smashing success, even attracting the attention of the local newspaper, which sent a photographer out to take a picture of me actually pumping gasoline into the tanks of the mile-long line of cars. They ran the picture in the paper the next day with a headline writer's marvelous caption: "Bill Anderson gives listeners gas." Who knows, maybe I did!

Becky and I really liked Provo. We found a small apartment in a nearly empty apartment complex not far from the station and, by trading out some advertising with the owners, we got our rent for free. We got involved with as many things as we could in the community, started going to ball games at BYU, shopping in the local stores, and taking long relaxing drives and walks up into the mountains. We especially enjoyed going up to the various ski resorts in the area, but despite Becky's pleadings and the offers of free skiing lessons from people all over the community, I never once put on a pair of skis. Not again. I had seen *Downhill Racer* once over at Vail, Colorado, and I told the Good Lord if He'd just get me down off that mountain I had been fool enough to go up that I'd never go back up there again. So far I've kept my word.

But Provo, for all its warmth and all its natural beauty and all the things we enjoyed about going there, was simply not a good radio town. There were two other stations in town at the time, plus we were less than fifty miles south of Salt Lake City, where there were a dozen or so more. That meant people throughout our listening area could also pick up strong, clear signals from most of those stations too, particularly from KSL, the Morman Church-owned station in Salt Lake. Something like ninety percent of the people who live in the greater Provo area are of the Morman faith, and even those who didn't listen to KSL seemed to be afraid to admit it when the rating services called. I once decided to conduct my own private survey and I got some people on the phone who actually had KFTN playing loud enough in the background for me to tell they were tuned to our station, but when I asked them which station they were listening to they answered "KSL." It was like they thought the devil was going to jump up and bite them if they said anything else. We clawed and scratched for every listener and every advertising dollar we could get, but with my living in Nashville and being out on the road in Timbuktu half the time, I often didn't take care of business at the radio station like I should have.

For one thing, I never could seem to get the right manager in place. I started out with a local manager who knew the community well and had an in with many of the local advertisers, but he only lasted until his wife became pregnant with their eleventh child. At that point he went to work at Brigham Young University because that was the only place of employment he could find with an insurance program that would cover a family with as many as eleven children.

I then brought a friend of mine in from another city who I thought was an excellent programmer and who, I felt, deserved a chance to try his hand at managing. Maybe he would have been good, but I never got a chance to find out. He disappeared one night under a cover of darkness, hoping his creditors would have a hard time picking up his trail. Last I heard of him he'd been in Alaska, been driving a truck for a living, and been in jail, not necessarily in that order.

My next attempt at finding a manager for the station ended when the man I had chosen applied for a license to operate his own beer joint and pool hall on the side. In staunchly conserva-tive, highly religious Provo, the manager of the local radio station does not sell radio advertising by day then pour Budweiser and rack billiard balls by night. So it was back to the drawing boards for the fourth and what proved to be the final time.

Manager No. 4 was someone I had known (or thought I knew) from his radio days in Nashville. He had worked for one of the country stations there and told me many times if the opportunity ever arose for him to work for me in Provo he'd love to go. After three managerial disasters, I thought it couldn't possibly get any worse than it had already been. Guess again, Whisper-breath!

The things that ended up happening to me because of this guy would fill a volume much thicker than this one, but I'll give you an idea:

The apartment complex where Becky and I had kept our small apartment filled to capacity not long after we started advertising for them on KFTN. One day the apartment manager came to me and said they simply didn't need the commercials anymore and, if we wanted to keep our living quarters there, he'd have to start charging us rent. I thought about it a while and decided since the station was struggling a bit anyway that perhaps the apartment was a luxury we could do without. So I told our new station manager to close out our lease and put my furniture in storage. I'd pick it up the next time I was travelling through the area and get it back to Nashville. Imagine my surprise several months later when the owner of the apartments filed a lawsuit against me for payment of back rent.

"But I gave that apartment up months ago," I protested on my next trip into town.

"Oh yeah?" he retorted. "Then who's been living there all this time?"

Try and picture the look on my face when I borrowed the key from him, walked upstairs, let myself into the apartment, and suddenly came face-to-face with all my furniture and many of my personal belongings. Not only that, but hanging on the wall right above my favorite reclining chair was a color picture of my station manager emerging from a hot tub clad only in a scanty towel and a devilish smile. Turned out that he'd kept the apartment for his girlfriend to live in, and when I confronted him and threatened to tell his wife what I knew, I got my second surprise. He didn't even have a wife. The lady I had thought he was married to all those years was just another girlfriend from another town somewhere that he'd been carrying along with him all those years. He didn't care if I told her or not. I chose not to.

This guy did a few other strange and insidious things. Once he told me our station's signal would greatly improve and we'd bring in many more listeners and advertising dollars if we constructed a new broadcast tower, one much taller than the relatively short one we'd been operating from. I knew what he said was true, but I told him I'd have to think it over. The expense would be substantial, and I just wasn't sure we could afford it at the time. In less than a week he took out a full-page ad in the local newspaper announcing "KFTN's New Tower of Power." When the tower I'd never said I'd build in the first place never went up, we were, of course, the laughing stock of the whole community.

But the greatest stunt my good buddy pulled on me (next to his selling twelve thousand dollars' worth of souvenir program books at one of the station's free Listener Appreciation Concerts when he'd been instructed to sell advertising in them and give the books away free to the fans . . . then stashing the money in dozens of paper sacks in the trunk of his car where he thought I'd never find it) was the time he and the sales manager came to me with the most tearful story I'd ever heard.

"Ole Fred here (actually I forget the sales manager's name . . . I've tried to!) is really in a lot of trouble, Whisper," my faithful station manager told me one morning not long before the apartment fiasco. "He's begged me not to tell you this, but I've just got to. You see, he's got five kids, and he and his wife have just found out that four of them have this strange, rare disease. The chances are that none of them are going to live more than just a few more years."

I was shocked.

"You know, he's not making a lot of money right now, and it's really getting tough on him to buy all the medicines the kids need just to keep them alive. He really needs your understanding and your help."

"What can I do?" I asked innocently, quite taken aback and touched by the story.

"Well, you know the such-and-such drugstore (I've tried to forget their name, too) that we've been trying to get to advertise with us? Well, we've talked to them about this, and they said they'd be willing to give Fred $250 worth of medicine for his kids each month for $250 worth of advertising on the station. It wouldn't cost us any cash money, and it could help keep his kids alive . . . maybe even for quite a while. He says he'll make it up to you somewhere down the line if you'll let him do it. And I know he will. What do you say?"

What *could* I say? I certainly didn't want the illnesses or possibly even the deaths of his children on my conscience. "Sure, I guess it'll be all right for a while," I answered.

On one of my next trips into town I happened to run into one of the managers from the drugstore walking along a downtown street. In casual conversation I happened to mention the advertising the station had been trading out in return for medicine.

"Medicine?" he said with a tone of surprise in his voice. "What medicine? I never traded advertising for medicine."

"Oh really? But haven't you been getting some commercials on our station?" I asked.

"Yeah, sure," he admitted, "but I've never given anybody any medicine for them."

"Well, what have you been giving us then?"

"Oh, a few wrist watches, some turquoise jewelry, maybe a clock radio or two. But I've never given your guys any medicine!" He seemed adamant.

"But what about Fred's kids?" I asked, concerned that they might not be getting the care they needed.

"Healthy as little horses, far as I know," the man replied. "I don't think they've ever been sick a day in their lives."

I wanted to throw up.

I finally gave up on trying to find somebody in the radio business that I could trust, and I sold KFTN after having struggled with it for six years. The bad news is that the radio station business broke my heart. I was totally disillusioned by something I loved. The good news is I've gotten it out of my system. I don't love it anymore.

My second attempt at conquering a world outside my own came upon me more subtly than did the radio business, and I was, as

Dean Booth so aptly put it, "up to my butt in alligators before I remembered that my original intention was to drain the swamp."

In March 1981, a restaurant called PoFolks opened on Nolensville Road in Nashville. You will remember from several pages and twenty years ago that I had written and recorded a song by that very same title, "Po' Folks." And since 1964 when I began hiring musicians to work for me, I had collectively called them either the Po' Boys or the Po' Folks, each name a spinoff from the title of my signature song. When the PoFolks Family Restarant (that's how they spelled it) opened for business in Nashville, it was naturally assumed by many in the community that I was only carrying my trademark name a step further and entering the food service business.

It wouldn't have been that unusual. Minnie Pearl had loaned her name to a fried chicken outfit one time and so had Eddy Arnold. Nashville was used to seeing Tex Ritter's hamburgers, Hank Williams Junior's barbeque, and Boots Randolph's nightclub and eatery. Bill Anderson's PoFolks Restaurants wouldn't have shocked anybody.

I was surprised, however, when "When did you start running a restaurant?" was a question I began having to answer nearly every day. I just shrugged my shoulders because for quite a while I was not even aware that there was such a thing as a PoFolks Restaurant. Then I began seeing bumper stickers around town that read "I'm Po But I'm Proud," and I thought, "Hey, somebody's been reading my mail!" One morning a couple of my band members climbed on board the bus to leave for a tour and brought with them some of the colorful bumper stickers, some brown craft-paper PoFolks menus, and a yellow clothing patch shaped like a mason jar with the inscription "PoFolks Have More Fun" embroidered in bright red letters. It was obvious that my employees had been inside this restaurant with the unmitigated gall to steal my copyright name. I was curious.

"Tell me about it," I prodded. "What's it like? How's the food? Should I sue them?"

"Well, they don't have your picture on the wall if that's what you mean," one of them answered. "It's country cooking, and I thought it was pretty good.

"Me too," chimed in the other. "I liked the inside of the restaurant. It has sort of an old-timey feeling to it, and they play country music over the sound system while you eat. My favorite part, though, was the Mason jars. They don't serve drinks in regular glasses. They serve them it Mason jars. I hadn't drunk out of a jar since the last time I was at my grandma's house!"

I hadn't drunk out of a Mason jar in years myself, but that's not the reason I called a friend of mine, Rita Whitfield, at PoFolks' Nashville advertising agency the next day. I had something entirely different on my mind.

"Rita, can you set up a meeting between me and the head honcho at that restaurant?" I asked. "I have a copyright registered in Washington, D.C., on the name Po' Folks, and I think I need to meet with the owner face-to-face. I might just have a lawsuit on my hands. Who knows, maybe I'll end up owning the place, and you'll be working for me."

Rita calmly told me that PoFolks was part of a chain of some fifteen or twenty restaurants scattered throughout the Southeast and headquartered in Greenville, South Carolina. She said she knew that the owner and president of the company, a Mr. Malcolm Hare, would be glad to meet with me the next time he was in Nashville. She'd be happy to arrange it she said. It turned out to be only a matter of a few days.

Mr. Hare told Rita he'd be glad to meet with me if our meeting could be held at the restaurant itself around six o'clock in the evening. I thought it was an unusual time to conduct business, but I said sure. Turned out Mr. Hare had a method to his madness. I arrived extremely hungry.

He further disarmed me when I walked in the door. I had my defenses up and tried not to smile when I walked in. After all, I told myself, I might be facing this man in a court of law someday in the not too distant future. But the aroma of hot, crispy fried chicken coming out of the kitchen and the sight of a cute little waitress in tight blue jeans, smiling and carrying a steaming plate of fresh homemade biscuits to a nearby table weakened me considerably. Then Mr. Hare, a short, dumpy little man with a quick smile and a big, round, telltale belly that revealed the fact he frequently sampled his own cooking, walked up, stuck out his hand, and with a grin the size of Texas spouted, "Howdy!"

I had no alternative. I stuck out my hand and howdied right back.

So this was what the owner of a restaurant chain looked like. He was dressed in blue jeans, an open-collar sport shirt, and a blue denim vest with a bright yellow "PoFolks" glowing from over his heart. He looked like he should be cleaning off tables. Instead he was the man in charge.

"Bill Anderson, it sure is good to meet you!" he grinned. "People have been coming in here ever since the day we opened wanting to know where you were and what you had to do with this place. I finally got tired of telling 'em you weren't connected with us at all and took to telling 'em you were back in the kitchen makin' biscuits. I hope you don't mind!"

I smiled in spite of myself.

"Boy, I hope you're hungry," he continued, pointing toward a large table in the center of the room. "I want you to sample some of our food."

And before I knew it I was staring right into the face of the biggest helpings of chicken and dumplings and turnip greens and cornbread I had ever seen. And I was telling the waitress, "Yes, ma'm, I believe I *would* like a Mason jar full of that good-lookin' iced tea." And every bite was just as delicious as it appeared.

I stuffed myself, we made small talk, and just as I was wiping my lips with the paper napkin and pushing my chair back from the table so as to get down to the business at hand, another cute little waitress arrived with the biggest platter of fried seafood I had ever seen in my life. There were fish and oysters and shrimp and deviled crab and hush puppies and cole slaw and I don't know what else. And right behind her marched another young waitress carrying fried chicken, country fried steak, a plate full of biscuits, a big bowl of gravy, and every vegetable imaginable.

"Oh, is someone joining us?" I innocently asked. "Like maybe the 101st Airborne?"

"No, this is for you," my gracious host answered. "I want you to try some of everything we've got!"

"Where am I supposed to put it?" I wondered, my stomach already pushing violently against the top of my jeans.

"You don't have to eat it *all*," he replied, "but take a taste of everything. We're really proud of our food. We think it's about the best there is!"

He wasn't far from wrong. I sampled everything I could, loosened my belt another couple of notches, and pushed my chair away from the table for the second time, attempting once more to shift gears and talk about what I'd come there to discuss.

"Mr. Hare, where did you come up with the name PoFolks for your restaurants?" I asked, trying to regain the businesslike composure I had begun losing some thirty-odd pounds ago.

"My name's Malcolm," he said, "not Mr. Hare." And he shifted his weight and slid forward in his seat. "Bill, I wish I could tell you I was riding down the road and your record came on my car radio and it inspired me," he grinned, "but I can't. I'm not really sure just how I picked out the name, but I'm glad I did. It sure fits."

"Well, it's been a pretty good name for me for about twenty years, too," I said. "Are you aware that I have it copyrighted?"

"No," he answered, "I'm not. But I have it copyrighted too. Do you spell yours P-O apostrophe?

"Yes," I replied, looking at the menu resting on the side of the table and realizing he did not.

"Maybe that's how I was able to copyright mine then," he interjected, leaning even closer and lowering his voice. "But, hey, let's don't get into that. I'm interested in knowing if you'd like to become involved with us in some way since everybody seems to think you are anyhow. Is that something you might be interested in talking about?"

I paused and shuffled my feet beneath the table. I had to admit it, the thought had crossed my mind.

"Well," I said slowly, trying to choose my words carefully, "I've been running all over the world promoting Po' Folks for the past twenty years. Maybe it's time for me to help us both get some good out of it. I know one thing—there's a lot of magic in that name. People everywhere identify with it, as long as they don't think you are putting them down by using it."

"Well, we don't do that," he assured me. "Here, have some Po Pie . . . hot apples, thick crust, real juicy . . ." I held up my hand and shook my head for him to stop. He signaled the waitress to put the pie on the table anyway. "Well then, if you're not gonna eat anymore, why don't we continue this little conversation over a cold one downtown at the Stockyard?" he suggested. "I think we might be on to something very interesting."

Suddenly suing PoFolks Restaurants for stealing my copyrighted name didn't seem so important, or even so necessary. The edge had begun to wear off the lawsuit somewhere between the hush puppies and the fried okra. Sometime in the vicinity of one o'clock the following morning in a corner booth in the Stockyard's downstairs Bullpen Lounge, Malcolm Hare, Roy Jones, vice president of operations at PoFolks, Incorporated, and franchisee for the Nashville market, and Bill Anderson, country singer, shook hands and agreed that the latter should indeed become the national spokesman for PoFolks Restaurants.

None of us was exactly sure what a national spokesman did or how he went about doing it, but at least the door was opened. The details could be hammered out by the lawyers and the business managers later on. All we knew was we liked each other, we all liked country music, we all liked country cooking, and we felt my association with a restaurant called PoFolks would never be questioned by anyone. It was a natural. I was excited over all the possibilities, and Malcolm Hare and Roy Jones seemed excited as well.

I phoned Bobby Brenner the next morning and told him of the strange turn of events. He decided that he and my accountant, Harvey Ginsberg, should come down from New York as soon as possible to talk with Malcolm and Company. But we admitted we'd be flying by the seat of our pants. Neither of us had the foggiest idea what would be expected of me in my capacity as spokesman, nor did we know what to ask PoFolks to contribute in return.

But there didn't turn out to be a lot of playing cat and mouse at all. Bobby, Harvey, and Malcolm quickly negotiated an agreement that was very simple and basic. PoFolks, Inc., would announce publicly that Bill Anderson, he of Po' Folks music fame, had signed a three-year contract to appear in radio and television commercials for PoFolks Restaurants and, in addition, had given the restaurants the right to use his photograph, signature and likeness in the endorsement of their products and services. I was also to allot PoFolks Restaurants a certain number of days each calendar year on which they could use my services as they saw fit. I would make myself available on those days to travel to the various restaurant locations around the country (of which there were exactly seventeen in four states at the time) and make personal appearances. For this PoFolks assigned to me a small amount of stock in the company, we agreed on an amount of compensation, and that's all there was to it. The contract was to run from June 1981 until June 1984.

I was happy as could be. I liked the people I'd met, I *loved* the food ("just like eatin' off Grandma's kitchen table," I'd come to tell folks, "not the dining room table but the *kitchen* table!"), and I especially liked the non-contrived feeling I got from being associated with something called PoFolks.

I had never been a corporate spokesman before, although I had endorsed products, and I knew there was a certain added value to an entertainer's being thought highly enough of that a big company (or even a small one for that matter) would want to hitch its wagon to his star. I had done radio and TV commercials back in the late sixties for Stanback headache powders and tablets and in the early seventies for Homelite chain saws, but nothing tied me so closely to them or them so closely to me as this new association would tie me to PoFolks.

I had also represented J.C. Penney through the line of clothing they had me and the band wearing on stage, and I'd done a bit of work for both Howard Johnson's motor lodges and Braniff International airlines at one time, but again it was nothing of this magnitude. I envisioned this new association as having unlimited possibilities, and it truly did.

My first official duties at PoFolks included the taking of pictures—lots of pictures. Pictures of me inside the restaurants and outside the restaurants. Pictures of me making biscuits and frying chicken and pouring drinks into Mason jars. Pictures of me with the owners and the managers, pictures of me with the guests. Becky and Jamey accompanied me to one of the photo sessions, and I have a marvelous picture of him hamming it up for the cameras by taking a big bite out of a PoFolks biscuit which Becky was feeding him across the table. I recorded some radio commercials "introducing" myself as the spokesman for PoFolks. I filmed an introductory TV ad, and we were off and running.

I was literally running because PoFolks was anxious for me to get out into the field and visit the restaurants, meet the managers, and shake 'n' howdy with the guests. (PoFolks has never to this day referred to the people who eat there as "customers." They're always "guests." I like that!) I visited every PoFolks location I could get to, and I learned more about the restaurant business in a few weeks than I'd ever dreamed I'd know in a lifetime.

Mostly I learned my perception of what a restaurant is was wrong. Every musician who's ever travelled the road (and this probably goes for every truck driver and salesperson too) thinks he can do two things: He thinks he can run a motel and he thinks he can run a restaurant because he has stayed in so many bad motels and he's eaten in so many bad restaurants! My first mistake was in thinking a restaurant was a place to eat. I found out quickly a restaurant is a *business*.

The association between me and PoFolks was immediately good for business, too, both theirs and mine. Crowds flocked to the autograph parties where I'd go into the restaurants and visit with the guests at their tables and hand out free autographed pictures. Sometimes I'd put on an apron and go back into the kitchen to "help out." Sometimes I'd wait on tables. Other times I'd roam around the store with a portable tape recorder soliciting comments from the guests which our advertising agency would later take into a recording studio and mold into radio commercials.

I would sometimes conduct media news conferences extolling the virtues of a dining experience at PoFolks. ("It's more than good food," I would say. "It's a good feeling!") The work I was doing was fun and it was accomplishing its objective. Sales were up, and PoFolks began to carve an image in the marketplace much more quickly than they'd ever have been able to do without the publicity I was able to generate.

The chain began to expand. From seventeen units in four states the company grew to forty-seven units in ten states by the fall of 1982, and the parent company couldn't keep up with the demand for new franchises. Sales in the stores were averaging well over a million dollars a year per unit, and some were grossing as high as two million. The stockholders of PoFolks, Incorporated, of which I had become one when I signed my contract, had a tiger by the tail, and we knew it. It forced us to make a decision.

Several large companies were watching us closely with an eye toward buying us out. The question was did we want to hang onto this monster and try to ride it through, or did we want to sell our interests to one of the available suitors and get out? We had to admit that in some places our manpower had become stretched painfully thin, and we couldn't bring good, qualified people on board and train them fast enough to keep up with the demand. We all feared that sooner or later operations within the restaurants would start to suffer. More capital investment was needed than we had available, and the very future of the concept seemed to be hanging precariously in the balance.

The Krystal Corporation of Chattanooga, the hamburger people, made a generous offer to buy us out, and right behind them stood the giant W. R. Grace Company expressing strong interest as well. At some point we had to give somebody an answer. From a personal standpoint, I faced the decision with very mixed feelings.

A few months earlier a tragic sequence of events had enabled me to purchase a sizable amount of stock in PFI to add to that which I'd been given. Some of the original investors in PoFolks, a father and his son, had been killed in the crash of a private plane out in Texas, and the family's block of stock was offered to me. I purchased all I could afford and made the rest available to some of my friends. I became a member of the Board of Directors of PoFolks, Inc., I was given a corner office in the corporate headquarters building when operations were moved from South Carolina to Nashville, and now I wasn't sure I wanted to give up all the excitement. I was in pretty tall cotton for a hillbilly singer from Commerce, Georgia.

Common sense prevailed, however, and I finally agreed with the other owners that everybody's best interests would be served by our stepping aside. The newspapers reported that we sold PoFolks to Krystal for twenty million dollars, but we never saw anywhere near that amount of money. Krystal took over the operation of PoFolks in November of 1982, and early the following year they took the stock public.

Had I been involved with PoFolks only as a stockholder and as their national spokesman, everything up to this point would have been fine. But a few months prior to the Krystal sale, I tried to conquer yet another world. It turned out to be the single biggest mistake I've ever made in my life. I became a partner with Roy Jones, the vice president of operations for PFI, in some of the franchises themselves.

I had watched other franchisees making tremendous profits in PoFolks and when Jones, who had an extensive restaurant background, asked me if I'd like to join him in some franchising ventures, I couldn't turn him down.

He and I formed a general partnership, sold shares to a group of limited partners who provided us with investment capital, and we went into the restaurant business. I personally helped select the site for our first unit, a run-down rattletrap of an old building in front of a very successful regional mall in Clarksville, Indiana, just across the Ohio river from Louisville, Kentucky. Everybody said we were crazy to put the first PoFolks that had ever been built north of the Mason-Dixon line into a building that had been operated as every type restaurant under the sun with no prior success. But the rent was low, and I just *knew* as soon the word got out about how good our food was all those folks who shopped at the mall would come beating on our doors. I was right.

The week we opened for business, I took my Po' Folks Band out into the parking lot on a sunny Sunday afternoon and, along with six or seven thousand other folks, we ate fried chicken and biscuits and sipped iced tea from Mason jars. We picked and sang country music until the sun was going down behind the trees, and all was well with the world. Becky had come up a couple of weeks earlier, and she and Malcolm had decorated both the inside and outside of the restaurant with all kinds of old signs, pictures, and artifacts— everything from antique sewing machines to battery-operated radios to posters from 1948 advertising Roy Acuff as a candidate for governor of Tennessee—and many of the people who came to our opening seemed as interested in her creations as they did in our food. I think it was the combination of things that made it work: good food and fast service added to Becky's colorful and innovative decor, plus me and the Po' Folks Band drumming up all the advance publicity and attention we could get. It became easy to see why our little restaurant was a success from day one. Looking back, that early success may have been both a blessing and a curse.

Within just a few months Jones and I began searching for another conversion site, this time across the river in Louisville itself. We found an old Roy Rogers Roast Beef house that had closed its doors, and before you could say "Gabby Hayes," we bought it, enlarged it, and turned it into a PoFolks. It became even more successful than our first.

We thought we could do no wrong. We were offered a chance to buy the huge territorial franchise rights for the area in and around Charlotte, North Carolina, and we did. Next we decided to exercise the option we had obtained earlier to build and open restaurants in east Tennessee. We built our first one in Bristol, and then, with Conway Twitty on board as an equal partner, we went west into his old stompin' grounds way out in Oklahoma. Conway had discovered our food and our concept through eating with us in Nashville, and being a lover of good ole country cookin', he just *had* to become involved. In the space of a little over a year, the Anderson-Jones-Twitty team was operating PoFolks restaurants in an area stretching all the way from Charlotte to Oklahoma City.

Roy Jones, who was the only one among us who knew beans about the restaurant business (or at least as that time we thought he did), said the only way he could possibly oversee a territory as vast as the one we found ourselves trying to take care of was if he had a helicopter. Things were going good, so what was one helicopter more or less? And one full-time pilot? We got ourselves one of each.

Jones played the role of Big Shot to the hilt, no doubt the only restaurateur in the country running his operations from a whirly-bird. Shoot, I got a big kick out of flying in it myself. Jones and the pilot would come swooping down out of an early morning sky and land a few hundred feet from my door in Lebanon, I'd climb aboard, and we'd take off to a PoFolks restaurant in North Carolina or Indiana or somewhere acting like we were Batman and Robin. We'd arrive at the restaurants for my in-store autograph parties, circle the parking lot a few times to attract a crowd, and then set the big black-and-gold machine down a few feet from the door. I'd bounce out and strut right into the big crowd of people, signing autographs and inviting everybody to come inside and chow down. After walking through the restaurant for a couple of hours and visiting with the folks who had come in for lunch, signing autographs and handing out free pictures, I'd take off for as many local radio stations, television stations, and newspaper offices as I could visit between two and five P.M. I'd do interviews and drum up publicity for my dinnertime visit back at the restaurant. From five o'clock until eight or eight-thirty, I'd be back in the stores doing my thing all over again.

When the last of the guests had gone, I'd visit with the waiters and waitresses for a while, sign autographs for them and their families, and pose for a few pictures. Then I'd take a quick walk back through the kitchen and thank all the people who worked there for their help, after which I'd head outside and climb back into the front seat of the helicopter. The pilot would start up the engine, we'd wave good-bye to the folks below, and head for my front yard. I'd be home and asleep in my own bed before some of the employees we'd left behind had closed up the restaurant and gone home to sleep in theirs.

(One morning after we'd brought the helicopter down into my front yard around two A.M., one of my good country neighbors stopped me downtown and asked me if I had heard any weird noises around my place the night before. He had been awakened, he said, by some strange sounds, looked out his window and seen a big revolving light easing down from up in the sky. He didn't want to frighten me, but it appeared to be right over my house! He was wondering if maybe I believed in UFOs. I told him no, I really didn't, but thanks for warning me and rest assured I'd keep an eye out for anybody that looked like they might be from another planet!)

Unfortunately, the glory days with the restaurants and the helicopter were short-lived. It soon became painfully obvious to me and to Conway that there was more to running a successful restaurant company than serving good cornbread and flying around the country in black-and-gold choppers. We had built a lot of restaurants, but we hadn't hired a lot of good people to manage them. Some of the stores were starting to get into some pretty deep financial trouble. Jones would give us pep talks, trying to keep us from becoming discouraged, and he'd tell us glowing tales about how many dollars were coming in the front door, but I noticed he never had much to say about all the dollars going out the back.

Pretty soon our restaurants were in worse shape than the original PFI had been in terms of both manpower and the financial strength necessary to sustain the operations. And there was no Krystal Corporation standing by to bail us out.

It had all seemed so easy in the beginning: Obtain from the parent company the franchise rights to a certain area. Sell some limited partnerships to investors who believed in us and in the PoFolks concept (and those were easy to find), and sign a few bank notes and equipment leases guaranteeing if anything went wrong and the company couldn't pay its bills that Conway Twitty and/or Bill Anderson and/or Roy Jones would step forward and pay them. That's all there was to it.

How could our company not afford to pay its bills? Weren't we making money every week in Louisville? Sure we were. Charlotte was lagging a little behind, but with all Jones's expertise he'd soon fix that. Besides, he explained to us, if we needed some cash in North Carolina, he'd just send some over from Kentucky. Somehow it never dawned on us to question a thing called "commingling of funds." There was a different set of limited partners in North Carolina from the ones in Kentucky, and taking money from one partnership and funnelling it into another was as illegal as sticking your hand in the cash register drawer, pulling the bills out, and seeing how fast you could run. But somehow that never crossed my mind.

Business at the restaurant we'd opened in Bristol was a bit slow, too, but the answer there, according to Jones, was just to open a few more units in the tri-cities market so it would become economically feasible to advertise on television. That would take care of that problem, nothing to it. Just keep signing bank guarantees and wait for the guests to come knocking the doors down to get in.

It wasn't long before the only people knocking on the doors were loan officers, finance companies, bank presidents, lawyers, and bill collectors. The stores in the Louisville market continued to do well, but it was taking all the money we could siphon off from there just to keep the doors open everywhere else. North Carolina, east Tennessee, and the one unit we'd opened in Norman, Oklahoma, were in dire financial straits. We had done a good job of expanding our little company but a lousy job of running restaurants.

We didn't just throw in the towel. We tried new marketing techniques, we tried making adjustments to the menu (lunch for $1.99, for example), but business didn't improve. We especially had trouble in the smaller towns around Charlotte where we'd branched out, places like Gastonia and Concord, North Carolina, and Rock Hill, South Carolina, towns that just weren't large enough to support an operation such as ours. We had tried to grow too fast and had done so carelessly. Our backs were against the wall, and we knew it. Our only hope was to begin closing some of the stores in an effort to halt the drain of cash.

But it was too late. Before Conway and I realized what hit us, we were personally signed to bank guarantees and restaurant equipment leases reaching well into the multimillions of dollars with no relief in sight. I didn't know whether to ride a bicycle or chop down a cherry tree because while Conway Twitty might have had many millions of dollars buried in the ground out at Twitty City someplace, I knew ole Whisperin' Bill didn't have anything of the sort. Our friend Mr. Jones was a big help. He left town and declared bankruptcy.

Enter the lawyers. Lots and lots of lawyers, and bankers, and financial advisors, and lots of hastily called meetings in all sorts of weird places and at all sorts of weird hours of the day and night. I couldn't recall everything that took place during those weeks now if I wanted to, and I don't really want to. Like a lot of other things in my life during this time, I've tried to forget. Neither Conway nor I had been aware of the degree to which the companies had degenerated. This was supposed to have been only a business investment on the side for each of us, not the major focus of our lives. He had his career to concentrate on, and I had not only my career but my extremely strenuous personal situation as well. How many baked potatoes we'd sold at PoFolks the preceding week and what had been done with the money was not high on either of our lists of priority knowledge. Perhaps it should have been.

I'm sure you're wondering about now just where my accountant and financial advisor was all this time. How could he have been doing his job looking after my finances and at the same time allow me to dangle so precariously over such a bottomless pit? Easy. At the same time I was up to my neck in PoFolks, so was he. He acquired the franchise rights to a large territory in Ohio and

Pennsylvania and opened several restaurants himself. Even his brilliant mind had been psyched out by the aroma of catfish and the glitter of distant gold.

The end result for me was that after much legal hassling and the payment of some exorbitant legal fees, Conway and I sold the parts of the businesses that could be salvaged and bit the bullet on the rest. It was a very large and very expensive bullet!

I found out throughout all these entanglements, though, that Harold Jenkins, a/k/a Conway Twitty, is a helluva man. Had he not been willing to step forward with a lot of long green folding money and been willing to accept large amounts of stock in the companies that bought us out, I might well have had to follow Jones into bankruptcy. Even as it stands, my little foray into the restaurant business has wiped out a large chunk of my life's savings. It'll probably take a while for me to finish paying off all the debts this little venture caused me to run up, but I'm trying. That's all I know to do, hang in there and keep trying. I'll make it, too, if the good Lord's willin' and the creeks—and the interest rates—don't rise!

When you take the financial disaster of my restaurant franchise adventure, add to it the frightful horror of Becky's automobile accident, and then figure in a couple of other minor calamities I've yet to discuss, you might see why I have on more than one occasion since 1984 taken down a map of the western hemisphere and searched to find a little island someplace where nobody has ever heard of Bill Anderson. I've given serious consideration to relocating there and telling people my name is Elmo Farnsworth and I'm a chicken farmer. But so far I've been unable to do that, for three reasons:

First, I don't want to teach my son that the way to solve problems is to run away from them. Second, I've never been a quitter, and even in the face of the most unsurmountable odds, I believe that sometimes the Lord uses adversity to turn us into stronger people. And third, with my luck Elmo Farnsworth would run into some fast-talking somebody on this little island and end up buying a radio station or going into the restaurant business there.

And I wouldn't dare wish that on the natives!

21

I am still the national spokesman for the PoFolks restaurant chain, which now includes over 140 restaurant units in more than twenty states, ranging from Pennsylvania to California. It's no secret that the corporation has had some recent financial problems and that these difficulties resulted in the company's filing for protection from their creditors under Chapter 11 of the federal bankruptcy law in December, 1987. The company stayed in Chapter 11 for only a little more than a year, however, and has emerged leaner, healthier, and with a clearer sense of direction and purpose than I've ever known it to have before.

I think the future for PoFolks is brighter than it's been in quite some time. Sales are up, spirit is up, and one of the nation's leading consumer magazines recently voted us the best full-service restaurant in the country in terms of price-value. That's a mighty strong foundation to rebuild on. Personally, I still believe in the restaurants and the concept now just as strongly as I did that first night inside the little store on Nolensville Road. Our food is still great, our service is second to none, and the folks who are running the company now—President John Scott and Director of Marketing Mike McNeil—seem to have a firm grip on where things stand and where they want things to go. I have not let the misfortunes of the company or my own miscalculations in the franchise business color my attitude or dampen my enthusiasm one bit. The mistakes I made were my own and not the fault of the parent company. Fortunately, they don't blame me for what happened, either.

I signed a new personal services contract with PFI when the original contract expired in 1984, and we renegotiated it again in

1988. I still record most of their national radio and television commercials and quite a few of the local ads for the individual restaurants, and I continue to travel across the country making personal appearances at the various restaurant locations. It was at the beginning of one of these promotional jaunts early in 1985, in fact, that I first experienced the horrifying pain of a ruptured disc in my back.

It was to be a three-day trip on board the Krystal Corporation's private jet. From Nashville our travels were scheduled to take us east to Winston-Salem, North Carolina; to Roanoke, Virginia; to Jacksonville, North Carolina; and finally into the Tidewater area of eastern Virginia. Before the trip was over I was to visit personally seven PoFolks restaurants, grant dozens of radio, TV, and newspaper interviews, and autograph menus, color photographs, and chicken wings belonging to hundreds of PoFolks guests. Actually I've never autographed a chicken wing, but I fully expect someday someone will ask me to.

We would be flying from Nashville into the Eastern time zone, which meant we needed to leave home at the crack of dawn if we were to get a head start on our day. I got up at five A.M. and by six-thirty I had shaved, showered, dressed, and tossed my suitcase and garment bag into the trunk of my car. I had driven the car out of the garage and into the driveway when I decided for no real reason at all to walk back up to the front door of the condo and give Becky and Jamey one more good-bye hug and kiss.

I put the car into park, opened the door, and was turning to throw my long, lanky legs out onto the ground when I felt something grab me like a vise on the lower left side of my back. I reached for the door handle to brace myself when an excruciating flash of pain shot like a lightning bolt down my left leg and out the ends of my toes. I've never been shot by a gun, but I can't imagine the pain feeling much different. Or hurting any worse. I tried to stand up straight and walk back toward the apartment, but I couldn't.

I must have looked like the crooked man who walked the crooked mile in the nursery rhyme as I half-crawled and half-duck-waddled my way . . . inch by inch . . . from the car back up the sidewalk toward the front door. When I reached the stoop, I tried bending over to pick up the morning newspaper and realized I couldn't do it. I was frightened.

Becky was up and helping Jamey get ready for school when I leaned against the doorbell and got her attention. She came to the door, took my arm and eased me back inside as I tried to explain to her what had happened. I asked if she'd try massaging my back to see if perhaps it were some type of muscle spasm that she could loosen. She tried, but it didn't do any good. I propped myself against the wall and tried to relax.

Becky handed me the phone, and I called the airport to talk with the pilots who'd be taking us on our trip. I told them what had happened and promised them I'd be there as soon as I could but that at this point I was afraid to trust myself behind the wheel of the car. I wasn't really sure I could even *get* behind the wheel of the car.

By all rights I probably should have cancelled the trip right then and gone directly to see a doctor. But these promotional trips involve so many people and so many carefully laid plans that I hated to rain on everybody's parade. I stayed inside trying to relax for a half-hour or so then gingerly made my way back outside, slid ever so carefully into the car, and drove on to the airport.

The one-hour plus that it took us to fly to Winston-Salem seemed like a month. I shifted my weight back and forth in the tiny airplane seat, I tried leaning the seat back, I tried standing up, but nothing helped. I was in an incredible amount of pain.

The midmorning interviews and my in-store visit at lunchtime in Winston went by in a miserable blur as did a very busy dinner hour spent inside the bustling restaurant in Roanoke. We then flew for another agonizing hour to Wilmington, North Carolina, and checked into a local motel. By the time I woke up the next morning from what little sleep I'd been able to get, I knew something was bad wrong and that I had to find some relief somehow.

I did a guest appearance on the leading early-morning TV show in Wilmington, and when the show went off the air the host, sensing my plight, graciously offered to phone his doctor and ask if he might come meet me at the local hospital. The doctor came, examined my back, had me bending and twisting all over the place, and then asked me if I'd like for him to give me a shot of cortisone. I had read over the years about cortisone being used to treat athletes with muscular problems, and I thought, sure, maybe it would ease my pain as well. Unfortunately, it didn't.

Somehow I was able to bite my lip, though, and make it on up to Norfolk, Virginia Beach, and Newport News to finish out the remainder of my three-day obligation, but I never once got comfortable. When my work was finally done, I flew home lying on my stomach in the aisle of the plane.

I knew something was seriously wrong, and I needed to get some answers. As soon as I got back to Nashville, I began making the first of what would turn out to be nearly two years' worth of visits to doctors, hospitals, and clinics.

I had a CT scan and later an MRI (Magnetic Resonance Imaging) scan that told the doctors I had a herniated disc between my fourth and fifth vertebrae on the left side of my back. It was bulging out from its normal position and pressing against the sciatic nerve, causing the pain to radiate down my leg and into my foot. I was told to get completely off my feet for two weeks, which I did. I was told to get a firmer mattress than the one I'd been sleeping on, and I did. I was told to begin exercises to strengthen my stomach muscles, and I tried, but the pain wouldn't allow me to do very much. I was told to quit wearing the cowboy boots I had worn for years and to begin wearing walking shoes or running shoes instead. I tried this, too, but as with all the other efforts, nothing really made any difference. Besides, I couldn't even bend over to tie the shoelaces!

I sought advice from orthopedists, neurological experts, chiropractors, osteopaths, and once I even travelled all the way to Missouri to visit a pain clinic where they admitted they couldn't cure me but could teach me how to live with the pain. While I was in Missouri, however, still another problem arose. I began bleeding from a large stone lodged in my right kidney. The doctors there didn't want to treat me and suggested I return to Nashville. I flew home, went directly from the airport to Baptist Hospital, and marvelled as a team of doctors smashed my kidney stone into a jillion tiny little pieces on a fascinating new piece of medical equipment called a lithotripter. In twenty-four hours the bleeding had stopped and the kidney stone was gone, but my back hurt just as much as ever. I was right back where I'd started.

Finally, I was told that nothing short of surgery on my back would give me any relief, and the doctors wouldn't even guarantee *that* to provide a permanent solution.

Back surgery frightened me, not only because of the operation itself, but because I had talked to so many people who had told me that surgery had not been the answer for them. Nearly every person I spoke with who'd had a back operation had also had a second back operation. Or a third. Singer Don Williams told me he had been pleased with the results of his initial surgery and I even went and talked with his doctor a couple of times, but it was only a few months later that I picked up the paper and read where Don had been forced to stop working the road due to the recurring problems he was having with his back. Later I was told even he had to have a second operation.

In the beginning my biggest problem with having back surgery was not because of me at all. It was because of Becky. There was just no way I could leave her to fend for herself for such a long period of time. The operation itself, the hospital stay, the lengthy, painful rehabilitation process could take months. I just couldn't do it. She was improving slowly, but she was still a long, long way from being able to handle life on a day-to-day basis. There was no way she could take care of Jamey, take care of herself, and take care of me. I had but one choice—simply to endure.

I began wearing a back brace for support and that helped, especially during the long nights standing on stage or taping television shows where I had to be on my feet and move around a lot. I traded my new firm mattress in on a flotation waterbed and noticed more improvement. If nothing else I slept better.

Something as simple as sitting on a sofa or in a soft, padded chair was painful. I went to one of the local PoFolks restaurants and borrowed a ladder-back, cane-bottomed wooden chair to keep at the dinner table. I sat in it when I ate my meals. When I wanted to watch TV, I'd push the chair into the living room and sit at a stiff ninety-degree angle like a mummy, afraid to move.

Driving a car was impossible without the use of a support cushion, and I went through several. When I had to go on the road, I'd often ride and sleep on the floor of the bus. It was awkward and extremely uncomfortable (the band members joked and said they loved it because they could walk all over me!), but I couldn't make it any other way.

Everybody seemed to have a solution. I happened to mention on a TV talk show one night that my back was hurting, and I got hundreds of letters in the mail the following week from people all over the country offering me suggestions that had worked for them or for somebody they knew. People recommended medications of all kinds, but other than one anti-inflammatory prescription shared with me by some friends at church, nothing gave me any relief. I deeply appreciated everyone's advice and concern, but none of it made the pain go away.

I never realized how much I'd always taken my back for granted. Or how the simplest daily task can turn into a monumental chore when your back hurts. There's never a minute of any night or any day when you're not aware of the pain and of your own limitations.

Fortunately, my back doesn't hurt as bad today as it once did. For that I am thankful. I wish I could brag about some kind of miracle cure, but I can't because I never found one. I never had the surgery. I came close to giving up and letting them cut on me one time after the pain got worse and Becky got better, but, thank goodness, she ended up talking me out of it. Mostly, I think, time just did its thing. Time and prayers. I can't say I'm "well" because I still hurt awfully bad sometimes. I still have to watch the way I move and the things I lift and the exercises I do very carefully, but I can say that I am better. For now I guess better will have to do.

All the while I had been struggling with my own problems and with Becky's, I had been only casually aware of some serious medical problems which were beginning to affect my oldest daughter, Terri. I had known for years that she, like both her father and her mother, had an unusually high amount of calcium in her body, and even though she had twice submitted to parathyroid surgery to help control the problem, I was not aware of some other complications that had arisen. Complications that her doctors in Nashville admitted exceeded their ability to control.

Simply put, the local doctors who saw Terri could not locate the source of some other problems that had arisen in her endocrine system. They felt her case was so rare and potentially so complicated that they applied for her admission to the National Institutes of Health in Bethesda, Maryland, a tax-supported research and treatment facility, for further evaluation. Not everyone who seeks admittance to NIH is accepted, so Terri was hopeful but fearful that they might not take her case. She was elated when the letter arrived telling her that she had qualified.

She took a leave of absence from her new job in the District Attorney's office in Nashville and was admitted to NIH for further study and evaluation in the spring of 1986. For two long, agonizing weeks she submitted to test after test, study upon study, as some of the most learned minds in the country tried to locate the cause or causes of her problems.

I flew to Washington and drove to Bethesda to be with her and her mother. No sooner did I arrive at the hospital than the doctor had *me* stretched out on a bed taking samples of my blood and asking all kinds of questions about me and my family and our medical backgrounds. They said they didn't want to rule out heredity as a possible contributor to Terri's condition. I said jokingly, "Well, I *do* have this back problem!" but the look on the doctor's face told me he didn't do windows, floors, or backs.

"We think we've located her primary problem," a Dr. Greenberg told us after I'd been in Bethesda a few days, "and we need to perform surgery. There is a rather large tumor (and he held up the forefingers and thumbs of each hand, forming a circle about the size of a grapefruit) on her left adrenal gland that needs to be removed. There is a chance the entire gland may have to come out. We won't know until we get in there. At this point we have no way of knowing whether or not the tumor is malignant, but we've got to get it out." The tone and urgency of his voice told all of us that we had no choice. "We'd like to operate day after tomorrow," he said.

The morning of the surgery was agonizingly slow. Bette and I, who through Terri's problems had been drawn closer to each other than we'd been in years, met at the hospital before dawn, hugged our groggy, blue-eyed daughter as the nurses rolled her out of her room to take her to the operating table, then sat down alone, each of us with our own thoughts, to wait. The doctors had told us the operation could take up to six hours. In a little over four they came out to confront us.

"Terri came through the surgery just fine," the surgeon, a Dr. Norton, assured us, "but we did have to remove the entire gland. This means, of course, that she now has only one adrenal gland to manufacture all the adrenalin and cortisol her body needs. We'll have to keep her on some pretty strong medication to help balance things out until the one good gland kicks in and takes over the work of two. Hopefully, that won't take very long."

"But what about the tumor?" I asked, wondering why he hadn't brought that subject up. Was there something he didn't want us to know?

"All we can do is wait on the pathologist's report," he answered. "We should know something in a couple of days."

In a couple of days? Although I had feared the worst all along, it didn't really hit me until the doctor said "in a couple of days" so matter-of-factly. "Your daughter may have cancer, yes, but you just relax and I'll let you know when I come back after the weekend. Have a nice day!"

He didn't say it *quite* that casually, but I guess I expected a bit more concern, a little more compassion. I mean, this was my daughter, my first-born child, a tall, beautiful blonde who had been Daddy's girl almost from the day she was born. I had rocked her and fed her and changed her diapers and taken her to piano lessons and sent her to college, and now at the age where she should just be starting to live, they were telling me she might have cancer. It was one of the most unfair things I had ever heard!

But who said life was fair? Some forty-eight hours later, the doctors verified our most dreaded suspicions. The tumor, they told Bette and me, had been malignant.

The two of us were stunned into silence. My first reaction was to reach for the remote control and fast-forward the tape. I didn't want to watch this movie anymore. But I could only stand there and stare at the floor. I had a thousand questions, but they'd have to wait. I couldn't have spoken a word even if I had tried.

Finally, when the doctors left the room and we were alone with the frightening truth, I asked Bette if, after we'd both had a chance to see and talk with Terri, she'd drive me to the airport. There was nothing else I could contribute by staying around. If I was going to fall apart, I preferred to do it in the privacy of my own home.

My ex-wife and I rode all the way from the hospital to Washington National Airport in silence, each of us quiet with our own separate concerns and our fears. She pulled the car up to the curb in front of the terminal and stepped out to give me a hand with my baggage. I walked around the car to the driver's side and reached out and gently laid my hand across her shoulder. Neither of us spoke a word.

Horns were honking and skycaps were hustling, planes were taking off and landing all around us, but we didn't even notice. I looked deep into Bette's eyes and I saw the saddest, most frantic combination of fright and hurt I think I've ever seen on another human's face. I squeezed my fingers into her shoulder blades and began slowly to pull her close. Surprisingly, she didn't resist; in fact, she leaned in toward me and laid her head on my chest. And the two of us, who had divorced when Terri was only eight, stood right there in the middle of a noisy, bustling airport in a strange city nearly a thousand miles away from home with our arms wrapped around each other and cried together for the first time in nearly twenty years.

Bill and Becky Anderson on *Tattletales* with host Bert Convy, Sherri and Mickey Spillane, Betty White and Allen Ludden

Becky applies Bill's make-up before a movie take

(Top) Bill with Mike Douglas and Carol Channing; (left) Bill and Sarah Purcell on *The Better Sex*; (below) Bill as a card dealer on *Alias Smith & Jones*; (bottom left) Bill and Jan Howard appear with Johnny Cash.

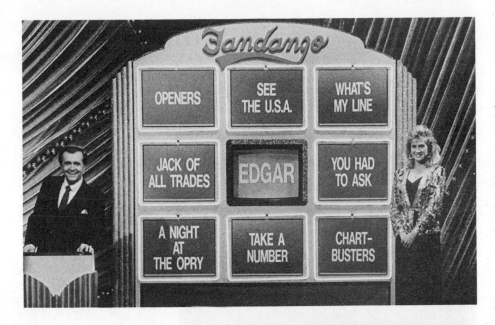

(Top) Bill and Blake Pickett on the *Fandango* set; (right) with Dr. Joyce Brothers; (below) on the set of *One Life to Live* with (left to right) Bobby Woods (Bo Buchannon), Mary Gordon Murray (Becky Lee Abbott), Wayne Massey (Johnny Drummond), and Bill.

(Top left) Ronnie Milsap calls 'em like he "sees" 'em at a softball game; (top right) Bill greets Roy Rogers; (middle) with Dr. Billy Graham; (bottom) Bill surrounded by his songwriting, singing awards.

(Left to right) Becky, daughters Terri and Jenni as Bill signs MCA Records contract

Proud parents Bill and Becky with Jamey in June 1978

(Top left) Commemorative marker in Commerce, Ga., in July, 1977; (bottom left) Bill and Barbara Mandrell at the CMA Awards, 1978; (bottom right) greeted by the Carters at the White House, 1978; (top right) Becky's mangled car following the accident.

Becky and Jamey Anderson, spring of 1982

(Top) The Anderson family enjoying dinner at PoFolks, 1981; (right) Bill receives a silver tray from Hal Durham commemorating his twenty-fifth anniversary with the Opry; (bottom) Bill and sister Mary at their mother and father's fiftieth wedding anniversary, 1983.

PART III

PART III

22

I've often wondered what the people must have thought who drove by our condominium on the Monday afternoon following Becky's accident and saw me out in the small clearing between the side of our apartment and the edge of the road playing baseball with Jamey. They probably thought I had lost my mind.

The wreck had happened too late on Saturday night for the news to make the Sunday paper, but by Monday morning it was not only on the front page of the newspapers but was the lead story on nearly all the local newscasts as well. Nobody expected me to be anywhere but at the hospital, I'm sure. And I would have been there except for the promise I had made to Becky and to myself long before: No matter what happens, Jamey's welfare and his security must always come first.

Sunday night had been a long one. After talking with Jamey about all that had happened, I had driven out to Lebanon and gathered up a few of my belongings, come back and moved into a small third-floor bedroom at the condo. It was a far cry from the spaciousness of the big house and master bedroom suite with its glass sliding doors opening onto the patio by the pool, which I had been accustomed to. But even though the room was small and the conditions crowded, I wanted to be there. I didn't want to be *anywhere* except with my son.

After Jamey had gone to bed early Sunday night, I drove back to General Hospital to wait. I knew I still had nearly thirty-six anxious hours in front of me before I would know for sure whether or not the medication the doctors were giving Becky had prevented any further swelling in her brain. Thirty-six hours to wait and wonder and think, and to hope and pray that my wife was going to live. Luckily, I didn't have to wait alone.

Jan Howard was at the hospital when I arrived. So were Mary Lou Turner and her husband, David. Jimmy Gateley and his wife, Esther, had come by. It really touched me to walk in and see these former employees and associates of mine, people who hadn't worked with me professionally for years but who cared enough about me and Becky personally to rally around us when we needed them most.

Charlie Douglas, the great radio personality and Grand Ole Opry announcer, was there with his wife, Martha. Kathy Woodard, who had been Becky's companion at the movie the preceding night and whom Becky had let out of the car only moments before the accident, was there with her mother. Our close friends Donna and Allen Whitcomb had been at the hospital since before dawn and weren't about to leave. Reverend Garry Speich, pastor of the church where Becky and I had gotten married and where we had maintained our membership, had been there since midnight, keeping a vigil all day except for the hours he had to be in his pulpit. One of the members of our church had come upon the accident only moments after it had happened, and when he found that Becky was the person in the car, he had immediately phoned the preacher. And what a great source of strength and comfort Garry was, not only then but throughout the long weeks and months that lay ahead.

One of my first thoughts upon arriving back in Nashville had been that I needed to get Becky moved as quickly as possible away from General Hospital and into Vanderbilt University Hospital or Baptist Hospital or wherever I could be assured she was receiving the finest medical attention available. At that time I didn't realize she was in the best possible place she could be.

In my mind (and, as I found out later, in the minds of most Nashvillians) General Hospital was just an ancient, decrepit, dingy-looking old red brick building in a rundown area near downtown, a place where people came when they either couldn't afford anything better or when, as in Becky's case, they had no choice. I was not aware of the state-of-the-art trauma center that had only recently been opened at General nor the level of expertise and care available there. One of the paramedics who had helped pry Becky loose from her crumpled car had the good judgment to take her to General even though Donelson Hospital was several miles closer. I'll always be grateful to whoever it was that made that decision. He probably saved my wife's life.

And the staff at General was so very patient and understanding. Not only were they giving Becky the best medical attention possible, but they took special care of me and the rest of our family as well. They gave Lynne and Becky's mom a private waiting room with a telephone the minute they arrived. Later, after I had gotten there, they provided all of us with special meals in a quiet room upstairs (I hadn't eaten since early Saturday night) where we wouldn't be disturbed. Word had spread rapidly through the corridors of the hospital that Bill Anderson was in the building, and the curious and the concerned had begun trying to move in closer for a better look. Sunday night the staff improvised for us an even larger family waiting area on an upstairs floor and provided us with coffee and sandwiches and later with pillows and blankets for several who chose to stay at the hospital through the night. They would later obtain for us several private telephone lines for incoming and outgoing calls, of which there were to be hundreds.

The hospital, referred to by many as "City Hospital" because the operation of the facility comes under the auspices of the metropolitan Nashville government, couldn't have treated the Andersons any better nor with more care and concern. Words can never adequately thank John Stone, the administrator, and Maggie Saltkill, his able administrative assistant, for all they meant to us during our stay. Not to mention the dozens of doctors, nurses, therapists, and support personnel who helped us through some of our most anxious hours.

I stayed at the hospital Sunday night until nearly one A.M. when I finally felt comfortable that Becky, who had by this time at last been transferred from the trauma center on the ground level to the intensive-care unit upstairs, was receiving the best care and most detailed attention possible. Her condition was still listed as extremely critical, but our spirits were buoyed by the fact that so far as could be determined her brain had not continued to swell. The doctors had explained to me that the medicine with which they were treating her was relatively new but that it was our only hope. Additional swelling in the left temporal lobe where the brunt of the blow had been struck could prove fatal. Over eighteen hours down now, less than thirty to go.

I drove back to the condo and fell down across the bed, but I was still tossing and turning trying to relax when the alarm clock I had set for six A.M. jangled loudly in my ear. I shook the cobwebs from my brain, shaved, showered, and awakened Jamey. It was my first morning of many attempting to be both his mother and his dad.

With help from Becky's mom, I saw to it that he got dressed, his hair combed, teeth brushed, and a scrambled egg, a piece of toast, and a glass of orange juice in his belly. Then I drove him to school.

I parked the car and walked beside him from the parking lot to his classroom. His first-grade teacher, Nikki McGowan, spotted me when I stooped to kiss him good-bye at the classroom door and moved quickly to my side. "I just heard about it on the news this morning," she said, sounding out of breath and looking frightened. "How is she?"

"The next few hours are the critical ones," I answered. "If they can keep the swelling down in her brain, then she's got a chance."

"Well, the boys and girls and I will sure say a special prayer for her this morning," she assured me, and I smiled. I wondered later what she would have said had this conversation taken place in a public school where prayers were no longer allowed. I thanked her, and my thoughts turned quickly to Jamey. What was his day going to be like? Did his classmates know? And how would they treat him when they learned? Kids can be cruel at times without meaning to, and I knew it.

"Just be gentle with him," I said to Mrs. McGowan. "There's a lot on his mind that he doesn't understand right now. Please . . . be gentle with him." She nodded, and I felt she understood.

As I turned to leave, Jamey's kindergarten teacher from the previous year, Mitzi Floyd, spotted me. She dropped a stack of papers she was carrying and literally ran to my side. Before either of us could say a word, I saw a tear begin to form in the corner of her eye and then start to trickle slowly down her cheek. She had been at the hospital Sunday afternoon and knew the seriousness of the situation.

Mrs. Floyd had been the ideal first-year teacher for our son. She had come and visited in our home before classes had started in the fall, trying to get an idea of what Jamey's home life was like so she could better understand and relate to his needs. She'd gone up to Jamey's room and listened to him play his drums, talked with him about his love for music and for airplanes, and once I had even taken her and her fiancé backstage at the Grand Ole Opry as my guests. She had gotten to know Becky, both as a friend and as a loving and caring mother.

For the longest time she just stood looking at me. Neither of us spoke a word. She seemed to be searching for something to say . . . and so was I . . . but it wouldn't come. Finally my emotions took over and, without thinking, I did something I had never done before in my life and something I will probably never do again: I reached out and hugged a school teacher!

By the time I reached the hospital shortly after eight A.M., I had already spoken with the doctors and nurses three or four times on the telephone. Nothing significant had occurred nor had there been any major change in Becky's condition during the night, which was good news. She was holding her own, and from all outward indications it seemed the medication was continuing to do its job. There appeared to be no additional swelling.

I parked my car just outside the emergency room door and walked swiftly through the lobby, past the elevators, and up the stairs to the intensive-care unit on the second floor. The head nurse cautioned me that I could go in only for five minutes, then quietly led me to Becky's bed, which was the one farthest from the door, right beside an outside window. It was colder by Becky's bed than anywhere in the entire unit, and her feet had come out from beneath the thin white blanket that covered her body. Knowing how much she hates to be cold when she sleeps, I instinctively covered her feet and gently squeezed her hand. I got no response.

She appeared to be connected to as many tubes and wires as she'd been the previous afternoon in the emergency room. With the light from the nearby window I could see the cuts, the bruises, the stitches even more clearly than I had seen them the afternoon before. They looked terrible. If I hadn't known this was my wife, I'm not sure I would even have recognized her. All sorts of strange machines were monitoring her breathing, her heartbeat, her brain waves. It looked eerie, but I knew each wire, each tube, each flashing green light on each TV monitor was relaying vital, life-sustaining information to the myriad medical personnel who were trying so hard to keep her alive.

"We have her by the window on purpose," the nurse softly told me. "With her type injury, she needs to be as cool as possible. This is the coolest spot in here." I didn't dare question her decision.

My five minutes passed in what seemed more like five seconds, and I was told I'd have to leave. When I reached the swinging double doors leading out of the ICU, I could see through the glass several newspaper, radio, and television reporters gathered outside in the hall waiting to talk with me. I had never felt less like talking with the media in my life, and when I reached them, I asked them to please try and understand that I just didn't have anything to say. Any medical information I had could be easily obtained through the proper channels at the hospital anyway. I wanted to go and be with my family and friends who were waiting downstairs. When we knew something more, I said, we'd let them know. Perhaps later in the day we'd even call a press conference. I was pleased when they understood and respected my feelings.

By the time I reached the newest of the family waiting areas the hospital staff had prepared for us, the phones were ringing off the wall. We had two incoming lines, one outgoing line, and operators on the main switchboard to screen the calls. As fast as Lynne or Donna or Kathy would hang up from one call, another would come in.

Many were from relatives or friends of ours scattered around the country. Some were from fans who'd begun hearing about the accident through their local radio stations and newspapers. Business associates called, other singers and performing artists, songwriters, booking agents, even total strangers called, just to let us know of their love, their compassion, and their prayers. Telegrams began pouring in, and by noon there were so many flowers that we began rearranging furniture in the little room to make space for them all. Radio stations called in from all across the nation, and while I wasn't up to granting any interviews, I asked the girls to express my deepest appreciation to each caller for their concern. My secretaries, Kathy Gaddy and Jeanne Chennault, said the phones never stopped ringing back at my office either. Each person who answered the calls kept a list of the callers. We still have those lists today. They serve as reminders of all the very special people who cared.

The calls taught me a lesson. I have often been guilty of not expressing my feelings to people at tough moments in their lives out of a fear of bothering them. Often I'd figure people in stressful situations, even close friends, would have enough problems without my interrupting them to let them know I was there if they needed me. But that was wrong. Each telephone call, each vase of flowers, each person who just came by and stuck their head in the door was one more pillar propping me up, keeping me from falling. I don't hesitate to offer my arms and my shoulders anymore. Like the old song says, no man is an island.

About two o'clock in the afternoon they let me pay another quick visit to the ICU. After being assured that nothing had changed, I quickly left the hospital to go pick Jamey up from school. I wanted to be in the first car in line when he walked out the door at 2:45 and I was. I asked him about his day, and before I got an answer he asked, "Can we play some ball when we get home, Dad?"

"Is that what you want to do?"

"Sure is!"

"Well, then of course we can play. But I won't be able to play for very long. I've got to be back at the hospital by four-thirty. Mom's doctor and I are holding a press conference. That's where we'll be telling the newspaper writers and the radio and television stations about Mom's condition. They'll put it on the news and into the papers so everybody will know how she's doing. I can't be late for that." He seemed to understand.

I've never played baseball with my mind and my heart so far away from the game. I know I pitched and I hit and I ran and I tried tagging Jamey out when he'd come sliding in under my glove at second base, but my body was the only part of me that was there. The rest of me was back at General Hospital in intensive care with Becky. Around four o'clock we put away the bats, balls, and gloves, and I drove back into town.

Dr. William Meacham, a Nashville-based but world-renowned neurosurgeon, had been called in to supervise Becky's case, and I had asked him to accompany me to the news conference. I knew I didn't have a clue as to how to answer all the medical questions the press would be asking. I needed some help.

I had met Dr. Meacham only briefly, had spoken with him on the phone but once, and had not up until that point been aware of his significance in the medical community. I quickly learned, however, that following a highly distinguished career at Vanderbilt he had recently reached retirement age and didn't practice there anymore. He kept his hands and his mind active by helping out in emergency situations at General, and our being fortunate enough to have him called in on Becky's case was, for us, a true godsend.

"Mrs. Anderson had a concussion and contusions (bruises) in several parts of the brain," Dr. Meacham told the assembled group of reporters, using lots of big words I was hearing for the first time. "There is no evidence of intracranial (inside the skull) bleeding that would necessitate surgery at this time. We don't know at this point whether or not she will develop a hematoma (a collection of blood outside of the blood vessels) which might or might not require surgery. Fortunately there is no paralysis. She is in intensive care, her condition is extremely critical, but I personally feel she will eventually make a full recovery . . . unless some complications should occur."

"A full recovery." That was the first time anybody had spoken those words, and they stunned me. I hadn't even thought about "recovery." I had been too busy thinking about "survival."

I didn't know then that even partial recoveries from head injuries were sometimes long, slow, and painful *years* in coming. When he said, "She should be the same person she was before the accident with no deficits," I assumed he meant in all aspects of her life. I have since learned that while the obvious physical deficits in a head-injured patient sometimes disappear over a period of time, many of the not-so-apparent emotional deficits, hidden away from all those except the few who know the victim best, may never go away at all.

But at the time I took Dr. Meacham's word at face value, and I'm glad I did. Because when the press conference was over, I went home, ate supper, tucked Jamey into bed, and for the first time since Friday night—when my world was so different from what it had suddenly become—laid my body down across a bed and went to sleep.

23

It's amazing how quickly the days and nights of my new life began to develop a pattern of sameness, floating by like so many cumulus clouds in a summer sky . . . nothing to distinguish one from the other except on the rare occasions when I'd force myself to ascertain whether it was Wednesday or Thursday, noon or midnight. Every day seemed to be a carbon copy of the day before until I learned to perform what were in the beginning mostly strange and unfamiliar tasks by rote.

It wasn't easy for a confirmed night creature to program himself to rise from his slumber at six A.M. Most of the six A.M.s I had seen in my lifetime I had seen from the flip side. I was usually crawling *into* bed, not stumbling out. And I hate to admit it, but when I had been at the condo with my little boy on school mornings during his year in kindergarten and the first few weeks of the first grade, I had often extended myself only to the point of rolling over in bed, giving him a big hug, and telling him to have a good day at school, then rolling back over and promptly falling asleep again. I rarely got up to check his lunch money, his shoelaces, or the work he was taking to school that day. Often I had heard the front door close when he'd leave to ride to school with his mother, but seldom had I actually walked out that door with him, climbed into the car beside him, and driven him to school myself.

After school I'd more than likely have seen him for the first time at the dinner table. After dinner I might have helped him a little with his homework and then gone up to his room and listened to him play his drums for a while before he went to sleep, but that's about it. I loved him dearly—from the moment he was born he was the light of my life—but I had somehow let my duties as a father begin to slide.

Now suddenly here I was waking him up in the mornings, seeing to it that he had his shower, clean clothes on his back, his hair combed, and some nourishing food in his belly. Since his school did not operate a bus service, I drove him to class, picked him up after school let out in the afternoon, and took him for a pick-me-up snack at the local burger barn. I had been used to seeing him dressed in clean clothes, but this was the first time I'd actually had to be master of the washer and dryer myself. At night I had always hugged and kissed him before he went to bed, but that was a lot different from my now reminding him to brush his teeth, helping him put on his pajamas, and kneeling with him to say his prayers. And quite a bit different from suddenly becoming the only one he had to turn to with fright in his eyes when strange things started going bump in the night.

(The time I spent with Jamey while he played his drums was always special to us both. I'd take my guitar up to his room, sit on the edge of his bed, and strum right along with him. From the day he was born—no, even before he was born—he has shown an uncanny ability to keep time with music. When he was just a toddler, he would sit in the middle of the kitchen floor and tap out rhythms on Becky's pots and pans with a spoon and a knife. For years every cake Becky baked came out bumpy. For a long time I didn't understand why until I finally figured out that it was because Jamey had put big dents in all her cake pans using them for drums. We bought him a set of toy drums when he couldn't have been much more than two years old, and he banged on them until they were in shambles. We had to buy him another set. Then on his fifth birthday we got him a scaled-down set of real, honest-to-goodness drums. For Christmas the year he was nine, he graduated from the scaled-down models to the full-sized set he plays today. He played drums behind me on nationwide television when he was only seven years old and on the stage of the Opry with me and my band two years later. I was born with a *love* for music, but Jamey was born with a genuine talent to *play* music. There's no doubt in my mind that he can go as far in music as his interest will take him. The natural ability is definitely there!)

But it wasn't until these first few days following Becky's accident that I learned how important it was going to be for me to become more a part of my son's everyday world than I had ever taken the time to be before. He had nobody but me. I *had* to be there for him. I had to change a lot of my habits and attitudes. I had to learn how to adapt my schedule to his schedule, my lifestyle to his lifestyle. I wasn't quite sure in the beginning just how well it was going to work out, but, surprise of all surprises, it was incredible. Jamey had said the afternoon I told him about Becky's accident that he and I would be spending a lot more time together, and he was right.

For one thing, I never went to the Grand Ole Opry without him. Every Friday morning he'd beat me to the morning paper so he could check the Opry line-up for the weekend, see what time I'd be performing and who my guests would be. He memorized all the sponsors' names and knew exactly which half-hour or quarter-hour portions they sponsored. I can hear his tiny voice now, yelling up the stairs while I was shaving, "Hey, Dad, tonight you're on at nine-thirty sponsored by the merchants on Music Valley Drive! And tomorrow night you're on at seven-thirty for Goo-Goo and at ten-fifteen for Little Debbie Snack Cakes!" And he'd start into the list of all the other stars who would be on with me.

One Saturday night I had a business meeting after the Opry and I had to bring him home after my first show and leave him with a sitter. I went back to the Opry, did my second spot, then went out to a restaurant for a bite to eat and to conduct my business. When I got home shortly after midnight, he was wide awake.

"What are you doing still up at this hour?" I asked him.

"I couldn't go to sleep," he replied.

"Why not?"

"Because you didn't tell me goodnight."

From that moment on I never ended a show at the Opry without saying "Goodnight, Jaybird." As long as I told him goodnight, in person or over the radio, I knew he'd go to sleep. I still do it today, whether it's on the early show or the late show, sometimes even if he's with me backstage. I don't want him to ever think his daddy forgot the importance of telling his son goodnight.

Taking care of Jamey was a whole new sense of responsibility for me, but it was also a whole new source of strength to know somebody so young and helpless had no one else in the whole wide world to lean on *but* me. Imagine, a six-year-old boy looking to *me* for answers. The only question was, where were *my* answers supposed to come from?

The mornings never varied. I'd get up, phone the hospital to check on Becky's progress, then wake Jamey up and see to it that he got dressed and ready for the day. After breakfast I'd help him gather together his belongings, and I'd drive him to class. On Wednesdays I'd travel the route more slowly so that I could call out and review with him the spelling words he'd be having on his test that day. Before his Bible test on Thursdays, I'd have him recite his weekly Bible verse to me several times as we drove along just to be sure he had it memorized. I never let him out of the car until I said "I love you," and I'd watch until he was safely inside before I'd drive away. It became our own special little ritual. I'm not sure who derived more comfort and security from it, though, him or me.

As soon as I was up the steep hill and away from the school grounds, I'd begin winding my way through the morning rush-hour traffic toward General Hospital. Most mornings I was able to pull up in front of the forbidding old structure just after eight o'clock. I'd rush inside and quickly try to get an update on Becky's progress from the doctors and nurses on duty, then head directly for the ICU, where I would hold her hand and talk to her for as long as I was allowed. She couldn't hear anything I was saying, of course, nor could she respond to me in any way. But I went and I touched and I talked anyway. And I thought of all the mornings I could have talked with her when she could have heard me and all the senseless time we'd wasted, arguing over where we each wanted to live. Standing beside her hospital bed, watching and listening to her struggle with every breath to stay alive, it all seemed so useless and so far away. I couldn't stay with her long, so as soon as the nurses ran me off I'd kiss her hand and head for the family room and my first of many cups of morning coffee.

I could set my watch by the arrival of Don Fowler, my close friend and booking agent, who'd be there by eight-thirty every single day, usually with a corny joke he'd picked up somewhere the day before, sometimes with a box of doughnuts, but always with a smile on his face and the offer of a helping hand. He'd be followed closely by John Johnson, the off-duty policeman who had witnessed Becky's accident and who had held her bleeding hand while she was still trapped inside the twisted wreckage of her car. John had begged her, "Lady, please don't die. I've never lost one yet . . . please don't you be the first!" He didn't even know who Becky was at the time, but thanks to his presence of mind and his speed in radioing for help, he was able to maintain his perfect record.

By nine o'clock every morning our little room would be packed. Becky's sister Judy had flown to Nashville from her home in Florida. The oldest of the four sisters, Sue, took her very first airplane ride and came over from North Carolina. Our dear friend and Jamey's godmother, Nan Henderson, flew down from Chicago. When Nan's husband and my fraternity brother, Don, had died of cancer a few years before, Becky had been the first person at Nan's side. Nan wasn't about to let Becky fight the biggest battle of her life without doing whatever she could to help. One or both of my daughters was in the room every morning. We became family-within-family during the long, anxious hours, each of us wrapping ourselves in the security blanket of the others' presence and holding on.

Sometime toward the end of the first week on one of my frequent visits to Becky's bedside in the intensive-care unit, I became aware of a machine I hadn't noticed there before. Evidently it had been in the room all along, but I hadn't paid much attention. It was a small, gray rectangular apparatus about the size of a cigar box, mounted vertically on a pole near the head of Becky's bed. At the top of the box was a small screen with a digital readout and various numbers were flashing on and off the screen in bright green . . . 65 . . . 67 . . . 58 . . . 60. I knew it was telling the attending physicians and nurses something, but I couldn't imagine what it might be. When a nurse walked by, I asked her what the little box was doing.

"We're monitoring her brain waves," she told me. "She doesn't appear to respond to anything around her, but this machine tells us that at least her subconscious is aware. Lean over close to her and tell her you love her and then watch the numbers."

I did as I was told. "I love you, honey," I whispered as I had done many times before into ears that seemingly could not hear me. Then I looked toward the screen. 67 . . . 74 . . . 81 . . . the numbers were rising.

"That's a good sign," the nurse said excitedly. "Her subconscious is aware that you are here and that you love her. When the numbers go up, it means we're getting a positive response. Keep repeating little things like that to her from time to time and watch the numbers. It's good for her to respond."

Suddenly the little gray box became the closest link I had to my wife. I'd speak, hold her hand, and watch the numbers rise. Judy and Sue and Lynne would get a few precious minutes with their sister occasionally, and they'd talk and watch the numbers go up too. Then we'd meet out in the hall and brag, "I got it up to 89" . . . "I got a 91" . . . like we were comparing our bowling scores or something. But it became a tangible something that we could grasp and hold onto. At that point, we needed all the hope we could muster. It didn't really matter that it came from a gray box.

One morning as I was leaving the ICU after playing the little numbers game, a lady on the hospital staff walked up to me out in the hall and asked me if I'd go with her to a room up on one of the patient floors. "What for?" I asked, fearful that perhaps she was intending to sing me a song she'd just written.

"I want you to see Becky's room," she replied. "We've redecorated it just for her. We've tried to make it as bright and as cheerful as we can. I want you to tell me if everything's all right."

"Whoa . . . wait a minute!" I exclaimed. "What do you mean, 'Becky's room'? She's still upstairs unconscious, for goodness sake. How can she have a room?" I didn't understand what was going on.

"Well, all I know is Dr. Meacham told us to get a room ready for her, and that's what we've done," the lady said. I shook my head in disbelief. How could Becky possibly leave intensive care? She needed somebody to attend to her every need twenty-four hours a day. She wasn't even awake! How could they even be thinking of moving her to a private room?

Dr. Meacham reassured me. "It won't be long until she'll be starting to wake up, Bill, and when she does she'll need to be in a room of her own. Don't worry . . . we'll have round-the-clock nurses with her, and she'll get all the care and attention she needs. You just relax."

"Are you sure? I just can't picture her in a private room in her condition."

"Trust me, she'll be just fine. But I do need to prepare you for a couple of things."

"Like what?"

"Well, first, a lot of times when people come to after suffering a blow to the head as severe as Becky's, they don't have very many inhibitions. I'm warning you, be prepared, she's liable to spout forth some words you didn't even know were in her vocabulary."

"I doubt that," I smiled. "I imagine I've heard 'em all."

"Well, just be ready. You might hear some more. Also, she'll probably say and do some things that don't make much sense for a while, but that's to be expected too. Remember, she's had a powerful blow to the head. We'll have a therapist working with her several times each day, and the other doctors will be monitoring her closely. She'll begin to come around, but it might be slow. Now, there's something else . . . something very important that I need for you to do."

"What's that?" I asked.

"I'm sure Becky has some favorite things in her life that are very special to her. Maybe a certain picture that hangs on the wall. Maybe a small item that sits on a shelf that has a special significance. Maybe there are certain songs that she likes to hear. I need for you to give it some serious thought and then bring some of her favorite things here to the hospital. Place them around her bed where, when her eyes begin to open, she can see them. Familiarity is a very important thing to a brain-injured person. We need to surround her with familiar things. Things that she loves."

Hmmm—familiar things that Becky loves. What were some of her very favorite things? What would she want to be there beside her most of all when she woke up? Of course I knew she'd want Jamey, but I couldn't possibly bring him. Not for a while anyway. But I *could* bring a picture of him. But which one?

I spent most of the night ransacking the condo searching for just the right picture of Jamey to take to Becky's bedside. Photography had been one of Becky's hobbies over the past few years, and she had hundreds of pictures she'd taken of Jamey pasted into scrapbooks, mounted in frames, and some still in packages from the photo stores. But I had to locate exactly the perfect one.

Finally, after several hours of digging, I found it. It was in a stack of pictures she had taken around the condo just a few weeks before, with Jamey dressed in a tan suit, wearing a white dress shirt and striped brown tie. He looked fantastic. The pictures had been taken outdoors, and this one was full-length, showing him standing up straight and tall with a marvelous twinkle in his eye and a big smile on his face. There was no doubt. This was the picture. But I wasn't about to take her just a tiny snapshot.

By the time I walked into the hospital room with the picture, it had been blown up to sixteen-by-twenty and was almost big enough to paper one of the walls. I decided to mount it on the mirror above her sink, directly at the foot of her bed. There was no way she could lie there in bed with her eyes open and not see Jamey's face smiling at her.

On the bedside table on her right I stood a small plaque that I had found hanging on her dressing room wall at the condo. It was a picture of a large hand holding a small, innocent-looking child. And the caption read, "I will not forget you . . . I have held you in the palm of my hand." It seemed appropriate since we all knew by the very fact that Becky had survived the severe injuries sustained in this horrible automobile crash that God surely *had* held her in the palm of His hand. I wanted her to see that plaque and read those comforting words as soon as she was able.

And then the doctor had said something about music. "Make a tape of some of her favorite songs," he had told me. "Just let the same tape play over and over again. You might get tired of hearing it, but it's familiarity to her. It's something she likes. It's important that she be surrounded with it."

Well, if you think *I* like country music, you should see Becky. She likes *country* music! Some of her fondest childhood memories are woven around the Saturday nights she spent as a little girl curled up on her daddy's lap listening to the Grand Ole Opry on the radio. Or the times when he'd come home after a hard day's work and put some Roy Acuff or Bill Monroe records on the record player and turn it up loud and hold her in his arms. Her daddy loved the pure country sounds, and he'd passed that love on to his youngest daughter.

Becky's very favorite singer of all is Mac Wiseman, a kind, gentle man from the Shenandoah Valley of southwest Virginia who can wrap his vocal chords around a folk ballad or a high lonesome bluegrass song just about as well as anybody and better than most. His clear, penetrating voice had echoed through our home on many occasions, and I knew Becky would want to hear Mac Wiseman sing more than anyone else.

Mac was more than her favorite singer. Both of us had also come to know him as a friend. Mac and I had toured together in England once when Becky was along, and a couple of years later he and his wife had gone with us on a cruise to the Caribbean. Both times Becky had hardly let the poor man get any rest. "Sing me just one more song . . . please, Mac!" she'd beg him every night after he'd already spent an hour or more entertaining on stage. And Mac would sit patiently backstage with his guitar and strum and sing her the old classics like "Put My Little Shoes Away," "The Knoxville Girl," and "The Baggage Coach Ahead."

Over the years we had obtained a lot of Mac's records for our collection. I gathered up every one of his songs I could find and spent hours dubbing onto cassette tape songs like "Jimmy Brown the Newsboy," "Footprints in the Snow," "Keep on the Sunnyside," and "I'll Still Write Your Name in the Sand." I carefully labeled each tape, put fresh batteries into the small cassette player I kept tucked away under my desk, and took the entire package to the hospital room where Becky would soon be moving.

A sweet-looking gray-haired nurse was putting the finishing touches onto the newly decorated room when I walked in with my goodies. She was busily moving in dozens of the beautiful floral displays that had been delivered to the family room downstairs, checking the bright new print curtains, and fluffing the pillows. She hardly seemed to notice that I'd come into the room. She went right on with all she was doing and never even looked up as I taped the big photograph of Jamey over the mirrored glass. She glanced my way but still didn't say anything as I placed the plaque on the nightstand. But she sprang to life in a hurry when I turned on the tape player to check it out and the volume knob had somehow been turned up as high as it would go. Mac Wiseman came on singing at the top of his lungs, "Catfish John . . . was a river hobo. . . ."

She backed up about three steps and looked up at me like she'd swallowed hemlock. It was obvious from the look on her face that she did not share Becky's appreciation for Mac Wiseman.

"I'm sorry, ma'm," I apologized, hurriedly turning down the volume. "I didn't mean for the music to come on so loud. But, you see, that's my wife's favorite singer and . . ." The little lady was staring a hole right through me. Her eyes looked like blown glass. I don't think she heard a single word I was saying. It was like she was in a trance.

"Anyhow," and I tried to slow down a bit and to smile, "you see, the doctor said I need to surround my wife with things she loves. And she loves . . . this kind . . . of . . . music . . . and . . ." I could tell I wasn't getting through at all. "She hates it," I thought to myself. "She hates this music so much she won't even talk with me about it."

Finally I decided there wasn't much sense in beating around the bush. "Look, lady," I said much more impatiently than I would have under normal circumstances, "I'm sorry if I've bothered you with this music. I'm sorry if you don't like it. But you might just want to try learning to like some of it. Especially if you're gonna be hanging around this room very much in the next few weeks. 'Cause I'll tell you something—my wife loves it and whether you like this music or whether you don't, you and everybody else who comes in this room are gonna be hearing an *awful lot* of it!"

She looked at me like I'd lost my mind. I reached down and turned the volume up again.

24

Phillip Todd Brasher was the eighteen-year-old boy who had passed out drunk at the wheel of his employer's pickup truck and crashed head-on into my wife's car at midnight, October 13, 1984. As so often seems to happen with drunks who are involved in automobile accidents, he barely received a scratch.

Brasher confessed later that he had been drinking since early that morning. He, his boss, and a friend had gone out to celebrate Brasher's birthday, he said, by riding around town, drinking some beer, and attending a gun and knife show at the state fairgrounds. He had eaten only a couple of small hamburgers all day while consuming "twelve or thirteen" beers and one last nightcap of hard liquor before staggering to the cab of the company truck and attempting to make his way home. He claimed not even to remember the violent collision of the truck and Becky's automobile.

Brasher spent less than an hour being checked for injuries at Donelson Hospital, and while Becky was fighting for her very life in the emergency room at General, he was back at the scene of the accident attempting to retrieve some of his personal effects that had been scattered by the impact. Sunday morning while I was frantically trying to locate an airplane to fly me from South Carolina back to Nashville, he was sleeping off a bad hangover in the quiet comfort of his boss's apartment. It would have been real easy for me to hate this man I'd never seen.

But for some strange reason, I didn't. I guess down deep inside I knew that hating him wouldn't unring the bell, wouldn't uncrash the cars. I wanted to expend my energies trying to help Becky get well, not being angry at Brasher.

Several things did bother me, though. First, the legal drinking age in Tennessee is twenty-one. Who sold this eighteen-year-old enough beer and/or liquor to get him into his drunken stupor? Second, upon checking, we found this was Brasher's third brush with problems caused by alcohol. Once in Georgia he'd been charged with driving under the influence, another time for public drunkenness, and yet his employer, Ronco Irrigation, Inc., of Atlanta, had entrusted him with a company truck to drive at his own pleasure. What kind of managers must they be? And why hadn't his parents or family members or his friends or *somebody* seen that this kid had a drinking problem and tried to get him some help? Why did it have to come to this?

Not long after the accident, while Becky was still in the early stages of her recovery and it was far too early even to begin thinking about punishment for Brasher or restitution from anybody, Brasher disappeared from Nashville. Nobody seemed to know where he had fled, but it didn't take us long to pick up his trail.

The driver's license he had presented to the police at the scene of the accident was from Michigan and listed an address in Gaines, a small town not far from Flint. We determined this must be his parents' home, and it didn't take Sherlock Holmes to figure an eighteen-year-old in this much trouble would probably run back to Mama and Daddy. Especially since it was also getting close to Christmas.

We located Brasher at his parents' home in Gaines, Michigan, early in January after he'd failed to appear at a scheduled General Sessions court hearing in Nashville. I learned quickly that it's not like we see it on TV, that there's a lot of red tape to go through in order to have a person extradited from one state to another to face legal charges. It can be both time-consuming and expensive, very expensive, and a lot of people who are in a position to prosecute often give up and never follow through with all the details and drawn-out legal proceedings. But even though I wasn't angry or bitter at Brasher personally, I just could not in good conscience let everything ride. Becky had suffered too much. We had all suffered too much. Somebody should be held accountable for all that had taken place and, even more importantly, we should be sure that it didn't happen again.

Having a good friend in the right place at the right time can sometimes come in awfully handy. Jim Hough, a feature writer for the *Lansing State-Journal* newspaper in Michigan's capital city, had over the years become a very close friend of mine and was one of the very first people to phone when he heard of Becky's close call. "If I can ever do anything to help," Jim had pleaded, "please let me know." Late in January I took him up on his offer.

"I need you to come up with a name for me, Jim," I said over the long-distance wire to Lansing. "I need to know who to call in the area around Gaines, Michigan, that can work with the Tennessee authorities in helping us bring Todd Brasher back to Nashville to face up to what he did. So far he's gotten off with something like forty-eight hours in jail for DUI, and now he hasn't shown up for his hearing. I don't think that's right. Can you help me?"

It turned out that Jim had had dinner the night before with the commander of the state police post in Lansing and had to make only one quick telephone call to set the wheels in motion. In a matter of just a few days officer John Johnson, who had been such a big help from the very beginning and had quickly become a close and valued friend, asked his superiors to allow him to be the one to fly to Michigan and bring Brasher back. Twenty-four hours later he and his partner were back in Nashville with Brasher in tow.

I saw this man who had wreaked so much havoc upon our lives in person for the first time in Probate Judge Jim Everett's courtroom in the metro courthouse a few days later. Nobody had to point him out to me. He looked about like I'd pictured him. He was tall and skinny, almost to the point of looking malnourished. His chin was set defiantly beneath his scruffy beard, his hair was long and unkempt, his clothes were ruffled, and he gave off an air of aloofness that bordered on cockiness. I didn't like what I saw, but then I hadn't expected to. Instead of his appearing to look repentant or sorry for what he had done, he stared with a glassy, nondescript look in his eyes while traces of an "I-don't-like-the-world" smirk creased his face. I glared at him constantly throughout the courtroom proceedings, but not once did he even so much as glance in my direction. Maybe I could learn to hate him after all, I thought, but I never did.

By this time, the charges against Brasher had been changed from simple DUI to aggravated assault, and Judge Everett had little patience with the young defendant. Noting that Brasher had registered a .17 percent on a blood-alcohol test immediately following the accident (in Tennessee .10 percent creates a legal presumption of intoxication) the judge said, "When you became eighteen, son, you became a man in many ways. When you become a man, you face a lot of consequences. That's what my daddy told me when I turned eighteen. This time you're going to have to face up."

Brasher's attorney, Arnold Peebles, argued however that "This boy is a child, virtually. Sentencing this young man won't deter a single other person from drinking and driving. The pressure on young people to join in and be part of a crowd is far more overwhelming than anything this court can do. We live in a society that totally condones and promotes the type of behavior he was involved in." I listened and tried not to agree. But I couldn't help but think the attorney was probably right. What a sad commentary on our times.

"What lesson did you learn from your previous DUI conviction in Georgia?" Assistant District Attorney Paul DeWitt asked Brasher on the witness stand.

"Not to drive drunk," was Brasher's curt reply.

"You learned that lesson one month before this accident?" DeWitt persisted.

"I messed up," Brasher said quietly.

I had to take the witness stand next, and for someone who has spent most of his life getting up and talking in front of people, you'd have thought I'd have been reasonably composed. I was anything but. I was nervous, my hands were actually shaking, and in reliving and retelling the story of that agonizing October night I broke down and cried. When Mr. DeWitt asked me to sum it all up in my own words and just tell the court exactly what I felt. I couldn't get the thoughts and the words to connect in my brain. All I could do was look up at Judge Everett from my seat there on the stand and whisper, "It's been hell, Judge. It's been pure hell."

The hearing was over in less than an hour. Judge Everett sentenced Brasher to three years in jail. Noting that Nashville cur-

Whispering

Bill Anderson

International Fan Club
PO Box 85   Watervliet, MI 49098

APPLICATION FOR MEMBERSHIP
(Please Print)

NEW _____ RENEWAL _____ BADGE ($1.50) _____

Name _____ Birthdate: _____ TNN _____ (yes/no)
                                                          (Mo./Day)
Street _____

City _____ State _____ Zip _____ VCR _____ (yes/no)

ANNUAL DUES EFFECTIVE JANUARY 1, 1991:

$10.00 FOR U.S. - **$11.00 FOR CANADA** - **$13.00 FOR OVERSEAS.** ALL CANADIAN
AND OVERSEAS MEMBERSHIPS MUST BE PAID IN U.S. FUNDS. BADGE: $1.50 EXTRA.

NEW memberships include color autographed picture, latest Journal, membership
card, PoFolks free meal coupon, badge (if ordered), miscellaneous souvenir.
Journals will be sent FOUR times a year plus letters and tour schedule updates
from a State Rep, four to five times per year. Special bulletins from time to
time.
RENEWALS will receive picture, membership card, PoFolks coupon, Journals and
Rep letters. Special bulletins from time to time.
PLEASE SEND YOUR MEMBERSHIP DUES TO THE ABOVE ADDRESS.

Referred by _____

rently generated more DUI arrests than many larger cities, including even Los Angeles and Detroit, the judge added, "We've got to send a message out that you can't drink and drive in Davidson County, Tennessee." He then told Brasher that when his sentence was completed he'd have to spend three additional years on probation with a revoked driver's license. "You can't drive to the store, you can't drive to church, you can't drive anywhere," the judge warned. "If you're caught driving, if you're caught on a speeding ticket, if you're caught sitting behind the wheel of a car in a parking lot, you'll serve the rest of that three years in jail."

Brasher was led from the courtroom by police officers and taken back to the metro jail to begin serving his sentence. I know he must have felt the judge was awfully harsh on him, but he knew and everybody in that courtroom knew he'd be eligible for parole as soon as he'd served twenty percent of his time. That would come to just a little over seven months. I watched him walk out the door and wished my wife had gotten off with a sentence that light.

25

I was all prepared for Becky to snap out of her coma, look up at me with a big grin on her face and say, "Well, hello there, you ole horse's ass!" After all, Dr. Meacham had told me that people who are knocked unconscious by blows to the head often wake up using strong, profane language, so I rather expected it. Barbara Mandrell had even told me how embarrassed she was to find out after the concussion she suffered in her automobile accident the month before Becky's that when she'd come to, she'd started ranting and raving at everyone around her. She couldn't help it. But when Becky, who never did want to be like everybody else, finally did begin slowly to regain consciousness, she was so extremely meek and mild that I almost wondered if it was really her.

She didn't snap out of it all at once. It was a gradual opening of the eyes that I noticed first, then a little response when I'd squeeze her hand that told me she could hear what I was saying.

One morning, several days after she'd left intensive care and had begun gradually waking up in her own room, the doctor asked her, "Who is that man sitting over there?" pointing to me.

"Oh, that's my husband," she said shyly.

"And what's his name?" the doctor continued.

"Paul Williams," she answered. "That's my wonderful husband, Paul Williams."

The doctor looked at me with a puzzled look on his face. I just shrugged. "She could at least have picked someone taller," I deadpanned.

I believe she was trying to say "James William," my full name, but come to think of it she's never called me that except when she's really been mad at me. Someday I'll have to ask her about Paul Williams.

"Mrs. Anderson, do you know where you are?" the doctor would ask.

"I sure do," Becky would answer. "I'm at a health spa in Florida."

"No ma'm, you're in Nashville, and this is a hospital. Do you understand that?"

"Really?" she would say, but in five minutes or less she couldn't remember what the doctor had told her. I was concerned, but the doctors told me not to worry; she was making all the progress she needed to be making at the time.

I'm told that people who suffer head injuries often become very blunt and outspoken, which I assume is a first cousin to the profanity Dr. Meacham had warned me about. Something evidently happens to the "little policeman" we all have inside our brain who often blows the whistle on us when we think something we shouldn't put into words but start to say it anyhow. Following Becky's accident, her "little policeman" must have gone on an extended vacation because she began saying everything that popped into her mind.

"Weight-Watchers would really do you a lot of good," she matter-of-factly told a slightly overweight nurse who came to her room one morning. And to her good friend and hair stylist, Donna Whitcomb, Becky said as she reached up and ran her fingers across the top of her shaved head, "Donna, this is the worst haircut you've ever given me! I'm not mad, but you can do a lot better work than this!" They both laughed.

One of Becky's nurses bore a slight resemblance to our housekeeper, Pam, and every time this particular nurse would come in her room Becky would call her Pam.

"No, Mrs. Anderson, I'm not Pam," she would patiently say. "My name is Gail."

"That's right," Becky would answer meekly but with determination. "You're Pamela Gail." The nurse finally quit trying to change Becky's mind.

There had never been a time since I'd known Becky when she had been as genuinely sweet, kind, and loving as she was during the first few days when she began to regain consciousness. She loved everything and everybody. But, for some reason, as she began waking up she seemed to be preoccupied with weight. It was probably because she had been on a strict diet at the time of the accident, had been walking several miles each day, and had been working out regularly at the health club. Dr. Meacham even told us later that Becky's being in such good physical condition aided her considerably throughout the recovery process.

One morning a therapist came in carrying a pair of white socks. He walked to her bedside, held up the socks for her to see and asked, "Mrs. Anderson, do you know what you do with these?"

"Sure I do," Becky answered. "You put them on."

"That's right," said the therapist. "Why don't you show me just how you put them on." And he handed her the socks, not knowing whether Becky would put them on her hands, her ears, or her feet.

He stepped back to watch as she carefully unfolded the socks, reached down and pulled one onto her right foot and up her right leg as far as it would go. Then she took the other one, pulled it on over her left foot and stretched it as far up her left leg as it would go. The left sock was decidedly longer than the right, reaching almost up to her knee. The right sock had stopped not far above her ankle.

"That's right, Mrs. Anderson," the therapist said, pleased that Becky had known exactly what to do with the socks. "Now, what do you call those?"

Becky never hesitated. She looked down at the smaller of the two socks and said, "This one you call low-calorie," she said, and then, pointing to the larger sock, she said, "and this one you call high-calorie!"

Becky gradually began to communicate with those of us around her a little more each day and seemed to be slightly more alert every morning than she'd been the night before. She would show flashes of memory in recalling something or someone from the past but she did not, as the doctors called it, "make memory." That is, even though something would happen around her and she would seem to understand it at the time, she would have no memory of it afterwards. I would come to see her every morning and then leave the room while the nurses gave her a bath and changed the sheets on her bed. When I'd return she'd say, "Well, hi, when did you get here?" She couldn't remember that I had been with her only minutes before, nor could she remember anything we might have talked about. She says now that the first day she remembers even being in the hospital is the day before she got to go home.

Fortunately, Becky has never remembered anything about the wreck itself. The closest she comes to remembering even the time frame in which it happened is recalling bits and pieces of the preceding Monday night when she and I went to the Country Music Association Awards Show together. Almost a full month is totally erased from her memory. In some respects that's probably good. She recalls nothing of the grinding crash, of her efforts to get off the road and out of the way of the onrushing truck, and for that reason she has not been afraid to get back behind the wheel of a car and drive. It was many long weeks before she did drive again, however, and in the beginning she was hesitant and unsteady.

She would drive only on the back roads for a long time, venturing out only as far as Jamey's school and back. For weeks I would follow along behind her in my car every time she drove just to make sure she could handle everything all right. Even when I began to grow comfortable with her driving the short trips, I'd have her telephone me when she'd get to her destination just to be sure she had arrived safely.

I probably had a tougher time with Becky's starting to drive again than she did. The first time I watched her slide in under the wheel I became quite emotional. I helped her pick out a new car and insisted that she get a large, heavy one. We both knew that had she been in a smaller, lightweight car the night of the accident she would have had very little chance of surviving.

She put fewer than twenty-five thousand miles on her new car in the first four-and-a-half years following the accident, but many people who have been in accidents such as hers never want to drive anymore, period, and often they don't. In that respect, we are lucky.

Becky didn't just lie in the hospital bed the whole time she was recovering. Dr. Meacham put her into a physical therapy program that required her to leave her room several times each day in a

wheelchair to go down to the first floor of the hospital's P.T. unit.
There the therapists would work with her on her basic motor skills,
helping her master such fundamental maneuvers as walking and
standing alone. But Becky was so cute and in such a gentle, playful
mood that she got *out* of doing a lot more therapy than she ever
got into.

The therapist would say, "Now, Mrs. Anderson, roll this ball
across the floor," and he'd demonstrate how he wanted her to do
it. "See how much fun it is!" he'd exclaim. And she'd reply, "Well,
it really does look like a lot of fun. But you seem to be enjoying it
so much you just go ahead and do it and I'll watch." I couldn't
keep from laughing. She had been conning me just like that for
years!

Becky was still in the hospital on my birthday, more than two
weeks after the wreck, but quite frankly, I had forgotten what day
it was. I had lots of other things on my mind, not the least of
which was her impending discharge. The doctors had told me they
wouldn't be keeping her in the hospital much longer.

I was extremely anxious about taking her home to the small
condominium where we would have absolutely no room for round-
the-clock nursing help. How could I possibly give her the attention
and the care that the twenty-four-hour-a-day nurses and doctors
had been providing at the hospital? And yet Dr. Meacham had
told me emphatically, "You *must* keep her in familiar surroundings!" which meant moving away from the condo was totally out of
the question.

I was deep in thought, trying to figure out a way around that
whole situation, when I walked into her hospital room the morning of November 1. I was totally taken back by the big "Happy
Birthday, Bill" banner that was taped to the wall, stretching the
entire width of the room. Before I could even express my amaze-
ment or my appreciation to the hospital staff who had painted and
hung the huge sign, all the nurses and doctors who had been
attending to our needs so beautifully throughout those long and
anxious days came parading into the room carrying ice cream and
cake and singing "Happy Birthday" to me. I was genuinely
touched. It was like for a brief moment I was back in the real world
again where little things and not just life-threatening things mat-

tered, and it felt good. In fact, I haven't had a birthday since that I've failed to remember those smiling faces and their warm expressions of compassion and understanding that came to me at a time when I needed them very badly.

It was almost a month after the speeding ambulance had brought my critically injured wife to the front door of the trauma center at General Hospital when Dr. Meacham told me she was physically well enough to go home. I wasn't sure she really was, but he had been right about everything so far, and I didn't figure I should start arguing with him now.

I have very vivid memories of the Saturday morning her mother and I went to check Becky out of the hospital and bring her home. The first thing we did after I had gone by the office and signed all the papers for her dismissal was to go back up to her floor and take vase after vase of beautiful flowers that friends and fans had sent her from all over the country and distribute them to patients up and down the halls. I didn't think the people who'd sent them would mind. I know they wouldn't have if they had been able to see the expressions on the faces of the young kids and the old folks alike when I walked in carrying some of those gorgeous arrangements. I felt like Santa Claus!

I went back to Becky's room and took down the big picture of Jamey that had hung for all this time over her mirror. I placed it carefully under my left arm. Then I gathered up the plaque and all the Mac Wiseman tapes and placed them in a box and tucked it tightly under my right arm. We made our way down the hall and out a side door to my car. Becky rode in a wheelchair with a half-dozen nurses and aides following along carrying her personal belongings and special mementos we didn't dare leave behind. Becky was thin and pale, and when she rose from the wheelchair to get into the front seat of the car her steps were slow and unsure. She wore a full-length light blue robe and a blue turban-style hat on her head. There was a blank but slightly questioning look in her eyes, a look I was to see hundreds of times over the following months and years.

I was extremely concerned about Jamey's reaction to his mother's coming home. I had taken him to the hospital to see her once while she was there, and his body had trembled and his tiny fingers had tightened around mine as we nervously made our way in through the emergency room entrance and down the hallway to a special room the hospital had provided for us. When Becky came into the room wearing the same turban-type hat she wore upon discharge and not able to be the laughing, fun-loving mother Jamey had known all his life, he grew even more tense and withdrawn. He and his mother had always been close, warm and affectionate toward one another, but now things were different. All the way home from the hospital I wondered which Jamey, the loving one or the reluctant one, we'd find waiting for us.

When I pulled the car into the driveway, I could see him peering anxiously through the curtains. As soon as he saw me, however, he closed the curtains and ran away from the window. I was afraid we were in for a tough time.

But my fears subsided somewhat when we reached the front door. There hanging in full view were a half-dozen brightly colored balloons with a big red ribbon tied around them and a note crudely lettered in crayon, that read, "Welcome Home Mom. I Love You." And the letter "o" in the word "love" was drawn in bright red and shaped like a heart. I smiled and breathed a huge sigh of relief. I knew I'd have to help get him through the next few months with a lot of tender love and care, but something told me standing there on the doorstep that my anxious little first-grader was going to make it through whatever he had to face just fine.

I eased Becky inside and up the stairs to the same bedroom where on that nightmarish Sunday afternoon only a few weeks before I had sat with my arm wrapped around my son's shoulders and told him of the fate that had befallen his mother. As I pulled back the covers and helped Becky into bed, I suddenly felt the urge to say, "Thank You, Lord," for I knew I hadn't been alone in that room the first time and I knew I wasn't alone in there now. Becky was a long way from being well. Our living situation was a long way from being settled. A lot of questions were a long way from being answered. But in spite of that my wife was alive, she was at home now in her own bed, and I couldn't help but feel I had been witness to a miracle.

* * *

It had all happened so fast. Just a few weeks ago everything had been so different. I was living alone in a big, secluded house on thirty-five acres of land out in the country, answering to no one. I slept as late as I wanted to, lay by the pool whenever I wanted to, watched TV half the night if I wanted to. In fact, I had bought a satellite dish, and during baseball season I would park myself in front of the television set and watch games I wasn't even interested in just because I could pick them up. I especially liked the night games from the west coast that didn't even come on until ten or ten-thirty Nashville time. They'd last until one or two o'clock in the morning, and I wouldn't miss a pitch. I became probably the only person in the whole state of Tennessee who cared whether the Seattle Mariners won or lost.

It hadn't been all fun and games in the beginning, though. When Becky first decided she couldn't live in the country anymore and packed her things and left the house in Lebanon, I hurt . . . bad! Even though the concern over our living arrangements had slowly been driving a wedge between us for quite some time, as soon as she was physically out the door I missed her something awful. And I missed Jamey more than words could ever tell. The first couple of months they were gone, I lay in my big bed alone many a night and cried myself to sleep.

And the house itself had so much of both of them in it. Everywhere I turned there was a reminder: a picture of Jamey laughing in front of the Christmas tree, a picture of him and me flying a toy airplane in the front yard, a picture of him riding through the fields on his tiny toy tractor right along behind me on the big tractor, a picture of the three of us hamming it up for the camera in happier days. Every time I walked past the open door to Jamey's room and saw the toy train he used to ride on and the tent he'd played inside and realized he wasn't there any longer, I'd fall apart. It was a pain like I had never known before.

Finally, after several months, when it became evident that my wife and my son weren't going to be coming back to stay anytime soon, I did the only thing I knew to do. I went through the house and took down every reminder of the life we had once had there together—every picture that had Becky in it and all but a few special ones of Jamey—and I stashed them all up in the attic where I wouldn't be tortured by them every time I wandered up and down the halls. I closed the door to Jamey's room where I couldn't see inside it every time I passed, and I pretended that part of the house didn't exist anymore. Because for me it didn't.

I decided I needed to go about trying to make a new life for myself, maybe make some new friends, and I did. I let them know that my house was there anytime they wanted to come over, and I played host to quite a few impromptu gatherings. I started keeping hours even more weird than the weird hours I'd always kept, I began drinking more than I ever had before, and I stopped going to church altogether. I grew increasingly defensive about where I lived and how I lived. "It's my life . . . I'll throw it away if I want to," I recited from my 1969 record hit. I was happy. Or at least I thought I was. I stood in front of the mirror and told myself how happy I was several times every day.

But in the space of a heartbeat, in the length of time it takes for a speeding pickup truck to crash into a barely moving automobile, my life had spun around another 180-degrees. Now, here I was suddenly back with my family again, but this time under a whole new set of rules and circumstances. Becky was at home, she had survived her life-threatening ordeal, the three of us were living together under the same roof again, but it wasn't like our problems had all magically disappeared by any means. In some respects, they were just beginning.

It's not easy to admit even now, but during the two-and-a-half years we lived apart I became selfish—selfish with my time, selfish with my attitudes, and very set in my new ways. At first, as much as I wanted to take care of Becky and be with Jamey, I still resented having to leave the big house and the wide-open spaces out in the country to move into an apartment.

And that's what a condominium is. By whatever name you want to call it, it's still an apartment. On the one hand, I wanted what was best for Becky, and Dr. Meacham had been explicit: "She *must* be kept in surroundings that are familiar to her, Bill. I can't emphasize that enough. I know you're crowded, I know you're uncomfortable, but I also know you want your wife to return to normal. Brain-injured people simply cannot begin to readjust to life if they are thrown into unfamiliar situations or strange settings.

Becky won't get well if you take her into a new environment." I had no choice.

But, at the same time, I despised it. I didn't figure I had spent twenty-five years of my life logging eight million miles in the back of a Silver Eagle bus, eating six million cheeseburgers, and signing four million autographs, just so I could come home at night and listen to my neighbor's stereo blaring rock 'n' roll music through the paper-thin walls of some cracker-box apartment. And then to be awakened at eight o'clock on Saturday mornings by the sounds of his washing his pickup truck on the lawn underneath my bedroom window, the doors to the truck wide open and the radio on a rock 'n' roll station screaming full-blast. I was used to thirty-five acres and six thousand square feet, remember? Where my closest neighbor couldn't hear my loudest TV. And vice-versa.

Now here I was living in this place, surrounded by people I didn't even know and didn't care to know, feeling like every time I so much as walked out my front door I was on stage. Neighbors peeking out of their windows, people honking their horns and waving at the real-life TV and recording star walking up the sidewalk. Suppertime halted by knocks on the door. "How's Mrs. Anderson?" they'd always ask first. And then, "While I'm here, would you mind signing an autograph for my mother's aunt's third cousin's uncle?"

I've never minded signing autographs, but I'll have to admit I resented very much these intrusions on my privacy, partly because I wasn't used to it and partly because so much of the time I was under such heavy mental and emotional pressure. I had to smile at a television camera all day, then come home and wash the makeup out of my shirt collars and iron clothes for the next day's taping half the night. Becky couldn't do it, of course; for a long time she could only get out of bed for an hour or so once or twice a week. The apartment was far too small for live-in help, and by the time I'd get home Pam would be so exhausted from having tended to Becky's and Jamey's needs all day that my best bet was simply to point her toward the front door as soon as I walked in and tackle whatever domestic chores remained by myself.

For a while Becky's mother was a big help, but she didn't stay in Nashville very long. She and Lynne, Becky's sister, had moved to Music City from their homes in North Carolina for the sole purpose of helping Becky establish and operate a small interior decorating business. Their company had gotten the contract to purchase and install most of the rustic decor inside PoFolks restaurants, but now with PoFolks curtailing their expansion, the business had slowed to a crawl. Her mom and sister soon felt their best interests would be served by moving back home. That left me feeling even more alone since neither of us had any other relatives living within several hundred miles.

At some point, even amid all the other pressures and obligations of my daily existence, I had to face the fact that my life and my business and my career had to go on. I still had to earn a living, and I had employees looking to me for their livelihood. I've never known how to make a living but one way, and that's by entertaining people. To do that, of course, I had to go back out on the road.

At first that was one of the hardest things I had ever had to do in my life, leaving Becky and Jamey. Pam would stay overnight while I was gone, sleeping on the couch, driving Jamey to and from school, caring for Becky's needs, but it was hard for me to relax, knowing I was hundreds, sometimes thousands, of miles away.

Yet, at the same time, I found a strange but comforting kind of peace back out on the road that had been missing in all the clamor and confusion of home. I loved Becky and missed her terribly when I was gone, but just as the condo was familiar territory to Becky, the road was familiar territory to me. With everything else around me having changed so suddenly and so drastically, I needed some familiarity in my life too.

I began especially to enjoy the hour or so every night when I was actually up on stage singing and performing. It was a chance for me to escape, to lose myself in my songs, to forget about the problems of my life for a while. My band members have since told me that I put on some of the best shows of my entire career during this time. I don't know. I don't remember very many of them.

I do remember that there was one song in my repertoire, though, that was almost impossible for me to sing. And I didn't realize just how impossible until one night near the end of a concert when a lady sent a note up from the audience requesting that I sing it. The song is "Five Little Fingers." It's one of the staples of my career.

I didn't think anything at all about singing it when I first read the lady's note, and since I've always tried to acknowledge requests at my shows whenever I can, I told the band to kick it off. Just as soon as the first words began to roll out of my mouth, however, I knew I was going to have trouble finishing it:

> *I came home last night to a dark and lonely cottage*
> *I took the wreath off the door and somehow I stumbled inside*
> *I just can't . . . I just can't, I said, live without her*
> *Give me one reason to live now that my darling has died.*
>
> *And then five little fingers touched my hand*
> *Five little fingers too young to understand . . .*

I had written and recorded those words more than twenty years earlier, back in 1964, and now they had almost come true. Except in my song the child was a little girl and a death had actually occurred. How may times had I sung those words without ever fully feeling, until after Becky's accident, their impact? Not really *knowing* what they meant? And now I had lived it, I had actually *felt* the touch of my son's five little fingers on mine. It chilled me to the bone, but somehow I got through it that night. I didn't sing it again, however, for a long, long time.

When the shows were over and the music had stopped and the last round of applause was no longer even an echo, when the last autographed picture was tightly tucked away under the last arm to leave the auditorium, and I was standing alone in the back of the bus changing clothes to the monotonous drone of a diesel engine, I'd start feeling guilty. Guilty for being where I was, for smiling, laughing, singing, while my wife lay helpless in a brain-damaged fog hundreds of miles away and my son tossed in an anxious sleep, wondering if he'd wake up the next morning to the sound of some strange voice telling him his dad was "in a meeting." Life began slowly to dissolve from the bright reds and greens and yellows of Becky's triumphant homecoming to the stark gray and deep purple reality of conflict piled upon unresolved conflict.

I wonder now if maybe I hadn't become a lot like the old mule the farmer couldn't get to plow. He began hitting the mule across the head with a big two-by-four.

"What are you doin' that for?" an onlooker asked.

"Danged mule won't plow," answered the farmer.

"Is hittin' him across the head like that gonna make him plow?"

"I dunno," the farmer replied, "but I figure I gotta get his attention first!"

The Great-Attention-Getter-in-the-Sky must have figured I hadn't been paying attention. And while I don't believe He *causes* bad things to happen, I do believe He *uses* what happens to us sometimes to correct our vision. It wasn't that I was blind, but prior to Becky's accident I *was* focusing my sights on a lot of the wrong targets. It's amazing how I began to feel Him slowly starting to turn me around.

It began with my back. Anyone who has ever had back trouble (and when my back was hurting I found that almost everybody I talked to either had back trouble or used to have it) knows that an ailing back is the stiffest and most painful early in the morning. Most mornings I hurt so bad I couldn't "climb" out of bed as I'd always done, so I began "rolling" out instead. Just rolling off the right side of the bed and onto the floor. Then I'd reach out and grip the edge of the wooden bedframe and begin to pull myself up . . . slowly, slowly, inch by inch. My first stopping place between lying face down on the floor and standing up would invariably be there at the side of my bed on my knees.

It had been a long time since I'd started off the days of my life on my knees. I had grown up knowing about God, attending Sunday School, church, youth fellowship, and the like, but my personal relationship with God seemed to have become less and less important to me over the years. It wasn't that I *believed* any less; it just seemed that I'd set aside smaller and smaller amounts of my time for thinking about Him and His purpose for my life. And I hardly ever just stopped and said, "Hey, thanks, God, for all you've done for me." But suddenly here I was every morning now down on my knees, by the side of my bed, in the still and quiet of an unspoiled day. I began talking to Him.

I don't know what I said, but it wasn't anything very fancy. I've never been very good at using big, highfalutin' words anyhow, so I just talked to God like He was my best friend. Like He was right there in that tiny apartment room with me. Which I know He was.

And I thanked Him for allowing Becky to live, for blessing my life with a wonderful son and two beautiful daughters, for having given me talent, fame, fortune, and the countless other bountiful gifts He had so graciously and richly bestowed upon my life. And I asked that through all my problems and turmoil He might grant me a whole new view of His purpose, a new freedom in my spirit, and a new power in my service to Him. In other words, God, can't we push the reset button and go back to square one in our relationship and start over?

No bolt of lightning came crashing through my window. No mighty voice spoke to me and told me what to do. But I began to notice that ever so slowly, a little bit here, a little bit there, my attitudes began to change. My view of the world and the conditions surrounding my place in it began to soften.

The apartment I was living in didn't grow any larger, but I gradually began to realize that it was a roof over my head, it kept me warm and dry, and I knew not everybody, even in Nashville, had that. I got acquainted with a few of my neighbors, and they turned out to be some pretty nice folks. Some of them even proved to be very understanding and extremely helpful. So instead of griping and complaining about things so much, I decided to give thanks. I still had my financial situation to deal with, of course, my back still hurt real bad, and my daughter's health didn't magically improve overnight. But gradually I began to notice that every day I'd wake up just a little bit more in control, just a little bit better equipped to handle whatever crisis fate decided to dish out that particular day. And it was a good feeling.

"Patience has never been one of my virtues," I truthfully wrote in my musical ode to romantic impatience called "I Can't Wait Any Longer," and I began asking God please to grant me more patience, to slow me down, and maybe to help me set my watch more to His time. I'd hum the melody to Marijohn Wilkin's and Kris Kristofferson's masterpiece "One Day at a Time," over and over, hoping the thought behind those beautiful lyrics would somehow carve itself a place in my consciousness.

It wasn't easy. I won't lie and say there were no days spent backsliding. I had a lot of those; I still have them. But ever so slowly my attitudes began to change, my bitterness began to mellow. My problems didn't go away, but for the first time in a long time I was able to call on a whole new source of inner strength from which to deal with them.

A former secretary of mine once taped to her telephone a sign which read: "God leads men into deep waters not to drown them but to cleanse them." For years I've heard sayings like "When God closes a door He opens a window" and "God breaks us in order to bless us." I began to think maybe that's what this was all about. Maybe God had decided He needed to get me flat on my back, literally and figuratively, in order to get me to look up. If so, I guess it worked.

I went out one day and had a copy made of a sign just like the one Roy Acuff has hanging on his dressing-room door at the Opry, and I came back and hung it on the wall at my office where I could see it every day. I look at it all the time. It's a reminder of the essence of the faith I'm trying real hard to live by every day. It simply says:

There ain't nothin' gonna come up today
That me and the Lord can't handle.

26

Some days it was a good thing that sign was hanging there on the wall where I could see it because in spite of my newfound strength, renewed assurance, and fresh inner resolve, I managed to spend a lot of my time during the first four years following Becky's accident simply hangin' on and gettin' by. I needed every reminder of my faith that I could muster.

Two ominous clouds seemed to be always hanging over my head. First, of course, was Becky's condition and the obligation I felt to help her as best as I could. Maybe "obligation" is the wrong word, because I *wanted* to help Becky, but in order to continue to do so, I was forced to stand toe-to-toe with the man in the mirror and answer some of the hardest, toughest questions I had ever had to face.

In the first place, who was I? And why was I here? Why wasn't I back out in the country living the lifestyle I had become comfortable with in the house that I loved? How many other men in my shoes would have sacrificed so much of their own lives, their own freedoms, in an effort to connect with their pasts? I didn't know.

And was that, in fact, what I was doing? Was my renewed commitment to my family born of rededication and love, or was I just trying to be a martyr of some kind? I had no idea.

And who was this lady lying there in her bed, and why did my whole life suddenly seem to revolve around her well-being anyhow? Hadn't our relationship been bent to the point of almost breaking for several years? And at this time and place in our lives, what were we to each other?

Were we living together under the same roof again because

together was where we'd each rather be than anywhere else in the world? Or were we simply together because a cruel quirk of fate had reunited us under a set of extremely extenuating circumstances? Was this the same lady I married many years ago, or was she now, through no fault of her own, a stranger that I didn't know and might never come to know? Was the love I had felt for her during her crisis drawn from the depths of faith and passion and commitment, and was it strong enough to sustain a truly happy and giving marriage for the rest of our lives? Or had I just been warmed by the flicker of a dying flame that had burned out long ago? Every day I wrestled with the questions, but very seldom did I go to bed at night knowing any of the answers.

I came to learn that my questions, while perhaps going a step beyond the ordinary questions a spouse might ask of himself or herself when faced with a head-injured mate in a normal family situation, were not in themselves really all that unusual. Dr. Philip Barry, writing in a paper entitled "Family Adjustment to Head Injury" for the National Head Injury Foundation, says that "The long process of recovery for a head-injured victim is shared by the whole family and not just the injured member." He says that the most obvious feeling a family member has to deal with is grief. And that grief, according to him, comes in four stages.

The first stage is shock—how could something like this possibly have happened in my life? The second stage is denial—it must be a mistake, which is exactly what I said to the bus driver when I first went up to the front of the bus to begin looking for a telephone. I had asked him if perhaps the call were not for someone else. Next comes anxiety—what do I do now? How can I possibly cope with all this disruption in my life? Then finally anger—anger at the victim for getting injured, anger at the doctors, anger at others involved in the accident, and even anger at God for letting this happen. "Perhaps the easiest person to be angry at is ourselves," he says, "and this can be translated into guilt. 'If only I had done something differently . . . if only I could do something more to help now.'"

I had felt every single one of these emotions, most of them several times, at one time or another following what happened to Becky. And I went through a lot of other feelings, too . . . isolation, abandonment, fright, frustration. I seemed to spend a lot of my time fighting with my emotions and they spent just as much fighting back with me. One day, though, I came to realize that the final and most important emotion for me to conquer was going to have to be acceptance. I had to come to a realistic understanding of what had happened, *admit* that it had happened, then plan what was going to happen from that point on and figure out what my role in it needed to be. The day I could finally reach the point of acceptance, I knew I could put all the other petty things aside and get on with the process of helping Becky get well.

My friend Sonny Smith, the former head basketball coach at Auburn University, helped as much as anybody in putting it all into perspective. I ran into him one day during the early period of Becky's recuperation and found that suddenly he and I had more to talk about than my love for sports and his love for country music. Sonny's wife, Jan, had suffered a stroke not long after Becky's accident, and Sonny, who is about the same age as I am, had been through much of the same trial and turmoil that I had. Jan survived her stroke, but it left her with some severe changes in her personality. Sonny admitted to me that one day he woke up and realized he was married to a virtual stranger.

"How have you been able to deal with that emotionally?" I asked him. "I mean you . . . yourself?"

"I've handled it by doing what I tell my ball players to do," he answered.

"And that is?"

"I tell them not to sweat the small stuff . . . and that *all* stuff is small stuff."

I thought about that for a while and realized that Sonny had hit the nail squarely on the head.

There were many things Becky wasn't able to do for herself when she first returned home from the hospital. In fact, the things she *could* do would comprise a much shorter list.

Most of her time was spent simply lying in bed. She was constantly in a tremendous amount of pain, particularly from headaches, and she didn't want people or movement around her. She ached and hurt so bad from the repercussions of the impact that she literally could not lie in a position where one part of her body even so much as touched another part. If one leg happened to brush against the other one while she was shifting her weight in the bed, she cried out from the pain. The same held true with her arms. She never seemed to get comfortable.

Her left leg was black and blue with bruises all the way from her hip to the top of her foot. Her left foot was totally numb, prompting an orthopedist to tell her later that she'd never be able to wear high-heeled shoes again. Today, she has practiced and perfected her balancing act to the point that she can and does wear heels, but she still can't wear boots or any other shoe that comes across the top of her foot. There's still an area about four inches wide circling all the way around the foot in which she has no feeling whatsoever.

For months after the accident Becky also always seemed to have an upset stomach. I took her to see an internist who checked her thoroughly and told her that it was no wonder her stomach was upset. Every internal organ in her body was inflamed and swollen. He could only surmise that it had come from her having been jolted with such violent force at the time of the crash. At the same time, every medical and law enforcement expert I talked with clearly stated that beyond any shadow of a doubt the seat belt she had been wearing had saved her life.

It was also many long months into Becky's recovery before she could sleep on a pillow again. Her head hurt so bad that she simply could not lay it down across anything as high or as hard as a pillow. She couldn't sleep on her back at all because of the myriad of cuts and bruises across the top of her head and down the back of her neck, but she finally devised a way to take a beach towel and roll it up with the soft side to the outside and then place it just so against her cheek bone in one tiny area that didn't hurt. For the longest time the only way she could sleep was by lying on her side and using the rolled-up beach towel for a pillow.

Several times during her first few months at home Becky would call for me to come into her room and see the most recent slivers of glass that had worked their way out from beneath the surface of her skin. Years after the wreck she was still pulling little reminders of the crash from under the skin on her fingers, her legs, and her scalp.

It was no wonder, then, that most of the time all Becky wanted to do was to lie still, alone in the dark, and rest. Her appetite dwindled to zero, and she lost a considerable amount of weight. She grew thinner than I had ever known her to be. When her appetite slowly began to return several months later, she realized her sense of smell was gone, and the only things she wanted to eat were sweet things. Naturally, with that, the weight returned, plus some.

The doctors explained to us that most of the things we think we taste are actually things we smell, but that sweets are, in fact, one of the few things we actually taste with our tongues. Therefore, sweets were about the only things she could taste and enjoy.

It was well into mid-1985 before Becky felt like trying to resume anything that resembled even a semi-normal existence. When she did, it was a case of her having to ease her way ever so slowly, ever so carefully back into the real world.

When, after months and months of isolation and inactivity, she finally reached the point where she felt like getting out of bed and venturing outside the condo for an hour or so each week, it seemed that even the simplest of tasks was often extremely tiring and difficult for her to master. She'd ask me to drive her to the grocery store, for example, but once we'd arrive there she'd have trouble making even the most basic decisions. Did she want to buy the Crisco or the Wesson Oil? The cherry fruit punch or the grape? *Redbook* or *Ladies' Home Journal*? The doctors had warned me that decision-making is often very taxing for brain-injured people, and I tried to be patient. After spending only a short period of time at the store helping her wrestle with decisions, I'd drive her home. She would often have to go back to bed for days.

On the rare occasions when Becky would feel like getting out of the condo at mealtime and going out to eat in a restaurant, I would try ahead of time to suggest both a place to go and a meal she might enjoy rather than watching her struggle through the ordeal of having to choose. "Let's go up to the Peddler tonight," I'd suggest. "They've got that great salad bar, remember? We can have a salad and maybe the six-ounce filet, a baked potato, and some fresh fruit for dessert." That seemed to make it easier for her to handle. If she absolutely could not decide some particular issue for herself, I would make the decision for her. Sometimes we simply made no decisions at all.

Her energy level was never very high. She would wake up early in the morning to see Jamey before I took him to school, but then it was back to bed for most of every day and on into the night. Becky has always been a night creature, though, and around nine o'clock in the evening she'd often wake up and be in her most alert state of the day. She'd watch TV (*The 700 Club* became her favorite program) until sleep would overtake her again somewhere around midnight. I had begun living and functioning on a schedule almost totally opposite from hers, however, what with my new duties as Mr. Mom, which meant days went by when we barely even saw each other. Seldom were we able to communicate on anything that resembled a meaningful level. Frankly, it wasn't a very fulfilling life for either one of us.

But I'll say one thing for Becky: In spite of all her injuries, her difficulties, and the seemingly insurmountable odds everybody said she faced, she never gave up. She never quit trying to improve, never stopped reaching and digging for that extra little something that might somehow bring her one step closer to being the person she knew she had been before the accident. To her eternal credit, she absolutely refused to accept the thought that she'd never be well again.

One psychiatrist in Nashville told her she'd never function at more than seventy-five percent of her former capacity. Becky's answer to that was "I'll prove him wrong." Written tests were administered by various doctors and clinics to determine her strengths and weaknesses in all different kinds of physical and emotional areas. When some of them would come back showing certain deficiencies, she'd say, "Well, you give me that same test again in a few months. I'll do better then." And she would.

I'll always give an awful lot of the credit for Becky's determination and her subsequent progress to a kind, insightful man that my friend Dean Booth brought to us, Dr. Tom Burns, a clinical psychologist who lived and practiced in Savannah, Georgia. Dean had known Tom since their college days together and, as an attorney, had seen the results of the work Tom had done with other head-injured patients over the years. Even though the distance between Savannah and Nashville would prevent daily contact between doctor and patient, Dean assured us early on that we'd never be able to find a more qualified doctor or more compassionate human being to whom we could entrust Becky's emotional and psychological recovery than Tom Burns. He was more than right.

Tom (he's such a down-to-earth person that neither of us ever felt the need to call him Dr. Burns) immediately gained both Becky's and my confidence and trust. For over two years he would rearrange his schedule at least once a month so that he could leave Savannah at a moment's notice and fly to Nashville to counsel with Becky. He is a soft-spoken, prematurely graying man in his late forties who, from the beginning, felt more like a friend than he did a doctor.

He'd fly out of Savannah on the last flight connecting to Nashville in midafternoon and would usually get to town around dinnertime. If Becky felt like it, the three of us would then go out to eat, talking about nothing heavy, nothing serious, but giving Tom a chance to size up Becky's progress since their last meeting. The next morning I'd drive to his hotel and join him for breakfast, trying to bring him up to speed on Becky's condition and her progress as I saw it. He'd confide in me things he might have sensed during his visit with her the night before and suggest things that I might do to help with her rehabilitation. Mostly he would remind and encourage me to keep everything in a positive, upbeat mood when I was around Becky. She didn't need anything negative bearing down on her, he'd say, and I'd promise to do my best. Later in the morning I'd drive him to the condo where he'd meet with Becky, have lunch, and stay until time for his late afternoon flight back to Georgia. And he'd always leave Becky "homework" assignments to work on between visits.

His main objective was to institute something called repatterning, an exercise he described to me as "building new patterns for damaged emotional muscles."

"The MRI scan showed us early on that Becky's most severe injuries lie in the prefrontal lobes of her brain," he said, "and that's the main circuit that carries information about the emotions. Right now Becky's not feeling very much emotionally. Nothing seems funny to her, nothing seems sad, nothing warms her or excites her."

I agreed with his assessment. Most of the time there was an empty, almost lost expression on Becky's face and in her eyes.

"I want to work on that," Tom would say. "Do you remember Patricia Neal, the movie actress who had the stroke several years ago?" he asked, and I said that I did. "Well, nobody ever thought she'd walk and talk and function normally again. But the doctors went to work repatterning her motor-skill areas, teaching her exercises and repeating them over and over again during the years following her stroke. Friends would come to her house and spend hour after hour moving her legs, moving her arms, teaching her how to function like a new person. I want to see if we can't do something like that with Becky's brain, see if we can't force it to bring other brain tissue into play. In other words, if one area of the brain is damaged, can we get new areas of the brain to take over and perform the functions of the damaged area? Can we connect some new circuits to replace the ones that are gone?

I admitted he was way over my head.

"It'll be sort of like physical therapy for the brain," he continued, "except instead of working on teaching *muscles* how to help a person *walk*, we'll be trying to teach *brain tissue* how to make Becky *feel* emotions. Nothing complicated, just simple things like funny, sad, angry. Frankly, I don't know if it will work or not. There hasn't been a lot of work done in this area. But I feel like it might be our only hope."

Who was I to argue?

He began by giving Becky, of all things, acting lessons. He told Becky to *act* . . . to *act* like she felt things emotionally even though she wasn't actually able to *feel* them at all. He set her up with something he called "feedback loops," encouraging her to practice over and over again *acting* like she could feel certain emotions until, in fact, she could. He told her to keep practicing these patterns again and again while he was away, to go for whatever emotion it was she wanted to revive, to pretend she *was* bringing it back time after time. Slowly but surely, with Tom's help and a large dose of her own gutsy determination, she began the long, tenuous process of retraining herself.

* * *

I said there were two clouds hanging over my head during the first couple of years following Becky's accident. Some days it seemed there were more than that, but there were two major ones. The first, of course, was Becky's condition, her injuries, her deficits, and the long, tedious process of her recovery. The second cloud was quite a bit different from the first but equally as foreboding. I knew that looming ahead of both of us somewhere out there on the not-so-distant horizon was a lengthy, complicated, and expensive legal battle drawn from the aftermath of the accident. I was in no shape to have to go through it, but try as I might I didn't seem to be able to wish it away.

There was no amount of money in the world that could ever have paid Becky, Jamey, and me for all that we had suffered and all that we had been forced to endure as a result of everything that had happened, but the judicial system in this country provides the opportunity for people to seek financial restitution when they feel they have been wronged. And with all the medical bills we'd already accumulated plus all the ongoing treatment we knew Becky was going to require for no telling how many years, our feeling was that Ronco Irrigation, Inc., and/or Phillip Todd Brasher, or some combination of the above should be held financially responsible. After all, they had been in the wrong. Brasher had been found guilty of operating a vehicle while intoxicated. And Ronco had allowed an eighteen-year-old with a past history of drunkenness to drive their company truck. Why shouldn't one or both of them have to step forward and help pay the doctors' bills, the nurses' bills, the hospital bills, and the upcoming goodness-knows-what bills that resulted from the havoc they caused?

But there was more to it than that. Becky wanted a strong statement made to the community on her behalf regarding drunk driving, and she felt, as I did, that the publicity we'd get from a court case would help the public focus on that issue. "People need to see what someone's drinking did to a perfectly healthy woman," she said. "I know nothing can change what happened to me, but it could keep all this from happening to another family. And that's important." I couldn't have agreed more.

* * *

While Becky was spending the better part of every day for nearly two years trying to get well, our attorneys were equally busy trying to settle our differences with Ronco and Brasher without any of us having to go to court. The opposing attorneys offered to pay us seventy-five thousand dollars, which admittedly is a lot of money, but at that time our medical bills had *already* totaled almost that much and we knew we'd only scratched the surface. For all we knew, Becky might not be able to work toward earning a living ever again. She was going to need constant physical and emotional therapy to aid her reentry into society, and that wouldn't come cheap. Whatever money she eventually received from the settlement on this case might have to last her a lifetime. Based on that, their offer was a mere drop in the bucket. We simply could not in good judgment settle for an amount that small.

So in an effort to get Ronco's and Brasher's attention and let them know we were serious, we filed a lawsuit against them for two million dollars, one million dollars in compensatory damages and another million dollars in punitive damages. That got no reaction. So we raised it to three million compensatory and one million punitive. They were still unwilling to negotiate a more equitable settlement.

I was relying on my Atlanta friend and attorney Dean Booth to advise me as to what I should do next, and he said I had no choice—I had to proceed with the lawsuit. If there is one thing I have learned during this most trying of times in my life, it's that lawsuits are much easier said than done. It rolls off the tongue real easy—"Let's file a lawsuit"—but what a can of worms it can actually turn out to be!

The two sides in this suit spent no telling how many costly hours, day after day, month upon month, researching facts, interviewing potential witnesses, taking depositions, filing and answering interrogatories, building their cases, preparing for a trial. They talked to each other periodically about settling the case without its actually ever having to go to court, feeling each other out as to how far the other side seemed willing to push or be pushed, but each time they eased off, playing cat and mouse with one another and with the court. For a long time I don't think either side actually thought the case would ever come down to an honest-to-goodness, full-blown courthouse trial, but once it turned into a big game of chicken and the longer it went on, the harder it became for either side to back down. Whether I liked it or not, I was on a collision course with a courtroom.

The case was set for trial in early October 1986, in the metropolitan Nashville courthouse, Circuit Judge Hamilton Gayden presiding. But even on the Monday morning that my attorneys and I actually walked up the courthouse steps and into the elevator bound for the fifth-floor chambers, I thought we'd meet the attorneys and principals from the other side in a hallway before we got there, reach an agreement on how to settle our differences, and get on with our lives. Regrettably, that's not what happened at all.

What I knew about courtrooms and courtroom procedure before that fateful Monday morning could have been written in large letters on one side of a guitar pick. When it was all mercifully over eleven gut-wrenching days and dozens of embarrassing front-page newspaper stories later, I knew only that being a participant in a courtroom trial ranked right up there alongside having kidney stones and root canal surgery at the top of my list of things I never wanted to sample ever again.

My first thought upon entering the courtroom was, well, it looks about like all the courtrooms I've ever seen on television. The walls were cloaked in dark walnut paneling that rose to the ceiling above the thin, brown indoor-outdoor carpet covering the cold marble floor. There was an elevated judge's bench on the wall to my right at what a performer might call center stage; a small, enclosed witness stand raised slightly off the floor to the judge's right, five or six feet in front of three windows that lined the outer wall; and an enclosed jury box with two rows of six padded swivel chairs pushed against the wall to the judge's left. In the center of the floor rested two long tables and six chairs arranged in an L-shaped configuration, whereby one table and three chairs faced the judge's bench, three chairs and the other table faced the jury box. To the right of the table facing the judge stood a small movable podium, maybe four feet high. I could see three microphones in the room, one at this podium, one at the witness stand, the other at the judge's bench. Each was mounted on an adjustable gooseneck stand.

Toward the back of the room behind a mahogany railing and a swinging wooden gate were several rows of church-type hard wooden pews, gallery seats for the press and other interested onlookers. The obligatory American flag and the bright red Tennessee state flag with its blue circle of white stars in the center hung on tall wooden poles with shiny brass eagles on the top to the rear and either side of the judge's chair. My immediate reaction when I slowly entered the austere chamber was to look around and see if I could spot Perry Mason. I knew he (or at least Judge Wapner) had to be in there somewhere.

The judge entered and began by introducing himself and making a few generalized remarks to all of us gathered in the room, none of which I can recall. He then called my attorneys and the attorneys for the defense to the bench and spoke with them in quiet legalese. I can only assume that he was making one final plea for them to step out in the hall and settle this whole mess like gentlemen. They obviously refused. He then announced that the first order of business would be the selection of a jury. I had never so much as even been called for jury duty in my life and had no idea how the jury selection process took place.

Some thirty or forty people had been summoned for possible duty that particular week, and they had been herded into the back of the courtroom shortly after all the attorneys, plaintiffs and defendants had been seated at the tables down front. They sat quietly on the pews, seemingly as nervous and as fascinated as I was.

Judge Gayden addressed them as a group from the bench and began telling them a bit about the case his court was preparing to hear.

"This is a very serious case," he said, "and it's going to be a very serious trial. Do any of you have any qualms about sitting on this jury?" Nobody raised a hand.

The judge then looked directly at me where I was seated alongside Dean Booth, Nashville attorney Richard Speight, a former college classmate and fraternity brother of Dean's at Emory University in Atlanta whom Dean had wisely suggested early in our preparation that we bring on board, and an associate from Speight's law firm, Mrs. Rose Cantrell. We had had to pull an extra chair up to our table to accommodate the crowd. The judge instructed me to rise from my chair and turn to face the room full of prospective jurors. "Do any of you recognize this man?" he asked. I'll admit I wasn't sure I wanted to hear their answers. What if nobody in the whole room knew who I was? Besides that, why was he asking? I was relieved and somewhat flattered when all but two or three hands in the room went up.

Judge Gayden then polled each individual person asking them where they knew me from. The answers were as varied as my career itself. Some knew me from country music, some from PoFolks commercials, some from game shows, others from soap operas. I was surprised that most of the blacks in the room knew who I was, but not surprised at all when a white lady with a distinctly northern accent, who said she was a molecular biologist at Vanderbilt University, stared at me blankly. I figured she probably thought a "Whisperin' Bill" was an invoice you get from a doctor who treats you for laryngitis.

"Are there any of you who could not be fair toward Mr. Anderson in a legal matter based on who he is and what you know about him?" Judge Gayden continued. Again no hands went up.

"Do any of you know Mr. Anderson personally or do you know him in any manner not connected with his profession as an entertainer and public figure?" he asked. One man answered yes, that his son had once played on the same soccer team with my son and indicated that he might feel uncomfortable having to serve on this particular jury. The judge allowed him to leave.

"Are there any of you who couldn't be impartial in this case based on the fact that it's a case where alcohol is involved?" he asked. "Are there any of you who have read about this case in the newspapers or heard about it on the radio or television who couldn't be fair based on what you might have seen or read?" The judge was certainly being thorough. No one responded to either one of his questions.

Deliberately and painstakingly the selection process began. Hours later, after prospective jurors were questioned by attorneys representing each side and dismissed for a variety of reasons, only twelve were left—ten women and two men. Eight of the women were blacks, both men were whites. Their ages ranged from the young man in the cowboy shirt and western boots on the back row who said he was in his early twenties to a lady who was probably close to seventy. I wasn't quite sure what to make of the final selection and I found out later neither were the attorneys. I just crossed my fingers and hoped for the best.

The court convened early Monday morning, but it was midafternoon Tuesday before the first arguments in the trial itself actually began. It was also an omen of the speed of things to come.

Looking back on it now, much of the trial is a big blur in my mind, and I'm not sure that it's not best that way. I took out the newspaper clippings recently and thumbed through them just to refresh my memory, and it hurt all over again. Real bad.

Most of what I remember is hour upon hour of painful testimony. Psychiatrists, psychologists, neurologists, plastic surgeons, dentists, attorneys, objections overruled and sustained, recesses, policemen, more attorneys, more doctors, more objections, more speculation, more memories, more hurt. Our objective was to prove that Becky had suffered severe, permanent, life-threatening damages for which we needed funds to provide ongoing medical treatment. Their objective was to prove that the damages were less than we claimed, the ongoing care less than we anticipated, therefore the money we were to receive should be less.

Todd Brasher was in the courtroom from the outset, but Becky was not, even though she was the focal point of the entire trial. Her doctors had pleaded that she would be unable to stand the stress and strain of being in court every day, so she was excused. Before the trial was over, however, we all knew she would have to come in and testify. But her not being there for the first several days caused the proceedings to take on a strange and eerie air of mystery as to just who this woman was that all this talk and testimony was about.

Nothing to do with the trial was easy on me (my back hurt constantly and I had to ask the judge for permission to get up out of my chair every fifteen minutes or so and walk around the room), but I think what hurt me even more was hearing doctor after doctor testify that my wife was not the same person she was before the accident and then telling everyone within earshot that she probably would never be the same again. "She suffers a twenty-five percent permanent impairment of her ability to make decisions and know joy and the fullness of life," one psychiatrist said. Another added, "If a person has not recovered fully from a head injury within two years, ordinarily there is no improvement beyond that point." I owned a calendar. I knew this was being said almost two years to the day after her injuries had occurred.

"Mrs. Anderson is a different person now than she was before the accident," Dean Booth told the jury. "She doesn't have any emotions, she has no energy. Everything she does she does out of sense of duty. She doesn't feel any pleasure, she doesn't feel any joy." And I remembered how Becky herself had once described the way she felt to a doctor who had asked. "I feel. . ." she said, searching to find just the right words, ". . .I feel like there's nobody home."

Dean talked about Becky's having lost her sense of smell and with it much of her sense of taste. He repeated a story I had told him about my having come home off the road one time and finding our refrigerator full of spoiled food. Becky had not even noticed, and it was a miracle that she had not attempted to prepare some of that food for herself and Jamey.

He told the jurors about Becky's vision problems, vertigo, and her "sudden, debilitating, and devastating" headaches. And he said, "Becky Anderson's life will be a continuous uphill battle. She will have to deal with life with her emotional hands tied behind her back. She will always sense that she is a visitor on this planet."

Tom Burns testified that Becky would "rehabilitate, but not recover" from her injuries. He explained to the jurors that damaged nerve cells do not regenerate like other cells in the body and Becky would "continue to live in a gray and colorless world." I listened but tried not to hear.

Police officer John Johnson recounted for the jury the explosive and terrifying moments following the crash when he arrived on the scene and reached his hand into Becky's car, took hold of her arm, and felt no pulse. "There was blood and glass everywhere," he testified. "I thought she was dead."

"I told her, 'I've got the ambulance coming,'" he continued. "I said, 'Lady, don't you die on me. I've never had one to die yet!'"

And on and on it went. More doctors painting more gloomy pictures, more recollections of the accident, more memories of the night that won't go away. For me, more fear of the future I had so little idea of how to face.

I had no role in the proceedings at all for the first several days, but I was there every minute the court was in session. I'd get up early each morning, dress, and drive Jamey to school. I'd fight the early morning rush-hour traffic into downtown and meet with the lawyers at Richard Speight's office around eight-thirty. We'd discuss our plans and strategies for the day then walk the five or six blocks to the courthouse.

When the testimony began each day at nine, I sat, I listened, I thought, and I reflected. Sometimes I'd try watching the jury, attempting to read their faces to see how certain points of what was being said affected them. Most of the time what I got in return was no expression at all.

I thought to myself how similar this was in many ways to working before a live audience in a concert setting. You sing, you tell a story, and you search the audience for their reaction. Many times their faces will tell you what you need to know long before they actually applaud or laugh. But not this group. "It's a tough room to work," I said in typical show-biz jargon in an effort to loosen up the attorneys when they'd question me as to how I thought a certain point had been taken by the jurors. "About the size of the typical crowd I draw, too," I joked, "and a darn tough room to work!"

One thing I'd never caught onto from watching courtroom scenes in movies and on television is that a trial doesn't just fall into place accidentally piece by piece. It's all carefully orchestrated beforehand—again much like I would plan out a concert show—with a certain witness scheduled to appear at a certain point and another to appear at another strategic point in the testimony. As I watched the proceedings unfold, I became aware that, to a degree, they were scripted. I quickly realized the wisdom behind it.

First, it allowed the attorneys to present to the jury a clear and concise picture of the evidence in some semblance of order. The jury could follow what happened from Point A to Point B without becoming confused. Second, it allowed peaks and valleys in the overall testimony which, in turn, allowed the strongest points in the testimony to stand out above other points that might not have registered as strongly with the jurors. Much like I wouldn't sing "Mama Sang a Song," "Golden Guitar," and "Five Little Fingers" all back-to-back on a show because they are all slow, sad songs, neither would a good attorney present psychiatrist after psychiatrist after psychiatrist in a case involving head injuries, even though each doctor might bring in his own special expertise to the court-room. Dean and Richard would call a doctor to take the stand, then follow the doctor's medical testimony by showing a videotape of another expert of some kind, then show the jury pictures taken at the scene of the accident, then move back to another live witness. It had a flow, a tempo, a purpose. Nobody in the room was as aware of how the evidence was being presented as I was, I'm sure, but then nobody else in that room made his living the way I make mine.

I was glad Becky wasn't there to hear everything that was being said, even though she could read it all the following day in the newspapers. There was no way I could isolate her from it com-pletely, but there were times when I wanted to.

I also was very surprised at my own reaction to the media cover-age of the trial. For someone who had spent most of his life working in a concerted effort to generate publicity for his career, I found myself to be painfully shy about my personal life being spread all over the front pages of the Nashville newspapers.

I'd see the morning paper, the *Tennessean*, before I ever left home each day, usually picking it up off my doorstep as soon as I woke up. I'd read the stories about the trial in private and take time to form whatever opinions I might have while I was shaving, taking a shower, and getting dressed. That wasn't so bad. But the afternoon paper was a completely different matter.

The first editions of the *Nashville Banner* usually roll off the presses in late morning, and by noon or shortly thereafter they are being hawked by vendors on every street corner in downtown

Nashville. Court would recess for lunch about that time each day, and I'd walk with my attorneys to a nearby restaurant to eat. There were several days when we'd pass vendors holding up the front page of the paper for passersby to see, and they'd be yelling, "Anderson Trial Continues . . . Read All About It," or "Doctors Say Becky Anderson Not To Recover," or something to that effect. I'd keep walking and try to pretend I was invisible.

In the evenings when I'd go to the market to pick up a loaf of bread or a tube of toothpaste, I'd pass by the newspaper racks and there it would all be again, the stories invariably shining from the top half of page one. Becky's picture, our picture, my name, her name. Why couldn't it all just go away?

For some reason, the whole time the trial was going on, I never felt like it was really happening to me. I could see, hear, feel everything around me, but it was almost like I was outside of my own body hovering over the courtroom watching everything that was going on.

And all the time the trial was unfolding I had this gnawing going on down deep in the pit of my stomach. It was apprehension. It was excitement. It was fear. And it wouldn't go away. It was a cross between the butterflies I had felt the first night I ever sang at the Grand Ole Opry and the stark terror I'd known one cold December day in 1976 when I had been a passenger in a small private airplane flying from Nashville to Columbus, Ohio, and the plane's electrical system had gone out.

I had just purchased the shell of a new Silver Eagle bus, and Custom Coach Corporation of Columbus was doing the interior conversion. They had been calling me for weeks to come up and select the furnishings for the staterooms, fabrics for the curtains, carpets for the floor, and the like.

Since there was no direct commercial flight, my road manager, Woody Woodard, located an twin-engine plane (I don't trust any plane with less than two engines!) that was available from the Gallatin Flying Service near Nashville, and Woody, my bus driver, James Price, and Becky and I, along with the hired pilot, took off early on a cloudy, wintry morning.

About an hour into the trip, I began to feel cold. "Ask him to turn the heat up a bit, Woody," I leaned forward and said to my friend in the copilot's seat. "It's kinda chilly back here."

"He can't," Woody replied. "The electrical system has just gone out."

I heard what he said, but the impact of his words didn't hit me. Not for a couple of more minutes. I knew we didn't have any heat, but I could live without that. I had no idea, however, that we also had no radio contact with the ground, no operating gauges to tell us how much fuel we had on board, and no electronic way to lower the landing gear. We were literally flying between Cincinnati and Columbus on a wing and a prayer!

In a minute the pilot turned around and asked James, who was sitting alone in the rear of the plane, to hand him some thick books that were stashed behind the back seat. James dug them out, passed them up to me, and I handed them to the pilot. The full meaning of the predicament we were in dawned on me when the pilot, cruising along at ten or twelve thousand feet and approaching the outskirts of Columbus, starting looking up instructions on how to land the plane with no landing gear. The books were the plane's operation manuals.

The pilot, a grizzled Marine combat veteran, decided against trying to land at our original destination, the busy, heavily commercial Port of Columbus airport. Instead, he opted for a smaller, less crowded field on the outskirts of town. He fiddled with the radio and tried to establish some kind of contact with the tower, but the radio was totally dead. He chose his only other alternative.

He lowered our altitude, came down over the runway of the little field no more than a few hundred feet above the ground and directly in front of the control tower, and dipped the right wing of the plane a couple of times. I noticed as he did so he was looking intently out the right window toward the tower.

In a minute someone in the tower flashed a bright red light up at us . . . on and off . . . on and off . . . and the pilot shook his head. He circled around the field, came back over the runway another time, and repeated the wing-dipping maneuver. Again we were greeted with a flashing light of red.

The pilot then pulled back the stick, and the little plane began to gain altitude again.

"What are we doing?" I asked nervously. All this time I had been sitting behind Woody, quietly holding Becky's hand and trying not to let either one of us think too much about what was going on.

"We've got to try to burn off some fuel," the pilot answered.

"How much do we have?" I asked.

"I don't know," came the answer. "The gauges are out. But we don't want to have a drop more than we'll need when we land."

"We're going to land?"

"We can't stay up here forever," he said. "The red light back there meant our landing gear definitely is not down. I had hoped maybe it was, but if it had been down the tower would have flashed us in green. We may have to come in on our belly. If so, we don't want a lot of fuel sloshing around in the tanks. We could go up in flames."

"What do you mean we *may* be on our belly? Is there any other alternative?"

"Well, according to this manual there's a hand-crank right over there somewhere," he said, pointing toward Woody's seat. "If our copilot here can turn that crank exactly seventy-two times, the gear is supposed to come down. Think you can do it?" he asked.

Woody nodded, flipped back a small cover, located the crank, and began to turn.

When Woody reached the seventy-second turn, he nodded toward the pilot and the veteran flier banked the plane and headed for the airfield. Again he buzzed the tower, hoping as we all were to see the green light flashing. But to our horror it came back red.

He pulled back on the yoke, and we headed up again. "I figure we've got enough fuel for you to crank that thing one more time— another seventy-two turns—then we've got to go whether our wheels are down or not," he said. Woody started turning the handle again.

By the time he reached the seventy-second turn, the pilot was already lining up the plane with the end of the runway. "OK, folks," he said to us all, "this is it. Seat belts good and tight. Everybody lean forward, heads down between your knees. Cross your arms over your chest and hold on tight. If there are any pillows back there, put them between your body and the seat in front of you. I'll put her down as easy as I can, but you may get tossed around a bit. As soon as we hit the ground and you feel us coming to a stop, get out and run as fast as you can. Even if we make the landing, there's always the chance of a fire."

Becky and I found a couple of small pillows and braced them against the seats in front of us. I could see the runway in the distance growing larger and larger, closer and closer. And then I saw the fire trucks. And the ambulances. They were moving out from their stations and lining up along the runway. And for the very first time I became awfully, awfully scared.

I took Becky's hand and said, "Well, at least we're together," and she smiled back at me and nodded. I could feel the plane rapidly losing altitude, could feel the pilot pulling back, pulling back, trying to slow our speed to the bare minimum he needed to keep us flying.

Suddenly, of all things, I thought of my mother. They say your life sometimes flashes before your eyes when you think you're looking death in the face, but mine didn't. I just thought about Mama. I could see her standing in her kitchen, leaning over the sink, washing dishes and singing an old hymn. I had seen her just like that so many times. "This is going to kill her," I remember thinking to myself. "Oh, God, this will be so hard for her to take. Please watch over Mama . . . and please let us make it!" And I closed my eyes and got ready to hit the ground.

A hundred or so feet above the runway, the pilot cut the engines completely, and we glided the rest of the way in with no power at all. I could feel the ground racing beneath us, I knew I was going to feel the jar of heavy metal scraping across the top of hard concrete at any minute. A plane skidding sideways out of control . . . sparks flying everywhere . . . noisy, ugly. How quickly could the fire trucks and ambulances get to us? How were we going to get out if the doors jammed? I waited.

I guess it just wasn't our time. Somehow the landing gear had come down, and we touched the runway riding the softest, most beautiful rubber tires I had ever felt beneath me. It was like bouncing on an air mattress. The last seventy-two cranks had evidently done the trick.

You have never seen five people get out of an airplane so fast in your life. We hugged and squeezed each other like we were at our ten-year high-school reunion. And I doubt there was one among us who didn't close his eyes and say a soft, silent prayer.

And now here I was sitting in the courtroom feeling the same uncertainty I had felt on that little airplane all over again, that same twinge of anxiety. I knew that just as we had been close to running out of fuel on the plane, just as we had been forced to come in for a landing whether the landing gear had been in place or not, each passing day in that room meant we were much closer to running out of doctors to testify, running out of policemen, dentists, and pictures to present to the jury. I knew that any minute now they were going to call Becky's name, and no matter what condition she might be in, she was going to have to come into that courtroom, ready or not, and get up on that witness stand in front of those twelve jurors, in front of the press, in front of a battery of antagonistic lawyers representing the other side, in front of God and everybody, and, landing gear up or landing gear down, she was going to have to testify.

So was I.

27

It happened on the second Tuesday of the trial, the seventh day I'd spent in the courthouse. Becky was called to the witness stand first thing that morning, and I was called as soon as she stepped down. It wasn't anything either of us said or did while we were testifying, but rather something that took place toward the back of the courtroom, *off* the stand, out of sight and out of earshot of the jury, that ultimately came close to turning the whole trial upside down. It was stupid on my part, and it could have easily caused us to lose everything we had been working so hard to gain.

I knew from slightly before the time court recessed Monday afternoon that Tuesday would be the day. There was nothing left for anybody else to add to all that had been said. Becky and I had to put it in our own words now. I didn't sleep a lot Monday night.

No matter how tough it was going to be on me, I knew it would be twice as tough for Becky, and I tried from the moment we got up Tuesday morning to let her know she could lean on me and count on me for all the support and help I might possibly be able to give her. I got up early, got dressed, saw to it that Jamey was dressed and had some breakfast, drove him to school, then drove back by the condo to pick up Becky. As we locked the front door and walked down the sidewalk to our car, I could tell she was nervous and apprehensive, yet I noticed a certain childlike quality about her that made me want to stand up next to her, wrap my arms around her, and dare the world to mistreat her in any way. "My God," I thought, "after all she's been through and now she has to go through this." But I never said that to her. Instead my message was, "Hey, when this is over, it will all be over. It'll all be behind us. This, baby, is the final chapter. We've made it this far, what's one more day?" I squeezed her tight, and we drove all the way into town holding hands.

I parked the car by a meter in front of the courthouse so Becky wouldn't have very far to walk. I helped her ease up the long walkway and the three tiers of wide marble steps leading to the front door of the imposing structure, then in through the lobby and over to the shiny brass doors of the elevators. A few people looked our way as we walked by, but there was no barrage of reporters or photographers waiting to greet us, and I was glad. My joy, however, was short-lived. As soon as the elevator doors opened on the fifth floor, the cameras started clicking. The press was there waiting for us en masse.

Word had gotten out that both of us were scheduled to testify that morning, and reporters who hadn't been all that interested in what the doctors and the lawyers and the policemen and the psychologists had had to say earlier in the trial wanted to hear everything Becky and I were going to tell the jury now.

I had deliberately stalled until it was almost nine o'clock on the dot before we entered the courthouse and rode up to the fifth floor. The judge had sent word that we could stay out in the courthouse corridor and wait until Becky, who would be testifying first, was called to take the stand. I later wondered if we might not have been better off waiting inside the courtroom because people were everywhere and most of them were staring directly at us. Photographers were lined up at the courtroom door, cameras poised, ready to strike. I guided Becky to a spot against the wall and told her to stand there. Then I positioned myself strategically between her and the battery of cameramen hoping that if they snapped their shutters all they'd get would be a big picture of my backside. "That'd serve 'em right," I joked, trying to ease Becky's tension. I knew they were only doing their job, but as I told one who had been a longtime friend of mine, "I'd appreciate it if you'd please just allow her a little bit of dignity." He understood, put his camera away, and walked downstairs.

When the bailiff came to the door and called Becky to take the witness stand, she clasped my arm tightly and the two of us began a slow, deliberate walk into the room where she had never been before but where her name had been spoken so many times over the past seven days. It couldn't have been more than a hundred feet from where we'd been standing together out in the hallway up to the small enclosed cubicle facing the jury box, but it seemed like a mile. Every pair of eyes in Nashville seemed to be focused on us—the hillbilly singer and his brain-injured wife.

Becky was wearing a plain gray dress and gray low-heeled shoes (she had not yet learned to balance herself in the high heels). She walked slowly and uncertainly. I guided her up the two or three steps leading into the witness stand, then stepped back as she put her left hand on the Bible, raised her right hand and repeated, "I swear that the testimony I give in this case will be the truth, so help me God." I took my seat some thirty feet off to her right at the counsel table with our attorneys. "She looks so pale," I thought as I anxiously stared at this woman who had for so many years been such a big part of my life. "Pale and disoriented. Almost like a child who has been left alone in a strange room with nobody she knows. She looks frightened, confused. God, this has got to be so tough on her. Please stay close to her and grant her Your peace!"

Becky never once lost her composure. Our attorneys asked her to tell the jury in her own words about the accident. She, of course, had nothing to tell because the entire terrifying episode had been erased from her memory. Then they questioned her about her current condition.

"Do you suffer frequent headaches?"

"Yes, sometimes very severe headaches."

"Do you have much energy? Can you tell us what a typical day in your life is like? How would you describe the way you feel most of the time?" And on and on and on.

Becky answered each question softly, thoughtfully. "I can't do the things I used to do," she said. "I can't be the person I used to be. So much feeling is gone. I thank God I've still got some mental ability. I can talk, I can think . . . but physically . . . it's so hard to get through each day. I feel like I'm just getting by."

Several times when she tried to give the attorneys as much information as she could, she began to ramble. At that point she'd catch herself and ask haltingly, "Did I answer the question you asked?" They assured her that she had.

Our attorneys were very patient with Becky, asking their questions patiently, quietly. They guided her gently from one topic to the next without abrupt changes in her thought processes, and she handled herself well. But when the defense attorneys took over and began their cross-examination, it became a different story.

Ronco Irrigation, whose headquarters was in Atlanta, had hired a short, dark-haired, nattily dressed, tenacious little Nashville attorney named Gary Blackburn to serve as chief counsel for the defense. His job was to do one thing . . . save Ronco as much money as possible. He was not hired to tread gently around me or Becky nor to assuage our feelings in any way. Ronco knew they'd have to pay us some money; they just didn't want to pay any more than they had to.

In his opening remarks to the jury the first morning of the trial, Blackburn sketched a big red dollar sign on a sheet of paper in full view of everyone in the room. "This is what this trial is all about, ladies and gentlemen," he said, "and don't you forget it. It's not about emotions, it's not about injuries, it's not about feelings. It's about *money*!" Throughout the entire trial he badgered, he prodded, he antagonized, he provoked, he taunted, he never let up. Even though I thought he might go a bit easier on Becky when she took the stand than he had gone on some of the other witnesses, I was mistaken. He lowered his voice a bit, but tactically he went after her with both barrels blazing.

He tried to confuse her, tried to play to her weaknesses, in hopes of catching her with inconsistencies in her testimony. He questioned her about her claim that her eyesight had suffered as a result of the accident. She told him she definitely did not see as well as she had prior to the collision. He moved swiftly to another subject, her interior decorating business, and he questioned her rapidly in an effort to disprove our claim that her illness had affected her business. Becky answered that she knew little about the company's finances even before the accident and said, "You can ask my accountant about that." Undaunted, Blackburn reached into his stack of papers and handed her a copy of some receipts. "Do you agree with what's written here, Mrs. Anderson?" he asked.

"I don't know," Becky answered calmly and honestly. "I can't see to read it."

I've been told by others in the legal profession that Blackburn is a good lawyer and I don't doubt that he is, but his cocky, almost condescending attitude toward Becky and me and our case in general rubbed me the wrong way at the time. My emotions weren't very far beneath the surface of my skin to begin with, and when in the course of the proceedings Blackburn sarcastically accused Becky of faking and exaggerating her injuries and then accused me of "putting on a show" when I took the stand, it was almost more than I could bear.

One minute he was saying Becky wasn't badly hurt because a couple of weeks prior to the trial someone connected with his office had seen us taking Jamey to an air show, in nearby Smyrna, and then the next minute he was suggesting things like, "Mrs. Anderson, maybe if you'd quit sitting around all the time and get out and try to enjoy life again you'd feel better." I never did quite figure out his logic on that one. And he repeatedly made a point of saying that he bet Becky would start to feel a whole lot better just as soon as the trial was over.

He made fun of the fact that during the Thanksgiving season following the accident I had sent turkeys to the homes of all the rescue and hospital personnel who'd saved my wife's life, simply as a small gesture of thanking them for all they had done. He tried to imply to the jury that my hiring of old college classmates Mr. Booth and Mr. Speight as my attorneys and the later hiring of another classmate and fraternity brother of theirs, Dr. Tom Burns, as Becky's psychologist, was some kind of immoral conspiracy on all our parts. Dean's answer to that was, "Who are you supposed to call on in times of trouble, strangers? No, you call on your friends."

Blackburn tried repeatedly to put Becky on the defensive while she was testifying. He sometimes spoke to her in a harsher tone of voice than I thought was necessary, and he appeared almost to be attacking her at times. When he did, I'd cut my eyes toward the jury to see if they showed any reaction to his tactics. Their faces were stone. Their eyes never wavered. I had no idea what was going on in their minds.

Blackburn almost pushed Becky a little too far at one point in her testimony. Dean had just asked Becky if she had been to see an eye doctor since the accident. Before she could answer, Blackburn stood and objected to the question, saying he didn't want Becky telling the court what the doctor might or might not have said.

Before Judge Gayden could rule on the objection, however, Becky turned to Blackburn from her seat on the witness stand and snapped, "I had no *intention* of saying what the eye doctor said to me!"

It was like her "little policeman" had stepped out of the room for a minute and before he could get back, Becky had pounced on Blackburn in a way that no one without a head injury would have ever dared attempt. I had to suppress a giggle because I had been on the receiving end of that same type of outburst myself several times over the past two years. I was glad to see Blackburn have to sit there and take it. Besides, if he had doubted the severity or the depth of Becky's injury before, he had to know based on Becky's reaction to his simple objection that she wasn't faking a thing.

I don't know how long she had been on the witness stand when it happened, but I assume it had been every bit of an hour, maybe longer. She had said about all there was to say, answered all the questions that could have possibly been asked of her, and there was only one thing left to do. "Mrs. Anderson," one of the attorneys said softly, "would you please step down from where you are and walk over to the jury box and show the members of this jury your scars?"

Becky never hesitated. Not once did she even question this demeaning request made at the expense of her dignity and her pride. Much like a sheep being led to slaughter, she did as she was told. A court officer came and helped her down from the witness stand and guided her across the floor to a spot only a few inches away from the six jurors seated in the front row.

I knew she had to do it. I knew the jurors had to see what they'd heard so much about. But I couldn't stand it. My heart kicked into overdrive, and every drop of blood in my body seemed to be racing to my brain. It took every ounce of restraint I could muster just to stay in my chair. I wanted to scream.

But I could only sit helplessly and watch as the jurors on the end of the front row and the six jurors on the back row all stood and leaned forward and peered into the face of the lady I love. Following instructions, Becky reached her hand up to her forehead, pulled back her hair, and twelve strangers gazed down into her eyes, across her face, and into her scalp, seeing for themselves the results of the grinding automobile crash that nearly cost her her life and left her with permanent reminders of an eighteen-year-old kid who had been out having fun celebrating his birthday.

I have never in my life had anger and hurt and bitterness sweep over me as fast as it did at that moment. And I hope I never do again. I totally lost control and started to shake and then to cry. "They've turned this into a sideshow," I said to nobody in particular, but loud enough for all those seated nearby to hear me. "This is like a circus . . . 'Hey, everybody, come look at the lady with the scars all over her head!' It's a dad-blamed circus!" I was livid.

Then I spotted Todd Brasher out of the corner of my eye. There wasn't one ounce of emotion showing on his face. He was looking straight ahead, his steely eyes fixed on the back of my wife's head while twelve strangers gawked at the results of his irresponsible behavior. He was the one, the only one, responsible for what was taking place. He was responsible for every tear I'd cried for the past two years, for every painful moment my wife had spent fighting for her life, for every piercing headache that had interrupted her sleep in the middle of the night, for every question my six-year-old son had asked, for every anxious moment he'd spent wondering where his mother was and when, if ever, she was coming home. This one man had caused it all. Now he was just sitting there staring. Not hurting, not crying, not remorseful, just staring. I looked at him until my eyes couldn't take it anymore. And in a voice as cold and as penetrating as I could summon, I said the first words I had ever spoken to him: "I hope you're happy, you son-of-a-bitch!"

He never blinked an eye. I knew he'd heard me, but he never moved a muscle. He just kept on staring straight ahead.

I knew my lawyers had heard me. I knew his lawyers had heard me. For the first few seconds I didn't even care. The jury hadn't heard me. They'd been too busy gawking and doing their job. But they would hear *about* it. Before it was over, everybody in the whole city of Nashville would hear about it.

I had to forget my outburst and calm down, and I had to do it quickly because as soon as Becky was through showing the jury her scars, her part of the testimony was over. She and her friend Donna Whitcomb left the courthouse immediately, and Donna drove her home. I wished I could have left with them, but it was my turn to testify.

By the time I reached the witness box, I had succeeded in putting my anger at Brasher aside. I took a deep breath of air, sipped a drink of cool water, stepped up onto the stand, and swore that I, too, would tell nothing but the truth, so help me God.

Richard Speight began the questioning and moved slowly and deliberately. He asked me to recount for the jury what I had done and where I had been the day of the accident. He asked me how I was notified, how I got back to Nashville, how I broke the news to my son. And he asked me to tell in my own words how my life had been so completely rearranged during the two ensuing years. I didn't really say anything new, nothing different from what I'd told many people during the time that had elapsed, but somehow telling it there in that courtroom, under oath, before God and everybody, it took on a whole new meaning. Emotional person that I am, there were several times during my testimony when I lost my composure.

I have always been a person who feels things very deeply. When I feel good, I always say that I feel better than anybody. Likewise, when I feel bad, I'm sure I feel worse than anybody. Or that's what I've told myself over the years. Like many other things in my life, my emotions have swung back and forth between being a blessing and a curse.

I don't doubt at all that my being a sensitive, demonstrative person has contributed to my ability to write songs. It's probably aided me in communicating my feelings to an audience as a performer as well. But breaking down and shedding tears in public embarrasses me. Before I took the stand, I prayed silently for it not to happen. But it happened anyway. The last thing I wanted to do was get up in that courtroom and cry. But I simply could not control it.

I told the jury everything that had happened from my viewpoint, the changes this accident had wrought in my life and in my and Becky's married life. "Becky has always been my best friend," I said, "but, to be honest, she's not the same lady I married." God, it hurt to say that, but it was the truth.

I felt like I was on the witness stand for a week, but in reality it wasn't much longer than an hour. I was afraid the whole time that as soon as I finished answering Mr. Speight's questions the defense attorneys were going to come at me tooth and nail, but when

Richard stepped aside, Gary Blackburn simply stood and said, "No further questions, Your Honor." Judge Gayden told me I could go back to my seat. I couldn't believe they were going to let me off that easy, that they weren't going to try and trick me, trap me, or make me out a liar for everything I'd just said, but I wasn't about to give Blackburn a chance to change his mind. I got down and walked back to my chair in a hurry.

Blackburn then rose and turned his attention to the jury. He paused for emphasis then softly said, "Ladies and gentlemen, what you have just seen is a professional entertainer at work. Make no mistake about it, Bill Anderson is a professional entertainer. He's tried to put on a show for you throughout this whole trial. He came in here with a script. I urge you not to be swept away in a wave of emotion. There's not a country music singer in this city worth his salt who can't bring a tear to your eye. That's their business."

I listened to everything he was saying, and I thought, "Mr. Blackburn, I wish it had been that easy. You don't know how badly I wish it *had* been a script. I wish it had only been a show. I wish I'd made the whole thing up. The unfortunate part is that it's all real. This whole thing is too, too real."

They called Todd Brasher to the stand on Wednesday morning following my testimony and my outburst in the rear of the court-room the previous day. I knew I was in for it.

His attorney was a flashy, constantly smiling yet almost sneering man with wavy hair and a shiny suit that made him look like he would have been more at home selling used cars down on Broadway than he was practicing in a court of law. His name was Jere Lee. Every time I heard it, I kept wanting to add "Lewis." He wasted no time in going for my jugular.

"Mr. Brasher, did Bill Anderson say anything to you yesterday while his wife, Becky, was before the jury?" he asked.

"Yes sir, he did," Brasher answered.

"Would you tell the jury what Mr. Anderson said?" Lee continued.

"He said, 'I hope you're happy, you son-of-a-bitch,'" Brasher replied.

I could hear the jury gasp from nearly forty feet across the courtroom. I could hear feet shuffle in the gallery, people begin-ning to whisper. I could see the shocked expression on the face of the elderly lady in the front row of the jury box. I could almost hear the pencils racing across the reporters' notepads as they hurriedly made copy of my profane expletive. I could see our whole case slowly sinking down the drain.

I'd have given anything if I could have reached out into the air and pulled back what I had said. But I couldn't. My dirty laundry was hanging out for everyone to see.

It made the front pages of both Nashville newspapers. People came up to me everywhere I went and commented on it. "I'd have said a whole lot worse than that if it'd been *my* wife" was a comment I heard more than once, and, "I don't blame you, Bill. It just proves you're human" was another. But I wasn't proud. I was embarrassed, I was ashamed, and I was sorry I had said it. Unfortunately, vocal chords don't come equipped with erasers.

The attorneys for both sides presented their closing arguments and made their final pleas to the jurors the first thing Thursday morning, the same day the papers carried their stories about my explosion. It had been eleven calendar days since the trial began. Everybody was ready for it to be over.

But I was nervous. It had all come down to this: the judge explaining to the jurors their options, their duties, and their responsibilities, and then twelve people going off together into a little room to try and sort out all they had seen and all they had been told. What was truth and what was fiction? What was as it had been represented and what had been exaggerated? Who were the good guys and who were the bad guys? What would I be able to tell my son when he was old enough to understand? "Son, the system in this country works. When people do something wrong, they are punished for it." Or would it be, "Son, if you're smart enough to hire a clever lawyer, he can get you out of anything"? I was wound tighter than a rusty E-string on a warped-neck Stella guitar!

As the jurors filed out of the courtroom to talk it over and try to come to some kind of a decision, I remembered all the stories I'd heard over the years about juries not being able to decide on a verdict, about them staying sequestered in hotel rooms for days at a time, about lengthy cases ending in mistrials and everybody having to come back and go through it all again. And even the old gag about there being no way a jury made up of twelve men and women could stay in a hotel room overnight and come back the next day and say "Innocent"!

Our case wasn't a matter of life and death or even a matter of whether I'd go to jail or be set free, but to me and my family what those jurors would come back into that room and say was doggone important. Their decision would be the last soliloquy in the final act of this entire two-year drama, and I wanted it to be right. And I darn sure didn't want to have to return and go through it all again.

I stayed close to my attorneys in the courthouse corridors for the first hour or so that the jury was in deliberation. Nobody talked much, nobody dared speculate on the outcome. Everybody seemed drained, lost in personal thoughts, not wanting to rewind the tape and study the replay until the man was out in the bottom of the ninth. There would be plenty of time for that, like the rest of our lives.

As the clock began to close in on noon, it became obvious that there would be no quick verdict. Dean, Richard, and I decided perhaps we should leave, get some fresh air away from the court-house and perhaps find ourselves a bite to eat. I didn't have much of an appetite, but I figured sitting in a restaurant staring into a coffee cup might at least help pass the time.

We went to a small restaurant nearby and sat picking at our food until nearly two o'clock when we decided it might be a good idea to walk back over to the courthouse. Dean looked at his watch when we got there and said he thought it might be best for him to start driving back to Atlanta. He wasn't sure that the jury wouldn't be out several more hours, or even possibly overnight, and he felt he needed to head for home. I shook his hand, thanked him for all he'd meant to me personally and professionally during this most trying time, and promised him I'd call him at home that night. In less than an hour I was on the phone trying to intercept him somewhere along the highway.

At almost the instant Dean left and Richard and I turned to walk back inside the building, someone ran up to us and said they had heard that the jury was ready. It was too late for us to try and catch Dean, but at least after nearly five hours of deliberation the jury had reached a decision.

When I stepped off the elevator on the fifth floor and walked back into the courtroom, I was convinced I had no emotions left. I thought for sure that eleven days of living suspended in midair had taken all my feelings away. But I was wrong. When the ten ladies and two gentlemen of the jury filed back into the room, my heart started pounding louder than any bass drum I've ever heard.

"Who is the foreperson of this jury?" Judge Gayden asked when everyone had been seated.

"I am, Your Honor," a lady on the front row stood and announced. "My name is Jessica Mickles."

Up to that point none of us had known whom the jury had elected as their foreperson, but we knew their choice could be significant. When Ms. Mickles stood, my first reaction was that her selection might just possibly be in our favor. I had learned during the jury selection process that she was a nurse, and I figured if anybody on that jury could understand Becky's plight it might well be her.

Yet I knew there was only so much the jury could have seen with their eyes. Becky had walked into the courtroom under her own power, she had answered all the lawyers' questions, and to most people she probably looked about as normal as the next person. Her bruises didn't show anymore, her stitches were out, she could walk and talk, feed and dress herself, and to the casual observer nothing appeared to be wrong. But had the jury been able to see beneath the surface? Had they been able to tell from what they saw and what they heard that all was not normal? That Becky's brain had been dealt a permanent, life-altering blow? That no matter how much better she appeared to be or how much better she might someday become, following a closed head injury a person is never the same again? Had they been able to see Becky with their hearts as well as their eyes? Ms. Mickles stood in the jury box with the answer on a piece of paper in her hand.

"Have you reached a verdict?" the judge asked.

"We have, Your Honor," she replied. I held my breath as she unfolded the paper and began to read.

"We, the jury, award to Mrs. Anderson the sum of one million dollars," she announced, "and to Mr. Anderson we give $235,000." It was less than we had asked for, but it was an award much larger than any of us had dared to hope for.

The room came alive with a gigantic buzz, and Judge Gayden had to rap his gavel several times against the wooden desk in front of him in order to quieten the crowd. As soon as things calmed down to a point where he could be heard, he thanked everyone for their help and their cooperation, and he spoke a few final words to the jury, thanking them again and telling them in essence that they could now feel free to discuss the case with anyone who might ask them about it but that they most definitely had a right not to talk about it at all if they so chose. The judge then gathered up his papers, turned and exited the room through a rear door to his left. Court was dismissed.

I couldn't believe it was over. As simply as that, it was all over. Yet it wasn't over. It wasn't over at all. In a lot of ways, it won't ever be over.

The minute I knew for sure that all the official business had been completed, I stood and grabbed Richard Speight and gave him a big bear hug. His closing arguments to the jury that morning had been brilliant, and I told him so. In my excitement, I squeezed him so hard he had to beg me to stop. I was about to squash his glasses.

I hugged his assistant, Rose Cantrell, and then my daughter, Terri, who came rushing up from her seat in the gallery. She grabbed me just as a photographer from the *Tennessean* aimed his camera through the door in my direction. A picture of the two of us locked in a happy but tearful embrace was on the front page of Friday morning's paper.

I wanted to get out of the courthouse as soon as possible, but there were a couple of other things I felt I needed to do before assembling my belongings and leaving. First, I wanted to talk to Todd Brasher.

I asked Richard to ask Jere Lee if I might speak with his client. Lee said it would be all right and returned with Brasher at his side.

I stood no more than a foot away and looked Brasher directly in the eye. "I want to apologize to you for what I said yesterday," I offered, and I stuck out my hand. Brasher looked at me for a moment without knowing quite what to say. I don't know what he was expecting me to say, but I don't think he expected me to apologize. He stood there awkwardly, then extended his arm and we shook hands.

"I hope you were telling the truth on the stand yesterday when you told the jury you hadn't had a drink since the night of the accident," I said.

"I was," he answered. "I haven't had a drink, and I don't intend ever to take another one. I haven't driven a car either." He paused again, as if he wanted to say something more but wasn't quite sure how. He looked at the floor, and he shuffled his feet. Then he looked back up at me. "I'm very sorry for what I did," he said softly.

I stood silently and looked into his eyes. His face was more clean-shaven now than it had been the first time I'd seen him nearly two years ago at the initial hearing. He was dressed in a sport coat and tie and wore a gold wedding band on the third finger of his left hand. He didn't look like a criminal at all. He could have been a guitar picker in somebody's country band. He could have been a disc jockey playing my records at a small radio station somewhere. He could have been my son.

I didn't hate him. I never had hated him. I had just been frustrated and hurt beyond belief by what he had done. "I really hope you're telling me the truth," I told him again. He didn't have to say a word. The look in his eyes told me that he was.

I stepped to the rear of the courtroom and asked the bailiff if I might use the phone. He led me into a small office, closed the door and left me alone.

I dialed our number at the condo. Becky answered on the first ring, anxious to know what had taken place. I told her quietly and calmly what the verdict had been and that I was on my way home. We both confessed later to having had strangely mixed emotions over the outcome. We were happy, we were pleased, but to think of celebrating the verdict like it was some kind of football victory seemed totally out of the question. We stayed home that night and had a quiet dinner alone.

I hung up the phone and walked back into the courtroom. Except for Terri, the room was empty. I asked her if she'd mind standing in front of the door and blocking the view of anyone out in the hall who might be trying to see inside.

As she made her way to the door, I stood alone in the middle of the quiet, imposing room . . . just me and my thoughts. It seemed like the nightmare had been going on forever, like there had never been a time in my life when I hadn't been consumed by some type of problem, some kind of crisis. Yet it had been only two years. Almost two years ago to that very day, in fact, when I had been standing in the emergency room at General Hospital praying that Becky might live. Earlier that afternoon, as the members of the jury had filed back into the courtroom, prepared to announce their decision, I had prayed again. Not for victory, not for money, but for the strength to be man enough to accept the jury's decision whatever it might turn out to be. All of my prayers had been answered. I dropped to my knees there on the floor of that deserted courtroom and thanked God.

The judge would, in a few days, cut the amount of the award the jury had given us by one-third, saying it was "outside the limits of reasonableness." It had been the largest award ever given in a case of this type in the history of Davidson County.

The money was important, of course, given Becky's need for ongoing medical treatment and my own stressful financial situation, but far more important than the money was the fact that Becky and I felt vindicated. A jury of our peers had said, "Hey, what happened to you folks was wrong. We know money can't ever make up to you what you've lost and what you've suffered, but we hurt for you and we hurt with you and this is the best that we can do." At the same time I felt their verdict was also going to send a profound statement out into the community, a strong, angry statement as to how they felt about drunk driving. We couldn't have asked for anything more.

I finished my brief prayer, stood up and tucked my shirttail in, straightened my tie, and tried to take on the appearance of a human being again. I picked up my briefcase and walked as straight and as tall as I could out through the big double doors and into the hallway. Terri joined me, and we made it as far as the elevators before we came upon a group of the jurors standing and talking with Gary Blackburn.

Throughout the trial these jurors had been instructed not to speak to me or any of the other principal players in the case, and we had been instructed not to speak with them. Were we to meet in the hallway during a recess or on a street downtown during a lunch break, we were each told to look the other way and to have no communication at all. As far as I knew, everyone had carried out these orders to the letter.

Now the case was over, and the judge had told them the rules didn't apply anymore. I had been in the same room with these twelve strangers for nearly two weeks, and somehow they didn't seem like strangers anymore at all. They seemed almost like friends. They looked at me as I approached, but nobody said a word. I figured it was up to me to break the ice.

"Thank you," I said to nobody in particular but to each of them as sincerely as I could. "Thank you for seeing with your hearts the things you probably weren't able to see with your eyes," and I reached out to the lady standing the closest to me and hugged her. She probably thought I had lost my mind.

Then I began to feel those dad-blamed uncontrollable tears start to well up in my eyes, but instead of wiping them away this time I turned to Gary Blackburn, "See," I said, pointing to the little drop of water slowly beginning to make its way down my cheek, "it's not a show, it's for real." He didn't say a word but reached out his arm and shook my hand.

"God bless you," he said softly.

That took me as much by surprise as my apology had taken Brasher. For a brief moment I wasn't sure exactly what to say. "Thank you," I replied. "Thank you very much." Somehow I sensed he meant what he said.

I turned and pushed the button for the elevator. It stopped and I got on. I rode in silence down to the first floor, got off, and turned right. I walked slowly through the vast marble corridors of the profound structure, out the front door, down the wide marble steps, and out onto the sidewalks of the city I love. There were no reporters this time, no photographers, no newspaper vendors shouting my name. It was almost a shock to discover that the sun was still shining, the stores still open, the city buses still running, life still going on. Mine had been on hold for such a long time.

I had about five blocks to walk to the garage where I'd parked my car. Terri walked quietly along with me, allowing me the luxury of talking when I felt like it and of being quiet when I didn't. I took a deep breath and thought to myself as I shuffled along, "Well, it's over. It's finally over. You've come through it, and you're still alive. A bit worse for the wear, perhaps, but still in one piece and alive. You've got your wife, you've got your family, and they love you. God loves you, too. What more could you possibly need or want? Besides that, tomorrow is less than twenty-four hours away."

I smiled at the thought. And then easing down the hilly sidewalk of Third Avenue, I stopped for just a moment and shut my eyes.

I tried hard to imagine the closing of a door.

28

The questions I get asked most often today go like this:

(1) What do you think of today's country music?

(2) Are you still making records?

(3) Where is Bill Anderson going from here?

I can give you my opinion on the first question. I'll answer the second one, and I'll tell you right now I don't have the foggiest idea about the third one. But that's OK. Where I'm going isn't nearly as important as how much fun I'm going to have getting there.

I think a lot of today's country music is pretty doggone good. At least it's a lot better than some of what was being passed off as country music a few years ago.

Much of what I hear when I listen to country music today is fresh, vibrant, and exciting. There has been a return to the more traditional sound, which I like, and there seems to be a new less-is-better philosophy within the record-making community. By that I mean the attitude in the recording studio today seems to be, hey, let's don't clutter up the records with a lot of unnecessary instruments and voices. Let's just go with the basics. To a large degree, for the first time in a long time, our industry doesn't seem to be ashamed to call itself "country."

The feeling I get when I look across the broad spectrum of country music today is that I'm looking at a rainbow—it's got a lot of different colors. It's everything from the carefully cultivated pop-country sounds of five former studio musicians calling themselves Restless Heart to the pure mountain soul that was born inside Ricky Skaggs. It's everything from K. T. Oslin looking and sounding like she's never been *in* the country to Reba McEntire and Patty Loveless looking and sounding like they never left. In many respects it's better musicians making better music then any of us ever made before.

But it's also a whole new breed of young musicians creating and playing the country music of today. It's a new generation of song-writers, record producers, and, for the most part, record execu-tives. What I find interesting is that so many of these people who are playing the music and making the decisions in our business now didn't grow up with country music at all. They weren't listen-ing to Buck Owens and Ray Price and George Jones back in the sixties. Their generation grew up on Elvis and the Beatles, the Rolling Stones and the Beach Boys. The melodies they first learned to pick out on their guitars had more than just three or four chords that were in most of our songs, and they learned to play them and play them well. When, in the course of time, they could no longer relate to the changes in rock 'n' roll, the heavy metal sounds and the outlandish lifestyles of the performers, many of these young people began tuning in to country music. They brought their natu-ral influences with them, though, and before long they were help-ing to create and shape a country music of their very own.

The first time I ever met Emmylou Harris, I asked her how she described her music. I couldn't quite figure it out. It sounded as country as anything I'd ever heard, but I noticed people outside of the traditional country music fans seemed to be embracing her style. "It's country music played with a rock attitude," she told me. I had to think about that awhile before I understood. I know now what she meant. There is a decided "rock attitude" in a lot of country music today.

Some of that, I think, has been good for our industry—the improved musicianship for one thing, the increased emphasis on higher quality recording techniques for another. Some of it, I'm not so sure. For example, lyrics have never been overly important in rock 'n' roll songs, and the lyrics to the many of the country songs in recent years haven't seemed to ring with the depth of emotion that they once did. I miss that. I don't mean that we should go back to singing, "I've Got Tears in My Ears from Lyin' on My Back in My Bed While I Cry Over You," but country music, unlike rock 'n' roll, has always dealt with the honest expression of human feelings. Sometimes in recent years, however, in an effort to create a more "positive" image for country music, I think our songs have tended to shy away from reality. On the one hand, one of the reasons country music's popularity has grown so over the past two decades has been the shift in emphasis from the "negative" song ("You Broke My Heart, Little Darlin'") to the "positive" songs ("Forever and Ever, Amen" and "You Were Always on My Mind"), but I wonder if maybe somewhere along the way we didn't start making music designed not to offend the listener rather than music created to attract the listener. Sort of like a ball team playing a game and trying not to lose instead of trying to win. Our industry was putting out a lot of records (and radio stations were playing them) that weren't really saying anything, songs that weren't cutting to the core of the everyday emotions people feel. A person twisting his radio dial and coming across a country station, perhaps for the first time, certainly wasn't offended by anything that he was hearing, but was he touched by it either? Many times I don't think he was. The end result was music I call plastic—easily forgettable pieces, devoid of emotion capable of reaching beyond the ear and embracing the soul. I like a pretty, positive love song as much as the next guy, but when a song says "I love you," I want it to stir something down inside me. I don't want just to *hear* the music, I want to *feel* it. There for a while it was hard for me to feel much from the country music a lot of folks were writing and singing.

I think musical historians may one day say the tide started to turn back toward country-music-with-feeling the day a talented, young, good-looking former dishwasher and short-order cook from Becky's hometown, Marshville, North Carolina, hung up his apron and picked up his guitar for good. His real name was Randy Traywick, and somewhere back in time some of his kinfolks were related to some of Becky's kinfolks because Becky's mama was a Traywick and in a town as small as Marshville everybody is related to everybody else who lives there anyhow. But the world came to know him as Randy Travis. He sang *country* music—about wedding bands and forever, about lost love and resurrecting memories—and he didn't apologize to anybody for doing so. Country music's new generation loved him, the girls thought he was cute and sexy, and so did the women. The older generation of fans felt that at last somebody was singing something *they* could understand. And country music began developing a new generation called the "new traditionalists."

Randy Travis's albums started selling in the millions, enough copies to put him on the best-seller lists right alongside Michael Jackson, Bruce Springsteen, and the others. But it never turned his head. In fact, the first time somebody told Randy one of his albums was on the pop charts, he is supposed to have said in all seriousness, "Well, get it *off* of there!" How could you *not* like somebody who said that?

I'm not sure about all these labels anyhow—"modern," "traditional," "new traditional." Frankly, I have never liked putting labels on music or on artists. Back when I was recording "Still" and "8 × 10" and "I Love You Drops" and they were No. 1 country hits and crossing over onto the pop charts, people labeled me "modern country." Yet today if you mention my name somebody will invariably say, "Oh, he's *traditional* country." Huh? Run that by me one more time. I didn't change. Who did?

Many of the fences and labels that have defined what country music is or what country music isn't over the years seem to have been torn down now, and I see that as a direct result of the rock influence. I also think it's healthy. If Tina Turner wants to record with Roy Acuff, nobody blinks. If a country record has a musical turnaround with a French horn playing twin harmony parts with a kazoo, who cares? At the same time, Randy Travis and George Strait and Ricky Van Shelton and Patty Loveless and Highway 101 and Keith Whitley have brought strong country roots and traditional convictions into the music, and by doing so they have helped create an homogenization of all the influences that make up today's country music—rock 'n' roll, country, bluegrass, and even rhythm and blues.

I just gave a long answer to a short question, didn't I? The question was, what do I think of today's country music? The answer is that I think there are only two kinds of music: good and bad. I like that which is good, and a lot of country music today, I think, is pretty darn good. I don't necessarily agree with all the practices within the country music *industry* today, but that's another story. As to the music itself, I'm excited about its present, and I'm encouraged about its future.

Pass the cornbread.

Yes, I am still making records. As long as I stay active in my show business career, I hope to be making records. I'm still a long way, believe it or not, from having written and sung everything I have down inside me. And what was it Rick Nelson sang in "Garden Party"? Something about "If memories were all I sang, I'd rather drive a truck." Me too!

For over twenty-three years I recorded for the same record company. It was called Decca Records when I first signed with them, but the name was changed to MCA Records in the early seventies. My first contract was for five years, from 1958 to 1963. It expired just about the time "Still" was the No. 1 record in the country, and that helped me negotiate another five-year deal that ran until 1968. I signed a third five-year contract then, only to have Bobby Brenner go in in 1972 and renegotiate it into a ten-year agreement. That contract, my last with MCA, was one of the first million-dollar recording contracts in country music history.

I don't know for sure how many records I have made, but over the years Decca and MCA combined have released somewhere in the neighborhood of eighty singles and close to fifty albums, including both the original releases and the later repackaging. Remember, back when I first started recording, an artist didn't go into the studio and record a complete album project then release singles from that album like they do today. Back then you recorded strictly for singles. Then if several singles became hits, the record company would package the hits together with some filler material they figured wasn't strong enough to be released as singles, add a few recognizable titles that had been hits for other artists, and call it an album. An album was not the staple of an artist's career then that it is now. It was more like a reward for a job well done.

When my contract was up with MCA at the end of 1982, I decided to go back home to Atlanta and team up with a man I had idolized as a boy, the legendary Bill Lowery. Since then I have recorded one album and several singles for his young but successful Southern Tracks label.

* * *

Bill Lowery has been renowned in music business circles for over thirty years as a music publisher, recording executive, artists' manager, and former president of the National Academy of Recording Arts and Sciences, but he was a country disc jockey during my growing up years, and I thought he hung the moon.

He didn't live very far from me when I was a teenager, and many's the Saturday morning when I'd go over to a little store called Hodges Appliance Company in East Atlanta and watch him and his countrified alter-ego, Uncle Ebb Brown, play country records on the radio, read commercials, and sell washing machines. Then when he'd get off the air around noon, I'd follow him over to the basement of his house and help him in any way I could with a small record label called Stars, Inc., which he was trying to get off the ground. I'd pack up records to mail to other disc jockeys around the country, I'd stack boxes up in the corner, I'd run errands. I didn't care. I just wanted to be around the music business and around Bill Lowery.

In the mid-fifties, Bill scored his first big hit with a song called "Young Love," which he published and released originally on his Stars, Inc., label with a young Atlanta singer-writer named Ric Cartey. Sonny James covered the record, sold several million copies, and the successful Lowery publishing empire was underway. A short time later Bill would publish Gene Vincent's classic "Be Bop a Lula," and he came within a whisker, or should I say a whisper, of publishing my "City Lights."

After I'd written the song on the roof of the little hotel in Commerce, the first place I thought to take it, naturally, was to my friend Bill Lowery. He liked the song, but he had the same reservations about it that we all had back in the late fifties: It was "too country." He tried producing a session with me on the song anyhow, but for some reason it just didn't come off. Before we could get back into the studio and try it again, Bob Tanner at TNT picked up both the song and a later recording I'd made of it in an unborn TV studio in Athens and the rest, as they say, is history.

We laughed about all that had happened over the years when Bill and I finally did get together in 1982, about how I was virtually the only artist from Georgia who had ever been successful in Nashville without having first served my apprenticeship with him in Atlanta, like Jerry Reed, Ray Stevens and countless others had done, and he welcomed me "back home" with open arms.

I cut my initial album, *Southern Fried*, on Southern Tracks in a recording studio built inside an old school house, not far from the first apartment my family had lived in when we moved from South Carolina to Georgia. The title cut from the album was almost a nationwide smash, rising into the thirties on the national charts. It was No. 1 in many areas across the South, and a lot of people north of the Mason-Dixon line even told me how much they loved the sound of the record and the beat of the song. But, unfortunately, they had a little trouble relating to lyrics that exclaimed, "How 'bout them Dawgs!" and "Roll Tide!" in most areas outside of Dixie.

I still record for Southern Tracks although I've never actually signed a recording contract. I would have signed one, but Bill never asked me to. I find a certain warmth in knowing there are still special people in the world like Bill Lowery and Bobby Brenner with whom I can do business and, in fact, to whom I can trust my entire career on just a handshake.

Bill even let me step outside his company and record an album for a new label called Swanee Records after I had joined Southern Tracks. It was intended to be an album strictly for TV sales and marketing in the beginning, but when Swanee later wanted to release a few of the cuts as singles for radio airplay, there was no problem at all. "You've always got a home here with me," Bill Lowery has said to me on many occasions. I treasure that highly.

I can't get off the subject of Bill Lowery without mentioning the night I was named to the Georgia Music Hall of Fame because that was the only time in all the years I've known this kind and gentle man that he looked me in the eye and told me a deliberate, bold-faced lie.

It was in September of 1985, and for the second year in a row I had been asked to come to Atlanta and host the annual Georgia Music Hall of Fame and Awards Show on statewide television. It was to be held for the first time at the prestigious World Congress Center in Atlanta and would be a black-tie affair with the governor and many local and state dignitaries in attendance. Bill him-self issued the invitation on behalf of the Georgia Senate Music Industry Committee, and I never thought twice. I accepted immediately.

As we were rehearsing in midafternoon on the day of the live telecast, I casually asked Bill if anyone would be inducted into the Hall of Fame that night. He said, sure, that every year the com-mittee named one outstanding Georgian in the world of music to the Hall of Fame. Previous winners had included Ray Charles, Brenda Lee, Little Richard, James Brown, Otis Redding, and oth-ers, and Bill said this year's winner was a jazz artist.

"What's his name?" I casually asked.

"Uh, Joe Williams," Bill said. "Yeah, that's it, Joe Williams. Great jazz trumpet player."

I had never heard of Joe Williams, but I figured the world was probably full of jazz trumpet players I'd never heard of, so I never gave it a second thought. I was too busy trying to learn my lines and define my role in the show. For all I knew Joe Williams was the greatest trumpet player who ever lived. I didn't know until nearly midnight that the only place Joe Williams ever lived was in Bill Lowery's fertile imagination and quick-thinking mind.

The show that night came off without a hitch. I managed to get through most of my part without too much difficulty. Then with about ten minutes left before we had to be off the air, I introduced state senator Nathan Dean, who, in turn, introduced Joe Frank Harris, the governor of Georgia, to present the biggest award of the night. As Governor Harris strode onto stage-left, I slipped off stage-right to watch Joe Williams get inducted into the Hall of Fame.

When I reached the wings, Bill Lowery was standing there. He smiled and patted me on the back and told me what a great job I'd done. Then he started making all kinds of small talk. In the background I could hear the governor speaking, but I couldn't make out any of the words he was saying. Bill was going on and on about nothing in particular, but I was listening. It never crossed my mind that he was only talking because he didn't want me to hear what Governor Harris had to say.

Suddenly, from out on the stage and over the drone of Bill's voice, I heard the words "Commerce, Georgia." That caught my ear and I turned toward the stage. "And he had a duck named Josh," the governor was saying. And I thought, "That's funny, so did I."

Suddenly I realized the governor was talking about me. "'City Lights,'" he said, "and 'Po' Folks' and . . ."

But it was still another split-second before it hit me. I thought he was just thanking me for hosting the show. A bit in detail, perhaps, but why else would the governor of Georgia be talking about me? Then suddenly I realized what was happening.

". . . And so, ladies and gentlemen, won't you please join me now in welcoming the newest member of the Georgia Music Hall of Fame . . . Grand Ole Opry star . . . and our emcee here this evening . . . Whisperin' Bill Anderson!" I could scarcely believe my ears.

The next thing I remember was Bill Lowery walking up behind me and shoving me out onto the stage. "Get out there, boy, that's *you!*" he said as the first notes of my record of "Bright Lights & Country Music" began to fill the hall. By this time the audience was on its feet, and I was in total shock.

I know I walked to the center of the stage and smiled and bowed and waved to my mama and my daddy who were sitting at a table just behind the governor's. "Did you know?" I mouthed to Mama, and she shook her head. "We didn't know a thing," they both told me later. They had come only because I was hosting the show and they wanted to be there.

The reason I know now how I acted after the governor called my name is because I have the show on videotape and I've watched it once or twice. Had it not been for the tape, I don't think I'd have remembered a thing that took place.

I walked toward the podium to receive my beautiful engraved Tiffany's crystal trophy from Governor Harris, but just before reaching the spot where he was standing I looked back over my shoulder at Bill Lowery, who was standing on stage behind me applauding like a proud papa. "Bill Lowery, you lied to me!" I shouted in his direction. "You *lied* to me!" He just stood there smiling and clapping his hands, his snow-white hair glistening in the spotlight.

I reached the podium and started to speak and here they came— those dad-gummed tears of mine that I never seem to be able to control. I struggled to keep my composure and somehow, through the tears, I managed to say thank you to all the special people from Georgia who had believed in me over the years and had touched my life in so many special ways. I thanked Mom and Dad, I thanked Bill Lowery, and then I thought of Becky.

She wasn't there. She was back in Nashville trying to put the pieces of her life back together. Trying to recover, trying to recapture that which had been so cruelly taken away from her, trying to learn how to live again. I thought of all the nights I had left her and my children at home and climbed on a bus to ride out into the night somewhere chasing my dreams. Of the nights when I would be home and we'd have a chance to spend some time together but I'd get an idea for a song I wanted to write, and I'd get up and leave her and close the door to my study and maybe not come out until morning. Standing there at that podium with the Hall of Fame trophy in my hand, my mother and father in the audience, the packed house still on its feet cheering, I appreciated my family and all they had sacrificed for me more than I had ever appreciated them in my life. I hurt because Becky couldn't be there. I hurt because I knew that even though I'd phone her as soon as the show was over and tell her the good news, she wouldn't be able to share my joy. She'd say she was happy and she'd say congratulations, but she couldn't feel the excitement. I knew that. And it hurt.

I ended by thanking my grandaddy who first taught me that all good things are a gift from God, and I hugged Bill Lowery's neck. "I forgive you," I said, "and I love you. But don't you ever lie to me again! I don't think I could take it!"

Where does Bill Anderson go from here? I get asked that question so often you'd think by now I'd have copyrighted an answer. But I really haven't. Remember, I didn't start out to be in this business in the first place. It all just kinda happened. One door would open and I'd walk through it, only to be staring another door in the face. The doors kept opening and I kept tiptoeing through them, trying to find out what was on the other side. Much of the time I'm *still* trying to find out what's on the other side.

Anytime somebody starts talking about where something goes from here, though, my mind wanders back to the mid-seventies and the afternoon I taped a half-hour television tribute to the great Tex Ritter.

It was in the last days of my syndicated series, the *Bill Anderson Show*, and I had devoted an entire thirty minutes to the music, the career, and the life of "America's Most Beloved Cowboy," one of my favorite people of all time.

The show had gone great. Tex had sung and spun yarns about his early days on the Broadway stage, his years in Hollywood, his marriage to his former leading lady, Dorothy Faye, and the legendary recording career that had culminated with his election to the Country Music Hall of Fame. We had shown some movie clips of him and Dorothy on screen together before they were man and wife, talked about the movie theme *High Noon*, which he sang and which won an Academy Award, and we'd even touched on his short-lived political career when he'd once run for the United States Senate from Tennessee.

"Tex, you've done it all," I said, in an effort to begin wrapping up the show. "You've been on Broadway, you've starred in the movies, you've recorded hit records, you've run for the Senate. Where do you go from here?"

Tex paused only slightly, just long enough for his eyes to take on their patented twinkle and his nostrils to issue another of his trademark half-snoring, half-snorting jolts, and he said slowly, "Well . . . Bill . . . Saturday, I'm going to Pennsylvania."

Sometimes when people ask me where country music is going from here or where Bill Anderson is going from here, I'll steal Tex's answer. "Saturday I'm going to Pennsylvania" somehow says that none of us really has any idea where anything is going from here, and even if we did, there wouldn't be much, if anything, we could do about it.

I do think I know, though, why most people wait until later in life than I have before they undertake the writing of an autobiography. There is no way for a person to write a book of this type while he's still as active in as many facets of his career as I am and have everything come out current and up-to-date when the book is released. Mel Tillis may have handled the problem best when he ended his book, *Stuttering Boy*, by simply writing, "To be continued."

A lot of times these days when I fill out a registration card checking into a hotel or when I have to list my occupation somewhere for some reason, I write "juggler." The dictionary says that to juggle is "to keep several objects in the air at one time by alternately tossing and catching them." One who juggles "performs tricks of dexterity." Yep, that's me all right, keeping about three careers in the air at one time, tossing them up and catching them before they hit the ground. At least three careers, sometimes more. Maybe I should have been like the folks at Kentucky Fried Chicken who say they do only one thing and do it right, but that's never made me happy. My fingers seem to do best when they're stuck into lots of different pies.

Even though I often try to climb several mountains at one time, I do try to keep my expeditions fairly well organized. In fact, as I look at my career today, I see it divided rather neatly into thirds.

I still spend about one-third of my time actively working in the music business. That includes recording, songwriting, and live performances. A few years ago I cut my concert schedule down from over two hundred dates a year to more like fifty or sixty, and I try to schedule most of those in the good weather months. I've decided I'll live longer this way. In fact, I find now that I actually look forward to climbing on board the bus instead of sometimes dreading it. I've always loved the shows themselves, but they're even more enjoyable now that they come at a much more manageable pace. I still work the Opry as often as I can, and I plan on hanging my hat there forever.

I continue to spend another third of my time today serving as national spokesman for PoFolks restaurants. Although the chain has had to face some tough times lately and has stopped expanding at the rapid rate it once did, I believe the concept is still as viable as ever and I'm going to do all I can over these next few years to keep spreading the story. Our food is still better than most you can find in a home-style restaurant anywhere, and our price-value is almost legendary in the food service business. I'm as "proud to be Po" as I ever was.

The other one-third of my career for the past six years has revolved around television and my involvement at the Nashville Network. I just wrapped up my sixth and final year of hosting a Monday through Friday, half-hour music trivia game show called *Fandango*. I've been the coproducer of another daily half-hour talent search program called *You Can Be a Star*, which is also ending after six years, and I recently served as executive producer on my first TNN special titled *An Evening with Lewis Grizzard*, a one-hour comedy show featuring the nationally known columnist, author, and humorist. For the past four years I have also produced the highly successful Lewis Grizzard comedy albums and tapes for Southern Tracks records.

The Nashville Network, the cable TV service owned by the same folks who own the Opry and the giant Opryland USA complex, has probably done as much or more than anything over the past few years to alter and expand the scope of country music, and I am particularly proud of my association with them. When TNN hit the marketplace amid much skepticism in March 1983, I was among the fortunate few who were invited to be on board.

Elmer Alley, who for years had served as program director of WSM-TV in Nashville, was given the task of assembling the programming ideas for this totally new broadcast concept, and one of the things he felt would be successful with the viewers was a game show built around country music fans and their knowledge of country trivia. Because of my experience at ABC-TV five years earlier hosting *The Better Sex*, I was the first person who came to his mind as a possible host for the program he later named *Fandango*.

It was the best thing that could have possibly happened for me. Since *The Better Sex* had gone off the air, I had been hosting a weekly syndicated series called *Backstage at the Grand Ole Opry* on a hundred or so stations scattered around the country, but I wanted to do more. The Nashville Network provided me with that opportunity.

In the beginning, there were a lot of people in the Nashville show business community who didn't think an all-country music TV channel was going to make it. I didn't doubt its success for a minute and said so. In fact, the night the network signed on with a star-studded gala, a reporter for *The Tennessean* called me aside in the lobby of the Opryland Hotel and asked me what I thought about all that was taking place. "Someday," I said, perhaps exaggerating a bit but trying hard to make my point by comparing the signing on of the Nashville Network to the first broadcast of the Grand Ole Opry, "someday people will look back on March 7, 1983, the way we've always looked back on November 25, 1925." The quote was in the next day's paper with the reporter's snide comment, "We'll see, Bill, we'll see."

Nashville was filled with dozens of people qualified to produce and direct *musical* programming when TNN first began broadcasting, but there was really no one within the local television community who had ever had any experience in the production of a game show. Realizing that game shows are a highly specialized field, TNN reached out and brought to town a producer from New York named Allen Reid, whose father had created and produced one of television's pioneer quiz shows, *The G.E. College Bowl* and who had himself over the years produced several game shows, most of them in Canada. Allen was hired by TNN specifically to produce *Fandango*, and he and I more or less inherited each other. "Bill, meet your producer" . . . "Allen, meet your host" . . . was the way it went. Normally, the producer selects his own host, but ours turned out to be a somewhat forced, although ultimately fortunate pairing.

In the beginning, though, Allen and I appeared to be another odd couple. He was an inventive but very demanding producer who loved the New York Mets and sushi bars. I was a laid-back hillbilly singer who followed the misfortunes of the Atlanta Braves, ate fried okra, and did game shows in his spare time. But over the six years we worked together, I think we were able to combine our strengths and become a very effective team. Allen taught me a tremendous amount about television and even more about how to host a game show. I taught him that "y'all" was just the Tennessee way of saying "youse guys" and that PoFolks fried chicken really wasn't going to corrode his innards. I'm still working with him, though, on the fried okra.

Not only am I a better game show host for having worked six years with Allen Reid, but it was also thanks to him that I got my first opportunity to learn a little bit about the other side of a television camera as well. Some six months after *Fandango* went on the air, he very generously invited me to join him and his wife, Mady Land, in the creation and development of his second TNN production, a competition show for up-and-coming young talent, called *You Can Be a Star*.

That turned out to be quite a learning experience for me. I never knew much about what goes on in a TV control room or in the day-to-day production of a television series. I always thought we guys who looked into the lenses of the camera did all the hard work. Not so. The front side of the camera is the easy side. The producer and his staff behind the camera on a well-organized television show earn every penny they make. It's extremely demanding, time-consuming work. I'm not sure I'd want to do it all the time.

I helped devise the format for *Star*, worked in the development of the scoring system which was used to rate the talent, and suggested to Allen that my band, the Po' Folks, would be the perfect group to play the music behind the young artists performing on the show. He hired them and even made my band leader, Mike Johnson, musical director of the show. They worked in that capacity for the entire six years.

Because of my hectic schedule and because of the fact that *Fandango* and *You Can Be a Star* often had to tape on the same day, I wasn't able to be quite as involved with *Star* on a show-by-show basis as I first started out to be. Toward the end of its run, about all I did was work with the Grand Champion winners in coordinating the recording sessions they won with Capitol Records. I'll always be grateful to Allen, though, for giving me the chance to learn about something I might otherwise never have known.

Fandango, for me, was truly a labor of love. Driving to Opryland for the tapings was much easier than flying to California for *The Better Sex*, and getting paid for hosting a game show based on country music trivia felt almost like stealing sometimes.

Just like on *Better Sex*, though, I never got to do the entire show by myself. They gave me a sidekick on *Fandango*, but not a pretty lady like Sarah Purcell. This time it was an antagonistic "talking juke box" named Edgar, and while he wasn't nearly as cute as Sarah, he kept things loose. His job was to do all the straight announcing on the show, describe the prizes, and, in between the serious elements, to zing me whenever he could and provide a bit of comic relief. He'd call me "Whisper-nose" or "Whisper-breath," and he'd make fun of my clothes and my singing and anything else he could key in on. Occasionally I'd break down and laugh at something he said, but his humor walked some pretty crooked lines:

"Hey, Bill, did you hear about the frog that got caught in the illegal parking zone?"

"No, I didn't, Edgar. What happened?"

"He got *toad* away!"

Well, it beat talking to a toy duck who could only squeak. Sometimes.

Edgar was never seen on camera as a person. He *was* the juke box. The source of his voice, however, became a hot topic. Everywhere I went people would ask, "Who's Edgar?" but I never would tell. At the end of each show Edgar, in his role as the show's announcer, would say, "The voice of Edgar is not . . ." and he'd name everybody from Ronald Reagan to Ronald McDonald, from Roger Miller to Roger Rabbit. People would write in all kinds of suggestions as to who they thought Edgar actually was, but most of them were way off base. They guessed Ralph Emery, Harold Reid of the Statler Brothers, Hank Thompson, and dozens of others, but we still wouldn't tell. The only people who ever guessed Edgar's true identity were those from the area around Indianapolis, Indiana, who remembered a crazy disc jockey from days gone by named Bill Robinson. Bill provided the marvelous voice for Edgar.

What very few people knew, however, was that Bill Robinson and I had been doing a routine very similar to what Edgar and I did on *Fandango* for years. Only it was in real life, and it was serious.

I first met Bill when he was a disc jockey on WMNI in Columbus, Ohio, back in the late sixties, and we immediately became good friends. He left country music radio for a while, moved to Lansing, Michigan, where he worked on an easy-listening music station, then got back into country at WIRE in Indianapolis not long afterward. We had stayed in touch over the years, found that we each possessed a bit of an offbeat sense of humor, and had pulled a few small long-distance gags on one another from time to time. But nothing like the one I pulled on him when he first called to tell me he had moved to Indianapolis.

"It's a great job, Whisper," he said to me excitedly the day he phoned. "Great station, great market, and I've found a super apartment here. I'm moving in tomorrow. Can't have any pets, but that's no problem."

Bells went off and sirens roared in my mind. "Can't have pets, huh?" I thought, and I asked him what his new address would be. Then I hung up and reached for my phone index.

I knew of a place that sold baby chickens by mail and would ship them anywhere in the world, guaranteeing they would arrive live and healthy. I couldn't wait to give them a call.

About four o'clock the next afternoon while Mr. Robinson was relaxing by the pool after having put in a hard day's work in his new town, at his new job, a delivery man walked into the apartment office with 150 of the cutest little chirping baby chicks you ever saw. They were addressed to the new tenant, Mr. William Robinson. Bill was paged and told to come to the office right away. Seems it had something to do with the rule regarding pets.

He went to the office, saw the baby chicks in cartons all over the floor, and knew instantly he had been had. He didn't wait around to meet with the manager. He paid the fifteen dollars or so in shipping charges (surely he didn't expect *me* to pay that!), grabbed the baby chicks, and took off like a herd of turtles back to his apartment. He watered his new pets, called a friend to ask what and how to feed them, then the next morning he signed on the radio station bright and early with a special offer to his listeners: "The first person who comes down here and reimburses me the fifteen dollars I paid in shipping charges can have 150 baby chicks absolutely free," he said. One of his listeners was there almost before the words were out of his mouth.

It didn't take him long to find out where the darling yellow chick-chicks had come from, however, and he was bent on revenge. I was scheduled for an outdoor concert at a park not far from Indianapolis in a few weeks and he knew it. He decided to get even right away.

Where he came up with this idea, I'll never know, but he went out into the community around Indianapolis somewhere and located about a dozen members of a motorcycle gang like Hell's

Angels. He told them I would be coming to town on such-and-such a Sunday afternoon and asked if he might hire them that afternoon to ride their motorcycles down to the park where I was performing. A couple of them turned out to be frustrated musicians, and they said sure, they'd love to come.

The day of the show, I was out onstage performing in front of a huge crowd. No one other than Bill had any idea that a motorcycle gang was within a hundred miles of the place. He made sure they were all hidden out of sight until just the right moment. That moment came when Bill heard me starting to get deep into one of my slow, sad, moving recitations. That's when he gave them the sign to crank up their engines.

I heard this big rumble and roar going on back behind the stage, but I pretended not to notice and kept right on going with my song. Suddenly I looked up and here they came, twelve of the raunchiest, scroungiest-looking human beings I think I have ever seen, dressed in black T-shirts, black jeans, red scarves around their necks, goggles over their eyes, their motorcycles thundering down the hill off to the right of the stage, throttles wide open. They got to where I was and rumbled right on past me as fast as they could go, only about two feet in front of the stage and not more than another two feet from the people seated on the front row.

It was like a big blur when they went by, racing from my right to my left. Then they stopped real quick, spun their bikes around, and roared back from left to right. They kicked up so much dust that even when they were out of sight I could barely see the crowd. And speaking of the crowd, they were like me—they had absolutely no idea what was going on. We all thought we were being invaded by somebody from a foreign country.

But my tormentor wasn't through. Just as the bikers passed in front of me the second time, he had someone up on the roof of the stage lower what appeared to be an old window shade down over the front of the little outdoor stage, completely shutting off my view of the audience. I don't know if anything was written on the outside of the shade for the audience to see or not, but on the inside of the shade where no one could see but me was a big picture of the back side of a human hand. All the fingers were tightly clenched into a fist with the exception of the middle finger, which was pointed straight out, fully extended. I got the message.

It was my turn next. When I got back to Nashville, I phoned and enrolled my friend B.R., as I've always called him, in some correspondence courses at a nearby college. In a few days I sent a collection agency out to see him because he hadn't paid his tuition. Next I ordered him a set of encyclopedias to use in his school work. I sent them COD, of course. Then he retaliated and did a few more things to me. One day in a charity softball game between my team and the disc jockeys from his radio station, he substituted a grapefruit he had painted white for the softball we had been using. It was my turn at bat, he was pitching, and when I swung and hit the "ball," it splattered grapefruit all over me, all over the catcher, and into the eyes of the umpire. I didn't laugh a lot, but he thought it was real cute.

Another time I was performing at the Fairgrounds Coliseum in Indianapolis, about the time I had out the record "Don't She Look Good (In the New Dress I Bought Her)," and Bill was emceeing the show. When I broke into that song, a big, heavy-set friend of ours named Jon Potter came waltzing out onto the stage—all 275 or so pounds of him—dressed in the ugliest looking dress you've ever seen and made up from head to toe to look like a woman. In his black leather spiked-heel shoes, he sashayed right up to the microphone where I was singing and proceeded to plant a wet, sloppy kiss right on my mouth. I knew immediately that Bill had put him up to it. The audience roared. I stopped singing and started trying to wipe off the lipstick and the awful smell of Jon's perfume. While I was trying and the crowd was laughing and snapping pictures as fast as they could, here came Bill out on stage followed by two St. Bernard dogs about the size of the Clydesdale horses. He camped right there between the two dogs, in the middle of that stage, in the middle of my show, and wouldn't leave until he had sold those dogs to somebody in the audience.

You can see that long before B.R. became Edgar and got paid for being a thorn in my side, he was playing the role to the hilt for free. When *Fandango* started, we didn't have to write any scripts. We had nearly fifteen years worth of real-life material to pick from.

Edgar and I did *Fandango* alone for the first four years we were on the air, and the trivia material on the show was drawn strictly from the country music field. At that point, Allen Reid and the network decided the show had gone about as far as it could go in its present form, and they felt some major changes were needed if the program was to continue. Their first decision was to redesign the set completely, then to upgrade the prizes from the can openers and tire tools we had been giving away to automobiles, boats, fur coats, and luxury vacations. They took me out of the flashy sport coats and sweaters I had been wearing on the show and dressed me in a subdued businessman's wardrobe from Botany 500. Finally, they decided to add a model, a pretty Mississippi lady named Blake Pickett, to the cast. They further decided to expand the trivia base by adding questions based on types of music other than country. I was skeptical of all the wholesale changes in the beginning.

Why did our successful little show (we had consistently been second to only *Nashville Now* as the highest rated show on TNN's Monday through Friday schedule) need another Vanna White? And why did we need questions about the Beatles and Frank Sinatra? Our viewers were more the Barbara Mandrell and Ricky Skaggs type, weren't they? I loved the new set and the improved prizes, but I didn't understand the thinking behind the other changes at all. But when the new shows hit the air, the ratings went up even higher than they'd already been. I relaxed and read the questions about Barbra Streisand.

Blake turned out to be a joy to work with. She had none of the ego problems I had always associated with gorgeous models, and there was no doubt that her long blonde hair, trim figure, and pretty blue eyes attracted male viewers to the show in bunches.

We taped *Fandango* only twice a year, five shows a day for thirteen days during one month in the fall and sixty-five more episodes the same way for a month in the spring, but it was on the air every day, five days a week, fifty-two weeks a year, and the exposure was tremendous. The actual time I had to spend in the production of the shows was kept to a minimum, allowing me to continue all the other facets of my strange and varied career. I was sad when after six seasons the network decided the show had run its course.

People often ask me if I enjoy hosting game shows more than I enjoy singing, and my answer is no. I don't think anything ever surpasses the feeling an entertainer gets when he walks out on a concert stage and performs before a live audience. Of all the things I do in my career, performing live is the one thing I'd miss most if I couldn't do it. But hosting *Fandango* on television was probably the next closest thing to performing in concert, and I enjoyed it tremendously.

For one thing, we taped the show in front of a live studio audience, and even though it was a relatively small one compared to what we might find in a concert hall, there was a lot of that same you've-only-got-one-chance-to-get-it-right pressure. Though a game show is videotaped, the tape is never stopped unless a technical mistake occurs, and, of course, the tape can never be edited in any place that might affect the outcome of the game itself. Therefore, we were wrapped in that "working without a net" atmosphere much like live TV, and I found it exhilarating.

Too, in hosting a game show, I got to call on just about every single part of my background. For example, I was constantly having to use the sense of timing I learned in radio. When the stage manager told me I had exactly ten seconds to talk leading into a commercial, I knew how to talk exactly ten seconds. I learned how to do that back at WGAU in Athens when I had to punch up the CBS news at the top of the hour. When I needed to get the studio audience to participate in the flow of the game, I could lean on my twenty-five years of experience working before live audiences to help me do that. And when I had to read a question with a few big words in it or when I had to call on a little old-fashioned intelligence in order to handle some particular situation, I could always pause and say a silent "Thanks, Mom and Dad, for making sure I got an education." I once had a school teacher who was fond of saying, "We are the sum of all our experiences," and that's definitely what you got when you saw Bill Anderson hosting a television game show.

The exposure I have received from being on national television every day, even on cable, has aided every other phase of my career as well. When TNN first signed on, I'd ask audiences at our concerts to raise their hands if they watched *Fandango*. In the beginning I'd get perhaps a twenty percent response. Today, with the network being available in almost half the TV households in the country, when I ask how many watch TNN it's more like eighty or ninety percent. Needless to say, the size of our concert crowds has increased accordingly. I haven't had a No. 1 record for quite some time, but you'd never know it from the size of the crowds at most of our concerts or the recognition factor I find in airports, shopping malls, and restaurants. I'm asked to sign far more autographs today because of my visibility on television than I ever was when my records were all going to No. 1 or when I was on ABC. Don't ask me to explain it, just let me enjoy it.

TNN has recently added a satellite radio network, TNNR, to its arsenal, and they have hired me to host a four-hour radio show every Sunday afternoon. I tell people that after almost thirty years in this business I'm right back where I started—playing records on the radio.

Actually, it's a little more than that, and it's a slightly bigger project than was *The Dinnerbell Jamboree* on WJJC in Commerce. The show is called *Yesteryear* and the concept involves my going back across the last thirty or thirty-five years of country music history and playing again the Top Ten records from a corresponding week in the past. For example, if it's currently the week of July 4th, I go back to four July-4th weeks in the past (one year per hour) and play the Top Ten records from that particular week in our chosen yesteryear. In addition, I try and recall anecdotes about the singers, writers, musicians, and songs involved in each of the hits. After all, I've been here since dirt, and I was there when a lot of the hits were born.

The show is loosely scripted, very thoroughly researched by a walking country music encyclopedia named Otto Kitsinger, and I'm free to read what Otto writes or ad lib just about anything I want to say. I have a telephone nearby and often call my friends in the business—artists, songwriters, producers—and talk with them on the air about whatever might be going on in their lives. In this day of jukebox radio, where so many stations play twelve or fifteen hits in a row back-to-back without giving any information about the singers and the music, we hope our show will be a refreshing change.

The shows are taped ahead of time and worked into my existing schedule, so I'm able to do them without having to alter my other careers very much. It's a fun project. I hope it lasts a long time.

* * *

Even though I always seem to be involved in some new phase of my career, I never stop working on the older ones at all. I have recently recorded a duet record and filmed a music video with a lovely lady from England named Toni Bellin. I know I'm prejudiced, but I think both the record and the video turned out great. Toni's husband came up with an exciting new arrangement on an old song and asked me if I'd drop by the studio the afternoon Toni was to record it and "whisper" a couple of lines on her record. I said sure, but when I got there and we went to work, he felt our voices blended so well together that he rewrote the entire arrangement into a full-fledged duet.

I've had a lot of success with duet partners in the past—Jan Howard, Mary Lou Turner, Roy Acuff, David Allen Coe—who knows, maybe the world is ready for a British accent to blend with a Georgia drawl. It's sure worth a try.

You see, that's what's so great about this business. There's always something exciting going on. Every morning you wake up with a chance to hit a home run. You might have gone to bed the night before batting zero-for-life, but that magic word or that magic phrase or that magic idea might just roll out of your brain and off of your tongue tomorrow. I don't know of any other profession where the opportunity for success is so great. I'm not saying the odds against it aren't high because they are, but they are never impossible.

Maybe that's what has kept me going all these years. Maybe that's why I'm still at it. Maybe that's why the word *retire* has never been a part of my vocabulary.

Minnie Pearl told me one time that she still gets butterflies every time just before she goes on stage. "If it ever gets to the point where you don't get butterflies," she said, "then it doesn't mean as much to you as it should."

I still get butterflies, too. Not just before I go on stage, but every day when I wake up with an idea for a song, or a concept for a television show, or a better way to market fried chicken rolling around in my head. I'm still enthused, I'm still excited, I'm still in love with this lady-in-red called show business. Maybe that's why I've pursued her for as long as I have. Maybe that's why I'll stay in the chase for as long as the Good Lord will let me, even though much of the time I don't have the foggiest idea where it is that I'm headed or what in the world I'm going to do if and when I get there.

29

How do you go about describing to someone whose life has never been touched by a head injury exactly what such an injury is and how it affects not only the person who receives it but everyone who lives around that person as well? It's not easy.

The National Head Injury Foundation estimates that in this country each year there are over 750,000 head injuries that require hospitalization. That's three-quarters of a million people killed or injured every twelve months just because they rode a bike with no helmet, didn't fasten their seat belt, ran through a traffic light, didn't stop at a stop sign, or maybe played football or hockey or some other sport with too much reckless abandon. They climbed that rickety old ladder "just one more time" before fixing it. Or they got behind the wheel of a car and drove "just a little bit drunk."

Becky's accident, her transformation from a warm, caring, loving person to someone who for so long could feel no emotions at all, to someone who lived each day of her life out of a sense of duty, to someone who was disoriented and confused for a period of years, taught me one thing above everything else: There is nothing human beings should value more than their minds.

Becky told me not long ago that she feels it's hard for the average person to understand what a head injury is all about because on the outside a head-injured person often doesn't appear to be injured at all. "In my case," she said, "my bruises were about gone, the cuts looked better, the stitches were out, I could get up and move around, I could talk, I could dress myself, I could feed myself, I recognized everybody, and people would say, 'Oh, you're fine now!' But that's not the way it was at all.

"Anybody can understand what it's like to be blind. You simply close your eyes and you are blind for a moment. But for people to understand a head injury, they really have to use their imaginations."

"How do you mean?" I asked.

"Well, just imagine for a minute that you are sitting in there in your study. Look around the room, notice how everything is complete and neat and orderly, just the way you arranged it. Every little item there helps in its own way to make your study the special, unique place that it is—your furniture, your books, plants, records, pictures, mirrors, TV set, all these things combine to make that *your* room. Then, imagine your room as your brain and all the furnishings in your room as brain cells."

"OK."

"Now, imagine you've gone out for a while, maybe to a movie, and when you come home a thief has broken into your room and stolen away from your room as much as he could carry. What he couldn't carry, he rummaged through and tore up and destroyed. Only a few things escaped his touch.

"That's what a damaged brain feels like. Like somebody came in and stole away everything they could, and what they couldn't steal, they rearranged. That's probably an amateurish way to describe it, but do you understand at all what I mean?"

I looked around my study. Everything was in its place. I looked at Becky. I understood the analogy.

Yet during her recovery I'm not sure I ever fully understood all that she was experiencing, in particular her single-mindedness about getting well. As she saw it, her one mission in life was to get well, period, and she was totally committed to doing whatever it might take. Getting well was all she thought about, all she focused on. She was so absorbed by this one thought that she didn't need to interrupt the process to explain to me what she was doing or justify herself to me or give me a daily report on her progress—nor did I ask for one—but I know now there was a lot going on that I was not aware of. I knew all the big things, of course—the visits to the doctors, the tests, the evaluations and prognostications—and when I could see little flashes of improvement in the way she felt and the way she acted from time to time, I just assumed the doctors and time were doing their thing. I didn't realize how much Becky had been helping both the doctors and time on her own. Had it not been for my writing this book and her willingness to share the various thoughts and feelings she'd had in her life since October 1984, I still might not know it all.

Becky knew for quite a while that I wanted to write a book, an autobiography about my life in show business but woven around the backdrop of her accident, the tumultuous years that followed, and the positive changes the whole episode brought about in both our lives. At first she was all for it. Then later, when she realized I would be telling some of the more intimate details of our lives and of her recovery, she turned against it. I tried to change her mind, but I didn't have a lot of luck.

I decided to go ahead and write the book anyhow, even if I never had it published. Writing it could serve as therapy for me if nothing else. Becky knew I was continuing to work on the project, but I never said anything to her about how it was or wasn't progressing. She never asked any questions. We both pretended the book didn't exist.

I can truthfully say, though, that I would never have published the book against her wishes. At some point in time I'd have pulled the plug and walked away. But I'm glad I didn't have to.

I first began to understand her feelings the day she came to me and said, "You don't have any idea of all the little mind-games I've played with myself to try and get better, do you?"

"No, I don't guess I do."

"I can't possibly tell you everything because there is so much to tell," she said, "but if you'd like for me to tell you a few things, I will." I was thrilled.

She began slowly but deliberately opening up and talking to me about many of the personal things she had felt and the secret things she had done to try and get well following the accident. It became apparent to me right away why she had felt the way she'd felt about the book: Deep down inside, she was embarrassed. Embarrassed about all the things that had happened to her. Embarrassed because she knew all this time she had been acting, pretending to be normal. And she knew she wasn't normal. She was afraid if I wrote the book she might be exposed.

"I don't want people to read your book and think you're married to a brain-damaged woman!" she repeated emphatically. But as her recovery progressed and she began to grow more and more confident that she *was* going to get well, she realized she didn't have to act anymore, that she truly was getting back to normal. That excited her, so much so that one day out of a clear blue sky she came to me, put her arms around me, and told me she was ready for the book to be written. She thought our story should be told. She hoped others might benefit from it.

I can say without a doubt that I am most definitely not married to a brain-damaged woman. At least not to one who is helpless or mentally impaired because of it. I am married to the strongest, most remarkable lady I've ever known, and by far the most determined. She has risen above all the odds, fooled all the experts, and built a totally new life out of the ashes of the old one. That's darn well worth writing a book about! Once she accepted that fact, she asked me if I'd like to "interview" her.

That's exactly what I did, just like back in my days as a newspaper reporter. I took a yellow legal pad, three or four sharpened pencils, made myself a pot of coffee, and sat down across from her at our breakfast room table. I asked her questions, lots and lots of questions, just like a reporter might do. She answered and I wrote. A few days later I interviewed her again. Then she sat down at the typewriter in Jamey's study and put a lot of her thoughts on paper herself and gave them to me. I realize now I could never have finished this project without her help. From the point of that first interview on, this became more than just *my* book. It became *our* book.

I have come to understand now, for the first time, that Becky's recovery has been divided into two very distinct and separate segments. The first two-and-a-half years following the accident were devoted to her resting and mending and getting well *physically*. The next two years were devoted to the *emotional* reconstruction of her body, her mind, and her spirit. It had to be done that way. She could never have worked on the emotional part until the physical part was intact. She would not have been strong enough to withstand the pressure and the strain.

The things she did to make herself get well and the way she forced herself to go about doing them totally astound me. And they astound her doctors as well. Not a person from the medical community who has seen her can believe the recovery she has made. This includes doctors ranging from neurosurgeons to internists, from orthopedists to psychologists. She has astonished and amazed them all.

First, here was a woman so badly injured both physically and emotionally that she admits all she wanted to do for days, weeks, months, and even years following her accident was to lie in bed and sleep. She knew intellectually that she had a husband and a little boy who loved and needed her, and she knew intellectually that she had once had a life outside the confines of her own bedroom, but emotionally she wasn't even able to care. All she wanted was to be left alone. "But at some point one day," she told me as we began our first conversation across the table, "and I don't even remember when it was, either Tom Burns convinced me or I convinced myself that I was never going to get any better if I didn't make up my mind to get up out of the bed and try. It was the first time I remember feeling any motivation at all. I wasn't ready to try it right then, but I told myself that one day soon I was going to make the effort."

"How did you manage?" I asked.

"Well, I didn't just bound out of bed the next morning and decide to conquer the world," she said. "The doctors had told me that the energy cell in my brain had been severely damaged, and I wasn't suddenly going to have a big burst of energy all at once. But every day I could feel myself gradually becoming stronger and stronger.

"At first, I didn't have enough energy to stay out of bed for more than a few minutes at a time. I'd get up in the mornings and help you get Jamey ready for school, but as soon as the two of you left I'd go back to bed. Many days I'd stay there until he got home.

"Tom told me to work on that, to try each day to stay up as long as I could, but I really had to force myself. I'd take my alarm clock and set it for a one-hour nap. Then I'd reduce that to thirty minutes, then twenty minutes. He said that by forcing myself to stay awake I would be training another part of my brain to take over the work of my damaged energy cell. Eventually, I didn't hit the snooze button on my alarm clock quite so often, and my brain did compensate. Of course, now I can keep a pretty normal pace."

"But go back to the beginning," I said. "Tell me what happened after you first made yourself the promise not to sleep so much."

"It was one night not too long after that, I don't remember exactly when, just before I turned out my light to go to sleep, I told myself, 'I am not going to sleep all day tomorrow! I'm going to get up and do something!' And I went to sleep with nothing but that one thought on my mind.

"The next morning when I woke up I remembered the promise I'd made to myself the night before, and I dragged myself out of bed. I didn't feel like it, but I *made* myself get up. I felt like I was sleepwalking. I stumbled toward the bathroom, and on the way I walked by a full-length mirror on my closet door. When I looked in that mirror and saw my reflection, I threw my hands up over my face. I couldn't stand to look. My expression was so blank, so empty. There was no life at all in my eyes. The muscles in my face were numb. I tried to smile and I couldn't. I honestly could not smile. I was horrified.

"I walked on into the bathroom, cleaned my face, brushed my teeth and combed my hair. I came back out and sat down in front of the mirror above my dresser and said, 'OK, now try and remember how you used to do it. You *used* to smile . . . now how did you do it?' I sat there for hours trying to bring back the feeling.

"For a long time nothing would come, but I kept on looking at myself and I kept on trying. It wasn't just the emotion of being happy that I couldn't feel. I couldn't physically remember how to smile. I couldn't get the muscles in my face to make that expression. Finally, I started talking to myself.

"'Now, Becky,' I said, 'you are not here in front of this mirror. You are at one of Jamey's Little League baseball games and he just hit the ball to center field. He's running toward first base. Now, what's your reaction?' And I *made* myself smile. I took my fingers and pushed up the corners of my mouth, *making* it look like a smile. Then I *made* myself do it again, over and over, again and again, *forcing* my facial muscles to move, *forcing* myself to be excited, trying so hard to remember how it used to feel back when it all used to come so natural."

"Did it work?" I asked her, excited that she was opening up such a big part of herself to me, sharing these immensely personal feelings.

"Something did," she said. "You see, Tom told me that most people who have the type injury I had don't want to do anything but sit and stare at walls all day—or watch TV—but I made up my mind that if I had to sit there and practice making expressions every day for the rest of my life that my son *was* going to see his mother smile again. My husband *was* going to see his wife smile again. If I had to imagine excitement and pretend I felt joy when I really didn't, then I'd just use my imagination and make believe. I was determined not to settle for anything less."

"So what happened next? What else did you do?"

"I practiced working on my smile for days. Every day I'd get up, go to my mirror, and practice. One day you told me a joke and I thought, 'That was really funny.' In my mind I thought I was laughing at what you had said, but when I turned toward the mirror, I was shocked. I wasn't laughing at all. I looked all glum and serious. I wasn't able to let you know how funny I thought your joke was. I told you it was funny, but there was no look on my face to show you I thought it *was* funny. After you left that day, I became even more determined.

"For hours I sat in front of the mirror and tried to smile. But I couldn't physically do it. My mouth had been busted and stitched, and my jawbone had been damaged. My teeth had been knocked out of line and broken or chipped. My eyelids had been cut, my forehead cut and bruised. None of my facial muscles were working."

"What did you do?"

"I took my fingers, and I pushed the corners of my mouth up. I tickled my mouth and lips the way I used to tickle Jamey when he was a baby and I would try to get him to smile. I thought pleasant thoughts. I thought of when I was a child playing. I thought of when I met you and of the night when we got married, and how we laughed when we came out of the church and that bus load of fans was standing out in the yard throwing rice at us."

"You know Bill Robinson put them up to that, don't you?" I asked. "They were fans in town on a tour from Indianapolis."

"Yes, and it was funny. Of course, knowing crazy ole B.R. did it made it even funnier. Then I thought of when you took me to New York for the first time, when we went overseas together, and I thought of the afternoon Jamey was born and the warm, loving look in your eyes. And I asked God, as I always do, to help me find a way.

"For months every time I was alone I would sit there in front of that mirror and work with my facial muscles. I remembered what Tom had told me about acting, and I'd imagine and pretend. Slowly but surely I seemed to make a little progress each day. I began to notice the feeling slowly returning to my face. When I heard or saw something funny, I was gradually able to react. When I was out and around people, I would constantly keep on my mind, 'Smile when you should.' It worked, too, because for months now I haven't had to think about smiling or laughing anymore. It all comes natural to me now."

"That's incredible," I said, totally captivated. "What other kinds of games did you play with yourself?"

"Well, on days when Jamey was at school and you were at the office or at the studio, I'd sit at home on the sofa by myself and imagine it was getting late and it was about time for you to be coming home. I'd pretend I could hear your key in the door, then I'd wait until you'd had time to step inside and I'd yell, 'Hi, honey! Have you had a good day? Supper will be ready in a few minutes.' And I'd pretend to be smiling, pretend to be in a good mood, practice telling myself, 'Now, when he comes in, remember you want to hug him, you want to smile, you want to be happy.' That's the only way I could remember to do it."

"Were these things Tom told you to do?" I asked.

"He gave me the game plan," she answered, "but I had to work out the step-by-step part for myself. Tom told me that I had been reduced to an infant in many ways, and that I'd have to go back in my mind and recall memories of the person I used to be. I could remember *being* an adult, but I needed to pretend I *was* one until it became a natural part of me.

"And I didn't just do any of these things *one* day. I did them *every* day, over and over again, day after day after day. I was trying to get to the point where they'd feel natural and come easy like they used to."

"How did you make it natural?"

"Mostly I'd just try to keep on my mind all the time, 'This is how I *used* to do it,' whatever it was; 'this is how it *used* to be.' And I'd try to work on only one thing at a time. In fact, I couldn't work on but one thing at a time. It was like I had a one-track mind. I'd get confused and distracted if I tried to do too much at once. I couldn't change trains of thought like a normal person can. I'd take a piece of paper and a pen and I'd write down the one thing I felt I could handle at that particular moment."

"Like what?"

"Well, let's say I needed to go to the grocery store, for example. I couldn't go by myself, you remember, for a real long time. You always went with me, but when I did start to get out and do a few things on my own, I would actually write down my whole routine ahead of time: (1) Leave house (2) Get in car (3) Drive to store (4) Park car at store (5) Remember to look for other cars, and so on. And then when I'd finally get inside the store, I'd start all over again.

"Remember, too, I didn't start off at first going back to the supermarket. For a long time I would only go to the 7-11 or one of the small drive-in markets. I couldn't go back to Kroger or H. G. Hill's or any of the big stores in the beginning."

"Why not?"

"Because there was too much in the big stores to confuse me. Too many choices. Too much activity that wasn't related to what I was there for. Delivery men would be bringing in drinks or bread or canned goods. Employees would be stocking shelves. People would be weighing fruits and vegetables. Other customers would be busy buying what they needed. And I was always afraid I might run into someone I knew."

"Would that have been a problem?"

"Yes, because my mind would have had to switch tracks—I couldn't just go from putting things in my cart to, 'Hello, how are you? It's good to see you.' I'd have had to remember to smile, to hold on to my grocery cart so I wouldn't lose my balance, to be careful not to lose my shopping list. Plus there were all the other things: Where is my pen to mark off the items I've already gotten? What time is it? When do I have to be finished so I can pick Jamey up at school? Where did I park the car? Do they carry the groceries out or do I? Then, do I have my purse or my checkbook? Will the ice cream melt before I get home? Will the milk spoil? Do I put the groceries in the trunk of the car or in the backseat? Do I have to go to the drugstore too, or should I buy the shampoo here? It's not on my list, but would Bill and Jamey like a watermelon tonight? I had to think of so many things other than the groceries I needed to buy. It confused me. It made me dizzy. And it made me tired.

"Even in the smaller stores where I didn't have to make so many decisions, it was confusing. I had to pretend I knew what I was doing. Many times I would pull into a parking space in front of a Minute Market or a 7-11, and before going inside I would mentally go through the process: 'OK, you walk in the door and down the aisle to where you find the can of peas you need. Then you take it to the cashier, get the money from your purse, pay for it, wait for her to put it in a bag, pick it up, and go back to your car.' I'd go through this in my mind two or three times before I'd actually go inside the store and do it. In the beginning I could only buy one item. After a while I could handle getting two or three.

"Later on, I got to where I could go into a larger store, but I still stayed away from the supermarkets. I would go into this little grocery near the condo and get a cart and walk up and down the aisles very slow, maybe even two times, just to get the feel of buying groceries. Then I would buy only what I'd need for dinner that night. This store was larger than the drive-in markets, but it had only one cashier and one or two employees stocking the shelves. Even at that it was very confusing. But I kept pushing. I kept telling myself that grocery shopping was just an ordinary thing that anyone could do. It embarrassed me that I couldn't."

I listened and I marvelled, wondering how many people finding themselves in the same situation would have put up such a fight.

"Tell me something," I said. "Buying things one item at a time or one meal at a time like you did, how long would it take you to buy a week's worth of groceries?"

Becky laughed. "Sometimes longer than it took us to eat them!" she said. "But I was determined."

"It wasn't only the funny things and the happy things that I had to practice reacting to," she continued. "For a long time I couldn't cry or feel sad either. And I knew that wasn't right."

"How did you handle that?"

"I'd try to watch something sad on TV. If that didn't make me cry or make me feel sad, then I'd think about a sad book. I couldn't actually read anything for over two years because my eyesight was so blurred, but I'd try to recall a book or a story I'd read earlier that had made me cry. Sometimes I'd even think back to the morning my daddy was killed and remember how much I loved him and missed him, but still I couldn't feel sad, I couldn't cry."

"What finally made you cry?" I asked.

"I'll tell you in a minute," she said, "but do you remember the day you came in the condo and the whole place smelled like onions? You nearly passed out before you could get back outside!"

Did I remember? I had threatened to go buy a gas mask!

"Well, I had been standing over the sink that whole afternoon peeling onions trying to make myself cry."

"Did you cry?"

"No, but I do remember the first time I did cry. It was about three years after the wreck. You had come home late one night, you'd flown in from California, I think, and it was around twelve or one o'clock in the morning. I was real tired, but I had forced myself to stay awake until I heard your key in the door. But then I didn't have the strength to get up and let you know how glad I was that you were home, so I just lay there. It made me sad to know that you had come all this way and I couldn't even get up to let you know I was glad you were home. I knew I had disappointed you. And I started crying. In fact, I cried myself to sleep.

"The next morning when I woke up, it still hurt and I started crying all over again. Then suddenly I realized, 'Hey, I'm crying!' I hadn't cried in over three years. And I got so happy about crying that I started laughing. I lay there laughing and crying all at the same time. I must have looked like a fool. When I quit crying, I tried to make myself start crying again, but I couldn't do it. In fact, it was six or seven weeks later before I was able to cry anymore."

"I'll tell you something *I* remember," I said to Becky as we continued to talk, allowing our thoughts to ramble across the jagged edges of the past four-and-a-half years, "I remember the first time you found you could smell things again."

"The time at the airport?" she asked. "Oh, I remember that too!"

I had been out of town on tour and was flying back home early one morning. Becky was well enough by this time to drive her car out to the airport to meet my flight. She had parked close to the terminal and walked to my gate. As soon as I got off the plane and hugged her neck real good, we started moving back through the terminal toward the baggage claim area. About halfway there I smelled something burning.

"Oooh, what's that?" I asked, never once saying I had smelled anything.

"Something's burning in here!" she said.

"How do you know?" I asked.

"Because it smells like . . .," she started. We both stopped dead in our tracks and looked at one another. She hadn't been able to smell anything for years. The doctors had said she would never be able to smell again. "Central nervous system tissue does not regenerate," was the way they had put it. But, as with everything else, Becky wouldn't take no for an answer.

"I did everything I knew to try and get my sense of smell back," she said. "I took hot baths with bath scents and I burned candles with incense. I put perfume on my nose and once I even put some of that awful-smelling oven cleaner in the oven and then stuck my head inside the oven to try and see if I could smell the fumes. But nothing worked."

And yet she had most definitely smelled whatever it was that was burning in the airport. With no prompting from me, she had said she smelled it. I don't know how it happened, neither does she, and neither do the doctors. But it happened. I put my arm around her and pulled her close. "Well, I guess God is still in the miracle business," I said. She put her head on my shoulder and began to cry softly.

I pushed my chair back from the table, opened the kitchen door, and took in long, deep breaths of fresh air. I needed a minute to stretch my legs and settle my brain. I walked across the room to pour myself a fresh cup of hot coffee. When I returned to the table and sat down, Becky started talking again without any prodding from me. In doing so, she cleared up one of the biggest mysteries of all.

"Did you ever wonder why I ordered all those things I'd see advertised on TV while I was lying up there in the bed?" she asked. I looked at her, stifled a laugh, nodded my head, and said, yes, and if she didn't mind, while she was at it, why didn't she just tell me the whole story.

Actually, it had nearly driven me crazy. For years our little condo had been running over with things like ginzu knives, bamboo steamers, vitamins, Bibles, wrinkle creams, more vitamins, Fats Domino record albums, Jane Fonda workout tapes, more vitamins, videotapes showing the most famous broken bones in the history of American rodeoing, and more vitamins. What I wanted was a vitamin that would make my wife stop ordering things from off television!

"I know you thought I was crazy ordering all that junk," she laughed, "but, trust me, it was part of my rehabilitation program."

"*Sure* it was," I said, and we both laughed.

"See, here's what I'd do: The ads would come on and I would see the phone number to call flash up on the screen or the address to write, but I deliberately wouldn't write them down. I'd keep repeating over and over to myself such and such a phone number, such and such an address, trying to teach my brain to remember what it was. I would memorize the amount each item cost and then, just to see if I'd gotten it right, I'd address an envelope or call the 800-number and place an order. Most of the time I'd get it right."

"Me and the postman will vouch for that!" I laughed. "You mean you nearly bankrupted us just to see if you could remember some phone numbers?"

"Well," she smiled, "I was working on my short-term memory. Sometimes I couldn't even remember the last words that had been spoken in a conversation or the ingredients I needed for a recipe. That was a way of strengthening that. But, actually there was one more reason I ordered all of those things, too."

"And, pray tell, what might that have been?" It was fun to be laughing and playing true confessions after all these years, especially since doing so was allowing me to see up close just how far Becky had come.

"Mostly I was trying to activate excitement," she said. "Every time a mail-order package would come I'd get excited, or at least I'd pretend to get excited and show some emotion. Do you remember the year I ordered all my Christmas presents by mail?"

I remembered well.

"I thought I was so clever until Jamey saw the postmarks and wanted to know why Santa Claus sent things from Miami!"

We laughed some more. And then showing another flash of the marvelous sense of humor that had been missing in her for years, she added, "And, hey, all that mail-order stuff wasn't bad. You've got to admit I feel a lot better than I used to. It must have been all those vitamins!"

Becky has always genuinely liked people, always enjoyed meeting new people and being around old friends, but she told me during the second of our interview sessions that for at least the first two years following the accident she went through pure agony every time people other than me or Jamey were around. I asked her why.

"Because I knew I couldn't react or respond to them like I used to," she said, "and I was embarrassed. When I became well enough to go to the Opry with you, for example, it would wear me out. Nothing physical made me tired, but the *thinking* did. I was always thinking, trying to change directions and keep up with the conversation, afraid that what I might say to people would be dumb. I'd go home afterwards and lie in bed and think some more—'I should have said this' or 'I shouldn't have said that.'"

"Well, you're not like that now," I responded, recalling a night only a few weeks earlier when we'd been at a large party and she had seemed so at ease. "What brought about the change?"

"I'm not sure, but I think it may have started with the telephone. I could talk to people one at a time on the phone and not have to face them in a group. Plus, I'd have more time to think about the things I was going to say before I said them. Once I got comfortable talking with people on the phone, it was a lot easier for me to talk with them in person. Of course, you know who played the biggest role in all that, don't you?"

I had no idea.

"Your sister."

"Mary? In what way?"

"Well, I didn't tell you this at the time," Becky confessed, "because I was afraid you'd get upset if you knew the size of the phone bills I was running up between here and Atlanta. But sometimes I'd talk to Mary in the morning, again at noon, and again for hours that same night."

"Why?"

"Because Mary was the one person I felt I could talk to. I could tell her anything and not feel embarrassed. I'd tell her something like, 'I did the stupidest thing yesterday. I put a roast in the oven and forgot it was there and burned it up,' and instead of Mary laughing at me or scolding me she'd say, 'Why, I did the same thing last week myself.' I could identify with her. She made me feel like I wasn't the only strange person in the world."

It made me feel good to hear Becky talking about my sister that way. I knew Mary had more than a little bit of background experience to draw from.

In 1981, a casual friend of Mary's in Atlanta—a lady named Darlene—had suffered life-threatening head injuries in an automobile wreck en route to Mary's house. The only identification Darlene had in her purse at the time of the accident was Mary's phone number. Obviously, Mary was the first person the authorities contacted following the crash.

Mary was working in those days as a registered nurse. Her specialty was psychiatry. Through a long and drawn-out procedure that covered several months, Mary ended up being appointed Darlene's legal guardian. That experience sparked in my sister a tremendous desire to learn more about head-injured persons.

"I found out quickly that even as recently as 1981 there was a very limited understanding of people with head injuries," she told me recently. "Doctors had just begun to learn how to keep brain-damaged people alive. They knew hardly anything about rehabilitation for them once they had survived.

"I began calling rehab centers all over the country trying to learn something, anything, about head injuries that would help me in dealing with Darlene. I actually visited three different centers, one in San Francisco, one in Boston, and one down in Texas, all of them new. And I tried to learn everything I could. In doing so, I became totally absorbed by the field. It was a new frontier, I was convinced of that, and there were times when I thought, 'Nobody's doing anything!' but I kept on digging.

"I was still in the process of trying to find additional help for Darlene when Becky had her accident. I had learned a lot already, but I wasn't sure just what to do with all I'd learned. Then, suddenly, Becky's need for help seemed to bring it all into focus. I prayed about it. I said, 'Lord, please let Becky live and show me what to do with what I've learned.'"

Her prayers were certainly answered. For over four years now Mary has been like super-glue, holding Becky's thoughts, feelings, and gradually returning emotions in place. She's been the one person Becky has always known she could turn to the whole time she has been struggling to get well. "From the very beginning," Becky says, "Mary made me feel like she had complete confidence in my ability to beat this thing and get well. Even when I wasn't so sure myself, Mary never once acted like she had lost faith in me. In between my visits with Tom Burns, Mary has been like my own private psychologist."

Mary has always been a take-charge kind of person. Without even asking me, she recently volunteered my services to the Georgia Chapter of the National Head Injury Foundation. "Oh, he'll be more than happy to serve on your Board of Directors," she told them, knowing that if I wasn't thrilled about it she'd be able to talk me into it anyhow. Turned out she didn't have to twist my arm at all.

For several years Mary served as the Administrative Head Nurse and Assistant Program Director of the Head Injury Rehabilitation Unit at Georgia Baptist Hospital in Atlanta. She left there recently but continues to work with their program as a consultant. She has recently become involved with a new rehab center called Meadowbrook and works in case management as a Certified Rehabilitation Registered Nurse.

When I was young, I used to wish I had at least a dozen brothers and sisters, but I had only the one sister. But God knew what He was doing. What I might have missed out on in quantity, I know now I more than made up for in quality!

"If you write too much in your book about how God has helped me through all this, people will think we are preachers instead of disciples," Becky said to me one morning during one of our talk sessions. "But I do hope you'll let people know that I'd never have made it without His help and without the prayers that I know were prayed for me by people all over the world. God has been with me this whole time. I'm sure of it."

"When did you first start thinking about it—I mean about God and the fact that He was with you?" I asked.

"The first day I remember being in the hospital," she answered. "Of course, I don't remember much about even being there, but I do remember waking up one day and seeing this doctor sitting at the foot of my bed. You were over across the room. I know now the doctor was Dr. Meacham, but I didn't have any idea who he was at the time or even why he was there.

"I asked him, 'Am I in a hospital?'

"He said yes, and he started telling me everything that had happened.

"'What are you going to do to help me get well?' I asked, and I will never forget what he said. He said, 'Honey, you don't need surgery, your vital signs are all OK, there's not much more I can do. It's really out of my hands. God is your doctor now.'"

"Did you accept that?" I asked.

"I accepted it without any question," she readily admitted. "God was with me even before the wreck happened. He's always been with me. Kathy has told me that just before I let her out of the car that night I had stopped for gas. When I got back in the car after paying the cashier, she says I told her, 'Kathy, fasten your seat belt. There are a lot of crazy drivers out on Saturday nights.' Not only did Kathy fasten her seat belt, but for the first time all night I fastened mine. I think God was looking after me even then."

"What about now?"

"Well, you know I'm so much more full of life now than I've ever been before. God and His grace have made me feel all my emotions deeper and more fully than I've ever known. I've learned that problems can become opportunities through Him. I've always been a Christian, but my desperate need of God's love and strength has brought me even closer to my faith."

Then she began to talk about the three ministers that she felt had played a large role in her recovery:

Brother Felix Snell, the preacher who married us and who came to be with me that frightful Sunday afternoon at General Hospital and who has stayed in close touch with Becky throughout this whole ordeal. Throughout her recovery he has dropped her little handwritten notes from time to time, just to let her know he was thinking of her and to remind her of God's unending love and grace. He continues to remain in contact with both of us even today. Brother Snell's love and concern and his prayers have helped sustain our entire family.

Reverend Jim Beasley, the preacher who baptized Jamey when he was only a few weeks old, called and came to see Becky several times both in the hospital and after she returned home, and she always seemed to feel better after his visits. He, too, continues to keep in touch.

And Reverend Garry Speich, our current pastor, has been one of Becky's greatest pillars of strength and hope.

When her eyesight was so bad she could hardly read anything, it was Garry who brought her copies of the *Upper Room* daily devotional guide printed in extra-large type. He would come to the condo and sit for hours talking with Becky about God's will and God's plan for her life. He assured her that God's time was sometimes slow but it was constant. Garry even went so far as to do some personal research on head injuries so that he might communicate with her.

"I know God gave us Jamey, too," Becky continued, "and all I had to do was look at my son and feel his love for me to become more determined than ever to push harder to become the mother I always was before. And you—don't ever underestimate how much your love meant to me through all of this."

"In what way?"

"You were always my rock to lean on. Just that special look in your eyes gave me the incentive to try and become the woman I was when you fell in love with me." And she reached across the table and squeezed my hand.

Becky says she also received a tremendous amount of spiritual strength and motivation from watching *The 700 Club* on television. I asked her what she derived from this particular program.

"Mostly I saw miracles that had happened in other people's lives," she said, "and it made me realize if God could work a miracle in them He could work one in me. He *had* worked one in me. I was a continuing miracle. That show also taught me I was free to ask for anything from God. That I didn't have to accept lying up in bed for the rest of my life. That if I was willing to ask for something and then willing to work for it, it was possible, through faith, to receive it."

I have never been much of a fan of TV evangelists myself, but I'm willing to rethink my prejudices a bit. There's no doubt that this one program was of tremendous value to my wife.

"What made you change your mind about being a part of my book?" I asked Becky the third or fourth time we sat down together. "Why are you willing to talk about yourself now and open up this way? Once you said you wouldn't do it."

"It's just one more thing coming back to life in me," she answered without hesitation, "one more step in bringing me back to who I used to be. But it didn't just happen overnight. I've been wrestling with it and praying about it for a long time."

"What do you think will be accomplished by it? Anything?"

"I don't know, but I do know that I want to share what has happened to me with other people who need encouragement, with someone out there who thinks he as reached the end of the line. I want that person to know that he can get better. It might take a lot of hard work, but things *can* get better.

"And, you know, it's not just the patients who need hope. Their families need it too. Sometimes the families suffer more than the actual person." She paused for a few seconds and looked up at me. "Oh, Honey," she said, "this must have been so hard on you."

I wasn't prepared for that. "Why do you say that?" I asked, a bit uneasily. I hadn't planned on talking about me.

"Because you had to feel everything that happened—the whole thing. Remember, for a long time I didn't have any feelings—I couldn't feel anything—but you could. I have lots of blank spaces, but you don't. You remember it all."

I paused to think. I wanted what I said next to come out right. "Well, everything I did for you, you'd have done it for me, wouldn't you?" I finally asked.

"Of course, I would," she said. "You know that."

"Well, why should you be surprised that I did it for you, I happen to love you. I happen to have *wanted* to take care of you."

"I know."

"Seems, too, like I remember something in our wedding vows about 'in sickness and in health.' Wasn't that in there somewhere?"

I didn't expect her to answer. We both knew what I meant. But she was right about my not having any blank spaces. There have been times when I've wished I had a few, but I don't have any. I remember it all—the good and the bad, everything that happened, it's all there. I remember every bit of it.

Becky said, "You know, my whole life I've always wanted to be the best at anything I've ever tried to do. It never mattered what it was—playing basketball in high school, giving a party for my friends—whatever it was, I wanted to be the best there was. I don't remember a lot of things about my daddy, but I do remember he always told me that anything worth doing is worth doing right. Otherwise, don't waste your time. When I realized what had happened to me in this accident, I wanted to be the best recovery patient that there's ever been."

I sat there and looked at her across the table. The light from the window was bouncing off her soft, blonde hair, grown back to the full length it had been four years ago before anything had happened. Her eyes were alert, alive and dancing when she said something funny, narrowed and reflective when she thought back to where she had been and how far she had come. To me she looked like an angel.

And I remembered a story she had told me once about lying upstairs in her bed in the condo not long after the accident and seeing a piece of lint hanging from the bottom of a chair that sat only a few feet from the side of the bed. "You know what a neat and orderly person I've always been," she said. "I never wanted anything out of order. But I lay there for months looking at that little piece of lint. I knew all I had to do was reach over about three feet or so to remove it, but I couldn't do it. I'd think every day, 'Now today I've got to remove that piece of lint,' but I absolutely did not have the energy or the will power to reach out and do it. Finally one day, after months and months of seeing it hang there, I was able to reach over and pull it off the chair. I held it until the next time I had to get up. Then I walked over to the trash can and dropped it in. It was a senseless little task, but it made me feel good. It was the first time since I'd been hurt that I felt like I had accomplished something."

I thought of all the things she had accomplished since then. How many light years had it been since the morning Tom Burns had told the court, "She will rehabilitate, but she won't recover"? Is that what he would say now if he were sitting here beside me, listening to Becky talk about being the best recovery patient there had ever been? Or would he echo the words of the clinical psychologist who sees her now, Dr. David McMillan, who had told me just a few days before, "Becky believed in the impossible and it happened. Who would have thought it? I sure wouldn't."

I've never heard of anybody giving an award for "Best Recovery Patient," but if they ever do and if they send me a ballot, I can guarantee you Becky Anderson will get *my* vote.

Epilogue

I'm writing these last lines of my book sitting in my study looking out the big picture window of the dream house Becky and I finally built and moved into just a few months ago.

Remember the nine acres of property we had purchased just prior to her accident? There's the most gorgeous yellow brick house rambling across that hillside now, nestled in among hundreds of tall, beautiful trees—maple, walnut, hickory. Just a few weeks ago the hillside was on fire with brilliant reds, bright oranges, vivid yellows. Does that sound familiar? Do I sound like I'm describing the house I used to live in in Lebanon? I thought I could never love another home as much as I loved that one, but I was wrong. We sold that place nearly three years ago, and it's long been out of my heart and off my mind. This is home now.

It was fifteen months from the day we broke ground to the day we moved into our new home, not because our contractor, Bill Frasch, was slow but because I wanted the building of this house to be a part of Becky's recovery. A final step in leaving the past behind and moving into the future. And it was.

Every time there was a decision to be made regarding the house, I encouraged her to make it. Or to at least have a voice in it. Do we want dark paint on the outside trim or light paint? A plain wallpaper in the guest bath or an attractive print? Light switches on this wall or that wall? I didn't care much about those kinds of things anyhow. I left it up to her, but for a reason: Decision-making is one of the most difficult things a head-injured person has to deal with. The more Becky was forced into making decisions, the better at it she ultimately became. Toward the end of the

construction she was designing the flow of the driveway, the place-
ment of the shrubbery, and probably telling the workmen what to
eat for lunch. Our neighbors must have thought our builders were
awfully slow, but there was a very definite method to the madness.
Today, the making of decisions gives Becky very little trouble at
all.

I've learned a lot over the past four-and-a-half years, not the
least of which is that loving a house—this house or any other
house—is not what life's all about. That's not what's important.
Life is about people, not about houses or any other material things.
It doesn't matter to me anymore if I live in a shack or a tiny
apartment or in a cardboard box. It's who I live *with*, not *where* we
live that really matters.

It brings to mind the opening line from an old song Jean
Shepard used to sing: "There's nothing so precious as something
you've lost . . . And found it somehow in the end." Becky and I
never lost our love for each other, but we had allowed some mean-
ingless things to stand in the way of it. Things that in comparison
to what we had with each other were really of no value at all.
And, then, how close we came to losing everything. Another
quarter of an inch, the doctors said, and Becky would have been
killed. I learned my lessons in a pretty painful way as it was. Any
more pain would have been unbearable.

Two small gray squirrels just romped across the lawn below my
window sill. The newest member of our family, Squirmy, the cat, is
on the driveway toying with some kind of tiny insect who dared to
try and invade her private domain and, sadly, is about to pay the
ultimate price. Jamey is in his fifth-grade class at school, Becky is
in the kitchen reading up on how to prepare low-cholesterol meals
for herself and her family, and all is well with the world.

For as long as I've been working on this book, I've wanted more
than anything else for it to have a happy ending. I haven't always
been sure just what kind of an ending it was going to have. I guess
when you write fiction, even fictional songs, you can create your
own characters, decide what it is that you want them to do, and
then you make them carry out your wishes as you write about
them. You want a happy ending, you make up a happy ending. It's

as simple as that. But that's not the case here. In an autobiography, the action takes place first and the writer simply reports on it.

I'm happy to report several things. First, Becky is doing just super, and Becky and Bill together are doing super, too. In fact, she told me just the other day that she's happier now than she's ever been in her entire life. I feel the same way.

"This may sound stupid," she said one morning when we were having a quiet breakfast together after I had taken Jamey to school and come back home, "but if it weren't so painful for you and Jamey, I'd go through it all again . . . if I knew in the end I'd be as happy as I am now."

We've both learned an awful lot in four-and-a-half years' time, including the fact that the Lord moves in mysterious ways. I had heard that saying all my life, but I'm a total believer now. He hasn't moved in mysterious ways with just me and Becky either. Take my daughter, Jenni, for example.

Earlier, I referred to her as a student at Western Kentucky University, majoring in goodness-knows-what, at the time of Becky's accident in the fall of 1984. At that time Jenni had no idea what she wanted to do with the rest of her life.

"But, Dad, when I walked into the emergency room at General Hospital that afternoon and I saw Becky, and I saw all the things those people were doing to try and keep her alive, and all the sophisticated medical equipment they were using, and how the doctors and the nurses were working so hard, racing against time to keep her from dying, it was like a bright light came on and I knew. I mean beyond any shadow of a doubt I absolutely *knew* at that very moment that I wanted to dedicate my life to doing just what those nurses in that room were doing. I wanted to be a nurse, to help someone like they were helping Becky."

Today, Jenni is Mrs. Charles Robeson, RN, and she works in the emergency room of a major hospital near Nashville. Who knows, maybe someday another mother of another six-year-old child will be rushed in. She'll need someone to help keep her alive, someone to care, and because of what happened to Becky, Jenni will know how.

Remember H. Randolph Holder, the man who wouldn't let me play any country records on his radio station? A few years ago he increased the power on his FM station to 100,000 watts and changed the format to, you guessed it, all country music. The call letters are now WNGC which stand for "We're North Georgia Country," a far cry from the night he wouldn't let me punch up even an hour of the *Louisiana Hayride*. The station has been successful, too. In fact, Mr. Holder told me last year a potential buyer had offered him as much as five million dollars if he ever wanted to sell.

And remember George Thompson, my fraternity brother who resented the years he spent in military school so badly he sent me back to the campus to steal the sign in front of the Commandant's house? I ran into him recently. He has just retired from a lifetime of service in, you guessed it again, the Army!

I think what I've learned above everything else these past few years is that life is to be lived . . . it is to be celebrated . . . it is to be held and cherished and appreciated and *lived* . . . every single moment of it, every single day. And it needs to be lived according to what really matters, what really counts, according to priorities.

Big houses and marble shower stalls and gold-plated razors aren't priority items. But holding my little boy's hand while he says the blessing at mealtime is. Taking him to school and helping him with homework and listening to him play his drums, those are priorities. Houses in the country on thirty-five acres of land are nice, but they aren't important. What's important is having a wife who loves me enough to stand at the airport waiting to meet my plane at midnight, dressed nicely, her hair combed, makeup on, and just a touch of her special perfume drifting through the night. Becky did that just last week, and it was important to me because it meant we were celebrating life.

I'm not going to lie and say these past few years have been easy because they haven't. Once or twice I came dangerously close to giving up and walking away, but I found the strength somehow to tie a knot in the end of my rope and hang on. I wondered at the time where the strength was coming from, but now I know. Like I say, the Lord moves in mysterious ways.

Back in the midst of all the agony and confusion in my life, my daughter, Terri, who was going through her severe health problems at the same time, gave me a beautiful and inspiring plaque to hang on my wall. It said:

Sometimes the Lord calms the storm.
Sometimes He lets the storm rage
And calms His child.

Terri and I could both understand and appreciate what the anonymous writer of that bit of wisdom was saying. Her storms have quieted down somewhat since that time, and even though the doctors continue to monitor her health closely, she appears to be doing much better. Some of my storms may still be raging. But *I'm* not raging and that's what counts.

I found another plaque for my wall not long ago while on tour out west. (You can hardly see my wall these days for all the plaques and signs hanging on it!) We were to be working this particular night near an Indian reservation, and I was whiling away some time that afternoon in a nearby curio shop. Down on the bottom of a tall wicker basket full of all sorts of handcrafted trinkets and toys, I found a little wooden sign no more than four inches tall and maybe about three inches wide. It was turned upside down when I first spotted it and I almost didn't reach down to turn it over. I'm awfully glad I did, though, because what somebody had crudely handpainted on that tiny piece of wood is probably the one thing that best sums up what this book is all about. And what I plan on the rest of my life being all about. It was almost as though it had been written just for me. It simply read:

It doesn't matter where you go or what you have.
What matters is who you have beside you.

Acknowledgments

There is no way I could possibly thank all the people whose lives have touched mine in a meaningful way over the nearly thirty years that I've been in show business. But, on the other hand, there are a few very special people who deserve more than the passing mention I have given them so far.

Not the least of those is Kathy Gaddy, the young lady who serves as my administrative assistant in all the various aspects of my career. Kathy has worked with me since she was fifteen, starting out by coming to my television tapings every night, welcoming the studio audience, and introducing me to the crowd. From there she graduated (?) to coming into my office as I might need her to help pack and mail out my new record releases to the radio stations. One day I discovered she was a pretty fair typist, and next thing she knew I had her coming to the office on a regular schedule to help me answer my mail. I don't remember ever officially hiring her. She just kept coming back and doing such a great job that one day I started referring to her as my personal secretary. A couple of years ago I came to realize that she was much more than a secretary, she was really my right hand and, to be honest, the brains of the whole outfit. I don't know how I'd manage to walk out my front door every day without her telling me in which direction to head.

Kathy's mom, Jeanne Chennault, worked with me for nearly twenty years herself, leaving in 1987 only because she felt the need to return to her home state of Texas in order to be closer to her family. Jeanne was my personal secretary for a long time, my bookkeeper, and the president of my fan club.

I didn't mention much about my fan club in these pages, but I want to say a few words about it now. A lot of people don't understand just what a fan club is or what function it performs in an artist's career. I can't speak for anybody else's fan club, but mine is a group of people who are devoted enough to me and my career that they spend their own time, their own money, to help support and promote me, my music, my television appearances, my association with PoFolks restaurants, and anything else that I might be involved with. The love and devotion I feel from these very special people is more meaningful to me than I could ever express. Jean Brown, from Coloma, Michigan, is the current president of my fan club, and I can't thank her and the state representatives and all the members enough for all they do.

I also want to mention my current group of PoFolks Band members because they are the greatest: Mike Johnson, Mike Streeter, Mark Johnson, Les Singer, Jim Brown, Lisa Harper Ramsey, and Laurie Harper Evans, plus our audio engineer Keith Durham. Now, gang, you can all say you've seen your name in a book! I love each one of you, and I thank you for putting up with the last two years of listening to me rattle on . . . sometimes endlessly, mile after mile on the road . . . about this book I've been working on.

To everybody who's ever been a part of my office staff or my band or worked with me in any other capacity, a special thanks as well. To every musician who's ever played on one of my records, every background singer, every engineer in the control room, every TV cameraperson, each of you has played a part in all that has been, and so much of it wouldn't have been without what you contributed.

To Tony Privett, thanks for believing in the idea of a Bill Anderson autobiography enough to introduce me to Chuck Perry of Longstreet Press. And to Chuck, thanks for editing my words and correcting my spelling and straightening out my punctuation, but most of all thanks for believing. Even more than that, thanks for understanding.

I can't close this book out without remembering the late John E. Drewry, former dean of the Henry W. Grady School of Journalism at the University of Georgia, whose encouragement will never be forgotten, although he wasn't quite sure at times just how proud he should be of a Grady graduate who took the wisdom he imparted and used it to compose hillbilly songs; a lady named Miss Cofer who taught me how to type in the tenth grade at Avondale High School; and the person who designed a word processor simple enough for me to semi-understand. My eternal gratitude to you all.

And last, but far from least, to my friend and compadre, Jimmy Gateley, my great red-headed drummer, Doug Renaud, and my bus driver and dear friend, James Price, all of whom brightened my life and then were taken from me long before I was ready to let them go, you are still loved, you are still missed, and you will never be forgotten.

Bill Anderson Discography

ALBUMS

Decca:

4192	Bill Anderson Sings Country Heart Songs	1961
4427	Still	1963
4499	Bill Anderson Sings	1964
4600	The Bill Anderson Showcase	1964
4646	From This Pen	1965
4686	Bright Lights And Country Music	1965
4771	I Love You Drops	1966
4855	Get While the Gettin's Good	1967
4886	I Can Do Nothing Alone	1967
4859	Bill Anderson's Greatest Hits	1967
4959	For Loving You (Duet with Jan Howard)	1968
4998	Wild Weekend	1969
3835	Bill Anderson's Country Style (Vocalion Label)	1969
5056	Happy State of Mind	1969
DXSB7198	The Bill Anderson Story (Double album)	1970
75142	My Life/But You Know I Love You	1970
75161	Bill Anderson Christmas	1970
75184	If It's All The Same to You (Duet with Jan Howard)	1971
75206	Love Is a Sometimes Thing	1971
75254	Where Have All Our Heroes Gone?	1971
75275	Always Remember	1971
75315	Bill Anderson's Greatest Hits Vol. II	1971
75293	Bill & Jan (Duet with Jan Howard)	1972
75339	Singing His Praise (Duet with Jan Howard)	1972
75344	All The Lonely Women in the World	1972
VLF3927	Just Plain Bill (Vocalion Label)	1972
75383	Don't She Look Good?	1973

Po' Boys: (1965-1973)

DL-74725	Bill Anderson Presents the Po' Boys
DL-4884	The Po' Boys Pick Again
DL-75278	That Casual Country Feeling

MCA:

MCA24001	The Bill Anderson Story, His Greatest Hits (Re-issue)	1973
MCA320	Bill	1973
MCA416	Whispering Bill Anderson: Can I Come Home to You?	1974
MCA454	Everytime I Turn the Radio On	1974
MCA2182	Sometimes (Duet with Mary Lou Turner)	1975
PS6152	Gentle on My Mind (Pickwick Label, Canada)	1975
MCA2222	Peanuts & Diamonds and Other Jewels	1976
MCA2264	Scorpio	1976
MCA2298	Billy Boy & Mary Lou (Duet with Mary Lou Turner)	1977

MCA2371	*Love & Other Sad Stories*	1978
MCA3075	*Ladies Choice*	1978
MSM35032	*Whispering Bill Anderson*	1979
MCA3214	*Nashville Mirrors*	1980

Po' Boys (1965-1973)
MCA-337   *The Rich Sounds of Bill Anderson's Po' Boys*

MCA Coral:
CB20002   *I Can Do Nothing Alone*   1973

Southern Tracks:
STL-001   *Southern Fried*   1983

Swanee Records:
SW-5007   *Yesterday, Today & Tomorrow* (Double album)   1984

RCA:
AHL1-4350 *Bill Anderson Hosts Backstage at the Grand Ole Opry*   1982

Independent:
NR11316	*On the Road with Bill Anderson*	1980
BAPF-001	*Bill Anderson Presents the Po' Folks Band*	1984
BAPF-002	*A Place in the Country*	1986

SINGLE RECORDS

TNT Records:
| TNT-165 | "Take Me"/"Empty Room" | 1957 |
| TNT-9015 | "City Lights"/"No Song to Sing" | 1958 |

Decca:
30773	"That's What It's Like to Be Lonesome"/"The Thrill of My Life"	1958
30914	"Ninety-Nine Years"/"Back Where I Started From"	1959
30993	"Dead or Alive"/"It's Not the End of Everything"	1959
31092	"The Tips of My Fingers"/"No Man's Land"	1960
31168	"Walk Out Backwards"/"The Best of Strangers"	1961
31262	"Po' Folks"/"Goodbye Cruel World"	1961
31358	"Get a Little Dirt on Your Hands"/"Down Came the Rain"	1962
31404	"Mama Sang a Song"/"On and On and On"	1962
31458	"Still"/"You Made It Easy"	1963
31521	"8 x 10"/"One Mile Over Two Miles Back"	1963
31577	"Five Little Fingers"/"Easy Come—Easy Go"	1964
31630	"Me"/"Cincinnati, Ohio"	1964
31681	"Three A.M."/"In Case You Ever Change Your Mind"	1964
31743	"Certain"/"You Can Have Her"	1965
31825	"Bright Lights & Country Music"/"Born"	1965
31884	"Time Out"/"I Know You're Married" (Duet with Jan Howard)	1966
31890	"Golden Guitar"/"I Love You Drops"	1966
31999	"I Get the Fever"/"The First Mrs. Jones"	1967

32077	"Get While the Gettin's Good"/"Something to Believe In"	1967
32146	"Papa"/"No One's Gonna Hurt You Anymore"	1967
32197	"For Loving You"/"The Untouchables" (Duet with Jan Howard)	1967
34490	"Stranger on the Run"/"Happiness"	1968
32276	"Wild Weekend"/"Fun While It Lasted"	1968
32360	"Happy State of Mind"/"Time's Been Good to Me"	1969
32417	"Po' Folks Christmas"/"Christmas Time's a Coming"	1969
32445	"My Life"/"To Be Alone"	1969
32514	"But You Know I Love You"/"A Picture from Life's Other Side"	1970
32511	"If It's All the Same to You"/"I Thank God for You" (Duet with Jan Howard)	1970
32643	"Love Is a Sometimes Thing"/"And I'm Still Missing You"	1970
32689	"Someday We'll Be Together"/"Who Is the Biggest Fool?" (Duet with Jan Howard)	1970
32744	"Where Have All Our Heroes Gone?"/"Loving a Memory"	1970
32793	"Always Remember"/"You Can Change My World"	1971
32850	"Quits"/"I'll Live For You"	1972
32877	"Dis-Satisfied"/"Knowing You're Mine" (Duet with Jan Howard)	1972
32930	"All the Lonely Women in the World"/"It was Time for Me to Move On Anyway"	1972
33002	"Don't She Look Good?"/"I'm Just Gone"	1973

MCA Records:

40004	"If You Can Live with It"/"Let's Fall Apart"	1973
40164	"World of Make-Believe"/"Gonna Shine It on Again"	1974
40070	"The Corner of My Life"/"Home and Things"	1974
40243	"Can I Come Home to You"/"I'm Happily Married"	1974
40304	"Everytime I Turn the Radio On"/"You Are My Story"	1975
40351	"I Still Feel the Same About You"/"Talk to Me Ohio"	1975
40404	"Country DJ"/"We Made Love"	1975
40443	"Thanks"/"Why'd the Last Time Have to Be the Best?"	1975
40488	"Sometimes"/"Circle in a Triangle" (Duet with Mary Lou Turner)	1975
40533	"That's What Made Me Love You"/"Can We Still Be Friends?" (Duet with Mary Lou Turner)	1976
40595	"Peanuts and Diamonds"/"Your Love Blows Me Away"	1976
40661	"Liars One—Believers 0"/"Let Me Whisper Darling"	1976
40713	"Head to Toe"/"This Ole Suitcase"	1977
40753	"Where Are You Going, Billy Boy?"/"Sad Ole Shade of Gray" (Duet with Mary Lue Turner)	1977
40794	"Still the One"/"Love Song for Jackie"	1977
40852	"I'm Way Ahead of You"/"Just Enough to Make Me Want It All" (Duet with Mary Lou Turner)	1977
40893	"I Can't Wait Any Longer"/"Joanna"	1977
40964	"Double S"/"Married Lady"	1978

40992	"This Is a Love Song"/"Remembering the Good"	1979
41060	"The Dream Never Dies"/"One More Sexy Lady"	1979
41150	"More Than a Bedroom Thing"/"Love Me and I'll Be Your Best Friend"	1979
41212	"Make Mine Night Time"/"The Old Me and You"	1980
10473	"Rock 'N' Roll to Rock of Ages"/"I'm Used to the Rain"	1980
51017	"I Want That Feelin' Again"/"She Made Me Remember"	1980
51052	"Mister Peepers"/"How Married Are You, Mary Ann?"	1981
51150	"Homebody"/"One Man Band"	1982
51204	"Whiskey Made Me Stumble"/"All That Keeps Me Going"	1982
52290	"I Wonder If God Likes Country Music"/"Ride Off in the Sunset"	1983
60059	"I Love You Drops"/"Still" (Re-issue)	1983
60115	"Five Little Fingrs"/"Mama Sang a Song" (Re-issue)	1983

Southern Tracks:

1007	"Southern Fried"/"You Turn the Light On"	1982
1011	"Laid Off"/"Lovin' Tonight"	1982
1014	"Thank You Darling"/"Lovin's Tonight"	1982
1021	"Son of the South"/"20th Century Fox"	1983
1026	"Your Eyes"/"I Never Get Enough of You"	1984
1030	"Speculation"/"We May Never Pass This Way Again"	1984
1067	"Sheet Music"/"Maybe Go Down"	1986
1077	"No Ordinary Memory"	1987
2011	"Love Slippin' Away" (Duet with Toni Bellin)	1989

Swanee:

4013	"Wino the Clown"/"Wild Weekend"	1984
5015	"Pity Party"/"Five Little Fingers"	1985
5018	"When You Leave That Way"/"Quits"	1985